Managing Iterative Software Development Projects

Managing Iterative Software Development Projects

Kurt Bittner

Ian Spence

⋏⋎ Addison-Wesley

Upper Saddle River, NJ • Boston • Indianapolis • San Francisco
New York • Toronto • Montreal • London • Munich • Paris • Madrid
Cape Town • Sydney • Tokyo • Singapore • Mexico City

The publisher offers excellent discounts on this book when ordered in quantity for bulk purchases or special sales, which may include electronic versions and/or custom covers and content particular to your business, training goals, marketing focus, and branding interests. For more information, please contact:

U.S. Corporate and Government Sales
(800) 382-3419
corpsales@pearsontechgroup.com

For sales outside the United States please contact:

International Sales
international@pearsoned.com

 The Safari® Enabled icon on the cover of your favorite technology book means the book is available through Safari Bookshelf. When you buy this book, you get free access to the online edition for 45 days. Safari Bookshelf is an electronic reference library that lets you easily search thousands of technical books, find code samples, download chapters, and access technical information whenever and wherever you need it.

To gain 45-day Safari Enabled access to this book:

- Go to http://www.awprofessional.com/safarienabled
- Complete the brief registration form
- Enter the coupon code 53J7-JWDK-LL61-GDKF-LCP2

If you have difficulty registering on Safari Bookshelf or accessing the online edition, please e-mail customer-service@safaribooksonline.com.

Visit us on the Web: www.awprofessional.com

Library of Congress Cataloging-in-Publication Data

Bittner, Kurt.

Managing iterative software development projects / Kurt Bittner and Ian Spence.

p. cm.

Includes index.

ISBN 0-321-26889-X (pbk. : alk. paper) 1. Computer software--Development--Management. I. Spence, Ian, 1961- II. Title.

QA76.76.D47B58 2006

005.1'068--dc22

2006009702

ISBN 0-321-26889-X
Text printed in the United States on recycled paper at R. R. Donnelley in Crawfordsville, Indiana.
First printing, July 2006

To Helen Guirr, Rose and Jamie Spence, and Laura Bittner,
whose patience and support made this project possible.

Contents

About the Authors

Kurt Bittner works for IBM on software development solutions strategy. In a career spanning 24 years, he has successfully applied an iterative approach to software development in a number of industries and problem domains. He was a member of the original team that developed the IBM Rational Unified Process and is a co-author with Ian Spence of *Use Case Modeling*, published by Addison-Wesley in 2002.

Ian Spence is a chief scientist and principle consultant at Ivar Jacobson Consulting, specializing in the adoption of the Unified Process and the iterative, use-case driven approach that it recommends. He has more than 20 years of experience in the software industry, including more than 10 years of experience in managing and participating in iterative projects. He is currently involved in the development of the next generation of lightweight software development processes and is a co-author with Kurt Bittner of *Use Case Modeling*, published by Addison-Wesley in 2002.

Foreword

Software development has come a long way.

Back in the dark ages of our profession, we clung to classical models rooted in traditional approaches to project management. Requirements were specified, then frozen, and it was off to the races. The cycle was clear: Plan the work, then work the plan. Results were, shall we say, mixed.

The problem often turned out to be a puzzling one. The software development organization could declare victory and demonstrate that they had delivered on the specified requirements. But from the business's point of view, the system was destined to be a failure, and this was often obvious from the moment of delivery. Why?

Because change happens. All significant software development efforts last sufficiently long so they are bound to suffer from changes due to the external environment. New technology bursts onto the scene, new competitors arrive, fundamental economic drivers shift, and so on. Sometimes you are forced by the outside world to innovate, and that forcing function doesn't always conveniently fall on software development project cycle boundaries. In today's fast-paced world, it is certain that if you build something precisely according to your initial set of requirements, you will build the wrong thing and fail in the marketplace.

Of course, there is also the problem of poor execution along the way, again due perhaps to ambiguities in the original requirements. But the argument, which has been made many times, is that you will fail *even in the face of perfect execution*. Because that approach is enough to drive any manager to drink, a new approach was clearly necessary, one that focused on business success, not just software development success.

If we now define a software development organization's success in terms of its ability to react to change, we have a new view of the problem. Change is expressed through requirements, so the fundamental issue facing any software development organization is its ability to deal with requirements flux. Moreover, changes to requirements arrive randomly; their scope and arrival time are externally determined. You may have a very neat project rhythm or cycle, but the changes to requirements will arrive asynchronously with that heartbeat. As with anything else in life that you can't control, what you need is a mechanism for coping. The message is clear: "Requirements change—adapt or die!"

That, in essence, is what iterative development is all about. It is software development's response to a fundamental business problem: delivering systems that have value. Yes, the "system" is a moving target. We have given up on the irrational belief that we can nail that target to the wall; we now work very hard to track the target and still hit the bull's eye.

Iterative development is a relatively new approach, having begun to gather momentum in the 1980s. Companies that embraced it in the 1990s found that they were doing a better job of delivering value than they had in the past with other methodologies. But, like all other advances in technology, the path was not always a smooth one; in hindsight, of course, it looks like a steady path "up and to the right." The reality is that there were lots of bumps in the road, some things that turned out to only look good at first, and many approaches that were tried and abandoned. What survived is the distillation of many projects' scar tissue, and we need to pay tribute to the managers who pioneered and persevered to give us a robust set of ideas for modern software development project management.

After a few decades, there is always a pause for reflection and summing up. Thought leaders sit down and try to capture, as best they can, the essence of what has been learned. Walker Royce did a great job in his 1998 classic *Software Project Management, A Unified Framework* (Addison-Wesley), and I attempted to add my own views on the subject in *The Software Development Edge* (Addison-Wesley, 2005). Now we have this addition by Kurt Bittner and Ian Spence.

Kurt and Ian are far from newcomers on the scene. They have many collective years of experience working with iterative development. Kurt was on the original Unified Process development team at Rational Software and led many teams applying the iterative approach. Ian's experiences are similar, having spent many years working with project teams applying iterative development. They have lived "in the trenches," and the guidance presented in this book reflects their experience.

They are also experienced writers. Their 2002 book, *Use Case Modeling* (Addison-Wesley), has already guided a generation of analysts and developers in getting requirements right. Their approach in that book was methodical and thorough, without being heavy and pedantic. It was a book that was written to be used, and it has been extremely well received. When I heard they were going to write the definitive book on iterative development, I jumped at the chance to be a reviewer.

They have not disappointed. This is a book for people who want to understand the principles and be successful in their practice. This is not a superficial popularization; this is "the real deal." I would recommend it to any software development manager who is serious about getting better at his craft. No matter how experienced you are, you will learn something from this book.

Great job, guys!

Joe Marasco
President and CEO
Ravenflow
March, 2006

Preface

"No plan survives contact with the enemy."
—*Field Marshall Helmuth von Moltke, 1800-1891*[1]

If we could plan perfectly, if nothing out of the ordinary ever occurred, if things always went as planned, there would be no need for iterative development. Iterative development is founded on the recognition that we need an approach that enables us to *make progress in the face of change, or perhaps in spite of change*. Iterative development is basically a *dynamic* planning and management approach that incorporates, even seeks out, new information to manage risks and deliver incremental value continuously throughout the project.

Iterative development is not particularly new. It has been around for a long time, and it has probably evolved independently a number of times. Because it tends to focus on situational responses, it has not tended to be well documented, and for this reason it has appeared to be ad hoc. Our goal with this book is to change that—to provide a systematic introduction to managing iterative development that you can apply to your own projects.

At the core of the iterative approach is the explicit management of risk as the guiding principle behind the project management approach. The project is divided up into a series of iterations, each of which is directed at mitigating a set of risks by implementing scenarios that will force the confrontation and mastery of the risks. Our goal is to take these concepts and breathe life into them by bringing them down to ground level. We aim to present a simple, straightforward, and practical approach to organizing,

---

[1] Von Moltke wrote a number of works on military theory. His main thesis was that military strategy consists of a system of alternatives because only the start of a military operation could be planned. As a result, he considered the main task of military leaders to consist of understanding all possible outcomes.

estimating, staffing, and managing the project, but one that can be applied to very small projects and yet be scaled up to very large programs. In doing this we aim to promote a pragmatic approach that attacks the problem of obtaining results in a predictable, repeatable, non-chaotic way.

Our experience is based on helping many companies adopt iterative development using the IBM Rational Unified Process (RUP),[2] but the techniques presented here are not only applicable to Unified Process[3] projects; they represent a general approach to any iterative software development effort. They are equally useful when managing an iterative project using Extreme Programming,[4] Microsoft Solution Framework for Agile Software Development,[5] or any other agile or iterative software development process.

This book is focused on making the techniques of managing iterative development understandable and accessible to anyone with a basic background in managing software projects. It strives to provide you with the practical guidance you need to start managing your iterative and incremental projects in a controlled, agile, and disciplined fashion.

The Challenge of Managing Software Development Projects

Managing software development projects is challenging: Responding to a rapidly changing business and technological environment means that teams are always pushing the limits of the possible. This pressure to deliver results is compounded by the fact that their are never enough of the right people with the right skills; the technology is evolving too fast. Yet teams must respond and succeed, for the stakes are very high. Almost everything done in the business world today requires software, so the success of the business often rests on the success of some team developing a solution that consists of a lot of software.

---

[2] See http://www-306.ibm.com/software/rational/.

[3] Other variants of the Unified Process include the Essential Unified Process (see www.ivar jacobson.com) and the Agile Unified Process (see http://www.ambysoft.com/unifiedprocess/).

[4] See www.extremeprogramming.org or www.xprogramming.com.

[5] See www.microsoft.com.

Software development projects must be able to respond with speed and agility to rapid and incessant change in both the business requirements and the implementation technology. Agility in software development is essential for businesses to succeed today and, more importantly, in the future.

The critical importance of software in supporting the day-to-day operations of businesses and providing competitive advantage is leading to another emerging trend: governance. In short, because business success rests on software success, business executives need to understand how their investments in information technology and software development are paying off. They demand visibility and accountability; the stakes are simply too high for them not to understand project status and trajectory. In addition, in many environments, the criticality of software to safety or business processes means that there is a need for auditability—a need to prove that what was done was authorized and approved. Governance of software development is also here to stay.

Finally, software development is a highly creative and collaborative endeavor in which success requires a fine degree of coordination between many people from many different disciplines, often working across different geographies and time zones and sometimes across cultural borders. The levels of invention and innovation that are fundamental to good software development mean development is not a mechanical process that can be fully planned at the start and then monitored during the execution. They also cause software development projects to exhibit frustrating diseconomies of scale—that is, a large project costs much more per line of code than a small project[6]—illustrating that the industry has still not learned how to manage creativity, novelty, and complexity very well.

Iterative development provides a solution to these three challenges—it provides an approach that is agile and responsive to the needs of the business while still providing the necessary controls and oversight needed to govern the development process and while fostering the creativity and collaboration needed to solve complex business problems.

---

[6] This is discussed in depth by Walker Royce in *Software Project Management: A Unified Framework* (Addison-Wesley, 1998).

Learning the Art of Managing Software Development

In every endeavor, *good management matters.* More than thirty years ago Frederick Brooks wrote something that still rings true today:

> *In many ways, managing a large computer programming project is like managing any other large undertaking—in more ways than most programmers believe. But in many other ways it is different— in more ways than most professional managers expect.*[7]

This quote succinctly highlights the two major traps that people fall into when considering the management of software development projects:

- Developers may fail to recognize the value added by professional management practices on a software project, seeming to feel that the role of the manager on a project is similar to the role of government in Henry David Thoreau's work *On the Duty of Civil Disobedience*: "that government is best which governs least."

- Managers may fail to understand that technical details matter and that they cannot be completely delegated; no project can be managed without really understanding the work being done.

To be successful, the software project manager needs to have a firm foundation in traditional management practices but also needs to know what makes developing software different from other types of projects. To manage the project, the manager needs to understand the work well enough to be able to tell whether the work is on track. At the same time, managers who understand only the technical work and not how to motivate and lead teams are also lost—they never get their teams working as a cohesive unit.

---

[7] Frederick P. Brooks, *The Mythical Man Month: Essays on Software Engineering, Twentieth Anniversary Edition* (Reading, MA: Addison-Wesley, 1995).

Managing software development is like managing anything else, only more so. The time pressures and resource constraints tend to be so amplified and the number of alternatives so dizzying that the manager's abilities are sorely tested. We have found that an iterative development approach is key to solving many of these problems. We have also observed that the difference between success and failure of a software development effort rests largely on the skills of the manager of the project.[8] This is not to discount the value of the rest of the team or the approach they follow; it merely underscores that few project teams can be successful without good management.

Who Should Read This Book

This book is principally for the people responsible for the successful delivery of projects that have a significant amount of software as part of their solution. These people have a variety of job titles and responsibilities, ranging from a team leader with informal day-to-day leadership responsibility for a small software development team, to a project manager managing the production of a major release of a software product, to a program manager overseeing many collaborating projects, each with its own project manager. In short, we target the people who must make decisions about what to do, when to do it, and why.

This book will provide benefits to all members of the project's leadership team and anyone else who is concerned with the overall business success of the project. It is especially relevant for those project managers faced with the challenge of managing an iterative development project, whether they are novice or experienced project managers:

- If you are a novice project manager, the pragmatic approach presented will provide you with the guidance that you need to successfully manage your project in a controlled iterative fashion and will give you a framework with which you can acquire the skills you do not already have.

---

[8] An observation backed up by the Standish Group's CHAOS Report; see http://www.standish-group.com/. We will return to the Standish CHAOS Report and the topic of project success in Chapter 2, "How Do Iterative Projects Function?"

- If you are an experienced project manager faced with your first iterative software development project, this book will help you to continue to exploit your existing management experience and best practices while transitioning to a more agile, iterative, and incremental software development approach. If you have tried iterative approaches but remain unconvinced of their benefit, we hope this book will fill in the missing information in a credible way, making you a believer in the approach.

- If you are the leader of a team that is working iteratively, this book will provide you with an approach to leading your team that will enable it to support and interact more effectively with the broader project management team and project board.

- If you are a project sponsor, program manager, or user representative, this book will help you to understand how to interact with, support, and exploit the benefits of the iterative development of the software projects that you commission.

- If you are the leader of a discipline team (such as requirements, architecture, and so on), this book will provide an understanding of the role the project management team plays in establishing and sustaining an iterative development environment within which your team can excel.

In this book, we bridge the gap between the two most common, and often adversarial, positions adopted with respect to the management of iterative development projects—the informal approach traditionally promoted by developer-centric methodologies and the more formal approach traditionally promoted by the project management community—by describing a single, layered, easy to use, agile, adaptive, and scalable approach.

We also broaden the scope of the discussion to include the sponsoring business itself, something that is often overlooked to the detriment of the result the project provides to the business. This is the area where software development projects ultimately compete with other investments for funding, a perspective to which our iterative projects must be aligned.

By adopting this holistic, management-aware approach we hope to bring together groups of people who often are not, unfortunately, aligned to achieve project success.

How This Book Is Organized

This book is intended to provide practical guidance on managing iterative projects and programs. The book is divided into two parts.

In Part I, "The Principles of Iterative Project Management," we present the basic principles of managing iterative software development projects. This part of the book focuses on the principles and best practices that underlie the successful management of iterative and incremental software development projects. If you are new to iterative development, Part I will give you a good foundation in the basics of iterative project management, although there are also some new insights for those already familiar with iterative approaches.

In Chapter 1, "What Is Iterative Development?" we explore what it means to develop software in an iterative and incremental fashion by examining how different project roles experience iterative development (for example, the developer, the customer, and the project manager).

In Chapter 2, "How Do Iterative Projects Function?" we discuss how an iterative and incremental project functions by examining what makes an iterative project successful and the key project characteristics that enable this success.

In Chapter 3, "Controlling Iterative Projects," we discuss how iterative projects are controlled. This chapter introduces the concepts of the time box, a standard project lifecycle for iterative development projects, and the objective measurement of results. It also introduces the phases of the Unified Process and explains how they facilitate controlled iterative development regardless of the iterative development method followed.

In Chapter 4, "Are You Ready for Iterative Project Management?" we discuss what you need to have in place before embarking on an iterative development project. This includes discussing some of the adjustments that often have to be made to team structures and personal attitudes to provide an environment conducive to and supportive of the adoption of iterative and incremental project management practices.

In Part II, "Planning and Managing an Iterative Project," we discuss how to plan, manage, and assess an iterative project, including how to plan projects and iterations, assess results, and adapt plans. We conclude by presenting how to adapt the approach to very small projects and very large projects and programs, and how to introduce iterative development to a new project team.

In Chapter 5, "A Layered Approach to Planning and Managing Iterative Projects," we examine the layering of the project and plans, which is essential to enable effective, controlled, iterative, and incremental development and to provide a scalable management solution. We also introduce the concept of an evolution as the mechanism for the iterative development of a major release of a software product. This chapter provides the framework for the more specific planning and assessment chapters that follow.

In Chapter 6, "Overall Project Planning," we describe how to create an overall roadmap for an iterative project. We examine techniques and mechanisms for planning the entire project lifecycle and the set of releases to be produced. We introduce some simple principles for lifecycle planning and use these to illustrate the process involved in creating an overall project plan.

In Chapter 7, "Evolution and Phase Planning," we present the principles for planning and managing an individual evolution and its phases. We examine the patterns found within an evolution and how to adapt these based on the forces at work on the project. This includes patterns of managing risks, estimating, and organizing the work into iterations.

In Chapter 8, "Iteration Planning," we present the principles of planning and managing an iteration within a phase. We examine patterns for managing an iteration and how to adapt these based on the forces at work on the project.

In Chapter 9, "Iteration, Phase, and Project Assessments," we examine how the assessment process works across the layers of an iterative project, looking in particular at the role of the iteration and phase assessments and how these affect the adaptive planning of the project and enable the entire project to be effectively controlled.

In Chapter 10, "A Scalable Approach to Managing Iterative Projects," we examine how to apply the principles and patterns presented in the previous chapters to various project sizes, concluding our "how to" guide for the planning and management of iterative projects. This includes guidance on how to scale the process down for the management of small and very small projects and up for the management of large projects and programs. Chapter 10 will be of special interest to those engaged in program management or those who find themselves working on projects that contribute to a larger program.

In Chapter 11, "Getting Started with Iterative Project Management," we conclude the book by providing advice on how to transition to an iterative software development process and how to introduce iterative development practices iteratively. This material will be useful to anyone embarking on their first iterative project or trying to introduce iterative management techniques into either projects or organizations.

In addition, we provide several comprehensive appendices.

- Appendix A, "A Brief Introduction to Use-Case Driven Development," provides a brief summary of the use-case driven development approach that is used to provide a concrete framework for the examples in Appendix C and throughout the book.

- Appendix B, "Outlines, Templates, and Checklists," provides detailed, reusable versions of the outlines, templates, and checklists referenced and presented throughout the body of the book.

- Appendix C, "Examples," provides a more detailed presentation of the example plans excerpted throughout the body of the book.

Acknowledgments

Our perspectives reflect the distillation of countless experiences and conversations that merge over time into a set of ideas. To fully acknowledge all such contributions that have led us to the ideas presented here would be impossible, but some contributions are worthy of note. Many of the ideas presented here emerged from discussions with colleagues including Grady Booch, Ivar Jacobson, Philippe Kruchten, and Walker Royce.

In putting these ideas into print, we are indebted to the many individuals who reviewed the manuscript in its various revisions: Liz Augustine, Sam Bayer, Eric Cardoza, Steve Earnshaw, Linda Fernandez, Brian Kerr, Chris Littlejohns, Joe Marasco, Graham Marsh, Mike Perrow, Neil Postance, and DJ de Villiers. We are also indebted to our editors at Addison-Wesley, Jessica D'Amico and Chris Zahn.

PART I

The Principles of Iterative Project Management

1

What Is Iterative Development?

"Iterative and incremental development is necessary to converge on an accurate business solution."
—Principle 5, Dynamic Systems Development Methodology, from Dynamic System Development Method *(Addison-Wesley, 1997) by Jennifer Stapleton*

As we discussed in the Preface, the need for iteration arises out of the need to predictably deliver results in an uncertain world. Because we cannot *wish* the uncertainty away, we need a technique to master it. Iterative and incremental development provides us with a technique that enables us to master this uncertainty or at least to systematically bring it sufficiently under control to achieve our desired results.

So what is it that makes a development process iterative and incremental? What does it mean for a project to work in an iterative and incremental manner? The *Collins Modern English Dictionary* provides the following definitions for the words iterate, iteration, iterative, and incremental:

> **Iterate** *vt*. — to utter or do repeatedly — **iteration** *n*. — **iterative** *adj*.

> **Increment** *n*. — 1. amount of increase 2. a becoming greater or larger; increase — **incremental** *adj*.

Assuming the terminology is derived from the general usage of the words, the question now becomes, "What does it mean for a project to work iteratively and incrementally by repeatedly doing things to create an increasingly larger and more complete product?"

In this chapter we address this question by examining what it means for a project and its team members to work iteratively and incrementally. We examine iterative working from the most common perspectives (project manager, developer, customer, and so on), thereby clarifying and illuminating what iterative and incremental development really is.

Iterating and the Scientific Method

Many activities are involved in developing a solution to a problem. We need to understand the problem, gather requirements for a potential solution, translate those requirements into a design, build the solution, and test it. This order is fairly natural and generally correct. Problems creep in, however, when we try to scale this approach up—that is, when we try to gather *all* requirements, then do *all* design, then *all* development, and then *all* testing in a strictly linear fashion.

Instead, we need to work more like scientists. The modern scientific approach is founded on the principle of direct observation: theories are proposed, and then experiments are designed and performed to test those theories. Based on the measured results, the theory is either rejected or confirmed.

How does this approach apply to software development? In a sense, many aspects of a software development project are theories or, more accurately, assertions that need to be evaluated. The plan itself is composed of many assertions about how long tasks will take to accomplish. Even the requirements are assertions about the characteristics of a suitable solution. Just because some stakeholders or subject matter experts say a requirement is valid does not mean that they are correct. We need to evaluate even the requirements to determine whether they define the right solution to the problem at hand.

This reasoning leads us to adopt a style of software development where the assertions inherent in the plan are repeatedly challenged and evaluated by the design and development of demonstrable versions of the system, each of which is objectively evaluated to prove that it reduces the project risk and each of which builds upon the prior version until the solution is complete.

This development style is more commonly known as iterative and incremental development, which we define as having the following characteristics:

- It involves the iterative application of a set of activities to evaluate a set of assertions, resolve a set of risks, accomplish a set of development objectives, and incrementally produce and refine an effective solution.

- It is iterative in that it involves the successive refinement of the understanding of the problem, the solution's definition, and the solution's implementation by the repetitive application of the core development activities.

- It is incremental in that each pass through the iterative cycle grows the understanding of the problem and the capability offered by the solution.

- Multiple applications of the iterative cycle are sequentially arranged to compose a project.

To be truly effective, the development must be both iterative *and* incremental. If development is iterative without being incremental, activities can be performed over and over again in an iterative fashion *without* advancing toward the project's goals, or in other words, without reducing risk and incrementally building the solution. Progressive risk reduction and a steady march toward the project's goals are the hallmarks of iterative and incremental development. For the sake of simplicity, when we refer to *iterative* development, we mean *both* iterative *and* incremental.

What Is an Iteration?

An iteration can be defined in the following way:

> **Iteration:** A self-contained mini-project, with a well-defined outcome: a stable, integrated, and tested release.

An iteration consists of a distinct set of activities conducted according to an (iteration) plan and a set of objective, measurable evaluation criteria. The release can be either an internal release or an external release.

Let's look at the three aspects of this definition in more detail.

The Iteration Is a Self-Contained Mini-Project

A software development project produces a new release of a software product by transforming a set of users' requirements into a new or changed software product. With an iterative and incremental approach, this process is completed little by little, step by step, by splitting the overall project into several *mini-projects*, each of which is called an iteration.

Each iteration has everything a software development project has: planning, the application of the core software development disciplines (Requirements, Analysis, Design, Implementation,[1] Test), and preparation for release. But an iteration is not an entirely independent entity. It is a small part of a larger project. It depends heavily upon being part of a project. We say it is a *mini-project* because it is not, by itself, what the stakeholders have asked us to do.

From the perspective of the development team, each iteration can be considered to be a self-contained project. This approach is very powerful because it enables the development team members to focus on meeting their immediate objectives and ensures that the results generated are frequently and objectively measured. The management team needs to ensure that the iteration objectives form a credible part of the larger overall project.

---

[1]   Throughout the book, we use the term Implementation to refer to the development discipline that encompasses the coding as well as the unit and integration testing of a component. This is the name used for the discipline within the Unified Process.

The management team needs to reinforce this way of working by ensuring that each iteration has the following:

- **Clear objectives**—Each iteration must have clearly defined objectives that are understood and agreed upon by all the parties involved in the project. This unifies the efforts of everyone involved in the project.

- **Measurable evaluation criteria**—For the objectives to function as the unifying theme for the team, it is essential that they are complemented with measurable evaluation criteria that enable the performance of the iteration to be objectively assessed.

- **A committed team**—The team must be singularly committed to working together to achieve the iteration's objectives. The team succeeds or fails as a whole, and all team members must do everything under their control to meet the objectives set for the iteration; all effort should contribute to achieving the iteration objectives.

- **A schedule**—As well as agreeing on the objectives for the iteration, the management must agree to its schedule and understand how it impacts the plans for the project as a whole. Scheduling an iteration can be as simple as setting the iteration's start and end dates and understanding how the iteration fits into the overall project plan.

- **An objective assessment**—To close out the iteration, it is essential that the results produced are objectively assessed against the iteration's objectives and evaluation criteria. Assessment should be conducted on a continual basis during the iteration and summarized at the end of the iteration. Without objective assessment it is impossible for the success or failure of the iteration to be judged and for the project to be controlled.

Doing these things ensures a well-defined and measurable result for the iteration that can be tied directly to the overall success of the project.

The Iteration Has a Distinct Set of Activities

Each iteration is unique. It involves undertaking a unique set of activities to produce a unique version of the product that objectively demonstrates that the iteration objectives have been met.

Because of this uniqueness, each iteration requires the production of its own iteration plan. The iteration plan contains the details of all the activities that the team is required to do to meet the iteration objectives. The amount and style of activity-level planning required for a project is dependent on many factors including the project risk, team size, experience levels, and the manager's own preferred management style.

For some projects, an informal plan describing the goals to be achieved and listing the tasks to be undertaken is sufficient; you can leave the scheduling and allocation of the activities to the development team. Other projects require more comprehensive plans that describe the activities and their allocation in greater detail to work out the dependencies between the tasks to be performed by the various team members. Regardless of the approach adopted, the principles of iteration planning remain the same:

- Establish the objectives and evaluation criteria

- Establish the resources available and schedule the activities

At any one time you work with no more than two iteration plans: one to manage the current iteration and one that is an evolving sketch of the plan for the next iteration. This limits detailed planning to those subjects of immediate consequence, avoiding the creation of unnecessarily detailed plans and encouraging the project members to focus on delivering immediate results.

As we shall discuss in Chapter 5, "A Layered Approach to Planning and Managing Iterative Projects," and Chapter 6, "Overall Project Planning," the iteration plans exist in the context established by the overall project plan, which is also developed iteratively and is adapted to the lessons learned from the execution of the iterations. The overall project plan is relatively high-level because all the details are pushed down into the iteration plans.

In Chapter 7, "Evolution and Phase Planning," and Chapter 8, "Iteration Planning," we look at the details of planning an iterative project and the iterations within it.

Each Iteration Results in a "Release"

To ensure that the project is making progress, each iteration is forced to produce something tangible: a "release." This release can be

- A prototype that is used to demonstrate some specific capability

- An "internal" release that is used to elicit feedback and that serves as the basis for further development and testing

- An "external" release that is shipped to customers in some form

The following is our definition of release:

> **Release**: A stable and executable version of a system.

The production of something executable during each and every iteration is so important to the iterative approach that some people even go as far as to assert that "The goal of an iteration is an iteration release: a stable, integrated and tested, partially complete system."[2]

In every iteration, all the software developed by all the teams involved in the project is integrated into a release. This series of releases provides the project with regular technical visibility points where the state of the project as a whole can be considered.

The idea that each iteration produces a release can seem confusing if you think of a *release* as something that is delivered to people outside the project team. When we use the term "release" we mean something that can be

---

2   Craig Larman, *Agile and Iterative Development: A Manager's Guide* (Boston: Addison-Wesley, 2003).

executed and evaluated, including things that are only evaluated internally such as prototypes, as well as external product releases. The early releases are incomplete versions of the system that demonstrate particularly important characteristics required of the system and address the major technical risks facing the project. As the project progresses, functionality is added incrementally to the software produced by the earlier iterations until sufficient functionality is available to enable the system to deliver real business value. After this point, subsequent releases can continue to be developed that implement additional capabilities.

The most typical kinds of releases, their purposes, and their time orders are summarized in Table 1-1.

Table 1-1   *Examples of Iteration Releases*

Release	Audience	Purpose
Proof of Concept	Internal	Demonstrate or investigate feasibility
Prototype	Internal	Demonstrate or investigate some capability
Intermediate Release	Internal	Elicit feedback from user representatives and demonstrate progress
Product Release (Test)	External	Elicit feedback from users
Product Release (GA[3])	External	Deliver value and business benefit
Product Release (Point)	External	Fix bugs and, occasionally, provide minor enhancements

An iteration's release becomes a product release when you decide to release it to an operational environment for unconstrained use by the user community. Many of the releases produced will have the level of quality and completeness required by a product release, but not all will be worthy of release. For example, the release might contain insufficient functionality to be useful to the users, or the users might not be ready to receive the release. Each consecutive release should be marked by

- A growth of functionality, as measured by the implementation of additional functionality during the iteration

---

[3]   GA or General Availability is often used to denote the first publicly available release of a software product.

- Higher quality, as measured by a reduction in the number of product defects

- Reduced risk, as indicated by estimate fidelity, risk magnitude, and stakeholder confidence

When planning an iterative project it is important to understand the purpose of, type of, and audience for the release to be produced by each iteration.

The Defining Characteristics of Iterative Development

A combination of these three elements gives iterative development its power:

- **An iteration functions as a mini-project**—This makes the iteration easily manageable and provides the entire development team with a clear, immediate focus. Structuring the project as a series of these mini-projects enables the inherent complexity of the project to be reduced by targeting specific issues and specific risks on specific iterations. It also helps to isolate the technical considerations from the management considerations, reducing friction between the various teams involved in the project and the amount of overlap within the project itself.

- **Each iteration comprises a distinct set of activities**—Each iteration deals with a specific and unique set of risks and, as a result, requires a unique set of activities in response to these risks. Each iteration focuses narrowly on resolving a set of issues and in doing so moves the project ahead. Successive iterations build upon one another, incrementally improving the performance of the project as the project incrementally builds the solution.

- **Each iteration results in a release**—This provides closure to a set of issues and risks by forcing the project team to produce something (the release), enabling the objective measurement and assessment of the project's progress. The series of releases, produced by the iterations, provides the project with regular technical visibility points where the state of the project as a whole can be considered.

Taken together, these three characteristics provide the foundation for successful iterative development of software and software-intensive systems. This approach also simplifies reporting to management: after each iteration, you simply report those objectives achieved, those unattained, and the remaining risk profile. These are things you can objectively state; they are not open to subjective interpretation. The scoreboard is visible and concrete, simplifying communication with stakeholders and senior management.

The Iterative Experience

Iterative development is, at its heart, a team-based approach to problem solving and solution development. It requires all parties involved—including the development team, the customer team, and the management team—to adopt collaborative techniques. To explore this idea, we consider how the adoption of iterative development affects the most common roles involved in a software development project.

If you consider the roles involved in software development, you will find that the roles fall into three broad categories:

- **The Core Development Team**—These are the people focused on formulating and developing the solutions identified by the requirements, including the application of the core development disciplines of Architecture, Analysis, Design, Implementation, and Test to develop high-quality components and solutions.

- **The Customer Team**—These are the people focused on defining the problems to be solved and the things to be built (including changes to business processes) to solve these problems. They must ensure that any solutions produced provide sufficient benefit to the commissioning organization.

- **The Management Team**—These are the people focused on making sure that the customer, business, and development goals are aligned, the right problems are being solved, the right solutions to these problems are being built, and the development is being undertaken in an effective, efficient, and controlled manner.

In the following sections we take a closer look at iterative development from each of the three perspectives outlined previously, examining how iterating helps the project achieve all of its goals and how it affects all of the people involved in the project.

Iterating from the Core Development Team Perspective

Let's consider project dynamics from the perspective of the core development team. This team is responsible for applying the development disciplines of Analysis, Design (including Architecture), and Implementation (including Unit and Integration Testing) to produce releases of the system that fulfill the customers' requirements. The requirements are considered to be the responsibility of the customer team, even though customer representatives or business analysts might be assigned to work directly and permanently with the development team. We will look at iterating from the customer team's perspective in the next section.

The Developer Perspective

The most common perspective taken on iterative and incremental development is that of the individual developer working on a small development team. After all, this is the perspective of the technical community that has produced the majority of the literature about iterative and incremental development. These developers have also provided most of the impetus for the adoption of these practices.

One of us recently attended a talk at a software developer symposium. The subject was iterative development using a specific interactive development environment. It soon became apparent that the presenter considered an iteration to be the iterative application of the "write test, write code, test code, fix code" cycle, applied over and over again, until a piece of completed, unit-tested code is available for inclusion into a release of some sort. And although it is true that these "development" activities embody many of the best practices recommended by the proponents of iterative development (such as test first, test often, and so on), the way that this presenter described their application would result in a very tight iteration, the duration of which could often be measured in minutes.

This view of an iteration as a single developer's cycle of "write test, write code, test code, fix code" is, of course, too narrow—it ignores much of the rest of the important work of the project team—but it is useful to continue to focus on the developer's perspective for a little longer.

Just as the symposium presenter described it, the tight feedback loop illustrates the natural way in which developers work on iterative and incremental projects. Individual developers follow their own rhythm and tend to perform analysis, design, and implementation in very rapid succession many times a day. At any one time, individual developers are making myriad tactical decisions as part of the fabrication and adaptation of the system's software. Individual developer activities tend to be synchronized around shared events, such as the daily build and system integration points. Group activities tend to be focused on architectural work, interface definitions, and the refactoring of the components.

When developers understand the limit of their responsibilities and their current objectives, their attitude is, typically, to roll up their sleeves and do whatever it takes to meet their obligations and deliver one or more working components to be integrated into some form of release. Each individual developer (or pair of developers, if practicing pair programming) develops an individual way of working within the framework laid down by the processes adopted by the project.

Progress and the Product Backlog

The individual developer is rarely interested in non-technical things, such as benefits realization, return on investment, or risk management. They achieve closure by regularly building real, executable code. Developers work by selecting sets of requirements and change requests to be analyzed, designed, implemented, built, unit tested, and then included into a release of the product. The overlapping nature of the developer's application of these disciplines is shown in Figure 1-1. The time and scale of the developers' iterative process can be measured in hours, days, or weeks depending upon the scale and complexity of the endeavor undertaken.

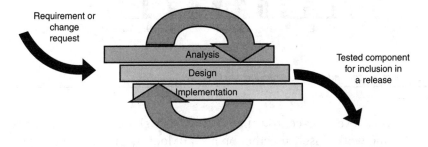

Figure 1-1 *Iteration from the developers' perspective*

Developers continue to work in this way, selecting and implementing small numbers of requirements or change requests from their list of outstanding tasks, until they have completed all items that have been assigned to them.

From the developers' perspective, the incremental part of iterative and incremental development is manifested in the increasing completeness and functional richness of the releases produced. This is contrasted with the (hopefully) ever-smaller number of requirements and change requests waiting to be implemented. This list of outstanding requirements and change requests is often referred to as the product backlog[4] because it represents the backlog of work waiting to be done. Each day the developers take more items from the product backlog, each day the build contains

---

[4] The concept of a prioritized product backlog was codified by and is central to the SCRUM iterative management method. See Ken Schwaber and Mike Beedle, *Agile Software Development with Scrum* (Upper Saddle River, NJ: Prentice Hall, 2001).

more implemented items, and each day some new work might be added to the product backlog. This daily, incremental progress through the work in the product backlog is shown in Figure 1-2.

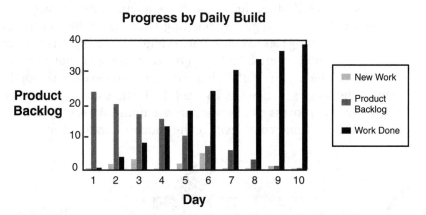

Figure 1-2   *Incrementally addressing a product backlog*

This developer-centric approach works well for small teams of developers who work closely together on a set of loosely interacting components and for larger communities of developers who work on a common code base, such as open source projects. To scale up to larger projects of closely inter-operating components—typical in larger development efforts—additional perspectives are needed.

The Development Team Leader Perspective

In contrast to the individual developer, the leader of the development team is concerned with the coordination and optimization of the work of a number of developers, each of whom is changing or implementing a number of components that must be integrated into a release that fulfills the team's shared objectives.

From the development team leader's perspective, an iteration is not just a cycle through the core development activities of analysis, design, and implementation; an iteration is typically a time-boxed mini-project that results in the production of a significant new release of the software.

Figure 1-3 illustrates how the team harnesses the work of a set of individual developers to produce an integrated release that is then used to generate feedback that shapes the change requests and requirements to be implemented in the next iteration and included in the next release.

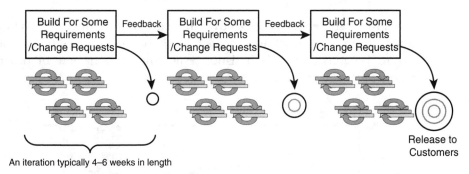

Figure 1-3   *Iteration from the development team leader's perspective*

Adapted from Craig Larman, *Agile and Iterative Development, A Manager's Guide* (Boston: Addison-Wesley, 2003).

The goal of an iteration is a release that integrates the work of the whole development team into a stable, integrated, and tested release of the system. For most iterations, these releases are internal releases—baselines created primarily for the benefit of the development team and used to provide closure to the iteration and measure the progress being made. These are "internal releases" not typically deployed to the users, though they are often shown to users to obtain feedback.

Typically there are three or more iterations leading up to the public release of the software. Each iteration in the sequence sees the production of a release of the system, starting with a small, partial implementation of the system in the first iteration that then grows incrementally with the implementation of more requirements, iteration by iteration, until the final customer release is produced. Figure 1-3 illustrates this development with the growing size of the circles representing the releases produced.

Connecting the Developer and Team Leader Perspectives

To many developers, iterative and incremental development is the progression through an almost infinite series of iterations, each of which causes the system to grow larger and larger until the customers are happy with it or decide to stop investing in its further development. From this perspective, as long as work is getting done and changes are being made, the project is making progress.

From the team leader's perspective, the work of a number of developers must *integrate*, or work together successfully, for progress to be made. Figure 1-4 illustrates this holistic development team view of progress across several iterations.

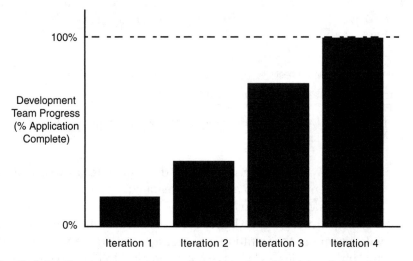

Figure 1-4   *Each iteration produces a more complete release than the previous iteration.*

In Figure 1-4 progress is measured by how complete the integrated working release produced by the development team is, not by the completeness of the specification or other documentation. The completeness of the application is calculated from the number of requirements that the integrated application can be shown to implement. In each iteration, the focus is on the production of a *working* release and not some set of project documents or un-integrated components.

It is essential that the team's progress is considered as a whole through the testing of the integrated release. We have witnessed a number of projects in which prodigious numbers of components were created and tested by developers but could not be integrated into even a partially complete product. In these cases the view of the project illustrated in Figure 1-4 never occurred because there was no objective evidence that any progress was being made toward the completed product.

The Need for Planning

To integrate the work of more than a few developers, some amount of planning must be done. First, work must be allocated to developers in a way that minimizes interdependencies so that the developers can work with some degree of independence, even though they are in fact interdependent on one another.

Second, the developers must have a way to agree on their interdependencies; for example, they must be able to agree on names of components and their interfaces. As the interdependencies become larger in number, the team eventually reaches a point at which informal interpersonal communication must be augmented with a record of the agreements made between the developers.

As these complexities increase, and as the effort to efficiently coordinate the work of the team members becomes more complex, the team leader will need a way to know what will be done when and in what order. This situation gives rise to the need for more formal planning, which in turn drives the need for estimation. The interdependencies between components owned by different developers initially create the need for more formal planning because the schedule can no longer be determined by simply either taking the expected development time for the most complex component (the case where all components are independent) or summing the development time for all the components (the case where all the components are so interdependent they can only be worked on one at a time). The dependencies between components must be understood to construct an effective schedule.

Iterative development is sometimes said to operate on such short time scales that there is no need for planning and estimating. This argument is specious; it is like saying that because we only take one step at a time, there is no need to plan our route because we can make continual decisions about where to turn next. As long as you don't care where you end up, this strategy works just fine, but the people paying for the project most certainly do have goals that they need the project to reach.

Planning and estimating is basically a mechanism for determining that the project is worth doing in the first place and for keeping the project on track after it has begun. Few of us would hire someone to repair our home without knowing how much it will cost and how long it will take with some certainty. Software development projects are no different: the people funding the project need to know how much it will cost and when it will be done. That requires both planning and estimates. We return to these topics when we look at the customer and management team perspectives later in the chapter, as well as in later chapters covering planning and estimating the overall project and individual iterations inside the project.

Iterating from the Customer Perspective

To achieve the full promise of iterative and incremental development, you must ensure that its adoption will affect more than just the technical and development communities. In fact, adopting iterative practices ideally has a profound and lasting impact upon all the business people involved in the project. It also fundamentally changes the way that these people specify, pay for, and realize the business benefits to be derived from the successful development of software solutions.

If the adoption of iterative and incremental development has no impact upon the business and the way that it realizes the benefits provided by the iteratively developed solution, then its adoption becomes just a technical assurance issue and is of little consequence outside the development team itself. To deliver its full potential, the way the project and its stakeholders interact must change as well.

Most of the literature on iterative and incremental development focuses on the developer and development team lead. Although the impact upon the development team is important, the true value of iterative and incremental development lies in the potential to dramatically improve business results. To achieve these benefits, the business—including 1) the customer representatives, 2) the business analyst team, 3) the end users of the system, and 4) the business leaders (sponsors)—must become an active participant in the project and will need to change the way that it interacts with the development team. In this section we look at these changes and their impacts. We consider these four aspects of the customer perspective individually and how the changes represented by iterative and incremental adoption positively impacts the business as a whole.

The Customer Representative

The adoption of an iterative and incremental approach by a software development project profoundly affects the way that customer representatives interact with the project's development team. As shown in Figure 1-5, each iteration presents the developers with the opportunity to elicit objective feedback on the appropriateness of the solution and the business impact that it is likely to have. By basing the feedback on demonstrations of working versions of the system, the communication is kept focused and to the point, enabling the development to converge upon a solution that meets the system's essential minimal characteristics.

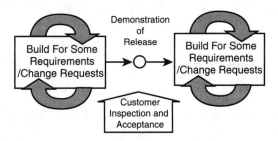

Figure 1-5   *The demonstration of each iteration's release enables objective customer feedback.*

Each iteration also gives the customer representatives an opportunity to comment on the work in progress and influence the future direction of the development. After reviewing a working release that illustrates the implications of the requirements decisions and the development team's interpretation of these requirements, the customer might decide to change the direction of the project or the prioritization of the remaining requirements.[5] Again, by demonstrating small amounts of working functionality, the team can focus on what would constitute an accurate business solution and what the minimum amount of functionality to achieve this result would be.

At each iteration boundary, the customer representatives have the opportunity to accept or reject the release produced by the development team

---

[5]   Of course, if the project is always changing direction at every iteration, it will go nowhere. If this seems to be happening to you, something in the basic assumptions for the project has gone wrong. When this happens, it is usually best to stop the project and reconsider what the project is trying to achieve.

and to adjust the direction in which the project is progressing. This empowers the customer team to become more involved in the project and to ensure that the solution will deliver the business benefit expected.

The rapid cycle of development, demonstration, and assessment provides many opportunities for the customers to become involved in the project. This iterative approach enables them to

- Take a more active and objective role in directing the project, actively steering the project to ensure that everyone involved in the project converges on a shared understanding of what would constitute an appropriate business solution

- Adopt a relationship with the project that is suitable for the amount of risk and trust in the relationship between the collaborating parties

- Act upon any lessons to be learned from their experiences to date—an opportunity that is also afforded the development team as a whole

- Maintain an objective assessment of the project's risks and progress to date

- Build confidence in the team's ability to deliver

The regular customer demonstrations also benefit the development team, giving them increasing levels of

- Understanding of the project as a whole

- Evidence of their convergence on an acceptable business solution

- Confidence in the acceptability of their plans

- Realistic expectations regarding the customer's requirements

The result is that the development project will no longer be a black hole into which money is poured in the hope that some software will appear at some vaguely specified point in the future. If the promised convergence and understanding does not result from the initial set of iterations, then action can be taken to either reorient the project or, if necessary, cancel it. This provides the business with an objective way of monitoring and adjusting its investments.[6]

The Business Analyst Perspective

There is some disagreement in the industry about whether the requirements work should be part of the iterative process. In our experience the true benefits of iterative and incremental development are only achieved when all team members, including those representing the interests of the business, are active participants in the project. This means that the requirements process needs to be tightly integrated with and executed to the same timetable as the iterative development of the solution.

Consider the following observations:

- There is no value in documenting requirements that will not be delivered. It is difficult enough to deliver a solution on time and within budget when you focus only on the work that absolutely needs to be done to achieve this goal. Spending time developing things that will not be delivered is a distraction and puts the project at risk. Rather than assuming this additional work "will help the next project," we suggest that the work be left to the project that it will benefit. Bear in mind that when a first project does not meet its objectives—a possibility heightened by unnecessary labor—there is often no "next project."

- Developers do not need to have all the requirements available before they start work. They just need enough requirements to drive their current work (in this case, the current iteration).

---

[6] Of course, this additional visibility comes with added responsibility for the business: it is imperative that stakeholders provide timely feedback when given the opportunity to review results. The iterative approach provides many opportunities for assessment and feedback, and timely and frank feedback is essential to ensuring more rapid time to market.

An awful lot of work can be done on a system before *all* the requirements have been completed because not all requirements are interrelated or of equal importance. A development team can easily solve the problem of how the system will support 1,000 concurrent users long before all the user interfaces are designed. In fact, the design of the user interfaces typically has little or no effect on the scalability of the solution.

- Requirements work tends to expand to fill the space available. On most projects, the ability for people to dream up new requirements easily outstrips the ability for any team to deliver them within the time and budget allotted.

Parkinson's law,[7] "Work expands so as to fill the time available for its completion," has never been truer than for requirements-related work. We have never seen a requirements team declare that they have found the full set of requirements before their allocated time has run out. In cases where the requirements team actually finds a sufficient set before the time runs out, they invariably invent more requirements rather than declare the task complete.

Defining requirements takes almost no effort compared to the effort needed to implement them. The real art in defining requirements is not to identify as many as possible but rather to find the minimum set of requirements needed to satisfy the business problem. More requirements are not better, and many a solution has been ruined by having too many features.

One of the basic assertions behind all iterative and incremental software development processes is that the only thing that matters is the delivery of a solution; anything that does not contribute to the delivery of a solution is superfluous and needs to be eradicated. The purpose of an iteration is to

---

[7] C. Northcote Parkinson, *Parkinson's Law: Or, The Pursuit of Progress* (London: John Murray, 1958).

produce a working version—albeit often a partial one—of the solution. To this end, the requirements to be implemented by the iteration must be known. This does not mean that all the requirements that will ultimately be satisfied need to be known before the development iterations start. Instead, we strive to have just enough understanding of the requirements to set a meaningful objective for the current iteration.

There are several models for the development of the requirements to drive an iterative development project. Let's consider four common models: waterfall, forward-loaded requirements / backward-loaded development, requirements pipeline, and just-in-time requirements.

Waterfall Requirements, Iterative Solution Development

In this case, all the requirements are defined before the iterative development of the solution starts. This pattern is shown in Figure 1-6.

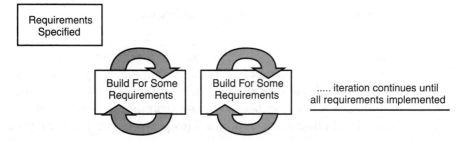

Figure 1-6   *Development iterations with requirements defined up front*

As you probably realize by now, this approach is less than ideal because it usually results in the definition of some requirements that are never implemented or the over-specification of some of the requirements that are. The approach creates unrealistic expectations and an ongoing atmosphere of antagonism and disappointment as the fact that every requirement cannot be implemented starts to dawn on the parties involved.

It also leads to the requirements team working in isolation, depriving them of feedback from the development team, which in turn tends to produce conflict between the requirements team and the development team. It also prevents the team as a whole from learning the lessons from the implementation of the first set of requirements and using them to improve the quality of the requirements and the whole team's effectiveness.

This pattern is often seen in organizations where

- The development team wants to iterate but has yet to prove the appropriateness of the approach to the business community. This is how many organizations embark upon the road to a more collaborative, iterative way of working.

- The development is being outsourced by a company unaware of iterative and incremental techniques to a company that has adopted them.

- The business has an adversarial relationship with the development team and does not trust the team to make any decisions or to work collaboratively with them.

- The business cannot prioritize the requirements and insists on treating them as a complete, indivisible set.

Although this approach is the historically conventional approach, it typically leads to an organizational structure that places team members into functional "silos" based on the type of work that they do. This creates barriers between team members, reducing communication and the teams' effectiveness in delivering solutions. This problem is usually compounded by the measurement systems that are put in place to reward people for doing work that is necessary but not sufficient on its own to deliver a successful solution. It is common for functionally organized teams to consider "success" to be the delivery of a good requirements document or a signed off software architecture document.

Although these things can be necessary for delivering a solution, they are not valuable in and of themselves. If the solution fails to be delivered, the completed requirements document has yielded no value. Although it might be necessary to organize reporting relationships along functional lines to promote skills development and career growth, the measurement of progress and results needs to be aligned with the delivery of the solution. This usually leads to a "matrixed" reporting structure in which everyone reports to at least two organizations: one functionally aligned for career growth and the other aligned with the project and its goals.

Forward-Loaded Requirements, Backward-Loaded Development

If there is any stability in the requirements, as shown in Figure 1-7, the development iterations can start well before the requirements work is completed.

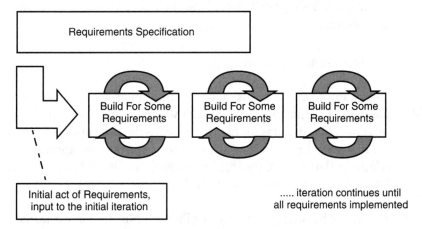

Figure 1-7   *Overlapping requirements specification and development iterations*

This appears to be a more iterative and incremental approach, but it still leaves the requirements and development teams working in different managerial silos with all the communication overhead and conflict that this arrangement can entail.

The Requirements Pipeline

There is a temptation to move to a pipeline model where, as shown in Figure 1-8, the requirements team works on the requirements for the next iteration while the development team implements the requirements defined for this iteration.

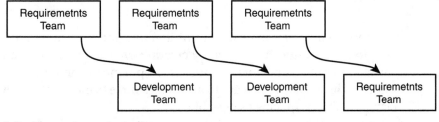

Figure 1-8   *The requirements pipeline*

The questions this pattern immediately raises include: Which iteration is the team working on? Do the iterations overlap? Is the team working on more than one iteration at a time? From a personal and project management perspective, how will people know which iteration they are working on or what their priorities are? We look at iteration from a management perspective in a later section.

Just-In-Time Requirements

Ideally, to provide the most agile, flexible, and focused development team, the requirements and development work are fully integrated into a single set of well-defined iterations. This extends the typical developers' model of iterative development to include the requirements specification of the release and its system testing. This extends the model of iteration shown in Figure 1-1 to that shown in Figure 1-9.

This way of working is the most effective, but it depends upon having an integrated, collaborative team that includes representation from the business and customer perspective, as well as that of the technically oriented development team.

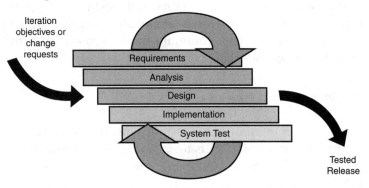

Figure 1-9   *Iteration with integrated requirement specification and system testing*

This approach takes the principles of iterative and incremental development to their natural conclusion by creating a single team focused on the effective, iterative, and incremental development of the entire business solution. This enables the team to adjust its course to ensure the delivery of business value as quickly as possible.

As you can see, the impact upon the business analysis team of adopting an iterative and incremental approach can be quite dramatic, as team members find themselves an integral part of the project team, working on the project for its full duration and not just in its initial phase. They also find themselves defining the requirements iteratively, often in a just-in-time fashion within the same iteration in which they are implemented.

The business analysts share the responsibility for delivering the solutions that they specify, and they participate at a depth of involvement in the project required to fulfill that responsibility. The requirements documentation, rather than being an immutable record of the "final" requirements that must be delivered, becomes a living contract between the business and the development team regarding what needs to be delivered to achieve a satisfactory resolution. When thought of as a contract, the requirements documentation infers obligations on both sides and is open for negotiation; the less trust between the parties, the larger and more complex the requirements document.

The User Perspective

The user perspective is very similar to the customer representative in that the users get to see periodic evidence of progress to ensure that the solution will meet their real needs.

If the project is to be successful, it is essential to involve the users in the demonstration and assessment of the releases produced by the iterations. We say "generally advantageous" because setting expectations is critical to getting useful feedback. Users can be confused if they don't know what they are looking at or what feedback you are hoping to get from them. Regular interaction with the users also helps remind the development team of its responsibility to deliver business value and not just sexy new technology. It also enables the requirements themselves to be verified as well as the system being verified against them.

The benefits of soliciting early user feedback, especially in the areas of usability and user-interface design, are illustrated by the following story. We think it offers a valuable lesson.

There once was an insurance company that appointed a visionary new IT director. The new IT director's first actions were to decree that

- *All new applications developed by the company would be designed and developed as Windows applications*

- *A PC-based Windows desktop was to be rolled out to all of the company's IT users*

- *All software would be developed using object-oriented development techniques*

The first major application to be developed under the new regime was a replacement for the old-fashioned "green screen" system that was used in the company's call center. The development went well, and the application was available for system testing on time and on budget. The visionary IT director was very impressed by the application, especially when its new user interface was demonstrated. The use of Windows—with a point-and-click user interface, a sophisticated help system, and 3D iconography—was so elegant that the IT director was heard to remark, "Fantastic! With this point-and-click interface and extensive bubble help, even I could answer the customer phone calls." Champagne corks were duly popped as the team celebrated the success of the project and the new IT strategy.

Unfortunately the visionary IT director was not one of the people whose job it was to answer the phone calls. That was the job for a different set of people who worked in very cramped conditions— with no room for a mouse and mousepad on their desks. The last thing they wanted was a graphical user interface that took many mouse clicks to achieve what used to be achievable with a single hot key. Add to this the fact that no one was allowed to start answering calls in the call center without extensive training, rendering the extensive bubble help redundant. Thus, the new system created a complete mismatch between the users' expectations, the physical and cultural conditions of the workplace, and the features delivered.

The users were expecting a new system to make their lives easier, but they received one that only made their lives harder. So much effort had gone into engineering the new user interface that no other new functionality had been delivered. The system never made it through user acceptance testing and its initial pilot.

The moral of the story is this: a clear understanding of the real problem being solved and the key high-level requirements for the solution is essential from the outset of the project. With this in hand, the team can plan iterations that demonstrate progress toward these goals, working out the details of the user interface and the rest of the "detailed" requirements. In our example, the IT director had the wrong understanding of the problem, but the development team assumed that he knew what was needed. Because he was "the customer," they delivered what he wanted, forgetting that the real users were the ones who really needed to be satisfied.

The Business Leader (or Sponsor) Perspective

From the perspective of business leaders, the value of iterative development lies in its ability to support the incremental commitment of resources to the project and to balance the investment in the project against the project risk and its chances of success. The funding exposure to the project can be limited to the current iteration. If the progress and risk reduction demonstrated by an iteration are insufficient, then the project can be cancelled or redefined without great loss to the organization. The funding of an iteration can be seen as the purchasing of additional information about the project before committing to further investment toward its completion.

Barry Boehm uses the analogy of stud poker[8] to illustrate the sponsors' perspective on an iterative and incremental development project. In a stud poker game, you can put a couple of chips in the pot and receive two cards, one hidden and one exposed. You can also see the other players' exposed cards. If your cards don't promise a winning outcome, you can drop out of the game without great loss. If your two cards are both aces, then you can bet heavily on a winning outcome. In any case, you can decide during each round whether to gamble more of your chips to buy more information about your prospects of a win or to fold based on what you already know.

---

[8] Barry Boehm, "Spiral Development: Experiences, Principles, and Refinements," Special Report, CMU/SEI-2000-SR-008, July 2000.

Similarly, with each iteration, more resources are gambled on the successful outcome of the project, and more information is available about the project's chances of success. If the project is successfully iterating and producing objectively measurable, proven increments, then the sponsors' confidence in the project will also increase incrementally, and investment will continue. If, during the initial iterations, the project looks as though it has been dealt a losing hand and faces insurmountable levels of risk, then the sponsors can drop out without great loss. In a sense, the cost of each iteration is somewhat like the premium on an insurance policy.[9] You are protecting yourself against the possibility of catastrophic loss (project failure) by buying information gained during the iteration. This parallels one of the standard approaches to risk management: buying insurance to manage risk.

As we shall see in Chapter 3, "Controlling Iterative Projects," the concept of using the iterations in this way to manage project risk is fundamental to the successful adoption of iterative and incremental techniques.

Iterative and incremental development offers businesses many benefits above and beyond those proffered by the more traditional waterfall development approaches. These include increased predictability, reduced time to market, higher quality solutions, increased project agility, and increased productivity.

The majority of these benefits will only be realized if the business itself starts to take a more active role in the projects and their iterations. This will fundamentally change the way that the business works with the projects, affecting everything from the way the requirements are captured to the way progress is assessed and, possibly most importantly, the way the projects themselves are funded.

Iterating from the Management Team Perspective

After you have the business and the development teams working collaboratively in a series of shared iterations focused on delivering value back to

---

[9]   In fact, only part of the cost of an iteration is an "insurance policy" because iterations also create value by implementing requirements. The cost of the information "insurance premium" is related to the repetitive activities of building and testing the solution and potentially being required to reimplement some functionality.

the business, you need to consider the management perspective and why it is important.

First, imagine a software development project without any management guidance. (Perhaps you've worked on one.) Such projects usually suffer from a lack of medium-to-long term direction; progress resembles a random path, and few team members are sure where they are going. Without mapping out the iterations, you have very little idea when the project will be finished, what resources will be needed to complete the project, or when these resources will be needed. Without estimates to help judge the cost of the project, it is difficult to get the customer and sponsor to commit resources for all but the most trivial project, and little information is available to indicate how the project is progressing toward the goal of delivering a solution.

It is very tempting to fall into the idealistic trap of thinking that if a team is committed to a goal, it will automatically self-organize and fulfill all its commitments to the organization as well as deliver high-quality software rapidly and effectively. In reality, even the best teams need some oversight to make sure that day-to-day work is progressing toward the longer-term goal. More importantly, it is the task of management to bring together the team that can do the work.

It is hardly accidental that poor management is the root cause of many project failures.[10] It is tempting to believe (as many non-managers do) that managing is little more than tending to the needs of some distant bureaucracy and that the role of the manager is to keep the bureaucrats at bay while the rest of the team does the work. In fact, much mediocre management does, in some way, resemble this picture. But if this is all the manager does, the project will probably fail.

Management is more than note taking, schedule keeping, and budget minding: providing leadership and direction are essential to achieving results. Proper management affords clear answers to essential questions:

- "Are we solving the right problem?"

- "Do we have the resources to deliver the solution?"

---

[10] See the Standish Group's annual CHAOS Report available from www.standishgroup.com.

- "Are we working on the right things, right now, to get us to our end goal?"

- "Are we fooling ourselves into thinking that we can actually deliver a solution within the time and resources allotted?"

Planning and measuring are not ends unto themselves but rather tools that help the manager to answer these questions. As our colleague Joe Marasco notes, good managers are aggressive skeptics: they seek out problems and confront them while they can still be managed and controlled. Management is the art of intelligent anticipation.

The Project Manager Perspective

As we have already established, an iteration consists of applying the core disciplines of software development to produce a demonstrable, executable release of the product under development and ensuring that the product will be grown incrementally across a series of iterations, each building on the product and lessons learned from the previous iteration. This is illustrated by Figure 1-10, which builds on the development team, customer, and business analyst perspectives shown in Figure 1-3, Figure 1-5, and Figure 1-9.

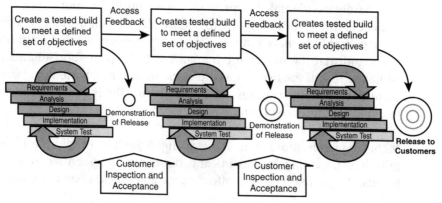

Figure 1-10   *An iterative project from the project manager perspective*

From the project manager perspective, each iteration appears to be a small, self-contained project during which all the disciplines of software development are applied to produce a release of the product that meets a specific, shared set of objectives. This idea that an iteration is a small project is consistent with most commonly used definitions of a project, such as:

> **Project**: A temporary endeavor undertaken to create a unique product, service, or result.[11]

Iterations are certainly temporary, typically lasting between four to six weeks,[12] and they definitely produce a discrete product in the iteration's demonstrable release.

At its simplest, the iterative planning process appears as a cycle of agreement, execution, and assessment:

1. Agree with the team and stakeholders on the objectives for the iteration, including evaluation criteria, timescales, and constraints.

2. Agree on a plan for how the team will achieve the objectives.

3. Execute the plan.

4. Assess the achievements of the team against the initial set of objectives and evaluation criteria.

5. Assess the impact of the iteration's results on the project as a whole.

6. Start the next iteration.

From the manager's perspective, these activities occur continuously throughout the project, as shown in Figure 1-11, and they form the basic pattern by which the work on an iteration is planned and managed.

---

[11] From the Project Management Body of Knowledge (PMBOK). See http://www.pmi.org.

[12] The actual length of an iteration will vary with the number of people on the project, which in turn varies with the complexity of the solution. Larger project teams require longer iterations to deal with the complexities of managing their communications. We cover this in more detail in Chapter 7.

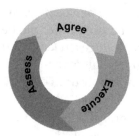

Figure 1-11   *Iteration from the management perspective*

Managers also provide direction to the project as a whole, organizing work so that each iteration progressively contributes to delivering the solution. To do this they must plan, execute, and assess the project as a whole and organize it as a series of contiguous iterations. The relationship between the two levels of management process is illustrated in Figure 1-12.

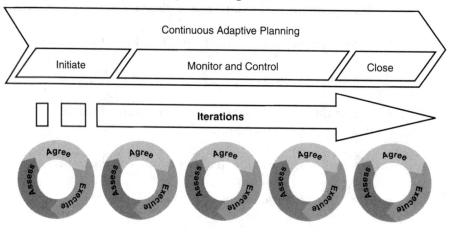

Figure 1-12   *The overall and iteration project management processes*

Part II of this book examines both the overall project and iteration management processes to be applied. For now it is sufficient to understand that the planning, monitoring, controlling, and management of iterative and incremental projects are fundamentally different from those of a non-iterative project in terms of the following:

- The dynamics of the project team interactions

- The nature of milestones

- The handling of dependencies

- The measurements and metrics

- The resources required

- The degree of parallelism in the project work

One of the most significant differences lies in the way that progress is measured. Instead of measuring progress by the completion of intermediate work products such as requirements documents, analysis models, and design specifications, progress is measured in terms of how many scenarios have been developed and tested. As shown in Figure 1-13, each iteration results in measurable progress toward solution delivery.

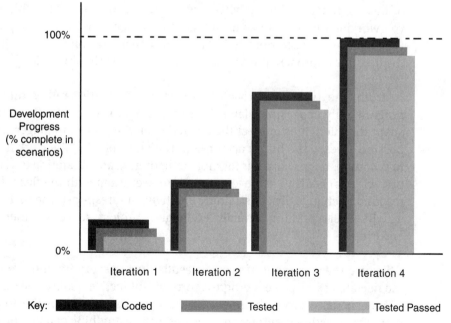

Figure 1-13   *Measuring increments in successfully tested software*

Shifting from subjective progress assessment (often in terms of documentation produced) to objective progress measurement (as measured by the amount of working software that has been produced) is the most fundamental difference between the iterative approach and other more traditional approaches. Analyzing trends arising from objective assessment of progress at the end of each iteration enables the project manager to take control of the project and to make changes to improve the odds of project success.

Iterations enable the project to become a series of smaller self-contained projects, each dependent upon the results and performance of the previous one. The feedback generated by assessment at the end of each iteration enables you to adjust the plans for the next and all subsequent iterations.

The Product Quality Perspective

These regular iteration assessments provide the mechanism for judging progress. At these *minor milestones,* progress is assessed against the goals and objectives set forth by the team in the iteration plan. One implication of this approach is that activity-based status reporting ("What things are you working on?") is not as useful as achievement-based status reporting ("What have you accomplished?" "How close to being done are you?"). With the iterative approach, it is very hard to hide the truth for very long.

In truth, the typical approach of measuring activities rather than real progress only causes problems. The project team needs the flexibility to adapt their activities to meet the desired goal; the project manager cannot possibly foresee the future accurately enough to plan all the work needed to accomplish the goals. It is far more enlightened and liberating to give the project team goals to achieve and to empower them with the flexibility to respond to change. By constraining creativity and responsiveness, detailed activity-level planning actually endangers project success rather than ensuring it.

Objective measurement of project results during every iteration removes the need to assess project progress through subjective quality assessments of intermediate products. Instead of judging the quality of the requirements by insisting that they be *signed off* before anything can be built, you can evaluate requirements by taking the first ones available and driving them through the development cycle within the iteration to produce working, tested code.

The way quality is measured fundamentally changes. Quality measurement is focused on the regular iteration assessments that provide continuous insight into the project. Retrospectives on the process and working practices regularly capture the lessons learned by the project and engender a culture of continuous process improvement within it. These observations can be immediately applied within the next iteration to improve quality and team performance.

Objective measurements are made in every iteration by testing the release produced, which provides management and quality indicators and measures project progress. This continuous integration and testing results in increasing test coverage as the project progresses because each iteration regression tests the requirements delivered by the previous iterations. This continually increasing test load is shown in Figure 1-14.

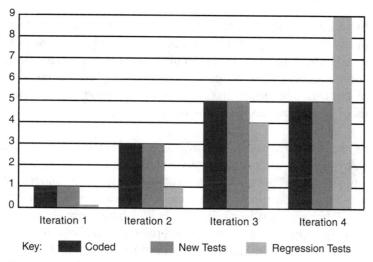

Figure 1-14   *Test coverage increases iteration by iteration.*

The result of engaging in testing in every iteration is that testing becomes the critical *guidance mechanism* of the project—it provides the information that is essential to steer the project in the right direction. This is a shift from the "quality verification" perspective that testing occupies on a conventional project. Rather than identifying problems after the fact, testing can actively change the outcome of the project!

The adoption of an iterative approach helps to improve the quality of the results delivered by the following:

- Reducing requirements misunderstandings early by forcing the requirements to be rapidly translated into things that can be observed and measured

- Reducing development risk early by proving technical approaches

- Accommodating and controlling change from the start of the project

- Providing a way to evaluate process effectiveness, schedules, team performance, and resource adequacy early in the project while changes can still be made

In an iterative approach, quality managers focus on the usefulness of the products and the processes, supporting the effectiveness of the team as a whole. The emphasis of the quality assurance changes from a focus on completeness to one of "fit for purpose." The project manager must let go of the misconception that "signing off on products and never changing them again provides higher levels of quality."

As we have discussed, iterative development follows an "agree/execute/assess" cycle in a very tight loop. Generally teams are pretty good at "agreeing" and "executing" but not very good at "assessing." The main role of team members focused on product quality is to provide the "assessment" part of the loop. They provide the mechanism by which the team learns about what they have just done so that midcourse corrections can be made in the next iteration. Without a continuous assessment function, the whole process breaks down. Testing is the meat of this process. Regrettably, many project teams do not adequately staff this important function.

Summary

Adopting iterative and incremental development techniques is not a purely technical decision that only affects the developers and other technical people involved in the project. It represents a fundamental change in the way that the project is conceived and progresses, a change that affects everyone involved in the project. Iterative development, therefore, requires changes in the way that the whole project team works and interacts, including changes in the way the project is managed.

From the perspective of the development team members, the adoption of iterative and incremental development is empowering, enabling them to actively and aggressively attack the project risks and challenges in whatever they judge to be the most appropriate manner. Managing iterations by setting clear objectives and objectively measuring results (and not dictating activities) ensures that they are free to find the best way to deliver results.

From a customer and business team perspective, the introduction of clear, meaningful objectives, combined with the ability to review demonstrable results, enables those who will ultimately use the new software to take an active role in the project and share its ownership with the development team. Iteration has a profound and lasting impact upon all the business people involved in the project and fundamentally changes the way that they specify, pay for, and realize the business benefits of software solutions.

From a management team perspective, each project is decomposed into a series of smaller projects, called iterations, each of which builds on the results of the previous one to incrementally achieve the overall project goals. This segmentation of the project introduces regular measurable milestones that keep the project on track while empowering the development team to create innovative and effective solutions, maximizing the project's probability of success.

2

How Do Iterative Projects Function?

"The joint was rocking, going round and round."
—*Chuck Berry*

Of all the characteristics of the family of modern, agile software development methods, the practice that makes the biggest contribution to the success of the method—and in most cases holds the whole thing together—is iterative development. It matters far less what method you select as long as you choose an iterative, incremental process.

In fact, if a project is iterating successfully, then it will probably be successful. It will certainly be under control and producing predictable results regardless of whether the project is using use cases, object orientation, aspect orientation, pair programming, or a test-first approach. The true value of many of these techniques is in the support that they provide for the successful iterative development of the solution.

Although there are many competing methodologies and processes promoting iterative software development, the iterations themselves always have certain key characteristics. As we saw in Chapter 1, "What Is Iterative Development?" iterations can be thought of as divisions of time inside a project, each of which has a clear set of objectives and results in a "release" of the product under development, a mini-project as it were.

In this chapter, we examine the key characteristics of successful iterative projects.

Iterative Development: Maximizing the Chances of Project Success

We adopt iterative and incremental software development approaches and manage our projects in an adaptive, iterative fashion for one primary reason: to maximize our projects' chances of success.

Defining Project Success

For a project to be successful, you need to be able to articulate what success means for the project. One commonly accepted definition is that used by the Standish Group in their series of CHAOS Reports: "Completed on time, on budget and with all the features/functions originally specified."[1]

Based on this definition, they classify projects into three resolution types:

- **Successful**—The project is completed on time and on budget, with all features and functions as originally specified.

- **Challenged**—The project is completed and operational but is over budget, over the time estimate, and has fewer features and functions than initially specified.

- **Failed**—The project is cancelled before completion.

Using these criteria, the Standish Group has analyzed US project performance since 1994 and produced some sobering results. Figure 2-1 summarizes these, showing that the majority of projects are still considered challenged or failed.

---

[1]   The Standish Group's annual CHAOS Report is available at www.standishgroup.com.

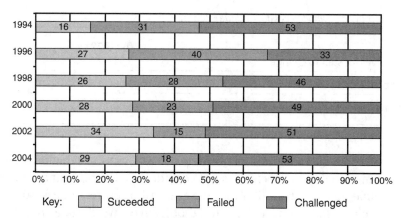

Figure 2-1   *The Standish CHAOS Report—Project Resolution History (1994–2004)*

Although we agree that most software projects are unsuccessful, we think it is for a very different reason than the causes explored by Standish. Increasingly, software projects and the solutions they deliver facilitate organizational change, which requires a clear change in the criteria for success. No longer are these projects being evaluated solely in the traditional terms of budget, schedule, and cost. The real success criteria are related to the business benefit produced, as measured by the business sponsors. This shift in emphasis is reflected in the results of a recent study in the United Kingdom that surveyed project managers for the success factors in achieving successful change,[2] which produced the results shown in Table 2-1. The lower the number associated with the factor, the more important it was considered.

Table 2-1   *Factors in Achieving Successful Change*

Factor	Average
Designing the system to have tangible business benefit	2.57
Communicating the reasons for change	3.08
Designing the system to benefit its users	3.30
Overcoming resistance to change	4.05
Training staff in new procedures	4.67

---

[2]   The State of IT Project Management in the UK 2002-2003. The final report from the Computer Weekly Project/Programme Management Survey. Report by Chris Sauer and Christine Cuthbertson, Templeton College, University of Oxford.

Table 2-1   *Factors in Achieving Successful Change*   (continued)

Factor	Average
Providing incentives for staff to change	5.33
Completing the project on schedule	5.68
Delivering the full functionality as specified	6.00

Note the clear distinction from the CHAOS Report in that delivering the full functionality as specified is not considered as important as delivering tangible business benefit. Although Standish is correct in asserting that most projects fail to meet their initial objectives, we think a more meaningful measure is whether they deliver business value in acceptable time. Measured this way, most projects still fail to measure up, but we think that software project teams need to shift their focus to delivering business value and not seek to optimize for hitting the original plan.

Ultimately a project should be judged upon the value that it delivers to the business that commissions it, the customers that purchase its products, and the users that use them. Rigidly implementing the initial set of requirements might be inappropriate if the business conditions have changed or if the initial understanding of the appropriate solution was flawed.

The business value delivered is a function of the project's cost, time, functionality, and quality, but unfortunately this function differs not only for each project but also for each stakeholder in the project. Our preferred definition of project success involves the delivery of an appropriate solution on time and within budget.

Many stories can be used to illustrate how the definition of success varies from business to business and project to project. One example that springs to mind follows.

Success?

For some projects, meeting the original specification is of marginal importance when compared to getting to market early.

A small company that we once worked with developed an initial single-user version of an insurance administration system primarily to act as a sales device to develop a presence in the market. The initial system was thrown away and replaced by an entirely new system.

The fact that the original system did not meet the real stakeholder requirements or even the original specification was not important to its success. By being first to market, the system set a level of expectation and created enough demand that it was worth investing in a scalable, functionally complete second version. The owner of the company went on to become one of the richest people in the country.

For other products, achieving a high level of quality pales in significance when compared to delivering an exciting set of new functionality. The classic case here is the enormous success and ubiquity of the Windows platform despite the many bugs and defects it contains.

For many projects, the idea of specifying all the functions and features up front is a hindrance, not a helping hand. Many of the iterative projects that we have worked on have been exploratory projects where the requirements have evolved alongside the development of the system and where the biggest risks have not been related to the definition of the functionality but rather to whether the type of application envisaged can be developed at all.

One of the most important parts of the project manager's job is to understand what the desired outcomes for the project are and what business results the project is expected to deliver. If time to market is the primary driver of business results, you will manage the project differently than if product quality is the driver of business results. Many project teams unfortunately isolate themselves from the business implications of the solutions they are developing and focus exclusively on the technical aspects of delivering the solution. What they are missing is that the solution they are building is part of a business strategy, and there are as many distinct solutions as there are strategies. You will most likely develop the wrong product if you don't understand the business context. Many techniques can be used to facilitate the development of a clear understanding of this context; one of our favorites is to develop a balanced scorecard[3] for the project. This technique is very powerful because with its consideration of the financial, customer, process, and learning and growth aspects of the project, it

---

[3] Robert S. Kaplan and David P. Norton, *The Balanced Scorecard: Translating Strategy into Action* (Harvard Business School Press, 1996).

provides a framework within which to consider and evaluate what success really is. We return to this subject in more detail in Chapter 6, "Overall Project Planning," when we consider lifecycle and release planning for iterative and incremental projects.

Success and the Iterative Project

The big advantage of the iterative approach is that it allows the project to adapt to both changing circumstances and the changing understanding of success that evolve as the project progresses. Many examples can be used to illustrate what happens to projects when the definition of success held by the stakeholders diverges from that held by the development team and what happens when people cling too tightly to their early assumptions and decisions. One example is the story of the visionary IT director and his graphical user interface that we used to illustrate the user perspective on iterative development in Chapter 1.

Another, sadly quite typical, example of what can happen when the stakeholders' and development teams' understandings of success diverge involves a large government IT development project where, to win the bid, the IT supplier produced a plan that laid out exactly which screens and components the developers would be working on months and in some cases years before the work actually took place. As the project progressed, and as the stakeholders' understanding of the true implications of the new system increased, it was pointed out that the original plan was seriously flawed and, along with the original statement of requirements, failed to address many of the biggest risks facing the project. The project manager refused to change the plan, holding onto his original assumptions and agreements as though they were holy writ. To the project manager, success required following and delivering to the original plan. The project did manage to deliver to the plan and fulfill the original contract but sadly did not produce a product that could be used successfully. In the eyes of the business, this was a failure, and so ultimately the project failed.

At the end of the project, there were a large number of outstanding change requests, many of which had been raised before the corresponding functionality had actually been implemented. The system itself became front page news because of its failure to deliver the correct services required to implement the government policies that led to its commissioning, and it is still used as an example of bad development practices by many people in the industry. Arguments still rage about which side of the partnership was ultimately to blame for the failure of the project. One thing is clear: there was no shared appreciation of what success really meant and no mechanism to adjust the project if its definition changed.

Ensuring that project success measures focus on business success and not on foolish adherence to the original plan is essential to ensuring that these stories are not repeated.

The most common example is that of the project where the requirements are signed off early in a project before the risks and problems are properly understood. The requirements themselves are then treated as an inseparable mass, all of which must be delivered to constitute success. The project then proceeds until the point where it becomes clear that either the project needs to be extended or requirements need to be de-scoped. This usually seems to occur after 90% of the project schedule has been used up and it becomes clear that 90% of the work is still left to do.[4] The reality is that there have probably been problems all along, and the project manager was not looking at the right measurements. More frequent assessment of actual results and basing earned-value measures on successfully completed tests and not production of artifacts or specifications are key to understanding what is really going on.

One of our favorite books on the state of the IT industry is *Crash: Learning from the World's Largest Computer Disasters,*[5] which is full of detailed stories of the type mentioned previously. Among the conclusions drawn by the authors is that adopting an iterative approach, which enables stakeholder expectations to converge and actively attacks the project risk, significantly increases a project's chances of success.[6] By iteratively establishing, sharing, and managing the definition of success and having the ability to adapt the project as this definition changes, everybody within the project benefits, and the probability of the project succeeding is greatly increased.

---

[4]   The classic 90% done, 90% left to do paradox that is observed on so many struggling projects.

[5]   *Crash: Learning from the World's Largest Computer Disasters* by Tony Collins and David Bicknell (Simon & Schuster UK, 2000).

[6]   Another one of their conclusions is that because the majority of projects are so late and their original estimates are so bad, the probability of your project being late and costing more than predicted is so high that if you are not prepared to spend at least three times what is originally estimated for the project, then you should not even start.

The checks and balances and the collaboration inherent in the iterative approach provide the mechanisms for achieving concurrence among the project's stakeholders, which in turn increases the project's chances of success. Continuous adaptive planning, resulting from the controlled application of the iterative approach, enables the project members to learn from experience gained during the iteration and enables them to react appropriately to any external changes that affect the project. This allows the project members to adjust to any changes in the stakeholders' understanding of the dimensions of project success or, as often happens, a change in the stakeholders themselves. It also allows everyone to discover the bad news early. If you are hatching a disaster, where there is no chance of success, you usually know it by the end of the second or third iteration. This information enables organizations to cancel poorly conceived projects early so that they can focus on projects that *will* deliver business results.

As we noted in the Preface, it is ultimately the people on the project who make it succeed or fail. By adopting an iterative approach, you enable all the people involved in the project to actively share in and influence the project's success.

Success and the Iteration: Gathering Evidence of Project Success

Each iteration has objectives that are set by the management team in collaboration with the development team (especially where technical objectives are specified) and the customer team (especially where the business- and requirements-related objectives are defined). These objectives provide the project with its direction and focus. The success of an iteration is based upon the teams' achievements when measured against the iteration's objectives and associated evaluation criteria.

The most common objectives for an iteration are to successfully implement and test a number of scenarios or a set of requirements and/or change requests, producing a new release of the solution that contains more functionality and is of higher quality than the one before. Establishing the right objectives is important in order to enable the project to have a singular focus on delivering working software; it is better to completely implement and test one key scenario or set of requirements than to complete the analysis and design documentation for all of them.

Objective measurement is essential to this way of working. It is the collection of objective feedback and the project's ability to react to and control this feedback that enables the successful management and control of an iterative project. This focus on the objective measurement of the iterations' contribution to project success enables us to avoid the two most pernicious problems associated with many unsuccessful attempts at undertaking iterative and incremental development:

- Using the iterative nature of the project as an excuse to never finish anything. The approach should not become a charter for procrastination that sanctions a "Don't worry—we can finish that in the next iteration" attitude.

- Allowing the results of an iteration to break or compromise results achieved by previous iterations. Each iteration needs to accept and build on top of what has come before. If the iterations are constantly in conflict with one another, then the project will never be completed.

By continuously monitoring the health of the project by assessing the results of the project's iterations, we enable its successful management and control. If the project is to be successful, then each iteration must

- Take a measurable step closer to the desired result

- Build and improve upon the results of the previous iterations

- Reduce the project risk

Each iteration will also do these three things in a demonstrable and objectively measured way. The success of an iterative project is therefore evident iteration by iteration. This progress can be measured and observed in many ways. We examine the most universal of these in the next section.

The Key Characteristics of a Successful Iterative Project

Successful iterative projects can be shown to be objectively and demonstrably converging on a successful conclusion: the production of an appropriate solution that will be delivered on time and on budget and that will address the real needs of the stakeholders.

A number of standard behaviors are exhibited by the majority of successful iterative and incremental software development projects that act as leading indicators of this success:

- Demonstrable, objectively measured progress

- Incrementally increasing functionality

- Continuously improving quality

- Continuous risk reduction

- Decreasing levels of change

- Increasingly accurate estimates

- Increasing enthusiasm, morale, collaboration, and effective teamwork

- Convergence on an accurate business solution

In this section we look at each in turn, examining its relevance to the iterative project and discussing the typical trends that a project can expect to display.

Demonstrable, Objectively Measured Progress

To be able to adopt an empirical approach to project management and control, we must be able to objectively demonstrate and measure how much progress the project has made. There are many possible ways to measure progress, including the following:

- Number of products and documents produced

- Number of lines of code produced

- Number of activities completed

- Amount of the budget consumed

- Amount of the schedule consumed

- Number of requirements verified to have been implemented correctly[7]

All these measures of progress have some validity and can be demonstrated in some way. But which is the best to use as the objective measurement of the progress made during an iteration?

The key here is to focus on the primary purpose of a software development project: to develop working, tested, and demonstrably functional software. The number of requirements that have been verified is the only one of these measures that is based upon the objective measurement and demonstration of working software. Other measures might provide an indirect measurement of activities completed but do not measure actual progress. Because each iteration should produce a stable, integrated, tested release, this task should be relatively straightforward and is typically the first measurement taken by any iterative project.

If we test the release produced by each iteration, we can objectively demonstrate that the project is making progress. If we record the amount of verified software that we have at the end of each iteration, we can start to track the true progress made against the schedule. Figure 2-2 shows a conceptual model of progress throughout a project, as measured by the percentage of the requirements that have been successfully verified at the

---

[7] It is worth noting that some requirements will be implemented correctly but will be found to be incorrect requirements—in other words, the development team implemented what the users asked for, but afterward it was determined that the requirements were not correct. Our concept of progress means real progress toward the final goal, so these implemented but incorrect requirements do not count toward real progress.

end of each iteration. The vertical lines show the iteration boundaries where the measurements are taken.

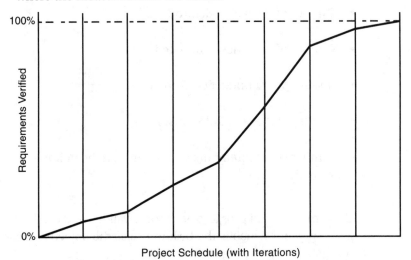

Figure 2-2 *Progress across a series of iterations*

In this example, requirements are "verified as complete" when they have been successfully tested.

This kind of measurement presents an accurate picture of the amount of software that the project has produced and keeps the project focused on producing a tested release in each iteration. Over the years, enough evidence has been gathered for us to assert that a graph of this progress over time will follow an S-curve.[8] Note that in this and subsequent diagrams, the shape of the curve might vary: some projects make good progress initially and then refine the results in later iterations, while other projects, especially those with significant technical issues, make progress slowly at first and accelerate later. The important observation is that results should be cumulative, with iterations building on their predecessors.

Figure 2-3 shows the cumulative growth of the amount of verified code produced by the project. The black line shows the typical code growth curve, and the shaded area shows the region of observed values. As noted previously, the actual gradient of the curve achieved by a project depends upon many factors including project risk, technical complexity, and resource availability.

---

[8] A conclusion also reached by Steve McConnell in his *Software Project Survival Guide* (Redmond, WA: Microsoft Press, 1998).

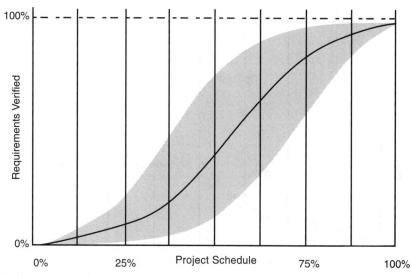

Figure 2-3   *The code growth curve*

> **Note**
>
> Both axes are defined as percentages. When considered as a graph of percentage progress against percentage time, we have found the S-curve (and the ranges shown) to hold true for the majority of successful iterative projects. If the graphs are drawn using absolute values, highly productive projects achieve a steeper gradient, illustrating that they deliver the full set of requirements earlier than less productive projects.

If we track the number of requirements implemented and verified during each iteration, this progress can be compared against the code growth curve to provide us with a simple indicator of project progress and its contribution to the overall success of the project.[9]

Figure 2-4 shows how the code growth curves can be used to interpret the results of even the earliest iterations. This figure shows that the project is slightly ahead of the expected curve and has the potential to finish early if the predicted mid-project acceleration occurs.

---

[9]   By tracking the amount of requirements verified at the end of each iteration and comparing this to the current scope of the project, this graph can be quite easily calculated and recalculated as the scope changes.

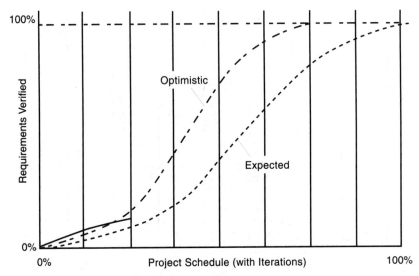

Figure 2-4   *Interpreting the results of early iterations*

As the project progresses and additional measurements are added to the graph, the actual code growth pattern for the project becomes clearer. Figure 2-5 shows the same project after the completion of five iterations. Here it can be seen that the project results are converging on the expected S-curve shape. Even a pessimistic reading of the trends shows only a very small shortfall in delivered requirements.

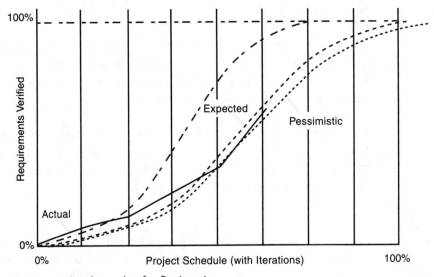

Figure 2-5   *Interpreting the results after five iterations*

On this and other charts, "complete" for requirements means that the requirements have been implemented and have passed all tests. This removes subjectivity from the assessment and makes measurement unambiguous. The line showing 100% represents the total number of in-scope requirements. If the scope changes, the graph must be recalculated to reflect how much of the new scope had been completed at the end of each iteration. This calculation is fairly easy if the number of complete requirements is recorded at the end of each iteration.[10]

Avoiding "Feature Creep"

On every project, requirements evolve and expand over time. This expansion of the original project scope is often called "feature creep," referring to the tendency for additional features to creep into the plan. It is natural as the users see results from iterations for them to think of new things that they would like. This disrupts the original plan if you have not accounted for a certain amount of it occurring. You can be making good progress according to plan, but if the number of requirements to be verified grows over time, you will begin to fall behind.

To some degree, there is no avoiding the problem, so you must have ways to deal with it. The solution will vary depending on your relationship with the sponsoring business. The simplest and least effective approach is to "just say no." Although this will keep you on your original schedule, it is ill-advised because the proposed new features represent valuable feedback that might make the solution more useful.

A second solution is to force ranking and prioritization of the new features against items already on the list. Ask the users what they are willing to give up to get the new feature. After ranking the features, you can then re-plan and decide what to remove from the plan if project length and resources remain the same. The sooner you have this discussion, the better. The natural time to have the discussion is at the end of each iteration, when you are revising the plans for the next iteration and the overall project.

---

[10] If you find you have to de-scope already completed requirements, then things have really started to go very wrong, but the graph will still be easy enough to recalculate.

We think a focus on frequent deliveries and getting value to the business sooner rather than later is essential to success, so we do not recommend extending the length of the current project to accommodate new functionality. Instead, we recommend staging a series of releases, with more important functionality delivered in earlier releases. We discuss how to manage staged releases in Chapters 5 and 6.

Incrementally Increasing Functionality

If the rate of code growth predicted by the S-curve is to be achieved or even exceeded, it is essential that the release produced by each iteration implements more verified requirements than the one before.

As shown in Figure 2-6, this increase in functionality is known as the increment, and it varies from iteration to iteration.

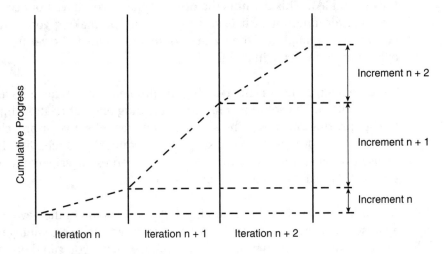

Figure 2-6   *Incrementally increasing amounts of completed software*

If the project is to continue to make progress, it is essential that each iteration delivers more demonstrable functionality than the one before and that the quality of the functionality delivered in earlier iterations is not compromised. There are many reasons why the increment produced by an iteration can differ from that produced by the preceding or succeeding iterations.

- **The amount of effort available to be applied during the iteration**—For example, one of the iterations might have far less effort applied to it because of team member illness or holidays.

- **The productivity of the team**—As the team gains experience and as working practices are tuned to fit the current project, the amount of time and effort required to implement and verify a set of requirements starts to decrease.[11] This increase in the team's productivity is one of the reasons for the acceleration in the middle portion of the code growth curve shown in Figure 2-3.

- **The stability of the requirements and the products produced by the earlier iterations**—If, because of the demonstration of an iteration's release, there are changes to the requirements that require existing code to be reworked and previously verified requirements to be discounted, then although much work is undertaken, the code growth produced by the next iteration can fall short of that originally predicted.

As illustrated by the S shape of the typical code growth curve, the increments achieved in the early project iterations are likely to be small. This is due to the costs and effort required to start up a project. The increments achieved toward the end of the project are also likely to be smaller due to the additional costs incurred by a project in transitioning to its user community (user support, training, optimization, bug-fixing, and so on).

Underlying all healthy iterative and incremental projects is the assumption that the project can continually build additional, high-quality increments on top of those it has built before. There are good reasons for the acceleration achieved by successful iterative projects in the middle sets of iterations

---

[11] The measure of productivity calculated in this way (by calculating the amount of effort required to implement a unit of requirements mass) is often called the project's velocity. We return to these discussions in Chapter 7, "Evolution and Phase Planning," and Chapter 8, "Iteration Planning," when we look at planning iterative projects and their iterations in more detail.

and sufficient evidence to establish the S-curve as the expected code growth profile for successful iterative projects.

Continuously Improving Quality

Another sign of a healthy iterative project is that the quality levels increase iteration by iteration. One way to measure the quality of the implementation is to assess the difference between the total amount of code developed and the amount of code that actually passes the system testing carried out within the iteration. The difference can be caused by two things: an under-staffed testing effort (more code is being developed than tested) or break-age (some code does not pass tests). Figure 2-7 shows a project's breakage across a series of iterations. In this case the amount of breakage (as shown by the double-headed arrows measuring the regression in functionality delivered) is reducing each time as the development team addresses problems found in the previous iterations and uses the experience and lessons learned from them to produce higher-quality code.

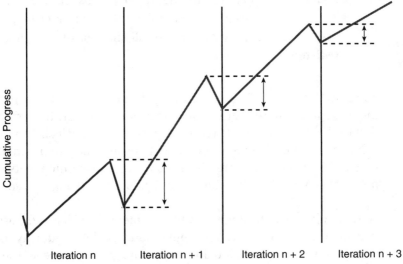

Figure 2-7   *Each iteration suffers from some breakage.*

One of the key attributes of a healthy iterative project is a steady focus on quality, which results in reducing levels of breakage across the iterations. A common dilemma faced by iterative projects is deciding whether to fix defects or add new functionality during an iteration. Figure 2-8 illustrates that the perceived progress in terms of requirements allegedly implemented is diverging from the actual progress, represented by the number of requirements successfully verified as complete by system testing. You can't figure out whether you are actually making progress unless you are measuring breakage.

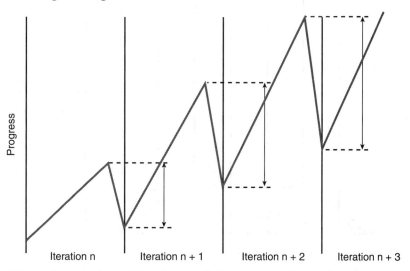

Figure 2-8   *Too much emphasis on adding functionality leads to degrading quality.*

In this case it is probably beneficial for the project to pause for breath and spend an iteration addressing the obvious quality issues and getting the two measures to converge.

Not every defect found during the system test will result in the functionality being rejected as unverified. Projects also need to keep an eye on the levels and types of defects being raised throughout the project. In early iterations it is less important that functionality is 100% complete and more important that the architecture is becoming progressively more stable. As a result, choosing the right things to test (architecture early, functional completeness later) is important. Selecting the wrong tests causes churn and forces the team to focus on the wrong parts of the project.

Figure 2-9 illustrates the defect trends one would expect to see in a healthy iterative project. Defects in the architecture or in the general solution approach are found in the early iterations; this is highly beneficial because it gives the project members time to address them before they threaten their ability to deliver. The number of new defects raised in each iteration is under control. Although more functionality is added during the mid-project iterations than during the early iterations, the releases are now of higher quality, so the density of defects is correspondingly lower.

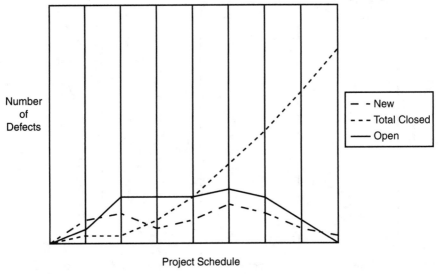

Figure 2-9   *Typical defect trends for a healthy project*

Over time, the project's defect density should start to fall. If each increment in implemented functionality results in a corresponding increase in the number of defects found, then the project has obvious quality problems and is unlikely to be able to successfully deliver. The ability of an iterative project to track the current level of quality and to react in an appropriate manner is one of the key enablers for success.

Continuous Risk Reduction

Another trait of a healthy iterative project is continuous risk reduction. The fundamental reason that a project iterates is to reduce the project risk. As shown in Figure 2-10, the resulting risk reduction should be observable across the project's iterations. In the figure, the risk reduction is superimposed over the typical project's code growth curve. This allows the risk reduction to be compared to the amount of code produced to reduce the risk, enabling assessment of the effectiveness of risk mitigation strategies.

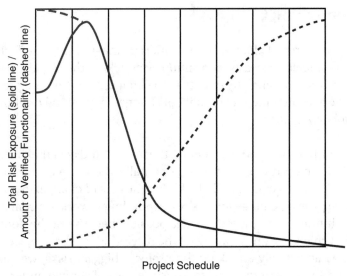

Figure 2-10   *Typical risk profile for a successful iterative project*

The key to the early iterations is to identify the small amounts of implementable functionality that will result in the most significant risk reduction for the project. Typically this means implementing the hardest areas of the system first because their intrinsic difficulty makes them high risk. At the end of each iteration, the total project risk should be lower than it was at the start of the iteration. If it is not, then the iteration was not successful.

The graph shows the project risk increasing in the first iteration; this is not because the project is not actively attacking its highest risks; rather, it is indicative of the fact that a project rarely understands all the risks it faces when it first starts. One of the key early lifecycle activities of any project is to investigate and analyze the risks that it faces. This leads to a period of risk exploration where the project risk exposure appears to increase as new risks are uncovered.

As we shall see in the following chapters, the principle of using iterations to address and attack project risks underlies the whole iterative planning and project management approach. *We divide projects into iterations to gain greater control over the project and to mitigate risk.*

Controlling Change

Some degree of change and rework is an inevitable side effect of producing testable releases early, continuously attacking the highest risk and continuously addressing any quality issues that arise. When the project members have accepted the inevitability of change, they can take action to minimize and handle it.

It is critical that you understand the impact and cost that accepting change will have on the project. Fundamentally, the more of the software system that has been completed, the higher the cost of change. In a successful iterative project, change and its corresponding rework are concentrated at the beginning of the project. This is possible because of the iterative nature of the project; by undertaking all the disciplines of the project simultaneously, while actively attacking the project's biggest risks, we gain the experience and insight required to bring the level of change under control. Figure 2-11 shows the change and rework trends that are typically exhibited by successful iterative projects.

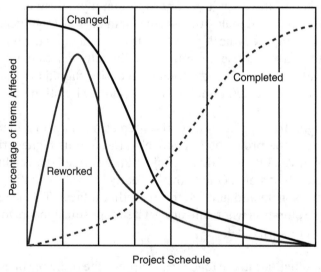

Figure 2-11   *Change and rework trends*

The percentage of items being changed shows the volatility that happens early in the iterative lifecycle. The reduction in items being changed shows an increase in stability. It is a fact of life for an iterative project that the products of the early iterations are likely to change as the understanding of the project as a whole develops. Early lifecycle artifacts are likely to be unstable, inaccurate, and imprecise.

As the project proceeds, work is undertaken to address these issues. The reduction in the amount of items being reworked shows an increase in the accuracy and stability of the work being undertaken by the project.

The increase in the number of items being completed reflects both of these trends but also an increase in precision. Early in the lifecycle, you would expect there to be a lot of rework of the produced items (typically between 35% and 100%). Later, as the amount of change decreases, rework should drop to below 25%. A key metric to watch is the stability of the interfaces between architecturally significant components (obtained by measuring changes on these interfaces). In the early stages, it is OK to have these move around a little bit as the architecture stabilizes, but interface changes late in the project are almost always a sign of deeper troubles. If you watch the rates of change on the interfaces, you will have a leading indicator of what is really happening.

The order in which components are implemented and completed is very important within an iterative project. The cost of changing something that has been substantially completed is much higher than the cost of changing plans for something that has yet to be implemented. As we shall see in later chapters, the decisions about what is stable enough to be implemented first and how to achieve sufficient stability to allow the project to progress are fundamental parts of the iterative planning process.

There is no way to eliminate entirely the possibility of major changes occurring late in the project lifecycle, but by adopting a risk-focused iterative approach to developing the software, we can reduce the probability of it happening.

Increasingly Accurate Estimates

For our iterative projects to be successful, they must be predictable. Not only each iteration taken in isolation but also the overall project considered as a whole must be predictable. Thus, accurate estimates must be available for both the short-term iteration activities and the long-term project performance.

An estimate is a prediction based upon probabilistic assessment.[12] Theoretically, the estimate should have an equal probability of being above or below the actual result, but statistical evidence[13] indicates that estimates are usually optimistic and are likely to be continually below the actual cost.

The margin of error inherent in estimates is best illustrated by the data collected by the Software Engineering Institute to support the COCOMO[14] cost model, shown in Figure 2-12. This shows how the project estimates (in terms of the project size and cost) become closer to the actual size and cost as they are made closer to the end of the project.

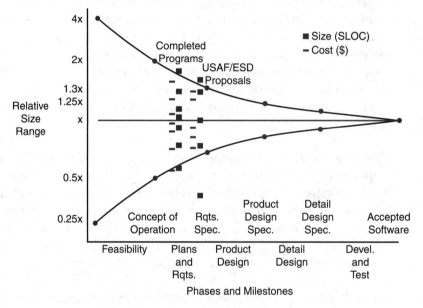

Figure 2-12   *The estimating cone of uncertainty*

Graph taken from the COCOMO II Model Definition Manual, available from http://sunset.usc.edu/research/COCOMOII/.

---

[12] Tom DeMarco, *Controlling Software Projects: Management, Measurement, and Estimates* (Upper Saddle River, NJ: Prentice Hall, 1986).

[13] See for example the results from the Standish Group's annual CHAOS Report (available from www.standishgroup.com) presented earlier in the chapter.

[14] This is an acronym derived from the first two letters of each word in the longer phrase Constructive Cost Model. See http://sunset.usc.edu/research/COCOMOII/. SLOC refers to "Source Lines Of Code," a common measure of the size of software.

In an iterative project, the estimates are revised during every iteration based upon the actual progress made by the project and the lessons learned so far. As we iterate through all the core software development disciplines, we gain experience and insight into all aspects of the project and create our own historical data upon which to base our new estimates. This allows the estimates to converge more quickly than in the waterfall model shown in Figure 2-13.

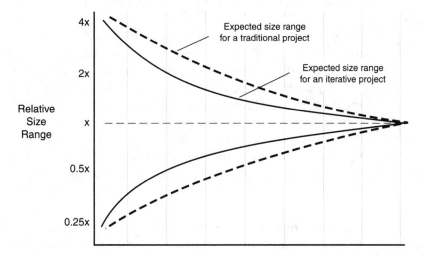

Figure 2-13   *The impact of iterations on the estimating cone of uncertainty*

Note

The accuracy of the initial estimate made at the beginning of an iterative and incremental project is no different from the accuracy of the initial estimate made at the beginning of any other kind of project.

The accuracy of an estimate can be measured in two ways:

- How close it is to the actual result

- The margin of error inherent in the estimate

As a project progresses through the iterations, the estimates should become more accurate in both dimensions. Successful iterative projects revisit their estimates during every iteration, producing a more accurate estimate for the work to be done in the next iteration and the remaining work for the project as a whole.

This is very different from the estimating practices that we observe on many projects. In fact the state of estimating in the industry is so bad that most of what companies call estimating isn't estimating at all. As Tom DeMarco observed in his 1986 book, *Controlling Software Projects:*[15]

> *[I]n many cases, the original project estimates don't involve any true estimating. Whenever there is an "expected right answer" conveyed to the estimator, the estimating process is likely to be stifled. Suppose your boss asks for a set of estimates and, each time you produce one, checks it against a little black notebook that you aren't allowed to see. If you're a political animal, you catch on quickly—soon you aren't estimating the work at all, you're just trying to guess what's written in the little book. Your reward is to be considered a team player. But you didn't build any estimating skills.*
>
> *There are many variations on the theme of the little black book. In some cases, upper managers convey their displeasure with raised eyebrows or by actually negotiating estimates. I have sat through sessions in which estimates were haggled as at a bazaar: "Fifteen months." "No more than nine." "I can't do it in less than a year, no matter what." "My final offer is eleven months." "You got it."*[16]

This observation remains true today. Even sophisticated parametric estimating models, such as COCOMO II, are often used to provide a justification for the negotiated result by tuning the parameters until an acceptable

---

[15] Tom DeMarco, *Controlling Software Projects: Management, Measurement, and Estimates,* (Upper Saddle River, NJ: Prentice Hall, 1986).

[16] Tom goes on to describe the various kinds of non-estimates prevalent in the industry at the time including such techniques as
- Next estimate = last estimate
- New estimate = last estimate + permissible slip
- Past slip = future negative slip
- Original estimate = expected right answer
- Your estimate = expected right answer + X

all of which appear to still be in use today.

result is achieved. The reality is that reductions in schedule without corresponding reductions in scope have the effect of setting the project up for failure from the start.

The fact of the matter is that the track record for estimating software projects is very poor, for a variety of reasons:[17]

- Software professionals don't develop estimating expertise.

- Teams don't make adequate provision to offset the effect of overly optimistic estimates.

- Software professionals don't have an adequate understanding of what an estimate ought to be.

- Teams don't cope well with political problems that hamper the estimating process.

- Software professionals don't base estimates on past performance, partly because there is a paucity of historical information.

- Teams don't continuously revise the estimates throughout the project.

- Teams don't do both course-grained and fine-grained estimates.

- People confuse precision with accuracy.

An iterative approach addresses all these issues by continually reestimating the remaining work as part of the assessment of each iteration. This continual reestimating and the effect it has on the accuracy of the related estimate of work to complete is illustrated by Figure 2-14, which shows the estimate to complete at each iteration boundary as an X with a corresponding floating bar to illustrate the margin of error.

---

[17] List derived from Tom DeMarco, *Controlling Software Projects: Management, Measurement, and Estimates* (Upper Saddle River, NJ: Prentice Hall, 1986).

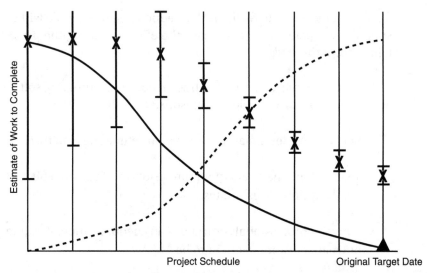

Figure 2-14   *Tracking estimates across a series of iterations*

The project can produce a higher-fidelity estimate at the end of each iteration because the project members can learn from the experiences of the previous iterations, which provide excellent historical data to use in the estimating process. The presence of more information on which to base estimates reduces the variability of the estimate. In addition, there is less work remaining to estimate, which further improves the accuracy of the estimates.

Continually reestimating the *remaining* work as part of iterative project monitoring leads to progressively better estimates as the project evolves. We return to the topic of estimating many times throughout the book as we examine how to plan and manage iterative and incremental projects in more detail.

Increasing Enthusiasm, Morale, Collaboration, and Effective Teamwork

Another force is at work in an iterative project that is more difficult to measure: the effect that iteration has on the team itself. The iterative approach, with its regular demonstrations, assessments, and retrospectives, provides a positive feedback loop that reinforces team building and serves as a built-in process improvement mechanism.

Iteration closure enables the development team to confront any issues that are interfering with the team's ability to deliver working software. These issues can then be dealt with during the next iteration.

The demonstration of working software at the end of each iteration brings the entire team to together and builds the development and extended teams' confidence that they can deliver.

The end result is that as the iterations pass, the team becomes a more effective, enthusiastic unit working toward the shared goal of delivering an appropriate business solution.

This is best illustrated by the way that the attitude of teams new to iterative development often changes as they begin to work iteratively. In most cases the iterative approach is adopted because the organization has been unsuccessful with more traditional approaches. Often a number of different "methodologies" have been tried, usually with ineffective results. Many team members will look at iteration as yet another approach that will ultimately fail. On all sides of the development organization, there will be initial cynicism toward the approach, with everybody doubting everybody else's ability to work in the collaborative fashion that is required for the iterative approach to succeed. Everyone will want to know, "Why is this different?" The difference is that the iterative approach provides greater visibility into what is really happening, and it forces issues to be dealt with when they arise. Problems do not go on forever without resolution; feedback is folded into planning the next iteration, and actions are taken to resolve issues. On traditional projects, a long time can pass before the team has executing code (the only real measure of how things are going), whereas on an iterative project there is executing code almost immediately.

For example, it is quite common for the developers to doubt the customers' commitment to the project and question their willingness to become actively involved in steering and assessing the project through the iterative elaboration of the requirements, providing feedback on the iteration demonstrations, and contributing to the iteration assessments. On the other hand, when approached to get involved in iterative projects, the customers often question the development team's attitude toward them taking a more central role in the projects and actually listening to their input.

In all the cases where the teams have wholeheartedly embraced the iterative approach, this "us and them" attitude has worn off within the first few iterations, and all the people involved in the project have started to function as a single team, sharing in each other's success and actively helping to address each other's concerns about the state of the project.

Convergence on an Accurate Business Solution

The biggest issue confronting software development projects is not how to deliver working software that meets a predefined set of requirements but rather how to deliver working software that actually benefits the business that commissioned the project and the users who will use it. Initial requirements statements are often flawed:

- People don't know what they want until they see it.

- People feel if they don't ask explicitly for something they won't get it, which causes the "requirements" for a system to turn into a list of everything that someone could possible want instead of what is really needed.

- When people understand the cost and implications of what they are asking for, they often do not want everything they are asking for.

Negotiation and building shared understanding are integral parts of the requirements process. The iterative development of the solution allows the key requirements themselves to be challenged by the demonstration of early versions of the system. This provides a firm foundation for increased understanding and a realistic basis for negotiating priorities. This bringing together of the various stakeholders' interpretations of the project and its purpose is one of the most powerful aspects of iterative development. To this end we should see the following perspectives converge iteration by iteration:

- What the customers think they need

- What the customers expect to get

- What the developers think the customers need

- What the developers expect to deliver

- What the users actually need

- What the developers are actually going to deliver

- What the customers are actually going to get

An illustration of what happens when this convergence doesn't occur is shown in Figure 2-15.

Figure 2-15 *The classic swing illustration of how different members of a team interpret the project's requirements*

This is a very old cartoon of which many variations exist. This one was found at http://www.badyear.com/images/cartoons/Tire_swing_cartoon.jpg.

To understand the convergence achieved by successful iterative projects, you must imagine all the different interpretations of the swing gradually morphing into a single illustration of a classic tire swing, constructed from a single rope and an old tire hanging from the right branch (which is what the user wanted).

The true power of iterative development is in the way that it objectively and measurably facilitates the convergence of the different stakeholder views. All the earlier characteristics we have discussed are in some way promoting and illustrating this convergence. The management approach that we discuss in the next chapter leverages these characteristics to provide us with a management framework that maximizes the project's chances of achieving its goals and iteratively demonstrating its success.

Summary

The iterative approach is quite simple in concept. In place of complex measures of *earned value,* based on intermediate artifacts and document-based deliverables, we substitute a simple measure of progress: running software in which a number of requirements have been implemented and verified. These completed requirements represent the real value that the project has earned.

To reduce risk, we consciously select requirements for implementation during the iteration that explicitly confronts specific risks. When choosing which risks to attack, we pick the hardest ones first.

There are some important side effects of doing this. Because each iteration builds upon the preceding one,[18] we make steady progress toward our goal of delivering a successful solution to the business problem. Because we make steady and demonstrable progress and because everyone is focused

---

[18] This progressive building upon the work of previous iterations is what distinguishes iterative development from mere prototyping. Prototypes are dangerous when they are used as "proof of concept" and then thrown away. Often these prototypes are toy implementations and don't significantly reduce risk. In iterative development the prototype is *not* thrown away unless it fails. If it demonstrates what was needed, it is incorporated into the system. This has the benefit of building the correct, scalable mechanism from the start. If work in the current iteration is being done to substantially replace the "prototype" that was written in a previous iteration, something is very wrong.

on the same thing—delivering an executable set of implemented and verified requirements—the morale of the team is higher, and the team is more productive.

Because we are continually integrating and testing the software, there is no "surprise" as the project nears its end when the team finds out that the pieces that they have been building do not work together. Over time, they will see that they are converging on the right solution, and so will the project's stakeholders.

This convergence is visible in many dimensions. Successful iterative projects all exhibit certain objectively measurable characteristics:

- Incrementally increasing amounts of verified functionality

- Continuously improving product quality

- Continuous risk reduction

- Reducing levels of change

- Increasingly accurate estimates

The objective measurement of these and other project characteristics enables the project to be successfully managed, monitored, controlled, and, most importantly, steered toward a successful conclusion.

The adaptability of the approach does not require that requirements be "frozen;" it is possible for the team to be flexible, and the end result might appropriately diverge from the original concept. In a world where organizations are continually adapting to change, this is the only approach that can possibly work. The benefit of having "sign-off" on requirements before the project starts is a fiction of an age long past.

The capability to adapt to change and to bring risk and uncertainty under control is the key benefit of the iterative approach. In following chapters we show how this works.

3

Controlling Iterative Projects

"O! thou hast damnable iteration, and art, indeed, able to corrupt a saint."
—William Shakespeare, Henry IV *Part 1*

To some people, iterative development appears to be uncontrolled development and a corruption of well established management practices aimed at establishing control over the project's schedule, scope, and cost.[1]

Iterative development is *not* uncontrolled development. On the contrary, iterative development actually allows for greater control than other development approaches: it provides more points at which progress can be evaluated and plans adjusted to adapt to new realities. But those people who associate re-planning with failure to manage are in for an attitude adjustment; they need to recognize that some re-planning is not only allowable but is in fact essential to achieving success. When applied correctly, iterative development provides a more rigorous and controlled project management environment—one that empowers the management team to take full control over its project, thus maximizing the team's chances of success.

---

[1] Although we're fairly certain that software development is not what Shakespeare is referring to here.

Only the inexperienced or naive would use the transition to iterative development to justify the removal of management controls from the project lifecycle. As Ivar Jacobson points out in *The Unified Software Development Process*,[2] the iterative lifecycle is not

- Random hacking

- A playpen for developers

- Something that affects only developers

- Redesigning the same thing over and over until developers finally chance on something that works

- Unpredictable

- An excuse for failing to plan and manage

Managing iterative projects can appear quite challenging because the disciplines of Project Management, Requirements, Analysis, Design, Implementation, and Test are interleaved in a way that provides no clear end to the activities of one discipline and the start of the next. This can be disorienting and sometimes results in a retreat to the familiar (but ineffective) pattern of sequentially organizing the activities in a "waterfall" style while using the terminology of iterative development. In other cases, the right degree of parallelism is never achieved, and the project teams simply work on many different disconnected threads of work without any coordination, with the result that they never finish anything.

These inept attempts at adopting an iterative approach are often used as proof that iteration will not work, forgetting that these same teams probably also failed at "waterfall" development. The problem is not with the approach but with the way that it is being adopted. It is just as if an untrained and inexperienced intern attempted an arterial bypass operation, something that skilled cardiac surgeons now consider commonplace. Adopting new approaches requires training and, more importantly, supervised practice and coaching.

---

[2]   Ivar Jacobson, Grady Booch, and James Rumbaugh, *The Unified Software Development Process* (Reading, MA: Addison-Wesley, 1999).

We divide a project into iterations to gain greater control over the project and to explicitly manage risk. To ensure that we are making progress, we force each iteration to produce something tangible that demonstrably reduces the project's risk. Over the course of the project, each iteration moves the project closer to its goal in a deliberate manner, removing different risks with each iteration. This deliberate march toward delivery is the hallmark of true iterative development, and it is what separates it from "random incremental" development, in which small parts of an application are developed incrementally but in an otherwise unplanned manner.[3]

During each iteration, you do a little from each of the disciplines. The challenge in planning and managing iterations lies in knowing what to do and when, how much from each discipline to do, and how to evaluate progress. Iterative development offers great promise in terms of reducing risk and improving time to market, but it requires changes at once subtle and dramatic in the way that projects are run. To understand these changes, you must first understand the basic mechanisms that are used to control iterative projects.

The Variables That Shape Projects: Scope, Quality, Time, and Cost

Most project management literature discusses the key variables that constrain a project: scope, quality, time, and cost. These are often presented as a triplet rather than a quadruplet, often as some kind of "iron triangle"[4] with the points labeled with whichever constraints the presenter is using to illustrate his or her thesis. The most common combinations are scope, cost, and time or quality, cost, and time, depending upon the point being made. We prefer to present this as a square (Figure 3-1) showing all four of the major project variables simultaneously.

---

[3] As is often the case when simple time boxes are used without an underlying architecture that is progressively built upon in a series of sequential iterations.

[4] Allegedly, people prefer a triangle because it is "sexier." See Max Wideman, "Triangles, Sex and Simplicity" (http://www.maxwideman.com/musings/irontriangle.htm). Mike Perrow also pointed out to us that the Roman statesman Cicero discovered what rhetoricians now call "the Ciceronian Triad," that is, things are best remembered in threes; four things are harder to recall, and only two things are often insufficient to prove convincing.

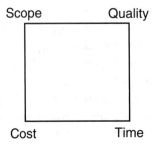

Figure 3-1   *The core project management variables*

The four corners of the square in Figure 3-1 represent the four core variables of project management:

- **Scope**—The scope of the product to be produced. For software projects, this is the number of requirements that the software must implement. This is what the CHAOS Report[5] measured in terms of features and functions.

- **Quality**—The quality grade required of the product to be produced. Quality is usually stated in terms of some reliability measure; mean time before failure is commonly used in real-time systems. Another popular measure is defects per thousand (or million) lines of code. One key measure of quality is fitness for purpose, which can be measured in terms of the relative priority of the implemented requirements and the number of them that were actually required. Defect-free code that does not meet any business need is not high quality.

- **Cost**—The total cost at completion of the project. This variable is sometimes referred to as resources because they are typically the single most significant aspect of a software development project's cost.

- **Time**—The time taken to complete the project, often stated in terms of some market-driven goal of having the solution ready by some specific date.

---

[5]   See the discussion of project success in Chapter 2.

The acceptable values for these four variables influence the way that a project is managed. Unfortunately they are not independent: if we increase the scope of the project, then it will typically require more resources and additional time if the quality is not to be compromised. Any changes made must be mutually compatible if the project is to be considered a success. Remember project success involves the delivery of an appropriate solution on time and within budget, which is a unique function of the project's scope, quality, time, and cost. As Max Wideman points out, "The interrelationships of these four separate variables are somewhat similar to a four-sided frame with flexible joints. One side can be secured and another moved, but only by affecting the other two."[6]

For a project to have any chance of success, these four core variables must all be mutually compatible, definitely attainable, and aligned to the stakeholders' shared understanding of project success.

Stakeholders: The Real Drivers of Project Success

Other forces drive the behavior of a project besides the scope, quality, cost, and time constraints to which it is subject. You should always remember that *it is really the stakeholders who drive the project.*[7] They are the primary source of requirements, constraints, and risks for the project. They supply the funding and audience for the project and will make the decision whether the project is worthwhile.

In our book *Use Case Modeling*,[8] we defined a stakeholder as

> **stakeholder**—an individual who is materially affected by the outcome of the system or the project(s) producing the system.

---

[6] Max Wideman, *A Management Framework for Project, Program and Portfolio Integration* (Victoria, BC: Trafford, 2004).

[7] Although people often talk about use-case driven, feature-driven, scenario-driven, or test-driven development, when discussing iterative software development processes, these are all mechanisms for defining and managing scope. These may well be the drivers for the software development process being followed, but it is naïve to think that these are the only forces working on the project and shaping project plans.

[8] Kurt Bittner and Ian Spence, *Use Case Modeling* (Boston: Addison-Wesley, 2002).

In addition, we have found it useful to classify stakeholders by the domain of the system that affects them most:

- **The Problem**—People in this group are affected by the problem or problems that the project intends to solve. They are typically the primary source of requirements; they confirm that the problem has been solved when they accept the product.

- **The Solution**—People in this group are affected by the solution because they have to support its operation or adapt their jobs to it in some way. These people might or might not benefit directly from the solution.

- **The Project**—People in this group are responsible for delivering the solution to the other stakeholder groups.

It is the risks, constraints, and objectives in these three domains that shape the overall project plan: the number, length, and style of the iterations; the disciplines that should be applied; the artifacts and techniques that are applicable; and the things that need to be done to prove to the stakeholders that real progress is being made.

Because nearly every project has stakeholders in each of these three domains, nearly every project has to handle risks related to each of them. Even more importantly, every project must satisfy its stakeholders that it is making sufficient progress to address these risks. Considering the project from the perspective of these three domains provides a means to simplify planning and management of the project's iterations. It also provides a framework for understanding and assessing project control mechanisms.

Controlling Individual Iterations

An iteration is like a little project: it has a beginning, a middle, and an end, and it has goals against which we can assess performance. These "mini-projects" are the underlying building blocks of the iterative project; controlling the iterations is the first step in controlling the overall project.

As mini-projects, the iterations are at the mercy of all the forces and constraints that affect the owning project. In particular, they are at the mercy of the four project variables: scope, quality, cost, and time. As mini-projects, they also must have objectives and success criteria defined for each of these variables.

You can exploit the nature of the iterations as small self-contained parts of a larger project to simplify the problem. This is done by selecting one of the variables to be fixed for the duration of the iteration. This enables the iteration to be controlled by varying one or more of the other variables.

The two most common variables to fix are:

- **Time**—Fix the duration of the iteration, creating what is known as a time box

- **Scope**—Fix the definition of what is to be delivered by the iteration, creating what is known as a scope box

In the succeeding sections we explore these two different approaches, looking at their strengths and weaknesses. We present these not to recommend them, because both have their own deficiencies, but to introduce alternative approaches before we present our recommended approach.

Time Boxing

Time boxing is a technique in which the overall project is divided into a series of iterations of usually equal length. The end of the time box acts mostly as an evaluation and synchronization point. During the iteration, a set of requirements is implemented or attempted to be implemented. At the end of the iteration, work is paused, regardless of the completion status of the requirements, and progress is assessed. If any work remains incomplete, it is simply continued in the next iteration.

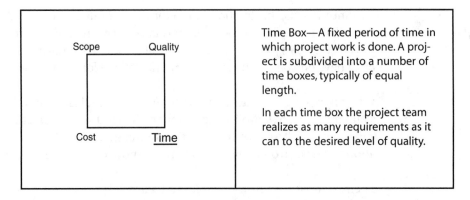

Time Box—A fixed period of time in which project work is done. A project is subdivided into a number of time boxes, typically of equal length.

In each time box the project team realizes as many requirements as it can to the desired level of quality.

Under the time-boxing approach, delivery *time* is the fixed component of the iteration plan, while *scope* becomes the main control variable. Because *cost* usually varies with time and scope, *quality* is sometimes used as a secondary control variable.

The iteration objectives are set by identifying requirements (usually scenarios) and work products that must be completed for the iteration to be considered successful. Quality is controlled by setting the quality level required of the products developed during the iteration. Typically costs are controlled by fixing the number of people working on the project for the duration of the time box.

We recommend time boxing as the foundation approach for controlled iterative and incremental development. Figure 3-2 illustrates how an iterative project appears as a series of time boxes, each of which consumes an amount of project resources. With a time box approach, the start and end points of each iteration are fixed.

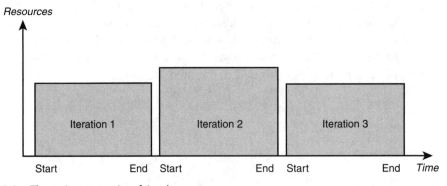

Figure 3-2   *The project as a series of time boxes*

To plan a time box, you select an appropriate amount of work based upon the priority of the requirements and the effort available. The effort available during the iteration is a function of the iteration's length and the size and skills of the team. As Figure 3-2 illustrates, the amount of resources expended can also vary between iterations.

Time-boxing iterations simplifies the planning process. As shown in Figure 3-3, the iteration can be thought of as fixed-size box with a fixed number of compartments, each of which represents an equal portion of the effort available in the iteration. The white boxes on the left represent the capacity of the iteration, while the shaded boxes on the right represent outstanding work items that need to be scheduled. The iteration planning process can be viewed as simply figuring out what outstanding work (the right side) will fit into the iteration (the left side).

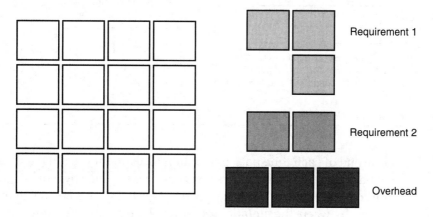

Figure 3-3   *The iteration as a fixed-size box, divided into equal-sized compartments*

By fixing the duration of the iteration and understanding the productivity of the project team, the number and size of the work compartments can be calculated. You can then estimate the effort to complete for the requirements, change requests, and other work items using the same units. The iteration's scope is then established by selecting requirements, change requests, and defects, starting with the highest-priority items and working down the list until work has been allocated to all the available compartments.

When the iteration is underway, the development team takes the individual pieces of work assigned to the iteration and completes them one-by-one in priority order. If the higher-priority items require more effort than estimated, then a proportional amount of lower-priority items are removed from the box to be addressed in a later iteration. Regardless of how the team is performing, the iteration time box boundary should be treated as immutable. Rather than changing the length of a time box, work is moved around between different iteration time boxes. The basic principles are shown in Figure 3-4. If the team is struggling to complete the work in the time allowed, then the lowest-priority items are removed from the time box to be addressed in the next iteration; if the team is doing better than expected and finishes all the work assigned to the iteration before the time box ends, then the most important work assigned to the next iteration is brought forward.

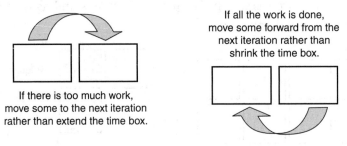

If there is too much work, move some to the next iteration rather than extend the time box.

If all the work is done, move some forward from the next iteration rather than shrink the time box.

Figure 3-4   *Time box boundaries are immutable.*

At the end of each time box, an iteration assessment is conducted, and the feedback is used to adjust the project plan. This is done by moving the work around between iterations. As shown in Figure 3-5, this can result in items moving between the iterations or even being removed from the plans entirely (hence the waste basket in Figure 3-5).

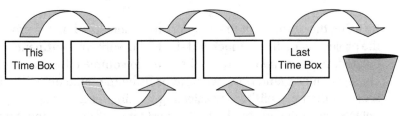

Figure 3-5   *Scope is managed by moving work between the iteration time boxes.*

Although it might seem that there must be circumstances where it would be beneficial to extend an iteration's time box to enable the team to successfully complete the iteration's objectives, this turns out to be dangerous because it leads to the time box boundaries becoming meaningless. When things start to slip, they are more likely to continue to slip rather than to be brought back under control. This tendency is worsened if you do not take the time to close out the iteration and learn the lessons from its execution.

Because iteration time boxes are clearly bounded, at the end of the time box, we call a halt to work and evaluate our progress instead of continuing to work until we are done. Time boxing establishes a sense of urgency and an awareness of schedule constraints. It also establishes a kind of *pulse* for the project—a regular meter against which progress can be measured.

When you first start to adopt an iterative approach, you might misjudge the appropriate length for your first few iterations. Our experience is that a duration of four to six weeks makes a good starting point for iteration length. If you find that this is too short or long, you can adjust the duration as you gain experience.[9]

When working in a time-boxed fashion, it is essential that you develop the most important requirements first so that only the least important requirements fall out of the plans for the project and do not get implemented. At the same time, you cannot keep putting things off; when this occurs, the project is in trouble, and if it occurs for long enough, the project is doomed. If too many unfinished requirements are left to the late iterations, the project will fall victim to its own procrastination.

Sometimes when you are behind schedule, the temptation to stretch the iteration just a little longer to accomplish the work can be very hard to resist. We think extending the iteration is a mistake for a couple of reasons. First, it's important to measure progress relative to goals. Stretching the iteration to accommodate slippage can give the impression that the original goals were accomplished as planned, which would not be true—doing so would be changing the rules after the fact. Second, it is really not disruptive to stop and take stock at the original iteration boundary and then replan the next iteration and continue the work. The honest thing to do is to accept that the iteration did not go as planned and take appropriate corrective action. Stretching the iteration tends to obscure the fact the project

---

[9] We talk about appropriate iteration lengths and how to get started in greater detail in Part II.

is off-track, even if only a little, and it's important to recognize where you really are.

Our suspicion is that teams want to extend the iteration boundary because they don't want to feel like they failed to achieve their objectives. Although we appreciate the value of positive feedback, we think that it is better to assess objectively. It could be that the iteration length was too short or the goals were too aggressive—the reasons behind the failure need to be understood. Stretching iterations to fit the work obscures what could be a systematic planning or scope management problem. We have found that iteration schedule slips usually end up being hidden and do not result in changes to the end date for the project, so stretching the iteration length usually has an unpleasant result at the end of the project when the project cannot be easily extended.

The most common cause for iteration slippage is the planning of iterations as mini-waterfalls combined with the late starting of the iteration's testing. We address the best ways to plan time-boxed iterations in Chapter 8, "Iteration Planning."

The keys to controlling iterative projects with time boxes are

- Estimating and prioritizing the work to be done

- Addressing the highest-priority items first[10]

- Assessing the iterations and acting upon the lessons learned

- Measuring the performance of and progress made during each iteration

- Adjusting priorities and scope based on actual results

Stakeholders usually find that time boxes produce very positive changes in the way that the project functions[11]—time boxes provide regular points in

---

[10] The trick here, of course, is to be able to establish the correct priorities. As we shall see, this topic forms an underlying thread throughout the rest of the book.

[11] Although it sometimes takes them two or three iterations to really understand the purpose of the time boxes.

the project where the stakeholders can clearly see project progress, and their predictability enables the stakeholders to plan and understand their involvement in the project. Stakeholders of the problem can begin to see how the evolving solution will meet their needs and can provide feedback to improve the overall solution. Stakeholders of the solution can see how the solution will affect their jobs and can begin to plan for the support and deployment of the solution. And, of course, stakeholders of the project can see whether the project is on track and making progress toward completion, or whether it is in trouble and requires attention or cancellation. This last possibility sounds harsh, but for a project that is not headed for success, the best outcome for everyone is to recognize reality sooner and take appropriate action to re-scope or cancel.

Scope Boxing

Scope boxing is a technique in which specific sets of requirements are selected and implemented as a set. The overall project is divided into a series of iterations of varying length. The end of the scope box still acts as an evaluation and synchronization point, but the iteration continues until all the selected requirements are complete. We do not recommend this approach because the variable length of iterations precludes the use of fixed periods of time as a control mechanism. We discuss the approach here because we have seen many people adopt this approach and claim that they are doing controlled iterative development. In our opinion this approach is not truly iterative and incremental, and it does not offer effective control over the project scope, schedule, or effort.

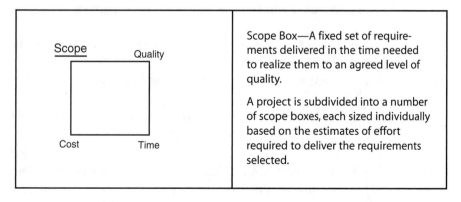

Scope Box—A fixed set of requirements delivered in the time needed to realize them to an agreed level of quality.

A project is subdivided into a number of scope boxes, each sized individually based on the estimates of effort required to deliver the requirements selected.

Often we see iterative projects attempting to use scope boxing to define their iterations. In scope boxing, the scope is fixed by selecting a set of requirements to be worked on until complete, without regard to fixed time limits.

With scope boxing, requirements are no longer moved around between the iterations; instead, the length of the iteration is adjusted to accommodate the time it takes to develop the set of requirements. Although this seems like a natural way to work, the absence of clear goals and time constraints leads to a diminished sense of urgency for getting the work done. The lack of deadlines means that there is little to keep the project on track, and as a result little tends to get done.

Scope boxing can appear simpler than time boxing because it collects a set of related requirements and then develops them to completion. In practice the lack of fixed milestones causes the effort to lose focus, and it often fails to actually complete what it sets out to do. It is easier to get started with scope boxing but very difficult to complete anything. It is also very difficult to manage a scope-boxing effort because there are few, if any, objective milestones.

The fundamental problems with scope boxing are related to controlling and tracking the plans:

- What do you do if you need to adjust the overall project plan to reflect what you have learned during the scope box?

- What do you do if the scope box is overrunning?

- How often do you revisit and revise the overall project plans?

- What do you use as intermediate milestones?

- Under what circumstances can you draw the scope box to a close before it has completed?

- When is it appropriate to pause for breath and learn the lessons from the project so far?

If you consider the use of scope boxes from each of our stakeholder perspectives, you will see why they are inferior to time boxes as a project control mechanism.

From the perspective of the problem stakeholders, project progress is irregular and unpredictable, and there is no opportunity to provide feedback before work is "done." From the perspective of the solution stakeholders, there are fewer opportunities to provide early input before functionality is "frozen" and hard to change. And as we have discussed, from the perspective of the project stakeholders, the project itself will suffer from a lack of direction and low morale due to a lack of motivation. As a result, we do not recommend scope boxing as a management technique and only present it here because we see people drawn to it and wanted to explain why it does not produce good results.

Guidelines for Controlling Iterations

As you have seen in the preceding chapters, there are many rules and behaviors associated with successful, controlled iterative development. These can be integrated with the concept of time boxing to provide some basic guidelines for working with iterations:

- Every iteration should be treated as a discrete time box.

- Iterations should be defined by their intended results and the evaluation criteria for these results.

- Every iteration should actively address and reduce project risk.

- During an iteration, the project team members should focus on meeting the objectives of that iteration alone, doing whatever they can to ensure the iteration's success, and no more.

- Every iteration should produce an executable release (either internal or external) of the software. The release should fulfill more of the project's requirements than the previous release (from the previous iteration).

- Every iteration should end on time. The time-box end date should not be moved.

- At the end of the iteration, its results should be objectively assessed; the team should be prepared to rework the solution and project plan as required.

Although these principles are useful and enable the control of individual iterations, they are not detailed enough to help plan a particular iteration or determine the objectives of the iteration. We need to introduce a few more concepts before we are ready to talk about how to decide which project risks should be addressed first and which requirements should be implemented in which iteration.

Controlling the Project as a Whole

It is usually insufficient for a project to be organized as a series of undifferentiated iterations: there are some risks and issues that need to be handled before others. Some kind of standard project lifecycle is required to provide a control framework within which the project can iterate effectively and to enable the state of various iterative projects to be compared.

In "Anchoring the Software Process,"[12] Barry Boehm specifically addresses this topic and defines a set of standard milestones for use with evolutionary, spiral, and incremental development processes. His intention is to provide a common framework, applicable to all software development processes, that defines a set of anchor points suitable for use by all software development projects.

The lifecycle anchor points that he introduces define a set of technical *milestones* suitable for use with all styles of iterative and incremental development:

---

[12] Barry Boehm, USC, "Anchoring the Software Process," November, 1995. Available at http://sunset.usc.edu/publications/TECHRPTS/1995/usccse95-507/ASP.pdf. An abridged version also appears in *IEEE Software*, July 1996.

- **Lifecycle Objectives (LCO)**—At this milestone, there must be conclusive proof that the project is viable: it solves a problem worth solving, and it is technically and financially feasible. To demonstrate that this milestone has been achieved, you must understand the scope of the project and the risks that threaten its successful conclusion. This requires there to be a credible plan and candidate architecture in place.

- **Lifecycle Architecture (LCA)**—At this milestone, the technical approach taken by the team needs to be proven and stable. To demonstrate that this milestone has been achieved, you must prove (by executing a partial solution) that you have a solution that works.

- **Initial Operational Capability (IOC)**—At this milestone, a usable version of the solution must be available to the user community, albeit in a prerelease form. To demonstrate that this milestone has been achieved, you must have a working, usable product that the users are prepared to receive.

This initial work on anchoring the software process was extended into a full iterative software development framework by Ivar Jacobson, Grady Booch, and James Rumbaugh,[13] Philippe Krutchen,[14] Walker Royce,[15] and many others to create the Unified Process and its commercially available derivative, the IBM Rational Unified Process (RUP). As a result, a common framework has evolved to help teams to plan a software development project and determine the goals of each iteration.

---

[13] Ivar Jacobson, Grady Booch, and James Rumbaugh, *The Unified Software Development Process* (Reading, MA: Addison-Wesley, 1999).

[14] Philippe Kruchten, *The Rational Unified Process: An Introduction*, 3rd ed. (Boston: Addison-Wesley, 2003).

[15] Walker Royce, *Software Project Management: A Unified Framework* (Reading, MA: Addison-Wesley, 1998).

The Unified Process extends Boehm's initial set of three anchor point milestones to define a *software development project lifecycle*[16] consisting of a set of four sequential phases,[17] each culminating in the achievement of a major project milestone.[18] These phases and milestones (shown in Figure 3-6) provide guidance and a roadmap for project planning and control. Together they define a project lifecycle suitable for the management of any iterative and incremental project.

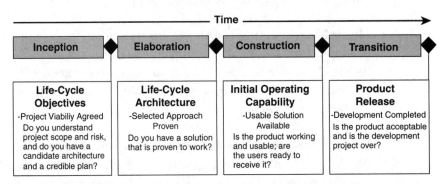

Figure 3-6   *The phases and milestones of the Unified Process*

---

[16] The PMBOK defines *project lifecycle* as "A collection of generally sequential *project phases* whose name and number are determined by the control needs of the organization or organizations involved in the project."

[17] In the context of the Unified Process, a phase can be defined as "The span of time between two major milestones of the process, during which a well-defined set of objectives is met, artifacts are completed, and the decision is made to go on to the next phase." Walker Royce, *Software Project Management: A Unified Framework* (Reading, MA: Addison-Wesley, 1998).

This is a more defined version of the PMBOK's definition: "A collection of logically related project activities, usually culminating in the completion of a major *deliverable.*"

[18] In the context of the Unified Process, a major milestone can be defined as a "System-wide event held at the end of each development phase to provide visibility to system-wide issues, synchronize the management and engineering perspectives, and verify that the goals of the phase have been achieved." Walker Royce, *Software Project Management: A Unified Framework* (Reading, MA: Addison-Wesley, 1998).

This is a more defined version of the PMBOK's definition: "A significant event in the *project*, usually completion of a major deliverable."

Note

Boehm did not include a milestone to represent the end of a spiral when he
defined the original set of lifecycle anchor points. The Unified Process introduces
a final milestone called "Product Release"—we have always found this to be a little
confusing because the product is actually released before the end of the project
during the Transition phase. We find it useful to think of this milestone as
"Lifecycle Complete" because it represents the end of a pass through the Unified
Process lifecycle and the set of iterations used to create and release the product.[19]

*Most importantly, the phases of the Unified Process lifecycle provide a way to
focus on, and therefore mitigate, specific kinds of risks.* At the end of each
phase, a particular class of risks will have been mitigated; if left unmitigat-
ed, these risks will cause serious problems as the project continues. The
types of risk associated with each phase are shown in Table 3-1

Table 3-1   *The Unified Process Phases, Milestones, and Risks Addressed*

RUP Phase	Milestone	Addressed Risks
Inception	Lifecycle Objectives (LCO)	Business Risks
Elaboration	Lifecycle Architecture (LCA)	Architectural/Technical Risks
Construction	Initial Operational Capability (IOC)	Logistical Risks
Transition	Product Release (PR)	Solution Roll-Out (Delivery) Risks

The phases help teams assign purpose to iterations and understand the particular kinds of risk that must be addressed before the project can proceed.

The Importance of Phases and Milestones

By defining the period of time between the predefined technical process
milestones, the phases enable you to focus even more on the state of the
project as a whole. Rather than identifying where the project is in terms of
being before or after a certain predefined milestone, you can simply say

---

[19] We look at handling multiple passes through the lifecycle and multiple product releases in
Chapter 6, "Overall Project Planning."

that the project is in this or that particular phase. As the project is planned, additional business milestones can be added into the project timeline to complement the predefined technical milestones, but the set of standard phases is maintained.

The milestones themselves serve many purposes. Most critically, their achievement provides concrete evidence of development status for stakeholders who have to make certain crucial decisions before work can proceed to the next phase. Milestones also enable management and the developers to monitor the progress of the work as it passes key points in the project lifecycle, and act as a series of checkpoints for the project as a whole. *At each major milestone, the stakeholder expectations are synchronized, project progress is assessed, and a decision is made about whether the project should be continued.*

Milestones need to be treated seriously—as a series of gates through which the project must progress in the defined sequence. It doesn't matter what phase the plan says the project is in; it is still in the first phase for which the milestone has not been met.[20] For example, if the Lifecycle Objectives milestone has not been met, then the project is still in the Inception phase, regardless of what the project schedule says or what the management team would like.

Unlike most other software process milestones, the Unified Process milestones measure the state of the project as a whole. Their focus is not on requirements snapshots, detailed designs, or architecture point solutions but rather on risk reduction and establishing the key principles that anticipate and accommodate systems evolution. This is the reason for calling the early milestones the "Lifecycle" Objectives and "Lifecycle" Architecture milestones.

Stakeholder agreement with the milestone goals is essential. This establishes mutual stakeholder buy-in to the plans and specifications and enables a collaborative team approach to unanticipated setbacks rather than the adversarial approach seen in most contract models. Consideration of the

---

[20] Our colleague DJ de Villiers notes, "On several occasions I have encountered a project team that claims for political reasons to be in phase X whereas they agree behind closed doors to really be in phase Y. This is probably the worst thing a project manager can do." Honesty in communication is essential.

business case at these milestones is an essential rather than an optional add-in.

The set of standard Unified Process milestones serves several purposes:

- Commitment points and progress checkpoints

- System-wide events that synchronize the whole team

- Measurements of the state of the project

Without them it becomes impossible to put the progress made by a project's iterations into perspective or understand whether the project has, in fact, been doing the right things. The phases and milestones of the Unified Process provide a way of assessing project progress so that you can ensure that the project is actually steadily progressing toward the delivery of a high-quality product and not wandering aimlessly through an infinite series of iterations.

Iterations, Phases, and Milestones

The definitions of *phase* and *iteration* are often confusedly and incorrectly interchanged because both are periods of time that result in the achievement of a set of clearly defined objectives. There are two major differences:

- The phases and process milestones are defined by the process and are common to all projects. The number and size of the iterations and their specific objectives are at the discretion of the project manager and the development team.

- End-of-phase milestones represent "toll gates" that cannot be passed without achieving specific results. The phases are not time boxes in the same way that iterations are. Iterations are concluded when the time runs out; phases are only concluded when their objectives have been met.

Each phase consists of one or more iterations, with the completion of each iteration representing a *minor milestone* for the project and contributing to the successful achievement of the phase's *major milestone*. As shown in Figure 3-7, iterations take place within phases. Each phase ends in a phase assessment where the project's progress is evaluated against the predefined milestone and a go/no go decision is made about the continuation of the project.

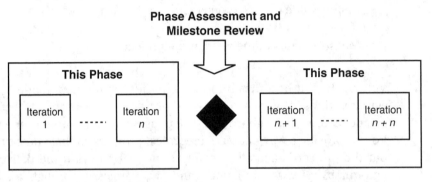

Figure 3-7   *Phases, iterations, and milestones*

Figure 3-8 shows the relationship of a set of iterations (I1, E1, C1, and so on) to their respective Unified Process phases, the relationship of phases to one another, and their conclusion, marked by the major process milestones. Each iteration concludes with a minor milestone, which is assessed at the iteration assessment. If the end of the iteration is also the end of a phase, there is also a major milestone, and some additional assessment is performed to make sure that the phase objectives have been met. We cover the subject of iteration and phase assessment in depth in Chapter 9, "Iteration, Phase, and Project Assessments."

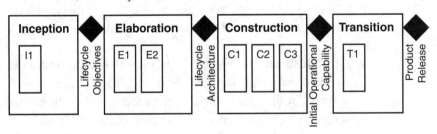

Figure 3-8   *The Unified Process lifecycle: phases and iterations*

In this figure, iterations are named with the first initial of their enclosing phase, plus a sequential number. For example, the first iteration in the Elaboration phase is named E1.

The Unified Process Phases

From a project management perspective, the Unified Process provides a *control framework* that guides the project management team in establishing appropriate objectives for their iterations and enables them to objectively assess the progress made by the project. Its use helps teams to effectively plan and manage iterative projects. It is also fundamental to the planning approach used throughout the remainder of this book, so fundamental that it is worth spending some time examining the phases and milestones in more detail.

The Inception Phase

The Inception phase has the following goals:

- To identify and mitigate business, project, and funding risks

- To assess the viability of the project, both technically and financially

- To agree to the scope and objectives of the project

- To form an overall plan for moving ahead

In the Inception phase, the main focus is on mitigating the risk that the project might be either economically undesirable or technically infeasible. For this, the team must explore the benefits and costs of the project so that a firm decision can be made about whether to proceed. At the end of the Inception phase, the stakeholders agree that the project is feasible and that the business case for the project is achievable if the project proceeds as planned. Everyone must agree that the project is viable—that is, that the project is worth doing, and the time and cost estimates are credible.

The Elaboration Phase

The Elaboration phase has the following goals:

- To bring architectural and technical risks under control

- To establish and demonstrate a sound architectural foundation[21]

- To establish a credible plan for the further development of the product

- To stabilize the requirements

The Elaboration phase's objectives are to prove the architecture[22] to be used in the product development (by verifying that the proposed architecture will support the solution) and to eliminate the project's highest-risk elements. At the end of the Elaboration phase, the project manager is in a position to plan the activities and estimate the resources required to complete the project. This is because the risks are under control and the architecture has been established and stabilized. Proving the architecture requires the development of one or more architectural prototypes that prove that specific technical risks have been addressed.

The Construction Phase

The Construction phase has the following goals:

- To bring logistical risks under control

- To complete the development of the solution

---

[21] Our thinking about software architecture has been strongly influenced by our work with Philippe Kruchten. For a good introduction to software architecture, see his article "The 4+1 View Model of Architecture," *IEEE Software*, 12(6), 1995.

[22] It is *very* easy to assess this subjectively in favor of moving to the next phase, and *every single time* the first Construction iteration suffers disastrously, just as stakeholders expect acceleration.

- To ensure that the solution is ready for delivery to its user community

- To achieve adequate quality as rapidly as is practical

This is where most of the "heavy lifting" of the project is done; it is where the bulk of the work occurs and where most of the effort, typically at least 50%, is expended. Because of the staffing increase and the extent to which working in parallel is required in this phase, entering the Construction phase with an unstable architecture (or no architecture[23]) is asking for trouble. Therefore, it is important that the team be honest about the stability of the architecture when exiting the Elaboration phase. It's not possible to work in parallel without a stable architecture.

At the end of the Construction phase, the development team believes that the product is sufficiently complete and of sufficiently high quality to deliver to users. It is ready for evaluation by selected stakeholders from the intended user community in a "beta" deployment with the intent of having real users evaluate its suitability for final release. To be able to successfully conclude the phase, the users must also be ready to accept the release.

---

[23] It may be only a slight exaggeration to say that the terms *architecture* and *architect* are thrown around so freely that they may have lost their meaning. Our simple definition is that the architecture is characterized by a set of critical choices that the development team makes about the solution. The dimensions of these choices tend to cover several major areas: concurrency, distribution, security, physical organization of the software components, and logical organization of the components. The architecture covers all these aspects (and more) and represents the major decisions that, if changed at a later date, will cause major disruptions to the schedule and may cause the project to fail.

For more on this approach to architecture, we recommend *Software Architecture: Perspectives on an Emerging Discipline* by Mary Shaw and David Garlan (Upper Saddle River, NJ: Prentice Hall, 1996), as well as any articles on the subject written by Philippe Kruchten.

The Transition Phase

The Transition phase has the following goals:

- To bring roll-out risks under control

- To deliver the solution to its end users

- To achieve user satisfaction and self-sufficiency

The Transition phase starts with the beta deployment and concludes with the final delivery of the solution to the customer or their support organization. This phase focuses on fixing remaining defects, training users, and, in many systems, converting data from older systems (or older versions of the same system) and running in a parallel testing mode for some period to ensure that the system is ready for final deployment. The phase concludes when the product has been successfully deployed and the maintenance and support responsibilities have been handed over to another project or department.

Alternative Views of the Phases and Milestones

To help understand how the phases shape the project, and to reiterate exactly what they mean, it is worth examining them from a number of different perspectives, including those of the three stakeholder domains we introduced at the start of the chapter.

As we look more deeply into the overall planning of the project and each phase, we continue to use this stakeholder framework to present simple, risk-based planning patterns that you can use to form your own project plans. These patterns, which grow out of the domain perspectives, make the Unified Process easier to understand by focusing on what we are trying to achieve and not on the details of the process being followed.

A simple way of approaching the lifecycle is to consider the key questions that need to be addressed by each phase and what artifacts the project needs to produce to answer these questions. This simple high-level risk- and objective-based view of the process is summarized in Table 3-2.

To understand how the lifecycle appears to the different stakeholder domains, it is worth examining what the project needs to achieve to assure each set of stakeholders that the project is under control. Table 3-3 analyzes the iterative project lifecycle from each of the three domain perspectives, presenting an overview of the *achievements* required in each domain to successfully complete the project milestones.

The three stakeholder perspectives—problem, solution, and project—are also useful for examining the activities that need to be undertaken by the project team. Table 3-4 provides an overview of the key *activities* to be undertaken for each area and each phase. By looking at the phases from these various perspectives, we can see how they unify all the elements of our iterative project, and we can start to understand the activities and achievements that are required of the iterations that take place in each phase.

Understanding how to correctly interpret the risks associated with the phases and the achievements associated with the phase milestones makes it easier to construct and validate your iterative project plans. You can select the appropriate activities to perform and artifacts to produce in order to demonstrate that you have mitigated the appropriate categories of risk and achieved the milestone for each phase. We return to the subject of planning phases and iterations in Part II, "Planning and Managing an Iterative Project."

Table 3-2   *A High-Level Overview of the Unified Process Project Lifecycle*

Inception		Elaboration		Construction		Transition	
	LCO: Viability Agreed		**LCA: Selected Approach Proven**		**IOC: Usable Solution Available**		**PR: Project Completed**
Risk Focus: *Business*		**Risk Focus:** *Architectural*		**Risk Focus:** *Logistical*		**Risk Focus:** *Roll-out*	
Questions:		**Questions:**		**Questions:**		**Questions:**	
• Are we building the right thing for the customer? • Is the solution feasible? • How much is it worth?		• Do we know what we are building? • Do we know how we will build it? • Do we agree on what it is? • How much will it cost? • How will the technical risks be mitigated? • Can we mitigate the technical risks?		• Are we getting it done? • Will it be done on time? • Is it good enough? • Do our assumptions and earlier decisions hold? • Are the users ready?		• Is it acceptable? • Is it being used? • Have we finished?	
Key Artifacts:		**Key Artifacts:**		**Key Artifacts:**		**Key Artifacts:**	
• Vision • Business case • Risks • Overall project plan • List of critical use cases[24]		• Use-case model survey[24] • Detailed descriptions for architecturally significant use-case flows and supplementary specs[24] • Architectural description • Architectural prototypes • Executed tests of the architecture		• Use-case descriptions[24] • Supplementary specifications • Designs • Code • Tests • Test results • Training materials • User documentation		• Installers, including data conversion • Customer surveys • Defects and their resolutions	
Outcome:		**Outcome:**		**Outcome:**		**Outcome:**	
• Agreement to fund the project		• A stable, proven, executable architecture		• A useful, tested, deployable, and documented solution		• The solution is in "actual use"	

---

24 As we shall see in the next chapter, use cases provide an ideal mechanism for managing the requirements for an iterative project. We have chosen to leave the forward references in place to make the table more useful as a reference when you are actually managing your projects.

Table 3-3 *An Achievement-Based Overview of the Unified Process Project Lifecycle*[25]

	Inception	Elaboration	Construction	Transition
Problem	• Problem understood • Value & scope of solution identified • Alignment with business' goals verified • Critical requirements identified	• Vision agreed upon • Requirements stable[26] • Success and evaluation criteria agreed upon	• Requirements correct • Ready to deploy • Acceptance criteria agreed upon • User documentation available	• Product accepted • Requirements complete • Product deployed • Users self-sufficient
Solution	• Technical feasibility assessed • Solution approach agreed upon • Candidate architecture selected	• Architecture proven • Executable architecture baselined • Critical components defined • Build/buy/reuse decisions made	• Implementation stable • Useful, quality product available • Product verified • Objective quality information available	• Product complete • Design complete • Code complete • Maintenance and support responsibilities handed over
Project	• Critical risks identified and assessed • Stakeholder responsibilities defined • Project objectives agreed upon • Project constraints established • Low-fidelity, lifecycle plan agreed upon • Costs estimated • Elaboration plans in place	• Risk profile well understood • Risks under control • High-fidelity, comprehensive lifecycle plan agreed upon • Construction plans in place • Accurate estimates for completion available • Resource profile agreed upon • Costs well understood	• Transition plans in place • Project under control • Impact of outstanding changes understood	• Stakeholders satisfied • Next evolution planned • Project closed down
Milestone	**LCO: Viability Agreed**	**LCA: Selected Approach Proven**	**IOC: Usable Solution Available**	**Project Completed**

25 We provide detailed explanations for each of these achievements in subsequent chapters when we examine management and planning for each of the individual phases.

26 Stable, but not "frozen."

Table 3-4 A High-Level, Activity-Based Overview of the Unified Process Project Lifecycle

	Inception	*LCO: Viability Agreed*	Elaboration	*LCA: Selected Approach Proven*	Construction	*IOC: Usable Solution Available*	Transition	*PR: Project Completed*
Problem	• Identify the architecturally significant requirements • Understand the target environments • Define the problem • Determine the value of solving the problem		• Stabilize the requirements • Detail the critical requirements • Elaborate on the vision		• Complete the requirements • Author user documentation • Manage changing requirements • Assess user readiness • Request change requests		• Perform acceptance testing • Train users • Market the solution • Manage change in the user community • Suggest improvements • Report defects and deficiencies	
Solution	• Explore possible solutions • Evaluate alternative solutions • Synthesize the architecture		• Prove the architecture • Develop prototype(s) • Describe the architecture • Describe component interfaces • Select components		• Develop components • Test and assessment • Refine the architecture • Optimize component design		• Deploy to end users • Prepare for support and maintenance of the system after it is delivered • Correct defects • Tune the application • Parallel operation and application migration	
Project	• Establish the project's scope • Plan lifecycle • Establish project costs • Build the business case • Identify the critical risks		• Track progress • Improve estimates • Plan development • Control risks • Elaborate upon the process • Establish the project infrastructure • Establish metrics • Resource the project		• Impact analysis • Monitor and control development • Plan deployment • Optimize process • Monitor risks • Collect metrics • Optimize resource usage • Control costs		• Assess the impact of change • Schedule changes • Hand over to production support • Monitor and control deployment • Close down the project	

Common Misconceptions About the Unified Process Lifecycle

The Unified Process lifecycle is often misinterpreted by people who are new to iterative development practices, especially those who have previously followed a waterfall lifecycle where the phases were aligned to individual process disciplines (for example, requirements, design, code and unit test, system test, and so on).

It is worth examining the most common misconceptions to ensure that we avoid them.

"Requirements" and "Design" Are Not Phases

Implementation and Test are not phases, either. All are *disciplines* that are applied in every phase. The most common error is to think that Unified Process *phases* are aligned to either the execution of one or two disciplines or the completion of one or two deliverables. The purpose of the phases is not to complete some discipline; the purpose of a phase is to mitigate (or eliminate entirely) some set of risks. Although these associations might have some validity, they are often misleading and result in unproductive or misguided efforts. *It is more correct and often easier to remember the risks associated with the phase,* as shown in Table 3-5.

Table 3-5 *Incorrect and Correct Interpretations of Unified Process Phases*

Phase	Incorrect Interpretation	Correct Interpretation
Inception	High-level requirements	Business risks
Elaboration	Detailed requirements and/or design	Architectural/technical risks
Construction	Implementation and development; team testing	Logistical risks (the risk of not getting all the work done)
Transition	Acceptance testing	Solution roll-out (delivery) risks

"Planning Completed," "Specification Completed," "Coding Completed," and "Testing Completed" Are Not Suitable Milestones

The *milestones* of the process are also often misinterpreted in a similar way to the phases. *It is more correct and often easier to remember the achievement associated with the milestone,* as shown in Table 3-6.

Table 3-6   *Incorrect and Correct Interpretations of Unified Process Milestones*

Milestone	Incorrect Interpretation	Correct Interpretation
Lifecycle Objectives (LCO)	Planning completed	Project viability has been confirmed by stakeholders.
Lifecycle Architecture (LCA)	Specification completed	The selected approach has been proven through developer testing.
Initial Operational Capability (IOC)	Coding completed	A usable solution is available.[27]
Product Release (PR)	Product available/deployed	The project is complete.

Other Common Misconceptions

There are a number of other common misunderstandings about the application of the Unified Process lifecycle, including the following:

- **Each iteration goes through the phases**—Phases contain iterations, not the other way around. Iterations are the smallest time period that is managed in a project.

- **You can't build any software unless you are in the Construction phase**—Some software is built in every phase. In the Inception phase, the software development effort is focused on proving that the proposed solution is viable; in the Elaboration phase, the software development effort is focused on proving that the technical approach is viable; and in the

---

[27] Typically in the form of a beta release.

Transition phase, the software development effort is focused on fixing defects and preparing the solution for final release.

- **You can be in more than one phase at a time**—No, phases do not overlap. Phases are achievement-oriented milestones that require the current phase's objectives to be completed before you can move on to the next phase.

- **You can't change the architecture after the end of the Elaboration phase**—You can change it, but not with abandon. At the end of the Elaboration phase, the architecture is *baselined*, which means that further changes will be subject to a formal change control process. If you feel that this is too constraining and that your architecture will be changing often after the end of the Elaboration phase, then you are fooling yourself by thinking that you're ready to conclude the Elaboration phase.

- **The phases don't apply to all development projects**—The phases apply to all projects but not necessarily to the same degree. Because the phases are each driven by specific kinds of risks, and because it is never possible to completely eliminate these risks, there will be at least some effort in each phase, if only to confirm that your suspicion that the risks are minor is true.

All these misconceptions can be avoided if you keep the purpose of the phases in mind and focus all your activities on addressing the projects risks by producing working software.

Objective Measurement of Results: Controlling the Iterations Within the Project Lifecycle

The final control mechanism that we have is the objective measurement of the results. As we saw when we were discussing time boxing earlier, it is the objective measurement of iteration progress and performance that enables us to steer and direct the project as a whole. Considering these measurements in the light of the Unified Process project lifecycle enables you to put the iterations' results into perspective and to know in which direction to steer your project.

Measurement and Iterations: Feedback Control for Projects

Iteration planning, when combined with iteration assessment and the objective measurement of project progress, provides a simple feedback-based control mechanism to enable the project management team to monitor and control their software development projects.

Figure 3-9 shows the basic feedback control loop used in many mechanical and biological control systems.

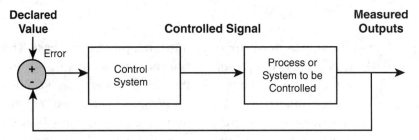

Figure 3-9   *Basic feedback control*

Considering that *software development* is the process we need to control in a software project and that it is the role of the management team to exert this control, we can see that the relationship between the management team and the iteration is essentially a relationship between the control system and process to be controlled. This is shown in Figure 3-10.

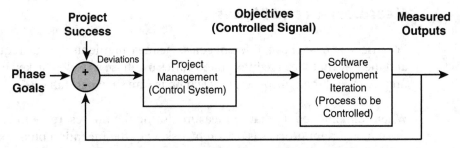

Figure 3-10 *Project management as a control mechanism for software development*

The feedback produced by objectively measuring and analyzing the outputs of the iteration enables the project management team to successfully control the project and steer the project team to the achievement of project success.

By assessing the measured outputs from the software development iterations against the project's success criteria and the current phase's goals, you can set the correct objectives for the next iteration to correct the course of the project.

This feedback-based control mechanism leads to many of the analogies used to illustrate how the management team "steers" an iterative project:

- Keeping a car on the road by continuously and minutely adjusting its direction

- Sailing a yacht from A to B against the wind by tacking

- Controlling where a super tanker finally ends its journey by making small adjustments to its course early on

Basically, the continuous small corrections that the management team makes to the direction of the project at the iteration boundaries help guide the project to a successful conclusion. This feedback loop enables the success of the project to be continuously observed and the contribution to the overall success of the project of each iteration to be assessed.

Measurement and Phases

Because the phases have different goals, the measurements that are required and the way that they are interpreted varies by phase as well. The key measurements, and their purposes, for each phase are shown in Table 3-7.

When thinking about what to measure during the phases, remember that the management process is driven by risk, with the Inception phase as the risk exploration period, the Elaboration phase as the risk resolution period, and the final two phases as a controlled risk management period.[28] With this in mind, we can reexamine the key characteristics of successful iterative development that we first looked at in Chapter 2, "How Do Iterative Projects Function?"

Table 3-7 *The Phases and Their Key Measurements*

Phase	Project State	Outcome	Key Measures	Measurement Strategy
Inception	The stakeholders are discussing the value and feasibility of the solution. The approach to be taken has been selected.	Project viability agreed. Agreement to fund the project (Elaboration at least).	Risk Exposure Stability Consensus Estimates	The focus during the Inception phase is on getting the project set up and establishing the measurement plan for the project as a whole. The first things to objectively measure are risk and estimates versus actuals. The measurement of stability and consensus are more subjective.
Elaboration	Demonstrable, executable versions of the system are being produced to actively mitigate the most serious project risks and prove the approach selected.	Selected approach proven. A stable, proven, executable architecture.	Risk Exposure Change Progress Estimates	As the project moves into Elaboration, there is a renewed focus on measuring progress in terms of verified requirements, the amount of change being requested, and the rework being undertaken. This complements the continued focus on reducing risk and improving the accuracy of the estimates.

---

[28] As discussed by Walker Royce in *Software Project Management: A Unified Framework* (Reading, MA: Addison-Wesley, 1998).

Phase	Project State	Outcome	Key Measures	Measurement Strategy
Construction	Deployable solutions that work end-to-end are being regularly produced.	Useable solution available. A useful, tested, deployable, and documented solution.	Quality Progress Velocity Rework	During the Construction phase, the emphasis changes to focus on quality issues, including the amount and cost of any rework being undertaken. The measurements are used to answer the question: Will the project be done on time and on budget?
Transition	The new system is being supported in the live environment. Feedback is being generated from actual system use.	Project complete. The solution is in "actual" use.	Quality User Satisfaction Adoption Levels Change Requests	During the Transition phase, there is a need to measure the user's perception of quality, the levels of user satisfaction, and the levels of adoption as well as to continue with the other measurements being collected about the project.

The first and most important measurement to consider is the project risk exposure. The risk profile of a typical, successful iterative project using the Unified Process lifecycle is shown in Figure 3-11. Here the key measurement point is the end of the Elaboration phase, by when the business and technical risks must be demonstrably under control. As a minimum, the project's "technical" risk exposure (as measured by the probability of the risk event occurring multiplied by the impact of the risk occurring) has been reduced to 20% of its highest value by this time.

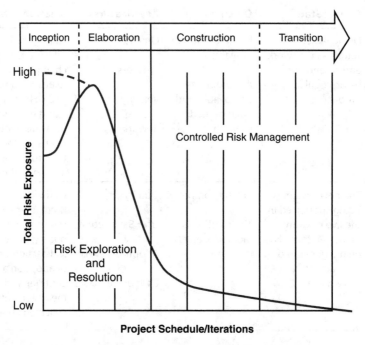

Figure 3-11   *The risk profile of a typical iterative project across its lifecycle*

In the series of graphs shown in this section, the number of iterations is not the important characteristic. The focus should be on the levels and trends observable at the phase boundaries.

This graph can be compared with the progress graph shown in Figure 3-12. This illustrates the basic underlying assumption of the Elaboration phase: that 80% of the project's risk can be addressed by the development of 20% of the solution. As we shall see in the following chapters,[29] selecting the correct 20% of the solution is part of the art of planning an iterative project. In some cases, it may take the production of more than 20% of the solution to demonstrate that the technical risks have been addressed. This is not necessarily a problem, but it does mean that the project remains at risk for longer.

---

[29] Most particularly Chapter 7, "Evolution and Phase Planning."

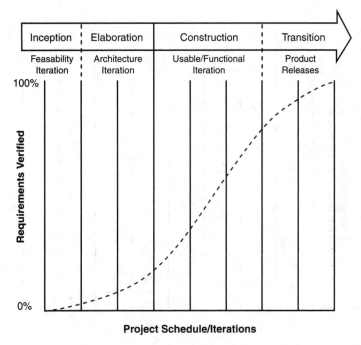

Figure 3-12   *The code growth profile of a typical iterative project across its lifecycle*

Figure 3-12 also illustrates how the project converges on an accurate business solution through a series of Feasibility Iterations, Architecture Iterations, Usable/Functional Iterations, and Product Releases.

We can also look at how the quality may vary across the lifecycle. Figure 3-13 shows how the amount of breakage typically varies across the lifecycle. During the Inception and Elaboration phases, the small amounts of code produced can have significant levels of breakage, but this should have damped down by the time the project enters the Construction phase. The expected levels of quality are reflected in the kinds of releases produced by the iterations. There is a general expectation that *proof of concepts* and *prototypes* will be incomplete and require rework.

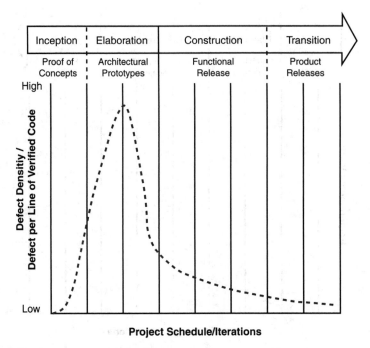

Figure 3-13   *Defect density across the lifecycle*

If there are significant levels of breakage in the Elaboration phase, then this can be addressed by tuning the architecture, replacing the deficient components, or training the people involved. The lessons can be learned and the project plans adjusted to reflect them. The project is still early enough in its lifecycle that there is time to address all the issues raised. In fact, a key objective of the Elaboration phase is to surface and address exactly these kinds of technical risk.

Degrading quality is often indicative of the selection of an inappropriate architecture for the solution. Every release produced by a Construction iteration should have all the completeness and quality attributes of a production release, which means that all the underlying key components must be working and working well. These quality trends are reflected in the amount of rework that the project typically incurs across the iterations. The typical trends are shown in Figure 3-14. If there are increasing or significant amounts of unaddressed breakage during the Construction phase, this is indicative of systematic quality problems that should have been addressed in the Elaboration phase.

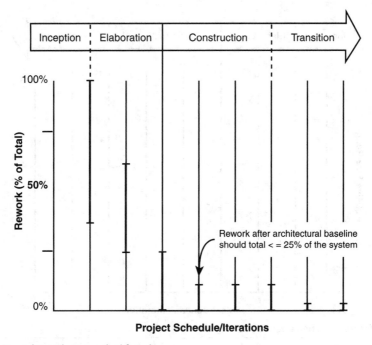

Figure 3-14   *Rework trends across the lifecycle*

The rework trends in Figure 3-14 are shown as expected bands rather than absolute values. Although some rework is to be expected for most iterations, the overall *trend* should be toward no rework. The conceptual prototype might be completely thrown away, and therefore the upper bound in Inception is shown as 100% rework. If the system is incorporating a large amount of legacy code, a smaller percent of rework will be observed. After the architecture is baselined, large amounts of rework are uncommon. Adding together the percent of rework from all iterations following the architectural baseline should result in a figure that is 25% or less of the total system code base. The percentages shown are relative to the total system developed to date and not just the content of the most recent iteration.

Another very important indicator of which phase a project is in is the accuracy of the estimates that it is producing. Figure 3-15 shows how the accuracy of the estimate to complete varies across the lifecycle. The most important point is the end of the Elaboration phase, where the estimate to complete should be within ±20% of the actual cost of completing the project.

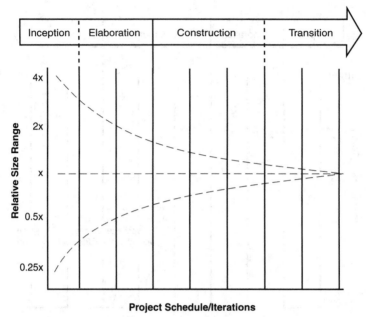

Figure 3-15 *Estimate accuracy across the lifecycle*

Controlling the Project Through Measurement

As a wise man once said, "You can't control what you can't measure." Objective measurement is fundamental to the effective control of iterative projects. The trick to achieving this effective control is to measure the right things at the right time.

Why do we measure at the iteration boundaries? We do it because it suppresses all the noise that would occur if we measured in real time during the iteration. For example, the testing that is undertaken in each iteration is expected to find defects, many of which will be handled within the iteration itself. Registering their creation and rapid closure would be counterproductive and would obscure the true project trends.

The key point at which the stability of the architecture must be assessed is on the boundary between Elaboration and Construction. At this point you can define measurement thresholds that will tell you whether you are before or after the Lifecycle Architecture milestone. You can also define optimum values for other measures that indicate that the project is being well managed and controlled.

At the end of Elaboration,

- The project's risks should be under control—typically the outstanding risk exposure should be no more than 20% of peak value.

- The project's estimate to complete should have a margin of error of no more than 20%.

- The amount of rework expected should be less than 25% of the system.

- The defect density should be no more than twice the acceptable level.[30]

Ideally this should be achievable with the production of 20% to 30% of the solution.

This level of precision is not achievable between the Inception and Elaboration phases or between the Construction and Transition phases because these boundaries are far more subjective.

Although the majority of these measures appear to be aimed at the stakeholders in the project domain, in particular the project's management team, they are useful to all the stakeholders. The stakeholders in the problem and solution domains are just as interested in the project's progress, stability, estimate to complete, and risk profile as those in the project domain.

Summary

In this chapter we introduced the basic concepts of controlled iterative development, including a time-boxed approach to delivering software-based projects that uses systematic reduction of risk as its organizing principle.

---

[30] Remember that every Construction iteration should produce a production-quality release, with an acceptable level of outstanding defects.

To help us understand this approach, we introduced three perspectives based on the domains that most concern project stakeholders: *problem*, *solution*, and *project*. These three perspectives provide us with a framework for forming goals for the project and its phases and iterations to ensure that the needs of stakeholders are met.

To enable the concept of time-boxed iterations to be applied effectively, a guiding iterative project lifecycle is required. We recommend the use of the Unified Process lifecycle for this purpose. The phases of the Unified Process define a risk-driven lifecycle providing an objective measure of the state of the project.

This set of predefined phases and milestones can be applied to many different kinds of projects: software development projects, process improvement projects, course development, and writing a book, for example. When you understand the basic framework, it is easy to choose the right set of activities from the Unified Process disciplines or from whichever iterative development process your team prefers.

The phases and their milestones are best understood in terms of the risks they address and the achievements that they represent. This is summarized succinctly in Table 3-9.

Table 3-8   *A Summary of the Phases and Milestones*

Phase	Focus	Milestone	Milestone Result
Inception	Confirm the scope and objectives of the project and bring the business risks under control.	Lifecycle Objectives (LCO)	Project viability has been confirmed by stakeholders.
Elaboration	Stabilize the product plans and bring the architectural and technical risks under control.	Lifecycle Architecture (LCA)	The selected approach has been proven through developer testing.
Construction	Build the product and bring the logistical project execution risks under control.	Initial Operational Capability (IOC)	A usable solution is available.[31]
Transition	Deliver the product and bring the roll-out risks under control.	Product Release (PR)	The project is complete.

---

[31] Typically in the form of a beta release.

We can also summarize some basic rules for phases, iterations, and milestones:

- Every iteration produces an executable release.

- Every iteration is a discrete time box.

- Iterations take place within the phases of the lifecycle.

- During an iteration, the project team members focus on meeting the objectives of that iteration alone, doing whatever they can to ensure the iteration's success, and no more.

- The results of every iteration are objectively assessed; the team should be prepared to rework the solution and project plan as required.

- The "anchor point" milestones are used to provide focus to the series of iterations.

- The milestones (and their phases) measure the state of the project in terms of its risk.

The final key component of our control strategy is the objective measurement of the progress and results of the iterations. This is what enables the project to be effectively steered toward a successful conclusion. Remember, you can't control what you don't measure. If a project is not objectively measuring and assessing the performance and results of its iterations, then it is not doing "controlled" iterative development.

In subsequent chapters we show how this control framework can be applied to the planning, managing, and assessing of iterative software development projects.

Are You Ready for Iterative Project Management?

"Iteration, like friction, is likely to generate heat instead of progress."
—George Eliot (English Victorian novelist, 1819–1880)

Thus far we have presented the principles of iterative and incremental development in a positive and enthusiastic manner. We hope by now that you are convinced that this is a credible way of developing software that significantly reduces project risk and increases the project's chances of success. At this point no doubt some of you are wondering, "If it's so great, why isn't everybody doing it?" and "Why do so many people assume that it is difficult to do?"

In our experience, iterative development is very easy to adopt,[1] but it does require the project team members to have the right sort of attitudes toward their projects and their work.[2] The fact is that adoption of iterative development practices requires subtle but significant change on the part of the

---

[1]   Remember that many people have been working in an iterative fashion for many years, often without the benefit of books like this that attempt to codify and support the approach. We both started using iterative approaches many years ago and found them so easy to use and so effective that we have dedicated many years of our careers to their application and promotion.

[2]   As we discussed in Chapter 2, "How Do Iterative Projects Function?" the iterative development experience is quite different from the one traditionally associated with waterfall software development projects, and it affects everybody connected to the project from the most senior business leaders to the most junior members of the development team.

project team members, especially if they have been working on conventional projects for many years. In short, these changes include the following:

- A new attitude is required toward uncertainty and change: teams must first recognize that change happens and there are always uncertainties, so in order to be successful they must purposefully work to manage change and reduce uncertainties. The second thing the team must grasp is that the only way to manage change and reduce uncertainty is through demonstration of real progress—no amount of studies, documents, artifacts, or plans will actually make risks go away; only by creating working software are risks reduced.

- A new attitude is required regarding the way that projects gather and address their requirements. The project team must start to focus on delivering immediate and realizable value back to the business.

- A new attitude is required regarding team working and accountability. The project teams will need to be assembled and encouraged to interact in new ways.

- Most significantly, a new, more progressive attitude is required for the estimation, planning, and management of the project itself.

With new attitudes in place, the adoption of iterative and incremental development practices becomes quite easy. If the project team has the wrong attitudes toward iteration, then as the opening quote implies, the early iterations are more likely to produce personal friction than project progress, in some cases generating enough opposition to prevent the project from being able to iterate effectively.

We return to the subject of "getting started" and overcoming the entrenched forces of organizational entropy in the final chapter of the book. For now we would like to conclude Part I with a brief look at some of the attitude adjustments that are required as a precursor to the effective adoption of iterative and incremental project management practices.

Value Delivery: The Key to Success

All arguments in support of adopting iterative and incremental development fail if the intermediate results produced by the project do not deliver real business value. Many software development projects are executed in a value-neutral setting[3] in which

- Every requirement is treated as equally important

- The delivery of technical components is seen as of equal importance to the delivery of usable systems

- "Earned value" systems track project cost and schedule, not stakeholder or business value

- A "separation of concerns" is practiced, in which the responsibility of the development team is confined to turning software requirements into verified code rather than delivering business value

- The actual desired outcomes of the project are ignored in favor of implementing the largest number of requirements possible

No wonder most projects are considered failures. Unfortunately this includes many iterative and incremental software development projects where the developers iteratively implement the requirements rather than iteratively solve problems. Many iterative projects fail to exit the Elaboration phase because of just such issues: although project members feel that they are iterating successfully, they never make the transition from iteratively addressing the technical risks to iteratively delivering usable versions of the system that provide realizable business benefit.

---

[3] Barry Boehm comes to much the same conclusion in his paper "Value-Based Software Engineering" (*ACDM SIGSOFT*, March 2003), where he argues that much current software engineering practice and research is done in a value-neutral setting.

Iterations Focus on Delivering Value

Delivering value is not the same as delivering code: it is easy to deliver a lot of code without delivering much business value. The code delivered and tested must do something useful for the business. One of the more interesting observations included in the Standish Group's CHAOS Report[4] is that even for the projects that are considered successful, only two-thirds of the implemented features were actually required. *This implies that a third of the software developed by the average successful project has no business value.* We clearly need a means for finding and implementing the requirements with the highest business value first.

Figure 4-1 shows that approximately 20% of the requirements have been implemented by the end of the Elaboration phase, but this alone says nothing about the value of the solution at this point. By the end of the first Construction iteration, the project has produced its first usable, complete release, which in this case implements about 50% of the requirements. If the project members have implemented the most important 45% of the requirements, then they may have produced a system that would realize as much as 80% of the potential value. If they have implemented the least important 45% of the requirements, then the potential value realized could be below 20%.

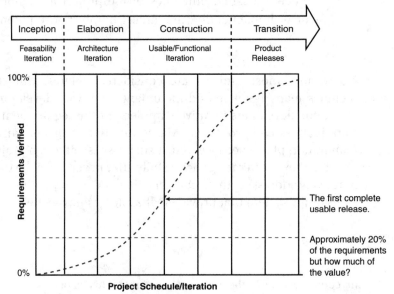

Figure 4-1   *How is value related to requirements verified?*

---

[4]   www.standishgroup.com.

The key to understanding the business value derived is to map the implemented requirements back to the desired outcomes for the project: a requirement not related to a desired outcome is clearly not important to the business. The connection to iteration planning is that early iterations should implement requirements related to more important desired outcomes, with one clarification: technical risk cannot be ignored. This apparent conflict can be resolved by recognizing that desired business outcomes require that technical risks are resolved early because a technically infeasible solution is incapable of delivering any desired outcomes.

As a result, planning iterations entails choosing the right set of risks and requirements for each iteration to ensure that the iteration's results make measurable progress toward the delivery of the desired business outcomes. As progress is demonstrated, as everyone can see that key technical issues are being resolved, and as the achievement of desired outcomes becomes more and more likely, confidence in success increases.

Use Cases: Unifying the Iterative Development Approach

The Unified Process lifecycle, introduced in Chapter 3, "Controlling Iterative Projects," defines a set of risk-related milestones to help steer the project. This lifecycle needs to be complemented with a development process that ensures that the iterations actually deliver value, not only to the project team but also to the business.

A common solution to this problem has arisen over the years: all the most popular and successful iterative and incremental development processes define the contents of the releases in terms of *executable, end-to-end behavioral threads of system usage*. Because every methodology seems to need to invent its own terminology, these *execution threads* come with different names: the various flavors of use cases, user stories, and scenarios are all mechanisms for capturing and defining the end-to-end threads of system usage and then driving the other development activities to ensure that verified usable systems are produced. They can all provide a business value perspective on the system requirements for use when planning the project's iterations.

For the purpose of providing additional examples and guidance within this book, we have selected use cases as the vehicle for capturing and defining the set of *end-to-end threads* to be developed. This is because they are one of the most widely known and used methods (and our personal favorite); in fact many of the other popular methods are compatible with or recommend a use-case driven approach.[5]

Desired Outcomes, Risks, Scenarios, and Iteration Planning

To make iterative development work, you need some way to work on scenarios, or independent threads of system usage. In our book *Use Case Modeling*,[6] we explain that use cases are a practical technique for describing scenarios because they provide a way of discussing system users' goals and how the system interacts with users to achieve these goals. Use cases are also helpful to people who ensure system usability, document the system's behavior, and design, develop, and test the system. They are especially useful for project management because they provide the end-to-end threads that are required to provide a value focus to the iteration and development plans.

Use cases structure and group requirements by user goals and business value. A use case contains a set of flows, which describe the interaction between the system and its actors. The set of flows provide a map of how the system can be used to meet the goals of the use case and a structured way of describing the set of end-to-end scenarios needed to drive the iteration planning and the development of the software. If you are unfamiliar with the concepts involved in use-case modeling, then we recommend that you read Appendix A, "A Brief Introduction to Use-Case Driven Development," before you start reading Part II of the book.

To use the use cases and their flows and scenarios to derive clear iteration objectives, you need to understand how they are related to the project's

---

[5] For example, Craig Larman (*Agile and Iterative Development: A Manager's Guide*, Boston: Addison-Wesley, 2003) and Alistair Cockburn (*Agile Software Development*, Boston: Addison-Wesley, 2001) both recommend the use of use cases with agile and adaptive development methods other than the Unified Process.

[6] Kurt Bittner and Ian Spence, *Use Case Modeling* (Boston: Addison-Wesley, 2002).

desired outcomes and the risks that threaten the project's ability to deliver them. Figure 4-2 illustrates the relationships between these concepts.

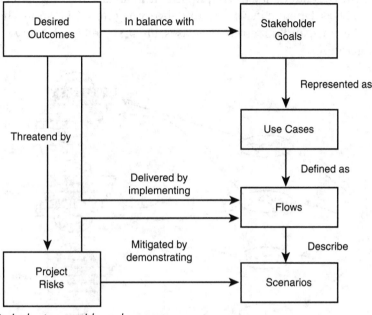

Figure 4-2   *Desired outcomes, risks, and use cases*

The use cases describe what the system will do to achieve the goals of the stakeholders when using the system. These stakeholder goals must be kept in balance with the desired outcomes of the project. This enables the use cases and flows to be appropriately scope managed and prioritized.[7]

Project risks threaten the project's ability to deliver the desired outcomes in a timely and cost-effective manner. Risks related to the development of the solution can be mitigated by choosing scenarios that force the confrontation of the risks. By mapping the risks to flows that mitigate them, iterations can be planned to ensure that every iteration reduces project risk and increases the business value realized from the solution.

---

[7] A use case captures a set of scenarios, each of which is described by one or more of its flows. All use cases contain a basic flow, which describes the set of normal, "happy day" scenarios. They also contain a number of alternative flows to describe variations, extensions, and exceptions to the basic flow. These can be combined with the basic flow to describe all the other possible scenarios. So, a scenario can be considered to be defined by a use case's basic flow plus zero or more of its alternative flows. Therefore, by scope managing the set of use cases and flows, we are scope managing the much larger set of scenarios.

The use cases provide meaningful subsets of the requirements that define end-to-end threads through the system that deliver tangible business benefit. They subdivide the requirements in an additive way that enables them to be assigned to iterations for delivery. Figure 4-3 illustrates how the flows of events, and not entire use cases, are assigned for delivery in the various iterations.

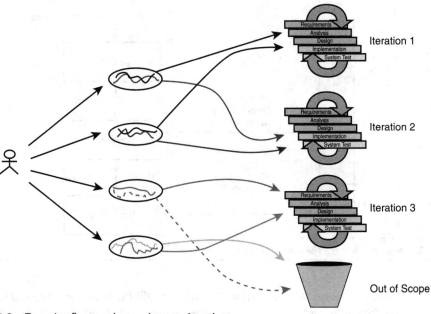

Figure 4-3   *Targeting flows and scenarios onto iterations*

Note

Many of the less important flows will often end up "out of scope." This handles the problem of over-enthusiastic requirements specifiers who over-specify a system loaded with lots of extra functionality that adds little value. This doesn't mean that these requirements will never be implemented; it just means that they will not be implemented at this time.

After use cases and their flows have been identified, their progression through the development lifecycle can be used to track progress and provide a suitable mechanism for the collection of the progress measures used to control the project. As shown in Figure 4-4, the state of each flow of events can be tracked through the development activities used to design, implement, and test the flow. Because scenarios are used to select the flows and because each scenario tells a complete story of how discrete value is delivered by the system, by delivering complete scenarios one-by-one, you are adding to the realizable value of the system each time one is completed.

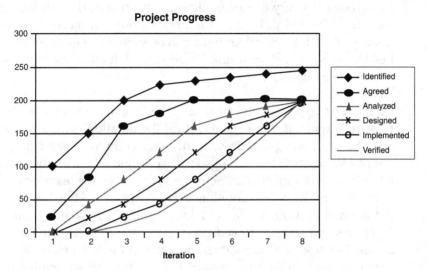

Figure 4-4   *Tracking project progress using use case flows*

The use of use-case flows—and the scenarios that they define—to plan, manage, and control the project gets the entire development team to continually focus upon the value delivered by the solution and enables everything done on the project to be tracked back to the project's desired outcomes and the risks that threaten its success.

Team Building for an Iterative Project

For a project to successfully iterate, the project team must be correctly staffed, and the team members themselves need to have the right attitude about the job at hand. Iterative projects require that the project team adopt a much more collaborative, opportunistic, self-directed approach to understanding the problem and developing the solution.

Team Skills and Attitudes

Because every iteration produces some tested executable code, every iteration requires a very broad set of skills. This means that iterative projects need to be staffed differently from conventional projects. On a conventional project, it is typical for testing to be staffed late in the project. On an iterative project, the team must have skills that span the entire software development lifecycle.

On an iterative project, the attitude of the team must shift as well: it needs to be fully focused on the goals set for the iteration, which means that it must be functioning as a single team with a common, shared purpose and not as a loose confederation of specialist teams, each with their own limited, role-specific objectives. There cannot be a "testing team" and a "development team" with different objectives. The team will fail if anyone says, "I did my part, but other people didn't do theirs, so it's their fault." Shared objectives and measures need to reinforce that the team succeeds or fails as one. Iterative development requires cross-functional teams whose team members are prepared to sacrifice their own personal ambitions for the greater good of the team. When the pressure starts to mount on the project, there are rarely sufficient specialist resources to enable the team to fulfill its project commitments. A good team is composed of members who ignore their specialties, seniorities, and job titles and work together as one to meet the team's commitments. For example, if there is a shortfall in the resources available to test the solution, the developers will stop the development of additional functionality and pitch in to ensure that the existing functionality is sufficiently tested to enable the iteration to be considered a success.

This presents a problem in organizations that enforce strict boundaries between disciplines and introduce organizational structures that emphasize the separation of the disciplines on a project (for example, developers are in one organization and analysts in another). This approach discourages sharing of information and working collaboratively. Regardless of organizational reporting structure, team members must put the project, not their "organization," first. This may require a shift in the way the organization is structured or at the very least a change in the way team members are measured or rewarded. On iterative projects, the individual specialties and internal team structures need to be made secondary to the iteration's goals to reinforce the notion of a single team focused on a common goal.

An iterative team works together in a manner similar to that of a football (soccer) team, where the team of 11 players has the desired outcome of winning the match. Each player has a specific specialization and role to play but must adapt this role to the specific demands of each match: defenders must be prepared to attack, and attackers must be prepared to defend. When the team is behind, you often see defenders turning themselves into makeshift attackers in an attempt to get a goal and bring their side back into the game. There are even situations where the goalkeepers (the most specialized role in a soccer team) must adapt their role to help the team succeed. Late in the game, it is not unusual to see them joining the attack for corners and free kicks and even occasionally scoring. The opposite situation also occurs when goalkeepers are injured or sent off; the team cannot continue without a goalkeeper, so one of the other outfield players often has to take on this role on behalf of the team. When the going gets tough, this is the kind of agility and adaptability that team members on an iterative project need to adopt.

The Leadership Team

Within an iterative development project, there are four keys areas of leadership that need to cooperate to enable the project to effectively iterate. Figure 4-5 shows the four key areas of responsibility that are required to support and lead the development activities. In an iterative project, there is no temporal disconnect between the activities of Requirements Management and Assessment. Although requirements work is more loaded to the front of the project and assessment more loaded to the back, it is essential for both roles to be active throughout the project. The same holds for the other leadership areas of Project Management and Architecture.

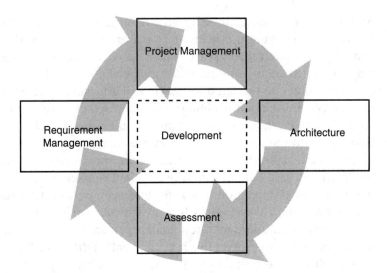

Figure 4-5 *The four leadership areas*

The leadership areas have the following responsibilities:

- **Project Management**—Planning, monitoring, and controlling the project. Leading the project as a whole, ensuring that
the project correctly balances the project variables of scope,
cost, quality, and time along with the personal agendas of the
people involved to maximize the chances of project success.

- **Architecture**—Setting the technical direction for the project.
Leading the technical aspects of the project; providing technical advice to the project manager and technical leadership to
the developers and other team members.

- **Assessment**—Ensuring that a suitable level of quality is
achieved in all areas of the project. Leading the quality and
testing aspects of the project; working with the project manager, the architect, the customers, and the rest of the development team to generate sufficient evidence to communicate
and ensure the quality of the products produced and the
processes used.

- **Requirements Management**—Ensuring that the customers are appropriately involved and represented within the project. Note that there is a strong connection between requirements and assessment: requirements specify the desired outcomes, and assessment ensures that the solution delivers these desired outcomes.

Throughout the project, each of the four leadership areas represents a set of continual responsibilities for ensuring the success of the project and the individual iterations. Each takes the lead in setting the agenda for one of the phases of the project lifecycle. Table 4-1 illustrates how the project leadership is shared across the lifecycle of the project.

Table 4-1 *Leadership Across the Phases*

	Inception	**Elaboration**	**Construction**	**Transition**
Project Management	**Sets the agenda** on behalf of the business to ensure that the project is viable and establishes the project's objectives, desired outcomes, and outline plans.	Verifies the business case and manages the project. Ensures that the team is working effectively and sharing the responsibility for the success of the project.	Leads and protects the development team. Monitors and controls the project.	Manages the transition of the product to the user community and ensures the successful closedown of the project.
Architecture	Defines the technical agenda for the project.	**Sets the agenda** to ensure that the technical risks are appropriately addressed, leading to the creation of a suitable architecture.	Leads the development of the solution and ensures its integrity and appropriateness.	Ensures that the integrity of the architecture is maintained.
Requirements Management	Works with the customers to understand the problems to be solved, scopes the project, and establishes the key requirements.	Works with the customers to elaborate and prioritize the requirements.	**Sets the agenda** on behalf of the project's customers and assists the customers in the review and acceptance of intermediate releases.	Assists the customers in the adoption of the solution and understanding their ongoing requirements.

Table 4-1 *Leadership Across the Phases (continued)*

	Inception	Elaboration	Construction	Transition
Assessment	Establishes the level of quality required by the solution.	Establishes how the application will be tested and verifies the appropriateness of the selected architecture.	Ensures the quality of the releases produced by the iterations. Provides insight into progress and quality.	**Sets the agenda** to ensure the overall quality of the final product and a seamless transition to the user community.

The classic mistake when starting out on an iterative project is to neglect one or more of the project's key areas of responsibility, typically assessment, preventing the iterations from closing the loop on the development of some verified, executable software.

During the Inception phase, one of the key responsibilities of the project manager is to ensure that the leadership team is working effectively and that the project team is working as a single team focused on successfully achieving the iteration's objectives. During the initial iterations, the project may well suffer from a lot of competing and jockeying for position as people attempt to uncover their role on the project. For those of you familiar with the Tuckman Model[8] of team development, you can expect there to be a lot of *forming* and *storming* during Inception. The project team will be *norming* during the Elaboration phase and should be *performing* by the time the project enters the Construction phase.

The project team will need to learn to work iteratively across disciplines, to share the responsibility for the iteration's success or failure, and to self-organize to efficiently address the project risks and any problems that occur. In early iterations, it is not unusual for miscommunication to occur between specialties within the project. For example, at an iteration assessment, the developers might say that they were unable to develop the appropriate components because they were waiting for the requirements

---

[8] B. W. Tuckman, "Developmental Sequence in Small Groups" *Psychological Bulletin* 63(6) (1965): 384–399.

[9] On one project we visited, the developers hadn't started work on building the iteration's release because they were waiting for the analysis modeling to be completed even though there was nobody on the project, apart from the developers, whose responsibility it was to take the requirements and develop an analysis model.

to be completed and delivered to them before they could start their analysis and design.[9] In this case, rather than actively addressing the problem or raising it as an issue when it occurred, the team chose to sit back and hope someone would notice and sort the problem out for them. Iteration assessments bring these problems to light, enabling them to be addressed in the next iteration. Over time these problems should be eliminated as the team starts to work as a truly integrated iterative development team.

Some projects and project teams will be too small to have four people providing the cross-discipline leadership to the project. In these cases, some of the areas of responsibility need to be combined. In our experience, some combinations of responsibility work well and others do not. As a rule of thumb, never combine the architecture responsibility with that of project management. This always ends up in some form of disaster for the project with either no management or no architecting taking place.

Unless you have a one-person project, we recommend always having a separate project manager and a separate architect: one to provide the team leadership and the other to provide the technical leadership. If there are insufficient resources to have separate leaders for requirements and assessment, then we recommend that you combine the requirements management with the project management and the assessment with the architecture.

To iterate successfully, the key management and development skills need to be in place. It is the responsibility of the project manager to ensure that all aspects of the development process are being covered throughout the project and to address any team and communication issues that arise during the iterations or their assessments.

We have already said quite a lot in the earlier chapters about the role of the management, requirements, and assessment teams in planning, measuring, monitoring, controlling, and assessing the iterative project. It is worth taking a few moments to look at the role of architecture in a bit more detail.

The Role of Architecture: Providing a Firm Foundation

Iteration rests upon the existence of a stable architecture: without it, the team cannot build the solution progressively, scenario by scenario, flow by flow, until it delivers the desired business value. Some practitioners find this focus superfluous and feel that architecture is a naturally emergent property of a well-partitioned system. The problem with this view is that to iterate productively, one needs to have a stable architecture, and achieving this requires specific focus in the early iterations.

Broadly speaking, the architecture of a system is intended to make it more resilient to change, increasing its adaptability to a broad set of changes and forces outside the system. Techniques for enhancing adaptability to change tend to fall into two categories: architecture-based and refactoring-based. Architecture-based techniques focus on identifying the product's most likely source of change, or extension, and using information-hiding modularity techniques to encapsulate the sources of change within architectural components. Then, when the change comes, it can be accommodated within the components rather than causing ripple effects across the entire product.

Refactoring is among a handful of techniques that can be valuable tools for shaping the architecture, but by itself, refactoring cannot produce a stable architecture. Refactoring is, in its essence, a technique for partitioning a solution in optimal ways to improve its structure, with the purpose of making it easier to develop and maintain. A well-partitioned solution is an essential aspect of a stable architecture. But there is more to architecture than just partitioning.

Architecture results from a number of decisions regarding the chosen technical approach: decisions related to performance, scalability, fault tolerance, security, and other architectural qualities. These decisions are really independent from the internal partitioning of the solution into a set of components. Refactoring-based change focuses on keeping the product as simple as possible and reorganizing the product to accommodate the next set of expected changes. Refactoring is always done within the context of a number of predefined *architectural* decisions.[10] Even within the most rigid and inflexible architectures, refactoring of the design and implementation are continuously undertaken.

Software architecture[11] encompasses the set of significant decisions about the organization of a software system. Such decisions include the following:

---

[10] Such as the previously selected programming language and execution platform.

[11] This definition is drawn from personal communication with Grady Booch, Philippe Kruchten, and Rich Reitman, and is inspired and informed by the work of Mary Shaw and David Garland.

- Selection of the structural elements and their interfaces by which a system is composed

- Allocation of behavior as specified in collaborations among those elements

- Composition of these structural and behavioral elements into larger subsystems

- Architectural style that guides this organization

Software architecture also involves

- Functionality and usability

- Resilience and performance

- Reuse and comprehensibility

- Economic and technology constraints and tradeoffs

- Aesthetic concerns (elegance)

The architecture constrains the design, implementation, and testing of a system by making certain system-wide choices to which everyone must adhere. At the cost of reduced individual choice, it ensures that the various parts of the system work in harmony. Without an architecture, anarchy tends to reign, and choices made by one developer tend to conflict with and invalidate choices made by other developers, often in unpredictable ways. The problem is compounded when the inconsistencies are subtle and create unpredictable modes of failure that are only discovered after the solution is delivered. As a result, proving the architecture is a significant milestone for any technology project. Get the architecture right before committing significant resources to the project and before worrying about completeness and precision in the requirements, test cases, design, and code.

It should be noted that within this definition, architecture is not purely the product of analysis and design. The creation of an architecture is a decision-making process and not a design process. The architecting of a solution cannot be achieved without implementation, prototyping, and testing. The architecture must be proven, and this can only be done by rigorous stress and performance testing of some form of executable, architectural baseline. Theoretical paper architectures are, for want of a better phrase, not worth the paper they are printed on.

Managers need to be aware of the architecture because it will affect the degree to which work can be partitioned and performed in parallel. Components define the degree of granularity of development: it is generally impossible (or at least impractical) to assign a single component to more than one team and frequently not more than one person. Poor partitioning of functionality between components will increase the interdependencies between project teams and will eventually threaten progress as developers are constantly forced to react to and recover from changes made by others.

Working with the Extended Team

As we saw in Chapter 1, "What Is Iterative Development?" when we discussed how the adoption of iterative and incremental development techniques affects the customer, the iterative project team extends well beyond the development team itself.

For iterative projects to be successful, they must work closely and collaboratively with the business throughout their duration. This may require significant changes to the way the business interacts with the project, the benefits of which will need to be sold to the business representatives before they are prepared to commit their time and energy to working more closely with the projects.

During the Inception phase, it is essential that the project manager and the requirements manager establish an extended team by engaging customers in the project. This might take the form of assigning a customer representative full-time to the project[12] to act, in effect, as the requirements manager and liaise with the business on the project's behalf, but this might not always be achievable or appropriate. The important thing is that this risk is addressed during the Inception phase and that the customer commitment and involvement in the project is established to the satisfaction of all parties.

To be able to contribute to the project, the customers and other stakeholders must understand the goals and approaches used on the project, as well

---

[12] As recommended by the advocates of Extreme Programming.

as the role that they play as part of the extended team. It is our experience that after the stakeholders gain experience of iterative development—by getting involved in the project's requirements gathering, planning, demonstrations, and assessments—and start to see that their feedback and opinions are valued and result in positive changes, they become enthusiastic supporters of the iterative approach. On successful iterative projects, it does not feel like there are separate business and development teams with conflicting objectives, plans, opinions, and agendas; it feels like there is a single extended project team uniting the business and development aspects of the project behind a single shared set of objectives and risks.

It is the responsibility of the project manager to create an inclusive environment where the customers and the developers can truly collaborate to solve the problems of and deliver value to the business through the innovative application of technology.

Iterative Attitudes and Values

As we discussed at the beginning of this chapter, iterative projects often require fundamental changes to the attitudes and values of the team members. Successful iteration requires the following:[13]

- **Commitment**—The whole team needs to be committed to making the project a success. This doesn't mean working silly numbers of hours or promising the customers more than can be delivered; it means just doing whatever it takes to work as a team and meet the iteration's objectives.

- **Focus**—The team needs to keep focused on the iteration's short-term objectives and not get sidetracked by other issues or activities. This is particularly true of the management team members, who need to stick to the iteration's set of objectives after they have been set and agreed to with the team. The time to change the project's direction is between the iterations, not during them.

---

[13] This list is similar to and influenced by the set of attitudes and values required for the use of the SCRUM iterative management approach, which were Commitment, Focus, Openness, Respect, and Courage, described in *Agile Software Development with SCRUM* by Ken Schwaber and Mike Beedle (Upper Saddle River, NJ: Prentice Hall, 2002).

- **Honesty**—Everyone on the team needs to be honest about what they have achieved and what they can achieve. The team needs to be open and honest about the project and the risks that it faces, sharing the problems and openly discussing any possible solutions.

- **Respect**—The team members need to respect one another and, most importantly, their customers.

- **Agility**—The team members must be agile and be prepared to adapt and change the way they work to facilitate the success of the project. There is no point in adopting agile processes that are adaptable to changing circumstances if the team members and plans are not themselves agile and adaptable.

- **Team Working**—Iteration requires the development team to truly function as a team. As we have seen, they must be able to put the success of the team ahead of their own personal agendas and ambitions. In an iterative project, the team succeeds or fails as a whole.

With the correct attitudes in place, the adoption of iterative and incremental development practices on your project becomes very easy. The fact that the project is iterating provides the perfect mechanism for the project team to learn how to work in an iterative fashion and tune their behaviors and processes to effectively support the project. We return to the subject of "getting started" in the final chapter of the book; for now, we would like to conclude this chapter with a brief look at the most important attitude change required—the project management team's attitude toward project planning.

Changing the Way You Think About Planning

Nowhere is the change in values more important than in the management team. If the project is to iterate successfully, it must be managed iteratively. This book prepares you intellectually for the challenge of planning and managing an iterative software development project, but successful iterative project management requires more than an academic knowledge of the subject.

The project manager must believe that an iterative approach is the best way to manage the project and must be prepared to set aside any inflexible, predictive, waterfall management practices that have been used before. This doesn't mean that you should throw away all the good management practices and experiences you have built up over the years. As all the earlier chapters have been at pains to point out, good, disciplined project management is essential to the effective application of iterative and incremental development techniques. It is just that you must put aside some of the conventional wisdom about planning to give yourself the freedom to fully exploit the flexibility and power of the iterative approach.

Conventional Planning Wisdom

The conventional approach to planning is prescriptive, based on the assumptions that the work which needs to be done can be predicted with great precision and that the unusual rarely occurs. This is true for many things—building a bridge over a highway or a standard family dwelling or a prefabricated commercial building, for example. These engineering efforts are technically predictable, and planning this kind of work is based on hundreds of years of experience. This experience has given rise to the generic project lifecycle shown in Figure 4-6, where the different types of project activities are aligned to the single phase that bears their name.

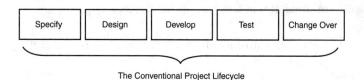

The Conventional Project Lifecycle

Figure 4-6 *The conventional project lifecycle*

This is the project lifecycle used as a reference model by the PRINCE2[14] management method.

This simple sequential lifecycle thinking, when applied to software development, gave rise to the popular "waterfall" software development lifecycle (shown in Figure 4-7).

---

[14] See Office of Government Commerce, *Managing Successful Projects with PRINCE2 (PRINCE Guidance)* (London: The Stationery Office Books, 2002).

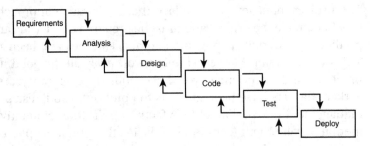

Figure 4-7   *The waterfall software development lifecycle*

Waterfall planning is founded on a complex system of interrelated beliefs:

- Products can be completely developed in one pass

- Requirements can be completed and frozen early

- All requirements are of equal importance

- Designs can be verified without building and testing something

- The entire project can be planned in detail with a high degree of precision at the start of the project

- Everything important can be known at the beginning of the project

- The project can "earn" value by only doing one discipline at a time

- Most importantly, if we follow the prescriptive steps of our process, then all the project risks will be addressed, and therefore one should measure teams on their ability to follow a plan and managers on their ability to create a plan

The focus of all waterfall methods is on optimizing the steps in the process to eliminate repetition and rework and to detect problems through detecting deviations from the plan. In short, the plan is usually regarded as perfect, and deviations from the plan are considered undesirable.

Why Conventional Planning Wisdom Is Wrong When Applied to Software

The short explanation is that almost every one of these assumptions is wrong when applied to software. Software development is an immature discipline, typically requiring extensive innovation and invention, rather than a mature discipline guided by generations of experience. Software projects are also typically unique in that we do not build the same things in the same way over and over again. We are usually building something new or rebuilding something in a new way—software is typically a response to the needs of a changing business. In addition, innovation in software development technologies proceeds at such a blistering pace that in addition to changing business conditions, the implementation technologies are constantly shifting.

In opposition to the assumptions underlying the waterfall methods, we find that[15]

- Problems are discovered too late to do anything about them.

- Predictive plans do not provide the flexibility and adaptability required to handle extensive unknowns.

- Early commitment to detailed requirements is counter-productive.

- Undertaking only one activity at a time separates teams, reduces effectiveness, and creates adversarial team relationships.

- Only obtaining feedback from the next sequential activity delays the detection of errors and problems.

---

[15] The nature of the problems inherent in the conventional waterfall approach to software project management is a topic excellently covered in many other books. We particularly recommend Walker Royce, *Software Project Management: A Unified Framework* (Reading, MA: Addison-Wesley, 1998).

- The plan does not adapt to the risks facing the project.

- Integration and testing are always left until the end where, more often than not, they are cut back in an attempt to meet the original delivery date.

- Design feedback is obtained late, usually leading to late design breakage, when it is too late to fix problems in the architecture.

- Because the objective feedback provided by demonstration and testing is only obtained late in the project, risk resolution typically occurs too late to be effective.

Many of these problems are succinctly illustrated by considering the progress and risk profiles of the conventional software project. These are shown in Figure 4-8 and Figure 4-9, respectively.

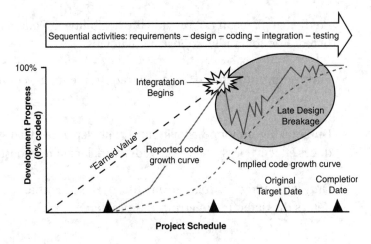

Figure 4-8   *Progress profile of a conventional software project*

Adapted from Walker Royce, *Software Project Management: A Unified Framework* (Boston: Addison-Wesley, 1998).

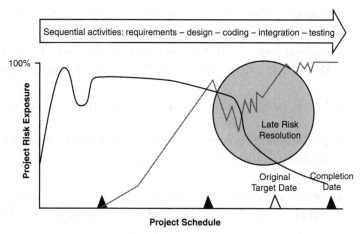

Figure 4-9 *Risk profile of a conventional software project across its lifecycle*

Adapted from Walker Royce, *Software Project Management: A Unified Framework* (Reading, MA: Addison-Wesley, 1998).

Note how the "implied code growth curve" extrapolated from the test results generated by the integration and system testing that takes place after the coding is "complete" diverges from the reported code growth curve that shows the speed of development of the untested code base.

The manifestation of these problems has led directly to the reputation of software development projects as typically being late and over budget. The adoption of waterfall practices also means that the problems are typically concentrated at the end of project, which is unfortunate because the majority of the budget has already been consumed and it is too late to fix the problems.

The failure of the conventional wisdom about planning, especially for high-value, high-risk projects, has led to the evolution of a more progressive school of thought and the foundation of iterative development.

Progressive Thinking About Planning

The progressive, adaptive, iterative approach is founded on the following principles:

- Proceed in small steps, continuing steadily by increments.

- The plans must adapt to the project's changing circumstances.

- The characteristics that distinguish the product or service must be progressively elaborated. They should be broadly defined early in the project and made more explicit and detailed as a better understanding of the project emerges.

- Large projects must be broken up into smaller projects.

- Requirements errors can be 100 times more costly to fix after deployment than at requirements time.

- Initial estimates have a large margin of error—most waterfall projects cost two to three times what was initially predicted.

- The first one never works; always develop things at least twice.

- Initial designs will be flawed.

- Requirements must evolve alongside demonstrable versions of the product.

- Teams need to own and be accountable for their achievements and plans.

- You should believe the project results, not the project plan.

- Detailed planning should be limited to the next milestone.

- Projects should adopt an active and aggressive approach to addressing project risk.

Aggressively attacking the project's risk requires the process to be agile, not prescriptive. The project must be able to do whatever is required to address its most important risks and must not be limited in the set of activities that it can apply. For example, if the most important risk facing a project is the integration of several commercial products, then writing the requirements for the integration does not significantly reduce the risk; only the creation of an executable prototype that demonstrates that the products can work together truly addresses risk.

To be effective, iterative and incremental development requires a progressive approach to project management.

Comparing the Two Approaches

The fundamental problem with conventional waterfall approaches is that they postpone risk mitigation to the point where it can become too costly to recover from the risks. The waterfall approach tends to mask the real risks to a project until it is too late to do anything meaningful about them.

Progressive, iterative processes were developed in response to the problems inherent in the waterfall approach. Instead of developing the whole system in one go, an increment is selected and developed, then another increment, and so on. The selection of the contents of the first increment is based on risk, addressing the highest-priority risks first. To address the selected risk(s), select a subset of the requirements to be implemented and tested. Develop the minimal set of functionality that enables objective verification (through a set of executable tests) that the risks have been successfully addressed. Then select the next highest risks to be addressed in the next increment and so on.

One of the great ironies of modern software development is that in the paper that led to the popularity of the waterfall approach to software development,[16] Winston Royce argued that projects should always go through at least two development cycles because the first version never works. He was actually arguing that projects should take a more incremental approach, not that they should adopt a prescriptive waterfall development approach. Progressive, iterative approaches take this principle one step further by splitting the lifecycle up into many smaller increments, each explicitly addressing the project's major risks.

The Unified Process lifecycle provides a risk-based framework that supports and enables the progressive, adaptive planning of software development projects. Progressive planning approaches require a decoupling of the phases and disciplines of the process. This is best illustrated by comparing where the disciplines are applied within the two approaches, as shown in Table 4-2 and Table 4-3.

---

[16] Winston Royce, "Managing the Development of Large Software Systems," from the *Proceedings, IEEE WESCON*, August 1970, The Institute of Electrical Engineers.

Table 4-2 *The Intersection of Lifecycle Phase and Discipline for a Pure Waterfall Process*

Discipline	Waterfall Lifecycle Phases					
	Requirements	Analysis	Design	Code	Test	Deploy
Requirements	✓					
Analysis		✓				
Design			✓			
Implementation				✓		
Test					✓	
Deployment						✓

Table 4-3 *The Intersection of Lifecycle Phase and Discipline for a Progressive, Iterative Process*

Discipline	Iterative Lifecycle Phases			
	Inception	Elaboration	Construction	Transition
Requirements	✓	✓	✓	✓
Analysis	✓	✓	✓	✓
Design	✓	✓	✓	✓
Implementation	✓	✓	✓	✓
Test	✓	✓	✓	✓
Deployment	✓	✓	✓	✓

You will note that *every discipline* has some role *in every phase*—this is not a mistake! The extent to which the disciplines are performed will vary, but they are always present no matter what the phase.

When adopting iterative project planning, it is important that the plans actively address the project's risks. To this end, in terms of the development process, anything can happen at any time. The development process needs to become an aid to planning and risk reduction rather than an alternative.

To illustrate what happens when a project is too dogmatic about applying certain activities at certain times, let us consider two insurance companies, both of which desire to improve their customer service by making some of their legacy applications directly available to their customers through new Internet client-based applications. Both companies are excited by new technologies that allegedly offer a simple and low-cost way forward. Both companies decide to pilot the new technology by developing an initial new application.

Company One follows waterfall development practices, so it needs to capture all the requirements of the new application in the first phase. They cast around for a business project willing to be the first adopters of the new, unproven technology. Not surprisingly, they cannot find many people prepared to gamble their projects on the new technology. Those engaged on business-critical, high-priority projects are particularly loath to add the new technology risks to their projects. This leads to the selection of a low-priority, low-risk, unimportant business application for development. Unfortunately, like many a low-priority, low-risk, unimportant business application, no one is interested in it, and the business application fails to get approval for continued development. The project team actually ends up developing six different requirements models for applications to test the new technology, none of which comes to fruition. In all this time, they do nothing to address the technology risks inherent in the project, and although the project goes on for more than six months, no technical resources are assigned to it because they are not needed until the next phase.

Company Two adopts a different approach. Rather than faithfully following their traditional waterfall development process, they decide to adopt an iterative risk-focused one. Now the biggest risk facing the project isn't that they have no detailed requirements specification or even that they haven't been allocated a business application to develop. The biggest risk is that the selected technology might not work. Everyone agrees that if it *does* work, there will be no shortage of applications ready to be implemented in a secure fashion over the Internet. To address the technology risk, they build an example application that enables the simple query and update of personal details across multiple legacy applications. They then demonstrate it against the live systems in front of the IT director and a selection of the company's business leaders. By the end of the demonstration, they have a queue of business applications waiting to be enabled by the new technology. This enables the business to select the project of most value as the first to be developed. This application successfully goes live for less than the cost of the extended requirements work done by Company One.

In this case it is obvious that the return on investment is much higher for Company Two than for Company One. The losses incurred by Company One are purely due to the selection of and adherence to an inappropriate development approach.

The fundamental differences between the two approaches are summarized in Table 4-4.

Table 4-4 *Comparing Conventional and Iterative Thinking on Planning*

Conventional	Iterative
Risk agnostic	Actively attacks risk
Predictive planning	Adaptive planning
Subjective measurement of progress	Objective measurement of progress
Delays integration and testing	Continuous integration and testing
Nothing runs until the end	Something executable produced every iteration
Difficulties at the end of the project	Difficulties at the start of the project

Now all this is not to say that waterfall methods are bad and should never be applied. In fact it is possible to see the waterfall as an extreme example of an iterative process, with only one iteration. And as with all things extreme, one should really have the basic skills in place before attempting it. It has always struck us as odd that iterative development practices are seen as more complicated and are typically adopted after people have experienced the supposedly easier waterfall approach. In fact the relationship should be the other way around, with project teams only being allowed to adopt waterfall practices after they have successfully demonstrated their ability to work iteratively. The "optimized" waterfall style process should only be applied when the project faces little or no risk and the team has done exactly the same kind of thing before.

Seven Habits of Successful Iterative Project Managers

Iterative project management requires the management team to embrace the attitudes and values required of the iterative development team and to exhibit these in their day-to-day management of the project.[17] They must actively promote the principles that underlie all progressive, iterative processes:

- Break large projects up into smaller projects, and then break the smaller projects up into iterations.

- Attack the greatest risks in the earliest iterations.

- Produce something demonstrable every iteration.

- Do not delay integration and test. Every iteration should include integration and test activities.

- Be prepared to make mistakes and explore blind alleys. Mistakes are to be encouraged if they reduce the project risk or challenge the project's assumptions.

- Plans must be adjusted based upon the lessons learned.

The application of these principles leads to changes in management behavior that are best summed up in the following seven habits of the successful iterative project manager:[18]

1. Steadily focused on advancing the solution in small but deliberate steps

2. Focused on generating results but not afraid to fail

3. Exercising adaptive planning continuously

4. Always risk-aware

---

[17] An excellent article with the same title as this section was written by Eric Cardozo and published in the Rational Edge e-Zine at http://www-128.ibm.com/developerworks/rational/library/1742.html.

[18] With apologies to Stephen Covey, author of the various *Seven Habits* self-improvement books....

5. Always open and honest

6. Focused on objective results-based assessments (not subjective opinion-based ones)

7. Singularly focused on delivering a working solution

If these seven habits reflect your existing management style, then you will find the transition to iterative project management fairly painless. If these habits are in opposition to your personal management style, then you might struggle to realize the benefits offered by the iterative approach.

Summary

Iterative and incremental development is more than just a development process: it is an attitude toward problem solving and solution delivery that requires the whole team to collaborate and share the project's risks, failures, and successes.

Going into the project with a "can-do" attitude is so important that if you and the leaders of your project teams (particularly the requirements manager and the architect) don't want to work in an iterative fashion, you should stop now. If you *do* want to iterate, there are a few simple things you can put in place to make the early iterations as painless as possible:

- A value-driven, end-to-end thread-based development process.

- A small collaborative leadership team covering the key areas of Project Management, Requirements Management, Architecture, and Assessment.

- Education and support for the stakeholders and team members directly involved in the project.

- A commitment to produce and use iterative and adaptive plans. It is essential that you don't fall back on conventional, predictive planning practices in an attempt to fit into the organization or give the impression that the project is easier and more predictable than it truly is.

In this chapter we also introduced use cases and use-case driven development as our reference process for use in examples and to provide a more concrete framework for the project planning and assessment guidance to come. This does not preclude the use of other development processes such as the Microsoft Solutions Framework, Extreme Programming, or any other agile, iterative method alongside the management approach presented here. It just provides us with a standard, well-defined vocabulary for use throughout the rest of the book.

PART II

Planning and Managing an Iterative Project

5

A Layered Approach to Planning and Managing Iterative Projects

"Planning is an unnatural process; it is much more fun to do something. The nicest thing about not planning is that failure comes as a complete surprise, rather than being preceded by a period of worry and depression."
—*John Harvey-Jones*

"Let our advance worrying become advance thinking and planning."
—*Winston Churchill*

No single plan can encompass all that needs planning within a project: in creating such a plan, one would obscure the essential contents with so much detail that no one could understand the plan. Plans must be simple and understandable while still being complete.

There is a little-understood mathematical fact that the more detailed a plan is, the less accurate it is. This runs counter to the conventional wisdom about planning that says that one deals with risk by having a detailed plan, the more detailed the better. Errors in estimates accumulate multiplicatively (because shifting dates affect the start dates of downstream activities), so if we have a 99% probability of each task completing according to plan, a 10-task plan is inherently more accurate than a 100-task plan, and that plan is even more accurate than a 1000-task plan.[1]

---

[1] We are indebted to Murray Cantor for this insight.

Probabilities of completing a project on schedule when each task has a 99% probability of completing on schedule are shown below:

$$P(1 \text{ task}) = 0.99^1 = 0.99$$

$$P(10 \text{ tasks}) = 0.99^{10} = 0.904$$

$$P(100 \text{ tasks}) = 0.99^{100} = 0.366$$

$$P(1000 \text{ tasks}) = 0.99^{1000} = 0.000043$$

From this list, we can see that a project with a thousand tasks has almost no possibility of completing exactly on schedule. So why bother to plan at all if you're encouraged to leave out so much detail? First, planning is a thought exercise that forces the consideration of possible outcomes and responses to those outcomes. Second, it is necessary to coordinate the work of interdependent resources. This does not mean that plans have to be extremely detailed; they merely need to be detailed enough to establish key evaluation points, at which observations will be made to ensure the project is on track, and to establish key synchronization points to hold the work together.

The solution to the problem of finding the right level of detail is to layer the plan. At each layer the plan refines the details of the layer above it to resolve the specific concerns of a particular set of stakeholders. Layering the plans also limits the extent to which change ripples through them, minimizing the need for frequent updates and revision.

This "divide and conquer" or "hierarchical" approach is a fundamental tenet of all human problem solving. It's the same as having different layers of abstraction, all of which nest nicely to describe the solution. At any level of abstraction, "all" the information is there. If you need more detail, you go to a lower level of the plans.

In this chapter, we identify the management layers that support and enable successful iterative projects, the management artifacts produced at each layer, the management responsibilities of each layer, and the mechanisms used at each layer for monitoring and controlling the project.

The Management Layers

Project management is seldom straightforward enough to be a simple linear process.[2] To solve this problem, most organizations and project management techniques identify management layers that simplify employees' responsibilities and enable them to work together to deliver business benefit to the organization. The most common layers include the following:

- **Organization-level Program Management**—This layer implements the organization's business strategy and vision. This layer commissions the projects and defines their overall targets and constraints. It sets the business context for one or more projects.

- **Overall Project Management**—This layer directs and manages a project, including the overall planning, monitoring, and control of the project and coordinating the development and delivery of one or more products.

- **Day-to-day Development Management**—This layer manages the tasks of product delivery: coordinating and overseeing the work of the development team and ensuring the quality of the products produced.

These layers represent levels of responsibility, accountability, autonomy, and decision-making authority rather than individual people, and they are present in all projects, no matter how small. These management layers interact in two major ways:

- The higher-level layers exercise control over the lower layers. For example, the organization-level program management layer charters and funds projects, which must deliver results to the funding organization.

---

[2] As we saw in the last chapter, linear, predictive, prescriptive planning and management techniques are not really suitable for software development or other creative endeavors.

- The outputs from the lower layers provide the inputs that allow the higher layers to function effectively. For example, the funded projects must provide evidence to the program management layer that they are on track and delivering results.

Iterative development practices are introduced below the development management layer because they are used to iteratively evolve the products to be delivered by the development layer. These relationships are shown in Figure 5-1. The introduction of iterations into the development projects gives us four layers of management. The activities at each level are shown as arrows because, although they are typically initiated in sequence, they take place concurrently.

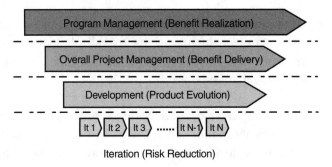

Figure 5-1   *The four management layers*

Adapted from Laurence Archer, "Implementing Rational Unified Process Within a PRINCE2 Environment" (Oak Management Services [previously Oak IT], 2001).

The more effective the management at each layer, and the better the quality of the communication between the layers, the more effective everyone involved in the project will be.

Each layer has a different focus and different goals. It is worth spending a little more time examining them before looking at how we can exploit them to facilitate the management of our iterative and incremental software development projects.

The Program Management Layer

A program is typically a collection of related projects organized to deliver a change in the overall capability of an organization. The program provides oversight to ensure that its constituent projects are coordinated and on track to deliver the intended results. When a project is not part of a program, the organization's senior management plays the same role, ensuring that the projects are on track and aligned with the broader business objectives.

This layer is focused on the sustained *realization of the benefits* offered by the solution as a whole, and its responsibilities extend well beyond the lifetime of the projects that develop the solution. The exact plans of each project are not important to this layer; what is important is the overall solution's value, the investment required, the delivery schedule, and the dependencies inherent in the project plans. The program management layer needs to coordinate its component projects to ensure that they can work together to deliver the intended organizational result.

The Overall Project Management Layer

A "project" is a management vehicle that organizes resources to produce some set of benefits within a specific time frame and with specific resources. Unlike operational business processes that are intended to go on indefinitely, a project has a defined lifespan; even though some projects seem to go on forever, they are all intended to conclude at some point.

The overall project layer is concerned with marshalling and managing the resources necessary[3] to deliver some desired business benefit. A project has a project manager who is responsible for the effective utilization of these resources to deliver the desired business result within the desired time frame, typically represented as a series of business-related milestones and delivery dates.

This layer is not concerned with the details of *how* to do the work that culminates in the achievement of a milestone; this is left to the next layer down. It is concerned with overall project risks and benefits, the time

---

[3] A project typically "owns" some set of resources, although it is also common to share some of these resources with other projects.

frames in which they will be addressed, and the resources needed to address them. By not focusing on the details of *how* these things are to be achieved, it is able to rise above the day-to-day details of the project to ensure that the effort is on track to achieve the desired results.

The "benefits delivery" layer is focused on incrementally delivering the benefits of the solution across the length of the project, as evidenced through a series of releases and prototypes. The details of how these are built are not important to this layer, but the areas that they address *are* important.[4]

The Development Layer

Projects typically develop products to deliver benefit to the business; this is certainly true of all software development projects. The development layer is focused on the definition, evolution, and delivery of *major releases* of the products required by the overall project.

Layers above this are focused on the coordination of resources *across* deliveries and with overall project oversight and funding. Whereas the overall project management layer is more general and externally directed with its focus on delivering business benefit back to the business and the program layer, this layer is more specialized and internally directed with its focus of developing deployable releases of software products.

The Iteration Layer

The iteration layer is focused on ensuring that the evolution of the required software products is undertaken incrementally in a controlled and managed fashion that actively reduces the risk facing the overall project. It is where the real work gets done. Each iteration focuses on incrementally evolving a software product. It takes a series of these iterations to develop a *major release* that can be successfully deployed.

---

[4] If you are an IT supplier, then you will typically find that the commissioning business has a business project that plays the same role.

As powerful as the major release is as a forcing function, additional controls are necessary to ensure that the project is tracking to the release goal. Because iterations focus on resolving specific risks at specific points in the project, they prevent risks from causing instability and wasted effort by ensuring that they are dealt with in the appropriate order—with the high-impact risks being addressed first.

The Role of the Layers

The top three layers are present in all organizations developing software. The fourth layer is added by the development team that wants to develop their software products iteratively.

For software development projects, there is a natural tendency to merge the development and overall project management layers based on the assumption that the project will only produce a single major release of a single software product. We have found this approach to be shortsighted; few projects deliver all their results in a single major release. For this and many other reasons we explore later, it is better to keep the overall project management separate from the development management. It is an essential part of managing the project to ensure that the benefits expected of each release are aligned across the layers and communicated to the entire project team.

At first it might seem that having four layers will create unnecessary bureaucracy. The introduction of these conceptual layers does not necessitate similar layers of management: we use them to simplify management practices by separating concerns, just as one would separate concerns using effective design techniques. The layers simply represent different management perspectives and interfaces.

Planning Through the Layers

As shown in Figure 5-2, each layer operates at a different level of abstraction with a different time horizon.

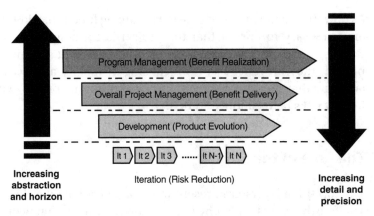

Figure 5-2 *The levels of abstraction and detail vary across the layers.*

The lower the layer, the shorter the time horizon and the more detailed, accurate, and precise the plans. A program plan may well stretch for a number of years, so it will be quite abstract and imprecise about long-term estimates. On the other hand, an iteration plan is focused on the next few (typically four to six) weeks and will be very precise about what exactly is to be done.

Traditionally, iterative project management guidance has focused solely on the lower two layers, and where it has attempted to address the upper layers, it has disregarded many of the important management and financial controls that are integral to controlling a business and that are at the heart of more traditional management approaches such as PMBOK[5] and PRINCE2.[6] It has also tended to give an unwarranted precedence to the development of new and innovative software solutions while disregarding the impact of business change and other organizational issues that often derail technically sound solutions.

Failure to discuss the impact of iterative development on the top two management layers has often made it difficult to sell iterative development to senior managers. Without support from senior management, iterative approaches can come into conflict with the programs and projects that they are supposed to support. For many senior managers the apparent lack

---

[5] The *Project Management Body of Knowledge (PMBOK)*, developed by the Project Management Institute (http://www.pmi.org).

[6] PRINCE (**PR**ojects **IN** **C**ontrolled Environments) is a structured method for effective project management. See http://www.prince2.com.

of management control advocated by many "agile" approaches is a cause for concern. They usually view those approaches as being in opposition to the visibility and foresight they need to ensure that project budgets are well spent.

We include the overall project layer in our discussions because iterative development has major implications for the planning and management of this layer. The nature of the planning, monitoring, and control undertaken for an iterative project is fundamentally different from that undertaken for a traditional project. The feedback provided by iterating will have effects far beyond the development layer. For iterative development to be effective, the overall project managers must also adopt a progressive, adaptive approach to project management and planning.

This is also the layer that is most affected by the layering itself. Project managers steeped in traditional approaches often cling to detailed planning as the primary mechanism for risk reduction, even though detailed plans offer no capability to mitigate risk. The growing consensus is that risk is only mitigated through the demonstration of results. To reduce risk and achieve better results, the overall project managers must be prepared to delegate and allow detail to be pushed down through the development layer to the iteration plans, where agile approaches are adopted.

The program management layer is isolated from the iterations by the middle two management layers, making it much more stable and unaffected by the particular techniques used to develop the products required to realize business benefit from its investments. There is, however, a role for iterative project management techniques in the management of programs, particularly those focused on technological innovation and the development of software-intensive products. We return to this subject in Chapter 10, "A Scalable Approach to Managing Iterative Projects," when we consider scaling up iterative project management techniques for use on large projects and programs. For now we focus on the integrated planning and management of the three project management layers.

Positioning the Unified Process Lifecycle

In Chapter 3, "Controlling Iterative Projects," we saw how important the Unified Process lifecycle is as a framework for controlling iterative development. As shown in Figure 5-3, each application of the Unified Process is known as an *evolution* and produces a major release of the product.

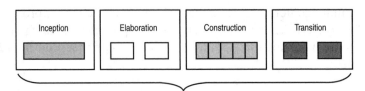

One evolution, deploying one *major* release

Figure 5-3 *An evolution is a single pass through the Unified Process lifecycle.*

The number and sizes of iterations shown here are purely illustrative and are not indicative of the relative lengths and numbers of iterations required by the phases, as we discuss in Chapter 7, "Evolution and Phase Planning."

Very few software development projects deliver a complete solution in a single release in the manner shown in Figure 5-3. Most projects deliver their solution as a series of major releases, each of which delivers benefit to their customers. These evolutions are *more or less* sequentially ordered[7] projects, each one building on the previous evolution as shown in Figure 5-4.

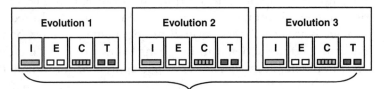

Multiple evolutions, each deploying a *major* release

Figure 5-4 *A solution delivered through several evolutions*

Note that this is a Unified Process evolution for each major release (Release 1, 2, 3, and so on), not for each minor bug fix or point release. During the transition of Release 1, minor enhancements, fixes, and emergency releases may be required (Releases 1.1, 1.2, 1.3, and so on). These would be the result of undertaking transition iterations as part of the first evolution.

There are cases where only a single evolution is required, but these are rare. From an IT supplier's perspective, this can appear to occur in outsourcing environments where a customer gives the supplier one well-defined evolution to produce and then brings the other evolutions in house. From the customer perspective, this initial delivery is still the first of a series.

---

[7] We say *more or less* because there is often some slight overlap between the completion of one evolution and the start of the next. For example, the Inception phase of the second evolution might overlap with the Transition phase for the first evolution.

The overall project layer is responsible for identifying and coordinating the development of an appropriate set of evolutions to meet its goals.

Layering the Plans and Milestones

Some people in the agile methods community argue that there is no need for planning beyond the current iteration, let alone the current evolution. As the quote from John Harvey-Jones at the beginning of this chapter observes, developing is more fun than planning, but planning is necessary to know where you are headed. The iterative approach enables the team to do something concrete within the current iteration, but without higher-level plans to illuminate the future, the current iteration effort could turn out to be misapplied and worthless in the end.

Given the complexity of coordinating multiple releases and possibly more than one development team, a mechanism is needed to simplify and focus the plans. We exploit the management layers to provide a simple set of plans; one for each layer, each focused on a different set of issues. This separation of concerns has many benefits, including the following:

- Reducing the management overheads by keeping the plans and control mechanisms simple and focused

- Keeping the detail focused on the short-term where it is required

- Providing plans with both the breadth and depth required to satisfy all the stakeholders in the project

- Enabling managers to manage and developers to develop

Figure 5-5 shows a simplified view of the planning elements at each of our project layers. The overall project is made up of development projects, each developing an evolution of the product to be produced. Each evolution is managed iteratively using the lifecycle of the Unified Process. Each Unified Process phase consists of iterations, which in turn are made up of planned and executed tasks.

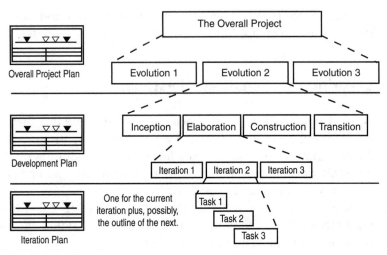

Figure 5-5   *Layering of project plans*

Although Figure 5-5 seems to suggest that there are a lot of plans, only three are active at any one time, one for each layer: (1) the overall project, (2) the current evolution, and (3) the current iteration.[8] The formality of these plans varies with the needs of the project, but in general each plan can be (and probably should be) no longer than a few pages.[9] We shall shortly see how this is possible, but first let's talk about each type of plan.

- **The Overall Project Plan**—For each project there is a single overall project plan. This overall plan is actually quite brief—it lays out the number of evolutions and releases needed to deliver the solution, including milestone dates, functionality delivered, risks to be addressed, and overall resource levels needed. The overall resources used and the business benefit delivered tie back to the Business Case developed for the

---

[8] In many ways this layering is akin to that which occurs when defining service contracts where plans need to be versioned and changes formally approved. Service contracts typically include a Master Agreement (akin to the Overall Project Plan), a number of Project Descriptions (akin to the Development Plans), and detailed Statements of Work (akin to the Iteration Plans) in order to restrict change control to the appropriate level. A similar separation of concerns is in action here.

[9] In this case we are purely talking about the plan itself, not the full set of project management documentation. Some organizations require a larger set of technical management plans (risk management, quality management, and so on) to be included in the planning document. Typically this makes the planning document longer than a few pages.

solution. The overall project plan acts as the roadmap for the project as a whole. Producing the overall project plan is the subject of the next chapter.

- **The Current Development Plan**—There is a single development plan for the current evolution that lays out the lifecycle milestones and goals for each phase, identifying the number and purpose of the iterations they contain. Where staffing levels vary across phases, the development plan lays out how many people are needed and what skills they need. As this evolution progresses and its results start to become apparent, the planning of the next evolution starts.[10] Producing the development plan for an evolution is the subject of Chapter 7.

- **The Current Iteration Plan**—There is a single iteration plan for the current iteration. This is a detailed plan describing what will be done during the iteration. The iteration plans tend to be the most susceptible to change because the iteration is where the real work happens, but because we do not plan every iteration at the start of the project, changes to the iteration plans do not ripple disruptively through the entire set of project plans. As this iteration progresses and its results start to become apparent, the planning of the next iteration starts. The production of iteration plans is the subject of Chapter 8, "Iteration Planning."

Many iterative project managers create a very rough draft of the plan for the next iteration alongside the iteration plan for the current iteration. The plan for the next iteration can then evolve as the current iteration is executed and its results become apparent. In this case at the end of the current iteration, the draft plan can be modified to become the plan for the next iteration rather than having to generate it from

---

[10] Although it is tempting to collapse the development plans into the overall project plan, our experience is that this causes far more problems than the benefit of a slightly reduced number of documents warrants. It also makes the overall project plan more volatile because it needs to be changed every time the development plans are tuned.

scratch. Also, as tasks are deferred and new data comes in, we have a framework—the draft plan of the next iteration—into which to fold these changes. If this approach is adopted, care must be taken not to over-plan the next iteration before the results of the current iteration are known.

As Figure 5-6 illustrates, the planning horizons and levels of detail vary across the layers. The detail of the plans increases as you move down the layers while at the same time the scope of the plan narrows. The overall project plan is typically visible to the entire organization, whereas the plan for an individual iteration is usually visible only to the people working on it.

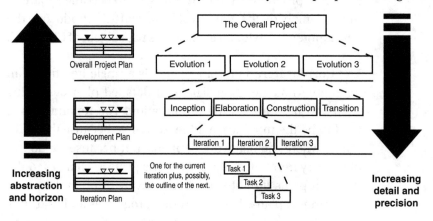

Figure 5-6   *The planning horizon and level of detail varies across the layers.*

The plans act like lenses in a microscope, with each successive lens refining the image and increasing the understanding of the small surface details of an increasingly precise area. At the same time, the layers are like the bulkheads in a ship, preventing problems at lower levels from forcing re-planning at higher levels. This simple planning concept enables the management of everything from very small projects to very large programs to be undertaken with the same general management approach.

The overall project plan has the broadest time horizon and focuses on decisions and commitments that affect the project as a whole, while the detail is pushed down through the development plans into the iteration plans. For the layering to work, you need to be able to outline the entire project in a robust, time-neutral manner that accommodates project over- and under-performance. To this end, you should focus the higher-level plans on commitments and achievements rather than on the tasks to be performed.

At the lowest layer, the current iteration plan lays out the team's work for the current time box. Task plans and detailed work plans are optional. These are sometimes used to help the people working on the task perform the work.

The key to understanding how the plans fit together is to understand how the milestones for the project are built up. Figure 5-7 shows the focus of each plan at each layer within the project.

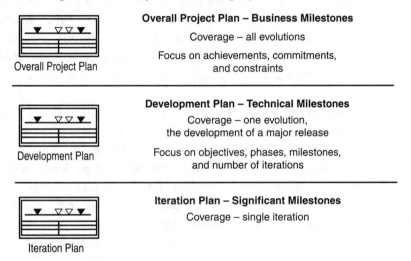

Overall Project Plan – Business Milestones

Coverage – all evolutions

Focus on achievements, commitments, and constraints

Overall Project Plan

Development Plan – Technical Milestones

Coverage – one evolution, the development of a major release

Focus on objectives, phases, milestones, and number of iterations

Development Plan

Iteration Plan – Significant Milestones

Coverage – single iteration

Iteration Plan

Figure 5-7   *The plans and their coverage*

The plans at the different levels share milestones.

- The Overall Project Plan focuses on business milestones and external commitments. It is primarily used by the senior management and other stakeholders to gain an understanding of what the project will deliver to the business and when it will deliver it. Business milestones are allocated to one or more evolutions, and they provide the linkage between business plans and development plans. In many cases the Overall Project Plan encompasses activities other than the development of the software. For example, it may shape not only the development plans at a lower layer also but peer marketing and change plans, too.

- The Development Plan describes how a single evolution will be developed and released. It provides a roadmap for the development team working on the evolution by introducing the technical milestones defined by the Unified Process lifecycle. These milestones structure and focus the project effort to reduce risk and ensure progress toward the delivery of a major release. The development plan sets the goals for each iteration and outlines the allocation of use cases, flows, scenarios, and risks to the iterations, ensuring that neither functionality nor technical issues fall between the cracks. Note: The specific content of each iteration is specified in its individual iteration plan.

- The Iteration Plan focuses on a single iteration, showing how the assigned requirements will be developed and how the technical risks will be mitigated. It provides the means by which the development team coordinates its work within the time box defined by the iteration. It is mostly an internal working plan used by the development team. Higher layers of management focus on the development and overall project plans.

All of the plans are goal-based[11]—that is, they focus on defining what needs to be accomplished and by when, rather than defining exactly how the results will be achieved. This gives the development teams flexibility in how they accomplish the goals while holding them accountable for their achievement. It is this change in emphasis that requires a project management paradigm shift from activity-based planning to goal-based planning. It is more important that the team members achieve a goal than that they complete a specified activity.

The milestones at any layer can be the following:

- **Allocated**—Shared between plans. Higher-level milestones must be delegated to the lower levels for completion.

- **Derived**—Lower-level milestones that contribute to the achievement of a higher-level milestone.

---

[11] This is also referred to as "result-oriented" or "achievement-based planning." What is important is that the focus is on the *what* and not the *how*.

- **Inserted**—Added to a layer because of the lifecycle process being adopted.

- **Emergent**—Lower-level milestones that assume greater significance as the more detailed plans solidify.

Planning is both a top-down and bottom-up activity, with some milestones being allocated in a top-down manner whereas others emerge as the plans for the lower layers become more concrete. Figure 5-8 shows that overall project milestones are allocated down to specific iterations. From the top down, goals are set, and overall project budget and timelines are established. Goals are typically defined in terms of results to be delivered and risks to be mitigated.

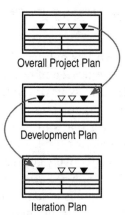

Figure 5-8   *The allocation of milestones down through the layers*

Although every overall project milestone related to software development will need to be allocated to an iteration for completion, other technical milestones will percolate up from iterations or evolutions to take on business significance. As an example, achieving a stable architecture proves that the solution is technically feasible which might be of great interest to the business. This bubbling up of technical milestones from the iteration and development plans to the overall project plan is shown in Figure 5-9.

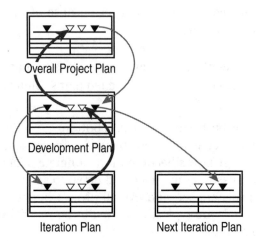

Figure 5-9 *Milestones can be allocated top-down or can emerge from lower-level plans.*

From the bottom up, work is defined to meet the goals established by the higher-layer plans.[12] The degree of detail of these bottom-up plans varies depending on the size and skills of the team and the contractual needs of the organization (some organizations require detailed plans to be defined and tracked). Lower-layer plans must map out the project up to the next project management review established by the layer above to provide the information needed to effectively control the project.

This goal-oriented planning is essential to keeping the plans at each layer simple, informative, and complementary, and it prevents them from degenerating into an enormous, unfocused, confusing array of activities and dependencies.

The principles are simple:

- Establish goals and criteria by which their achievement will be evaluated.

---

[12] Top-down plans are generally optimistic in nature, whereas bottom-up plans tend to be pessimistic. Undertaking both simultaneously provides the balance needed to arrive at challenging but achievable plans. One should always start with a top-down plan and verify it against the emerging bottom-up plan. This reconciliation of top-down and bottom-up plans is sometimes referred to as the "round-trip gestalt." Sometimes situations arise where, when you get to the middle, things cannot be made to agree. You should not paper over this eventuality. This is where the real project management comes into play.

- Let the development team determine how it will meet the milestones.

- Don't measure success based on whether a plan of sequenced activities is being followed but on whether the goals are being achieved.

In this layered approach, the detail of the activities to be performed is held in the iteration plans, enabling the other plans to remain simple and goal-focused.[13] This provides the opportunity for progressive project management—the iteration plans contribute toward milestones in the development plans, which in turn provide input to the overall project plans. This reflects the typical approach to planning: defining where you want to be and then defining steps along the way. The details of how you make these steps are pushed down into the iteration plans and made visible in the higher-level plans only as required by the stakeholders. In many cases the details of the lower-level plans come from the development team itself rather than the management team.

The key to successful project planning is balance: this is both a balance between the management and technical areas of the project and between the need for long-term and short-term plans. In the layered approach, this balance is achieved by confining the detailed planning to the current iteration and keeping the higher-level plans focused on documenting the achievement and commitments made by the project as a whole. Then, as the iterations complete, their results can be assessed and the higher-level plans adjusted to represent and react to the realities of the project.

Positioning the Other Key Management Artifacts

An artifact is a byproduct of work. Artifacts have many roles in the project:

- They assist in completing the work to be done.

---

[13] Long-term, detailed, activity-based planning is based on the assumption that a project manager knows what needs to be done and the order in which things need to be done. In creative endeavors like software development, this is impossible for anyone to determine precisely beyond the very short term. Goals, however, are entirely a different case.

- They act as a vehicle for communication within the project team and with the project's stakeholders.

- They provide evidence that the work was done.

Apart from the products to be explicitly developed (for a software development project, this is the executable software), the other project artifacts are only of secondary importance. Never confuse the map with the territory. We don't do the work to produce the artifact—it is the work itself that is important. On the other hand, an artifact can sometimes help us avoid the need to do the work over again because no one wrote down the result.

To manage the project, a number of management artifacts are needed to provide the project's terms of reference, set the management strategy, plan the project, and assess how the project is doing. Apart from the set of project plans, the majority of these are unaffected by adopting a layered, iterative approach. Table 5-1 summarizes the project management artifact set and discusses how they apply at different layers.

Table 5-1   *Planning and Management Artifacts*

Type of Artifact	Purpose	Examples	Layer
Terms of Reference	Define the project goals and objectives	Business Case Vision Contracts Acceptance Criteria	Held at the overall project layer, reflecting the evolutions and products to be produced.
Management Strategy	Define how the project will be conducted	Project Approach Quality Plan Measurement Plan Communication Plan Technical Plans[*]	Held at the overall project layer and shared by all evolutions and iterations.
Project Plans	Plan the project	Overall Project Plan Development Plan Iteration Plan	One type of plan for each layer.
Monitoring and Control	Track and report the state of the project	Iteration Assessment Phase Assessment Project Assessment Project Closedown Exception Reports	These will pass between the management layers. The frequency of the iteration assessments should negate the need for other kinds of regular status assessments.

[*] Such as the Configuration Management Plan, the Change Management Plan, and for Rational Unified Process projects, the Development Case.

The scope of this book is restricted to the planning and assessment of the project. Elements of the terms of reference and management strategy are only discussed where they are affected by the introduction of iterative development practices.

Distributing the Management Responsibilities

The layering of the project also affects the ways that the management responsibilities can be distributed and delegated. The typical assumption is that either there is a single project manager covering all the layers or each layer has a separate manager, but as we shall see, the roles can be combined to fit the circumstances and skill set of any particular project.

Key Management Roles

Three levels of management responsibility are required on any iterative and incremental project, and these levels reflect and align to the layering of the plans and the project. This separation of management responsibilities is shown in Figure 5-10.

Overall Project
Manager

Development
Lead

Iteration
Lead

Figure 5-10   *Key management roles*

These three management roles distribute the responsibilities of the Unified Process's single Project Manager role.

Between them, these three areas of responsibility encompass all the required levels of management, from the planning and execution of the iterations through the technical planning of the evolutions to the overall planning of the project as a series of evolutions delivering business benefit and supporting business change.

There is a temptation to group all these responsibilities into a single generic project management role, but this causes various issues when applying iterative project management practices in practice:

- It makes it more difficult to map the identified responsibilities onto the typical project's management structure. It is very rare for one person to take on all these responsibilities for anything other than the smallest of projects.

- The process doesn't scale. For a large project, there is usually a management team rather than a single project manager. If all the responsibilities are lumped together into a single role definition, it makes it difficult for the members of the management team to understand their particular responsibilities.

- It collapses the business and technical aspects of project management into a single role, making it much more difficult to persuade technical staff to take on any planning or management responsibilities. Typically, technical staff members enjoy the idea of being a development or iteration lead but lack the management experience or qualifications required to be the overall project manager.

- It makes it harder to integrate the iterative approach into an organization's existing management frameworks.

The three roles are summarized in Table 5-2, and fuller descriptions are provided in Appendix B, "Outlines, Templates, and Checklists."

Table 5-2   *A Brief Overview of the Management Roles*

Role	Responsibilities	Comments
Overall Project Manager	Responsible for the planning and management of the entire project, including: • Overall project planning • Budgets and finances • Setting the management strategy • Liaising with the steering committee and senior management	This is the purest of the three management roles with its focus on managing overall project risk and ensuring that the project delivers real business benefit in a timely and coordinated way. It is often combined with that of the development lead when the management team is instantiated for small- and medium-sized projects.
Development Lead	Responsible for the planning and management of one or more evolutions (of a software product), including: • Phase planning • Defining the number, size, and objectives of the iterations • Estimating the evolutions	More technical and specialized than the overall project manager role, this role is focused on the delivery of working software and naturally requires a more hands-on, in-depth involvement in the creation of the software. It is often combined with the iteration lead role when the management team is instantiated for small projects.
Iteration Lead	Responsible for the planning and management of one or more iterations, including: • Iteration planning • Team leading • Estimating individual activities	The least managerial of the roles, this role is focused on leading the team to the successful completion of an iteration. It is often combined with the development lead when the management team is instantiated for small projects.

Assigning Management Responsibilities

The *roles* define sets of responsibilities that need to be filled on the project, but these roles are different from people; people can play more than one role. Different projects will assign the management responsibilities in different ways to support project risk, size, politics, capabilities, and personal preferences.

In fact, almost any assignment of the three roles is possible. The right assignment for a project is the one that plays to the strengths, career aspirations, and personalities of the individuals involved while reducing project risk.

The most common patterns we have observed in organizations are illustrated in Figure 5-11.

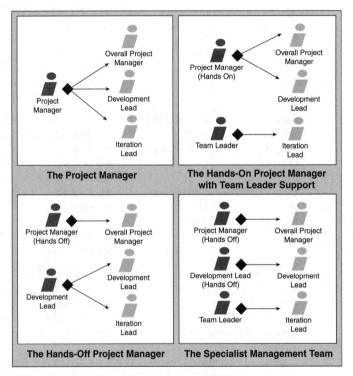

Figure 5-11   *Distributing the project management responsibilities*

The dark figures represent the actual human resources, and the lighter figures represent the assigned sets of responsibilities.

Note

There is always only one Project Manager—the person charged with the overall leadership and execution of the project.

The Project Manager

Here a single person assumes the full management responsibility for the project. This is only really appropriate for small projects where the management and leadership overhead is, by the very nature of the project size, quite small.

This requires the project manager to be highly skilled in both the business and software development areas of the project because this person will be undertaking both the broader, business-focused project management responsibilities of the overall project manager and the more technical, specialized responsibilities of the development lead and iteration lead.

This pattern is suitable for small projects and larger projects where the project only has software development responsibilities.

The Hands-On Project Manager with Team Leader Support

In this case the management responsibilities are split between two collaborating individuals: a hands-on project manager and a supporting team leader.

Leading the management team is a hands-on project manager who takes on the responsibilities of the overall project manager (dealing with the project's steering committee and producing the management artifacts required to manage the project as a whole) and the development lead (producing the more specialized management products including the development plans). This person is supported by a team leader who handles the more detailed aspects of the iteration planning and provides day-to-day leadership to the development team.

This is the most common pattern we have seen. It is very rare for a project manager to undertake the detailed activity-level planning required to plan an iteration or provide the low-level technical leadership required by a development team. This is true as much for traditional waterfall projects as it is for iterative and incremental ones. The agile nature of iterative development makes it even more important to have strong day-to-day team leadership, which reinforces the need to separate the more generic project management responsibilities from the leadership of the iterations.

The Hands-Off Project Manager

Again, in this case the management responsibilities are split between two collaborating individuals. This time we have a hands-off project manager supported by a development lead.

Leading the management team is the project manager who sees himself or herself as a more "traditional" project manager, dealing with the financial, budgetary, and schedule aspects of the project, providing the interface to the business and the project's steering committee, and producing the management artifacts required to set the direction and standards for the project.

This person is supported by a more specialized development lead who produces the more technical management artifacts (including the development plans and the iteration plans) and provides the day-to-day leadership to the development team.

This pattern is quite popular because the overall project manager is often the project manager for a portfolio, or set, of development projects and development teams. To cope with the management load, this person delegates the day-to-day management of the development projects and iterations to a development lead.

The Specialist Management Team

In this case there is one person for each role. This option is not recommended unless the people involved have other roles on the project. In this case the development lead can take on a purer, more hands-off management role, delegating the more detailed iteration planning and day-to-day team leadership responsibilities to a team leader.

There are many other patterns where the management responsibilities are combined with other project roles, such as the other three leadership areas (Architecture, Requirements Management, and Assessment) that were identified in Chapter 4, "Are You Ready for Iterative Project Management?"

For example, in one large project we worked on, where there was a hands-on project manager supported by a number of specialized team leaders, the iteration leadership was rotated around the team leaders on a phase-by-phase basis: the Inception iterations were led by the team's

Requirements Manager, the Elaboration iterations were led by the Architect, the Construction iterations were led by the Development Team Leader, and the Transition iterations were led by the Deployment Manager. This was particularly powerful when the overall project needed to plan and manage a series of partially overlapping evolutions to meet its sequence of delivery dates and integration points.

Generally the patterns reflect that although there is only one project manager, this does not mean that this person manages every aspect of the project on his or her own.

Working as an Integrated Management Team

There are some other important management roles that need to be considered and integrated into the management of the project:

- **Project Sponsor**—The person supporting the effort to solve a particular business problem. Usually responsible for committing resources and the delivery of results.

- **Business Representative**—The person ultimately responsible for deciding which requirements to implement and when. Sometimes this is a single business person seconded to the project, and at other times this is a number of business people with whom the project's Requirements Manager must liaise and coordinate. Typically the most senior business representative is part of the project's steering committee. This role is often referred to as the Customer in agile software development methodologies.

In some organizations these people are brought together with other external stakeholders to form a project steering committee.[14]

---

[14] This is not something we would necessarily recommend because it is often a colossal waste of time and energy. We mention it here because it is a fact of life for many projects in many organizations. Rather than define individuals' responsibilities as members of the "steering committee," we prefer to see their responsibilities defined as part of the project team.

- **Project Steering Committee**—An extended team commissioned by the Project Sponsor to oversee and guide the project. Typically responsible for setting priorities and approving management artifacts.

The project sponsor and the members of the project steering committee are usually drawn from the business or the program management layer and act as the interface between these areas and the project.

For the project to be *joined up*, management must work as a team to plan and assess the project. As we have seen, planning needs to be undertaken simultaneously in both a top-down and bottom-up fashion. This requires input from all management roles at all layers of the project. They will also have to work together to monitor and control the project, ensuring that the layers and plans are coordinated and aligned throughout the project's lifespan, not just at the beginning when the various plans and team are authorized to proceed.

Management Through the Layers

The final area of management affected by the introduction of a layered, iterative approach is that of monitoring and control, the mechanisms that are used to keep the layers balanced and aligned. The layers assist in controlling our iterative projects by providing a framework for establishing the appropriate levels of control and decision making.

Tolerances Through the Layers

The best way to manage through the layers is to set and apply tolerances. These are related to the project drivers: scope, cost, time, and quality. Most organizations set tolerances in all these areas. If the project exceeds or looks like it will exceed its tolerances, then the deviations are reported up the layers, and the higher-level plans might need to be adjusted. As shown in Figure 5-12, the key to the application of tolerances in a layered, iterative approach is monitoring and understanding the impact of the performance of the individual iterations.

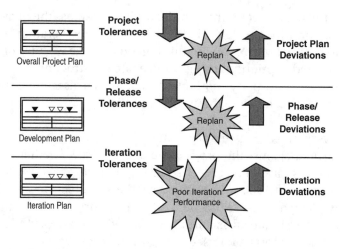

Figure 5-12   *Poor performance triggers reporting up the management layers*

Example project tolerances include the following:

- **Time tolerance**—Up to two weeks slippage is allowed.

- **Quality tolerance**—No major release can have any priority-one defects and no more than three priority twos.

- **Scope tolerance**—All the essential requirements and at least 50% of the highly desirable requirements are included and verified in the evolution's release.

- **Cost tolerance**—No more than £300,000 or $550,000 or €435,000.

Tolerances should be both positive and negative—for example, target date, plus or minus two weeks.[15] The overall project plan tolerances are set for the project as a whole by the project sponsor on behalf of the business or owning program. The overall project manager sets the development plan tolerances. These tolerances typically apply to the phases of the project and the releases to be delivered to the business. Finally, iteration tolerances are derived from the development plan.

---

[15] Negative variances are not necessarily good. Usually if a project is under-spending, it is not meeting its recruiting goals, which in turn is *not* a good thing because it indicates an inability to get work done in the future.

The tolerances set for the iterations will vary across the phases. If we find a major, priority-one defect in the first Elaboration iteration, especially if it is in a third-party component, this is good because we have plenty of time to get it fixed. A priority-one defect in a late construction iteration, especially if it is in a third-party component, is more of a disaster because there is little time to fix it before the system goes live.

At every iteration assessment, the cumulative results of the iterations are measured against the project tolerances to see whether any higher-level tolerances have been exceeded. If the project exceeds or looks like it will exceed its tolerances, then the deviations are reported up the levels, and new plans might need to be made, or the project might have to be cancelled. This is known as putting the project into *exception*. In this situation, exception reports are raised to report the exception up the layers. At each layer, there is enough flexibility to handle minor exceptions without affecting the layer above.

Be careful when allowing low-level exceptions to precipitate major higher-level re-plans. This should be done when necessary, but nothing is more disruptive to a project than a high-level re-plan. This is because paralysis sets in while everyone down in the ranks awaits the impact on their lower-level plans. Needless to say, the crucial elements here are good communication and the better judgment of more senior managers as you go up the layers. It is also necessary to construct the higher-level plans in a robust and adaptable fashion to mitigate this risk.

Trends should be continuously analyzed to spot indications that the tolerances will be exceeded in the future if things carry on the way they are. This enables the plans and processes to be adapted as needed, improving the project's chances of staying within tolerance and avoiding exception. The trends should also be monitored to spot any sharp changes to the curves. These need to be examined and explained because they might also indicate that there are problems in the project.

Estimating Through the Layers

Estimating techniques can be applied through the layers, just as planning is.

Before committing to a project, some form of overall estimate is required. It is impossible to build the business case without an estimate of the overall effort and cost involved. Just as the plans at the overall project layer are abstract, any estimate created for this layer will also be error-prone and imprecise, but it will provide a context for the execution of the project and the establishment of overall project tolerances.

Working within the constraints of the overall project estimates, you can create a more accurate estimate for the completion of the first evolution of the project and then the first iteration. As you iterate through the project, you will collect actual performance measurements from the completed iterations and use these to revise and challenge the estimates at the higher layers in the same way that the iteration results are used to challenge the higher layer's plans.

Continually challenging and recalculating estimates in this way makes the estimating process iterative as well as recursive, with the performance against the lower layer's short-term estimates being used to tune and recalibrate the higher layer's longer-term estimates. Table 5-3 provides a concise overview of estimating across the layers.

Table 5-3   *Estimating Across the Layers*

Layers	Scope	Estimate	Comments
Program	The cost of delivering and sustaining benefits	Low fidelity; low precision estimates of total cost, effort, and schedule	Estimates of the total cost of achieving and sustaining the expected business benefits.
Overall Project	The project in its entirety	Low fidelity; low precision estimates of total cost, effort, and schedule	Estimates of the total cost of the software, hardware, and other products. This involves estimating the effort, cost, scope, schedule, and resources for the project as a whole.
Development	An evolution in its entirety	Medium fidelity; medium precision estimates of the total cost, effort, and schedule for an evolution	Estimates of the cost and effort associated with producing the software and its components. Estimates of the number, size, and duration of the phases and iterations.
Iteration	An iteration in its entirety	High fidelity; high precision estimates of the cost and effort of the artifacts to be produced and activities to be undertaken within an iteration	Estimates of the effort to be applied and the activities to be undertaken within an iteration.

The overall project plan identifies the products needed to successfully deliver the required business benefits, and it estimates the cost, effort, and schedule that will be required to deliver them. This in turn requires the scope of changes to be estimated. Doing this entails estimating all the costs associated with the project (hardware, infrastructure, training, and support, among other things), not just the software development components. Each planned release must be estimated so that an appropriate understanding of the scope, cost, time, and resource needs of the complete project is available. This overall project estimate will be a low-fidelity, low-precision estimate that bounds the total costs for the project as a whole. We return to the subject of estimating the project as a whole in Chapter 6, "Overall Project Planning." For now it is sufficient to focus on how the layering of the project enables the estimates to be refined and tuned to facilitate the management and control of the project.

To verify these estimates and enable the project to proceed, more detailed estimates will be required for the near-term work, especially the first evolution of the software products.

To create an estimate for an evolution, two decompositions of the software project are used:

1. Estimates for each element (software components or documentation) the project will produce, summed to produce an overall estimate of the effort and resources involved. Various methods are available for this sort of estimation including COCOMO II.[16] These estimates are created based upon the current knowledge of the project's scope and the current state of any of its artifacts.

2. Estimates of the number and size of the iterations that the evolution is expected to have. In addition to scheduling enough time to complete the software development, other activities related to running the project should be considered such as staff training, resource acquisition times, team leadership, recruitment, and so forth. As we discuss in Chapter 7, the Unified Process lifecycle provides guidance and figures to help with this kind of estimating.

---

[16] See http://sunset.usc.edu/research/COCOMOII/.

As the iterations are completed, the results achieved and the experiences of the team are used to tune the estimates for the evolution. For example, as the size and extent of the use cases become apparent, you can start to create and maintain estimates for the implementation of each flow. As you gain experience implementing the initial flows of events in earlier iterations, you can use this experience to make more accurate estimates for the completion of the remaining flows. This in turn creates a more accurate estimate for the completion of the project.

As the iterations proceed, the effectiveness and capability of the team will become more apparent. If you find that the amount of effort applied to each iteration falls short of estimates—due, for example, to having underestimated the organizational overheads on the project or the availability of shared resources—the schedule, number, and size of the iterations can be adjusted to more accurately reflect the productivity of the team.[17]

Finally you must create estimates for the work that can be included in your first iteration. At the iteration layer, you can create detailed estimates for the activities to be completed in the iteration and use your experience to create and track detailed estimates for the work to be completed. When creating estimates for the iteration layer, you can take into account the actual personnel being asked to undertake the work and ask them to provide their own estimates for the activities they are assigned.

For iteration time boxing to be effective, you need fairly accurate estimates of the work to be undertaken in the iteration before the iteration starts. These fine-grained estimates are essential to the iteration planning. We return to this subject in Chapter 8. The estimates for the other layers are also needed if the project plans are to be adapted in light of the iteration results.

---

[17] Some organizations like to refer to the *velocity* of the team (the volume of requirements that can be executed within a week) and use this as the measure of productivity. Given a known velocity and a known requirement mass, the time to completion can be estimated. This is one form of lower-level estimating. Unfortunately it typically neglects the falls in velocity that can be expected at beginning and ends of projects as reflected in the code-complete S-curve (see Chapter 2, "How Do Iterative Projects Function?" for details). Nonetheless, it is a very good measure for refining the level-2 estimate during the construction phase.

A number of benefits are associated with estimating at all three layers:

- **Complementary validation**—By estimating at all three layers, you create a set of complementary estimates that can be used to validate each other.

- **Appropriate levels of accuracy and precision**—By adopting a layered estimating model, the estimate for each layer can be kept at an appropriate level of accuracy and precision. Detailed activity-level estimating is restricted to the iteration at hand.

- **Evolutionary estimates**—Initially you create coarse-grained estimates for the overall project and its key products, and then you produce more detailed estimates for the first evolution, its artifacts, and its iterations, and finally you cross-validate them by comparing the estimates generated at each layer. The same goes for the estimates and actuals gathered for the iterations. The feedback loop created by validating across the layers enables the estimates to evolve alongside the project plans and even the gathering of measurements.

- **Improving quality and accuracy**—The quality of an estimate is related to its accuracy; an estimate that is within 10% of the actual value is very accurate and therefore of good quality. The best way to improve the quality of an estimate is to learn from the experience of executing the plans. As the project progresses, you will start to gather actual measurements of the cost and effort required to accomplish certain tasks. These can be compared against the original estimates to track the estimating accuracy and to challenge the estimates for other similar items. By revising the outstanding estimates based upon the actual costs of undertaking similar work, you can improve the accuracy of the remaining estimates.

These benefits are only achievable if the actuals recorded for each iteration are fed back through the layers to refine and adapt not only the estimates but the plans as well. If, for example, all the tasks undertaken within the first iteration are found to have been underestimated by 50%, the team's performance must be analyzed and the information used to revise and adapt the project's higher-level estimates and plans. If the variance in performance exceeds the project's tolerances, then the project must be put into exception and its future as a viable concern reconsidered.

Monitoring and Control

The purpose of establishing management controls is to ensure that the project produces the specified results with appropriate levels of quality within the agreed timescales and costs while ensuring that the project remains viable against its business case.

At each management layer, you need to be able to

- Monitor progress

- Compare achievement with the plan

- Review plans, options, issues, and risks against future situations

- Detect problems

- Initiate corrective action

- Authorize further work

- Capture and act on relevant external changes

- Observe and analyze measurements and their trends

This means there must be monitoring and control mechanisms at each layer. The mechanism at each layer is fundamentally the same: regular assessment events with the escalation of critical problems through exception reports.

Monitoring and controlling the project works from the bottom up, with the most frequent events taking place at the iteration layer where regular iteration assessments are conducted in which the success or failure of the iteration is assessed against its objectives and estimates.[18]

At the development layer, Unified Process phase assessments are conducted in which the state of the evolution is assessed against the phase-specific technical milestones.

At the overall project layer, additional project management reviews might be needed. These are scheduled as part of the overall project plan and are typically aligned with the significant business milestones or funding gates for the project. You may find that the development phase reviews are sufficient if you are engaged in a simple software development project with little maintenance, business change, or other related concerns.

Some projects will find the need to undertake additional periodic assessments, but this is usually an indication either that the iterations are too long or that there has been a breakdown in the relationship between the management layers.

At each event, there should be an honest and open assessment of how the project is progressing and the current situation. This enables the state of the project to be communicated up through the layers. These assessment events are also the mechanism for the higher layers to communicate any changes or issues that have arisen that could affect the development project itself. Senior management is also responsible for ensuring that relevant external changes are brought to the attention of the development project and that action is taken.

At each layer, management has the authority and responsibility to make adjustments to the plans, provided that they stay within the defined tolerances and do not invalidate the business case. If their tolerances are exceeded, then they will need to inform the management of the layer above, where more drastic corrective action may need to be taken.

---

[18] Many projects will also undertake more frequent reporting and team events (for example daily, weekly, or bi-weekly progress meetings) to keep the iterations themselves on track. The point here is that these are an optional complement to the iteration assessments, which must be performed.

Table 5-4 summarizes the purpose, timing, and attendees for the various management events. This includes the startup and closedown events that are typically used to complement the iteration, phase, and project assessments.

At all project layers, progress is controlled and monitored through objective measurements and project tolerances, especially in the areas of

- Quality

- Change control

- Risk management

- Schedule

- Milestone achievements and progress

Iteration assessments are the key to monitoring and controlling the project; at these events, evidence of project results are gathered, consolidated, and then compared against plans and tolerances to assess any threats to the project as a whole.

The challenge is to know when to put the project into exception[19] because this is when changes will ripple up the layers. When exceptions occur, decisions about corrective action and possibly even the continuation of the project must be made. To understand how management by exception works, it is important to understand where the decision-making authority lies and how the decision makers are involved in the project. Table 5-5 provides an overview of the decision-making roles and their authority levels. This complements the view of the decision-making events presented in Table 5-4. Note: in reality, many of the responsibilities are shared between the layers, which may give the impression of overlap between the entries in the tables.

---

[19] Skill is required to judge when tolerances have actually been exceeded and when the situation is recoverable within the context of the existing higher-level plans. For example, the early releases created within the Inception and Elaboration phases might exceed the overall quality tolerance for the evolution, but due to their position in the evolution's lifecycle, this might be acceptable.

Table 5-4   *A Brief Overview of the Management Control Events*

Event	Description	Attendees				Timing	Key Decisions	Notes
		OPM	DL	IL	Others			
Project Startup	Event to officially start the project	Yes	Opt.	N/A	Sponsor	At the beginning of the project prior to the commencement of the initial evolution	Whether to start the project. Identification of key constraints and overall project tolerances.	Often combined with the initial evolution's Evolution Startup
Evolution Startup	Event to officially start the evolution	Yes	Yes	Yes	Business Rep	At the beginning of the evolution	Whether to commence the evolution.	Will also start the first iteration.
Iteration Assessment	The formal assessment and reporting of an iteration's success or failure	Rec.	Yes	Yes	Selected functional area leads, other team members, and at least one user representative	Every iteration (typically every 4 to 6 weeks)	Whether the iteration is a success, a qualified success, or a failure. Whether the plans need to be adjusted.	For small projects, the entire team is typically invited to the iteration assessment.
Phase Assessment	A lifecycle milestone review for the development project	Yes	Yes	Rec.	Sponsor, Architect, Requirements Manager, Quality Rep, Business Rep	At the end of every Unified Process phase	Whether the phase has been successfully completed. Whether the evolution should continue.	The most formal development review. Builds on the iteration assessments to take a broader view of the evolution's state.

Event	Description	Attendees				Timing	Key Decisions	Notes
		OPM	**DL**	**IL**	**Others**			
Project Assessment	A milestone review for the overall project	Yes	Rec.	N/A	Sponsor, Steering Committee	As required by the overall project milestones	Whether the milestone has been successfully completed and the benefits realized. Whether the project should continue.	Typically approves the plans and funding for the next stage of the project. Used in conjunction with the phase assessments to provide steering committee / senior management control point.
Project Close-down	The event to formally close down the overall project	Yes	Opt.	N/A	Sponsor, Steering Committee	At the end of the overall project	Whether the project has been a success. Whether the project has finished.	An evolution closedown is not required because this is done as part of the Transition phase review.

Key to the Attendees column: OPM—Overall Project Manager, DL—Development Manager, IL—Iteration Lead, Opt.—Optional, Rec.—Recommended, N/A—Not applicable

Table 5-5   *Key Areas of Decision-Making Responsibility*

Role	Areas of Responsibility	Authority
Project Sponsor	Changes in business value delivered	Final authority on overall scope changes
	Changes in schedule	Final authority on overall schedule changes (such as delivery dates)
	Changes in project costs	Budget holder Approver of capital expenditure
Project Steering Committee	Changes in project boundaries (changes in scope, schedule, or cost)	Consulted and advised on changes and variances Final authority on whether the project should proceed
Business Representative	Changes in scope	Final authority on detailed scope changes Prioritizes the requirements on behalf of the business and by doing so helps the Requirements Manager set the agenda for the Construction phase
Overall Project Manager	Changes in evolution boundaries	Can alter the project's business milestones Can alter boundaries between evolutions Consulted and advises on changes to delivery dates and iteration boundaries
	Changes in project costs	Defines the cost profile for the project Consulted and advised on changes
Development Lead	Changes in evolution scope	Can alter boundaries between phases and iterations Can alter iteration lengths and the number of iterations Consulted and advises on changes to delivery dates and business milestones
Architect	Changes in evolution and phase boundaries	Analyzes the risk related to the requirements Primary source of estimates of technical risk, impact, and complexity Sets the agenda for the Elaboration phase.
Iteration Lead	Changes in iteration scope	Can alter the scope of iterations Advises on overall scope changes

Summary

Rather than a single, highly detailed plan to manage the project, a number of plans, each focused on a different perspective, are more useful:

- One overall project plan that is goal-oriented and benefits-focused to sketch out the overall timeline and structure of the project. The main purpose of this plan is to define the business milestones and articulate the project as a series of evolutions and major releases.

- One or more development plans, one for each evolution, to describe how some subset of the overall project objectives will be achieved by the development of working software. The main purpose of these plans is to provide a roadmap and context for the iterations used to develop an evolution.

- One or more iteration plans, focusing on how an incremental set of functionality will be developed and delivered within the context of an evolution. The main purpose of these plans is to plan how the team will achieve its objectives within the iteration time box.

These plans are related by budgets, estimates, milestones, and achievements, with major milestones from one level rolling up to the next higher level. These milestones provide a roadmap for the development of the system.

The "detailed" plan is the iteration plan, which describes the details of the work to be performed over a relatively short time period: typically a four- to six-week period. Because details are restricted to an individual iteration, the effort of adapting to change is limited to the lower-level plans, and planning rework is held in check. The higher-level plans exist to record commitments and enable impact analysis.

To facilitate the creation of the plans, estimates need to be created at each layer. These estimates are then continuously revised throughout the project based on the results and performance of the completed iterations to tune and adapt the plans.

To match the plans and estimates, management controls are also established at each layer in the form of iteration, phase, and project assessments. These continuously monitor the state of the project and enable the appropriate controls to be applied at each layer, minimizing the knock-on effects of unpredictable team performance.

Planning and managing at these three layers enables the iterative approach to scale up to very large programs or down to very small projects. It enables the management responsibilities to be distributed effectively across the management team according to the project risk and the management skills and resources available. Planning and managing at these three layers also frees project teams from having to create and maintain detailed plans that almost immediately become out of date. It enables them to take an agile approach in their day-to-day work while retaining the key measures, milestones, and controls that enable effective management.

At first impression, the layering of planning and management can be quite confusing because very similar concepts are used at each layer. In fact it is this recursive nature of the concepts that makes them so powerful. Table 5-6 provides a useful summary of each layer and acts as ready reference for some of the terminology used throughout the rest of the book.

Table 5-6 *Layering Summary*

Layer	Purpose	Results	Plan	Role	Gateway Review	Estimate
Program	Benefits Realization	Business Benefits	Program Plan	Program Manager	Out of Scope	Out of Scope
Overall Project	Benefit Delivery	Changes and products that offer clear business benefit	Overall Project Plan	Overall Project Manager	Project Assessment	The project in its entirety.
Development	Product Evolution	Product Releases	Development Plan	Development Lead	Phase Assessments*	An evolution in its entirety. Estimates for the individual components and requirements that make up the evolution.
Iteration	Risk Reduction	Releases (Major or Minor)	Iteration Plan	Iteration Lead	Iteration Assessment	An iteration in its entirety. Detailed estimates for individual activities, tasks, and changes to artifacts.

This book focuses on the iterative project itself, which is covered by the three lower layers of our model. For this reason, elements of the program layer are not covered and are shown as out of scope in this table.

* Sometimes referred to as Lifecycle Milestone Review

6

Overall Project Planning

"There is no such thing as a favorable wind for the man who has no idea where he is going."
—Seneca (4 BC–65 AD)

The mantra of iterative development is *release early and often.* Frequent, tangible, working releases are at the heart of the iterative approach. And yet, frequent releases alone are not enough to ensure that the project will reach its desired goal. Each successive release must contribute toward the desired result. Unfortunately, saying this and achieving it are two very different things; you need a way to reason about where you are going, the commitments you have made, and a long-term view of the project that enables you to place intermediate results into context.

The last chapter introduced a layered approach to planning, including using the overall project plan to set the agenda for the project as a whole. The overall project plan is a *lightweight plan* summarizing the long-term direction for the project that identifies the *major releases* to be produced and business benefits that will result from them. The value of the overall project plan is that it presents in simple and understandable terms a picture of the whole project, one that ensures that the project remains relevant to the organization as a whole, enables the project to be integrated with any strategic or program management plans, and provides the context for the successful iterative development of the software products required.

The fundamental questions in overall project planning are the following:

- Should the solution be delivered in a single release or as a series of smaller releases over a period of time?

- When does the business need specific capabilities, and when will it be ready for the solution?

- Which requirements must be delayed to allow the delivery of the most important ones?

- When can these decisions be made?

- What is the latest date decisions can be made without impeding the business?

- How can the work be organized to accomplish it all with the time and resources allotted?

In the process of answering these questions, you will develop an overall roadmap for the project: an overview of all the major releases, their goals, major requirements and risks, and a strategy for how and when you will make critical decisions.

If the project requires the solution to be delivered as a series of major releases, then each release can be driven by a "development project" with its own lifecycle. We call each of these "development projects" an "evolution" because it is a special kind of project designed to evolve the solution closer to its ultimate goal.[1]

In this chapter we look at mechanisms for planning the entire project lifecycle and the set of major releases to be produced.

---

[1] The use of the term "evolution" helps us to distinguish the major releases (and the full lifecycle "projects" responsible for them) from the various minor and spot releases and the iterations that produce them. Each evolution goes through an entire Unified Process lifecycle (Inception, Elaboration, Construction, Transition) to produce and deliver its major release.

Evolution and Release Planning

One of the first planning decisions to make about a project is its release strategy. As noted in the previous chapter, it is very unlikely that any software development project will be able to deliver its software in a single release. Generally the project will stage the release of the product, delivering the software as a series of major releases with provision for additional point releases to address quality issues and make minor enhancements.

Consider a project that is expected to take two years to deliver all the required functionality. The project could be planned a series of 26 four-week iterations, each of which produces a release to be deployed, but it is unlikely that the business would actually want to receive 26 releases of the product. This would probably be a more frequent release schedule than the business could tolerate.

Alternatively, as shown in Figure 6-1, the project could be planned as a single Unified Process evolution resulting in a single major release toward the end of the expected two-year development period.

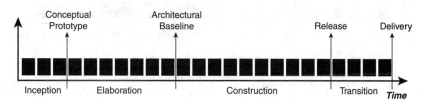

Figure 6-1   *A single Unified Process evolution with a single late delivery*

This strategy is undesirable as well because it does not deliver value to the business frequently enough.

As shown in Figure 6-2, to achieve an earlier delivery, the Elaboration and Construction phases could be shortened, and the majority of the project time could be spent in the Transition phase.

This pattern assumes that all the technical and architectural risks can be successfully addressed in the first few iterations. The project would then deliver its first release at the end of the Construction phase. It would then deploy a new release every four to eight weeks as it progresses through the Transition phase.

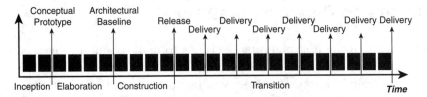

Figure 6-2   *A single Unified Process evolution with early delivery and extended Transition*

A better approach is to adopt a staged approach to the releases. Rather than addressing the entire project as a single evolution, the project releases could be staged and planned as a series of evolutions, with each evolution resulting in the planned delivery of a major release of the product. This results in a series of releases as shown in Figure 6-3.

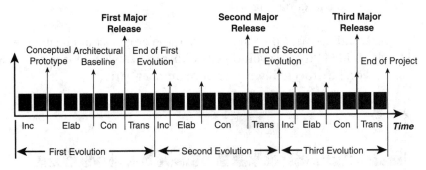

Figure 6-3   *Planning the project as a series of evolutions*

The number of evolutions (major releases) required is usually dictated by business concerns, balancing the rate at which the business can absorb new capabilities against the need for new capabilities.

In addition to introducing a series of evolutions, you will want to exploit the layering of the plans to simplify the overall project plan for the project. Rather than planning the details of all the iterations, the overall project plan should focus on the major releases of the product and the associated commitments made to the business. The details of the individual evolutions and associated iterations are pushed down into lower-level development and iteration plans, keeping the overall plan understandable.

Balancing Risks Across Multiple Evolutions

Delivering a software product in multiple evolutions can also help to manage project risk. It enables the business and technical risks to be spread across a number of evolutions. This risk balancing is often required to enable a project to adapt to time, scope, cost, and resource constraints while meeting its delivery commitments to the business.

For example, if the overriding success criterion for a project is to be the first product to market, it might be sensible to defer mitigation of architectural risks until after the initial delivery. In doing so, however, you must be prepared to accept that a significant portion of the product might need to be rewritten if the architecture changes substantially. More than one company has released an initial product quickly only to find itself saddled with unhappy customers and problems to fix but without the time or resources to make the necessary architectural changes for long-term success. On the other hand, more than one company has failed to deliver at all in its quest to develop an architecture suitable of supporting everything that could ever happen.

Evolution planning, as part of the overall project planning, helps to avoid these situations by explicitly describing the release strategy and allowing for conscious trade-offs of business and technical risk. Figure 6-4 illustrates how risks can be moved backward and forward across a series of evolutions.

There are two strategies for balancing risks across evolutions:

- **Pulling risks forward one evolution or more**—Architectural risk can be brought forward, for example from Evolution 2 to Evolution 1. This makes the initial evolution's Elaboration phase more difficult but simplifies the Elaboration phase for the second evolution. This is what happens on a lot of new technology projects where the first evolution builds the architecture to support a whole series of further evolutions and releases.

- **Pushing risks back one evolution or more**—Architectural risks can be moved backward, reducing the overall benefit of the earlier evolution. For example, architectural risk might be deferred to ensure that the product is delivered in a timely manner. In some cases it might even make sense to build the first release on "throw-away" technology and then re-architect and re-platform the entire solution as part of the second evolution.

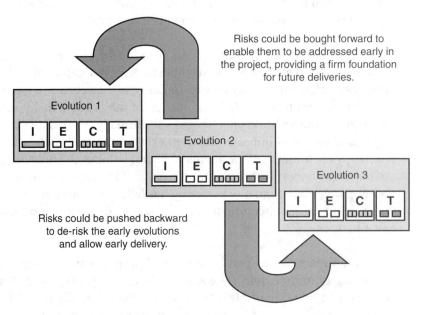

Figure 6-4   *Balancing risks across a series of evolutions*

Alternatively, if there is significant business value to be gained from a very small amount of functionality, production risks can be pushed backward to later evolutions. This would reduce the scope of the first evolution but enable it to be delivered in less time.

In the previous example (Figures 6-3), risk balancing across the three evolutions enables the time spent initially in Inception and Elaboration to be reduced from that shown in the single-release approach (Figures 6-1 and 6-2).

Regardless of the risk management strategies adopted, each evolution goes through an entire project lifecycle (Inception, Elaboration, Construction, and Transition) to deliver a major release. The Inception phases for the evolutions after the initial one can be very simple because the value of the solution has already been established. In these cases they are limited to establishing the scope for the new evolution.

As we shall see in the next chapter, balancing risk in this way affects the length of the phases and the number of iterations in an evolution. For now we focus on the higher-level release planning required to identify the number of evolutions the project should have.

Handling Sequential Evolutions

As shown in Figure 6-3, the evolution cycles can be arranged sequentially, but as shown in Figure 6-5, they more commonly overlap.

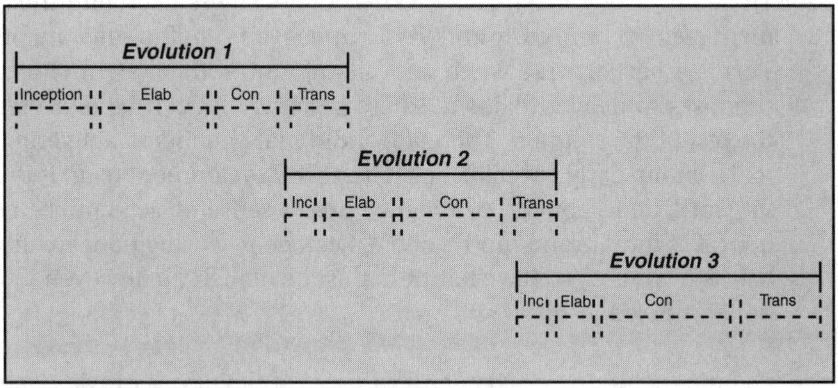

Figure 6-5 *An overlapping series of evolutions*

Unlike the Unified Process phases, evolutions are not strictly sequential and can overlap to optimize the project plans, enable the efficient use of resources, and reduce the total elapsed time for the project.

There are, however, some rules that apply when planning evolutions:

- An evolution cannot complete a phase before the previous evolution has completed the same phase.

- An evolution should not enter the Elaboration phase before the previous evolution has exited its Elaboration phase.

- The more overlap, the more work that occurs in parallel and the more potential for conflicting changes.

The most typical pattern is for the Inception phase of a subsequent evolution to overlap with the Transition phase of the prior evolution or even with the later iterations of the Construction phase of the prior evolution. This is because the Inception, Construction, and Transition phases do not affect the architecture of the overall solution, so dependencies are greatly reduced, enabling work to proceed in parallel.

Planning for Multiple Evolutions

There are strong incentives for both the business team and the development team to have early and frequent deliveries of the software products.[2] This is especially true when a small amount of the system's functionality promises to deliver major business benefits that can be delivered before the rest of the solution. There are additional benefits to delivering a minimal solution early: it builds belief that the development team is doing useful work, and it builds confidence and a sense of accomplishment that improves morale and motivation. Of course, releasing poor-quality results has its own risks, so the evolution must be of high quality even if the functionality is reduced.

Planning solution delivery across a series of evolutions provides a roadmap that shows how the project will deliver value over time. This provides a number of benefits:

- It enables earlier solution delivery and deployment. There might be valuable elements that could be delivered early without waiting for the entire solution.

- It provides a focus for the architectural work in each evolution.

---

[2] This is in addition to the frequent production of releases by the project's iterations. Here we are talking about the actual delivery to a live environment for unconstrained use.

- It avoids the need to adopt a "big bang" approach to change. The business change and system migration might need to be undertaken more gradually.

- It enables the project to be split up into a number of smaller sequential projects. The complete solution might simply be too big to deliver in a single release.

- It enables the need for maintenance and support to be factored into the plans.

- It enables the project to be aligned to the organization's budget cycles. Given the uncertainties of organizational budgeting, no project or program should go more than one budget cycle without showing concrete results.

Making conscious decisions about when and how releases will deliver value enables the business to coordinate them with any broader business plans. Even though evolutions beyond the first one might be only vaguely defined at the start of the project, it is useful to have a planning framework in place that enables more than a single evolution to be factored into the overall project plan. This is also useful for obtaining stakeholder commitment: stakeholders can see up front that any additional functionality can be included in a later release and doesn't just go "into the waste basket."

There is an additional benefit to delivering a solution over a series of major releases: it is a powerful motivator. Each major release provides a clear end-point toward which everyone works, one that is often missing if the development is planned as an undifferentiated series of ongoing iterations. It also overcomes the natural tendency to want to keep "perfecting" the solution. The evolution's release date acts as a forcing function for the delivery of tangible results and the completion of a development cycle.

Factors That Affect the Number of Evolutions

Even for simple systems where the majority of the functionality can be delivered in a single evolution, there is still a need for maintenance and support releases to provide business continuity and to enable user feedback and other issues to be addressed. As a result there is still a need for an overall project plan to coordinate the releases. The decision to have one or more evolutions depends on a number of factors, as shown in Table 6-1.

Table 6-1   *Factors That Affect the Number of Evolutions and Major Releases*

Factor	Response
The length of time the business can wait for a solution The commissioning organization's sense of urgency The budget cycle and funds available	Break solution into a number of releases (each delivered by an evolution) to ensure timely delivery.
The size and complexity of the deployment The window of opportunity for deployment The infrastructure and technology cycles	Break solution into a number of releases (each delivered by an evolution) to integrate the delivery with the other projects and suppliers.
The degree to which the requirements can be deployed separately The degree to which different stakeholder communities require different capabilities and services	Group cohesive requirements together and deliver each set in a separate release, each delivered by a separate evolution.

The ability to break the overall solution into a series of evolutions depends on having independent parts of the system that can be delivered separately or on the ability to deliver the solution in a series of progressively more functional releases. In some cases, having very frequent releases based on the individual iterations is a possibility, but even in these cases a multiple-evolution approach is generally preferable.

One danger of releasing too frequently is that it can lead to a level of overhead disproportionate to the amount of business benefit delivered, resulting in "upgrades" that deliver little or nothing of real value. The ability to continually release small amounts of functionality depends upon having a stable architecture for the solution, which provides consistency across the series of releases. This stability reduces the pain of upgrade problems as the product changes from release to release. If the architecture cannot be stabilized early, or if the functionality of the solution cannot be partitioned, a single large release is the logical alternative. A single large release is riskier but might be necessary to prevent having to upgrade users from one incompatible release to the next.

The Composition of the Overall Project Plan

The overall project plan's focus is to plan the achievement of the desired outcomes and the delivery of benefits to the business over time. It provides a view of the major products, time scales, and costs for the project. This includes summarizing the following:

- Desired outcomes

- Compelling events

- Business milestones

- Project commitments

- Project dependencies

- The approach and strategy to deployment

- The management approach to be followed

By focusing on achievements and business events rather than the techniques or processes to be followed, the plan can be kept succinct so that it will not collapse under excessive detail. To provide sufficient context for the management and control of the project, this plan must consider broader issues:

- How many major releases should the project produce? How frequently should the project deploy a new release?

- How should the project be organized?

- How much of the project is IT related? Who is responsible for the non-software development aspects of the project?[3]

---

[3] Other non-software development products are often required to enable the benefits to be realized. This can include such things as marketing, sales, training users, decommissioning existing systems, installing new hardware, and changing business processes.

- Who is responsible for ensuring that the system developed delivers real business benefit? Who is responsible for measuring this benefit?

- Who is responsible for supporting the system after it has been developed? How long will the system be in use? What is the intended product lifecycle?

- What are the business's plans for using, selling, and marketing the software products produced? What commitments has the project made to the business?

- How much will the whole thing cost? How will the ongoing project responsibilities be funded?

The key to effective long-term project planning is to understand the project's desired outcomes, business benefits, and the corresponding business changes and other follow-on effects.[4] Every project needs to deliver real, measurable business benefit back to its commissioning organization, which entails more than just building a software product.

The Style of the Overall Project Plan

Nothing in the style or content of the overall project plan warrants special treatment; it should reflect the organization's planning standards. The only real difference between a project that is adopting an iterative approach and one using a conventional approach is that the layering inherent in the planning of iterative projects will be exploited to remove unnecessary detail in the higher level plans, enabling the overall plan to focus on business commitments, notable achievements, and management decision points.

An interesting side effect of this approach is that it often transforms senior management's impression of iterative projects from an initial impression that iterative projects are uncontrolled technical development projects

---

[4] For example, the long-term support and ownership costs (total cost of ownership).

with no "proper" long-term plans, little visibility of what is going on, and ineffective management controls. The overall project plan provides the appropriate amount of visibility and information to enable senior managers to feel that they have appropriate control over the things that really matter to them. Our experience has been that to senior management, iterative development is just a means to an end, a method, a technique. Senior managers really don't care what underlying techniques are used to develop the software.[5] They do care if the project is out of control, and they do care if there are no long-term plans in place to illustrate where the project is heading. If all you have is a plan for the next iteration (four to six weeks) and nothing else, they will become very concerned.

Appendix B, "Outlines, Templates, and Checklists," provides an outline for an overall project plan suitable for use with iterative and incremental software development projects.

The Principles of Lifecycle Planning

A simple set of patterns and principles underlies all forms of lifecycle planning. Figure 6-6 summarizes these principles and presents the basic pattern.

Because all flow charts tend to oversimplify reality, we offer Figure 6-6 with some trepidation. Although the elements of the figure are shown sequentially, this is only an indication of the order in which they are typically completed, not the order in which they are addressed. These principles must be continuously applied and maintained throughout the entire life of the project.

The first three principles ground the project in reality by defining the objectives, risks, and constraints that apply to the project. They establish the target for the project and the criteria by which all project decisions and adjustments will be tested throughout the project's lifetime.

---

[5] As Joe Marasco notes, "If you told them you were using witchcraft, their only concern might be that you use a suitably competent witch."

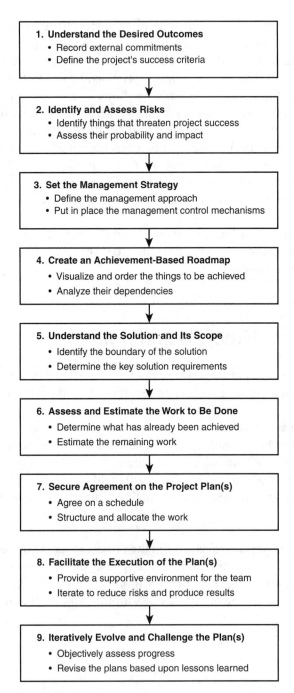

1. Understand the Desired Outcomes
- Record external commitments
- Define the project's success criteria

2. Identify and Assess Risks
- Identify things that threaten project success
- Assess their probability and impact

3. Set the Management Strategy
- Define the management approach
- Put in place the management control mechanisms

4. Create an Achievement-Based Roadmap
- Visualize and order the things to be achieved
- Analyze their dependencies

5. Understand the Solution and Its Scope
- Identify the boundary of the solution
- Determine the key solution requirements

6. Assess and Estimate the Work to Be Done
- Determine what has already been achieved
- Estimate the remaining work

7. Secure Agreement on the Project Plan(s)
- Agree on a schedule
- Structure and allocate the work

8. Facilitate the Execution of the Plan(s)
- Provide a supportive environment for the team
- Iterate to reduce risks and produce results

9. Iteratively Evolve and Challenge the Plan(s)
- Objectively assess progress
- Revise the plans based upon lessons learned

Figure 6-6   *The principles of lifecycle planning*

1. **Understand the Desired Outcomes**

   Make sure you understand what you want to achieve. Focus on the value to be delivered and to whom it is to be delivered, not the activities to be undertaken or the artifacts to be addressed.

   Make sure that you define what "success" means for the project. Determine the project objectives. Analyze the potential benefits and develop an understanding of the project's business case.

2. **Identify and Assess Risks**

   Anticipate the obstacles that stand in the way of the project achieving its desired outcomes. Also consider any constraints on your freedom with regard to planning, managing, and executing the project.

   Analyze project risks and create initial mitigation and contingency strategies for the most significant ones.

3. **Set the Management Strategy**

   Determine the approach to be taken to managing and controlling the project. Of particular importance are which processes to follow, how results will be measured, how progress will be reviewed, how events will be reported, and how decisions will be made.

   This involves selecting or developing the procedures that will be used to monitor, control, and report on the project.

The next three principles establish the roadmap for the project. This is a low-precision but high-fidelity plan that provides the big-picture view of the project. This enables the day-to-day progress made by the project to be put into perspective and the individuals undertaking the project to be empowered and understand their responsibilities and dependencies.

4. **Create an Achievement-Based Roadmap**

   This is the low-precision view of the overall project plan often referred to as the project roadmap or project map.[6] It shows the fundamental things to be achieved,[7] their order, their dependencies, and possibly

---

[6] The idea of a "Project Map" comes from Alistair Cockburn, *Agile Software Development* (Boston: Addison-Wesley, 2001), 125.

[7] Some people would primarily use artifacts at this stage in the planning cycle, but in our experience, this changes the focus from the value to be delivered to the process to be followed.

which ones are to be deployed together. It might show the major products to be produced, the dates by which the achievements must be achieved, and the relative magnitudes of effort needed to achieve each goal. It does not show who will do the work or how long the work will take (which is why it is called a roadmap and not a plan).

The roadmap should be fairly stable because it is independent of the techniques to be used or the length of time that the achievements will take. It provides a simple view of the steps to achieving the project's desired outcomes. Regardless of the size of the project, it should be possible to illustrate the roadmap on a single piece of paper.[8] The detail will be added iteratively as you identify the *how* to accompany the roadmap's *what*.

5. **Understand the Solution and Its Scope**

Determine the project scope and start to define how the solution to be developed will achieve the objectives outlined in the roadmap.

Determine the boundary of the solution and the quality and other *ility* requirements that apply to it. This is where the use cases and other requirements artifacts are important.

Investigate the project dependencies and understand the requirements that the proposed solution will place upon the operating and business environments where it will be installed.

6. **Assess and Estimate the Work to Be Done**

Assess where the project is and what it will take to complete it.

Assess the current state of the project (no project starts from nothing) and estimate how much effort the project will take (produce a rough guess using your experience or any appropriate top-down estimation method) to achieve its objectives.

Determine the resources needed and the time(s) when they are needed to successfully execute the project. This information is particularly important because it is needed to support resource forecasting

---

[8]   This kind of achievement- or goal-based planning and its representation on a single sheet of paper is explored in more detail by Erling S. Andersen, Kristoffer V. Grude, Tor Haug, Mike Katagiri, and J. Rodney Turner in *Goal Directed Project Management: Effective Techniques and Strategies*, 3rd ed. (London: Kogan Page, 2004).

and capacity planning. This will be particularly important to the program management layer.

The final three principles enable the more detailed project plans to be agreed upon, executed, tested, challenged, and improved.

7. **Secure Agreement on the Project Plan(s)**

   Identify dates for the milestones lying within the current event horizon and define the tolerances related to each milestone. Lay out the work: assign the milestones in the roadmap to the lower layers of the project and to the evolutions, releases, and iterations within the lower-level plans. This is where the milestones are aligned across the layers.[9]

   For each "sub-project" identified, apply the appropriate lifecycle to ratify the plans and introduce additional milestones to control the technical aspects of the project.[10]

   Add any additional management review points required to control project risks.

8. **Facilitate the Execution of the Plan(s)**

   Within the framework established by the achievement-based roadmap, project plans, and management strategy, the team needs to start executing the project as soon as it can. Planning without execution produces nothing.

   The basic execution mechanism is the iteration: all work will be undertaken by a project team executing an iteration plan. It is at the iteration level that task and activity lists are created and the actual individual pieces of work are scheduled. At the higher levels, it is enough to understand the purpose and objectives of the iterations.[11]

---

[9] For the overall project, this is where the stages and evolutions are identified.

[10] This is where the Unified Process (UP) lifecycle is introduced for the evolutions identified. The UP phases and milestones are introduced to provide a framework for controlling the individual evolutions.

[11] On many occasions we have encountered project teams doing nothing but waiting for the overall planning to be completed. This is a waste of valuable time and resources! There are always things that the team can do during the initiation stage; the project should start iterating immediately to provide the information required to create credible high-level plans and to start to reduce the project risk.

The *high-level plans* will be inherently stable and will provide the framework within which the iterations can be executed, progress can be tracked, and objective assessment of their impacts undertaken.[12]

9. **Iteratively Evolve and Challenge the Plan(s)**

As we observed in the Preface, "No plan survives contact with the enemy." Although we make plans, we need to understand the forces that will cause reality to deviate from our plans so that we can respond appropriately to keep progressing toward our goals. This is the most important thing: *progressing toward the goal, not adherence to a plan.*

The overall project plan (created in steps 1 to 7) is only a sketch that will be elaborated, expanded, and adapted as the project progresses. Its main purpose is to provide the vision and roadmap of where the project is going and what it is trying to achieve. This will enable the project team to place their progress and experiences into the larger business context and understand whether they are headed for success or failure. It is only these more abstract plans that enable us to act appropriately upon the results of the individual iterations and to continually monitor, adjust, control, and adapt the project to maximize its chances of success.

There are many reasons why the project might need to be re-planned:

- The business has changed, requiring some very large changes to the project

- The development team has an unexpected change in productivity

- The number of use cases, flows, and scenarios has been underestimated

---

[12] You do not have to wait for all the lifecycle planning to be completed before you can start your iterations. In fact all you need to start the first iteration is the desire to undertake the project. You can then bootstrap the project by executing an initial iteration to reduce the project risks and provide clarity to the forming plans.

If you find that your plans are overly optimistic and need to be updated, make sure that you are being realistic in your revisions and exorcise the optimism from the plan. At the same time, you don't want to be overly pessimistic either. Use the data from the completed iterations to adjust your estimates of productivity to assist in creating more stable and credible high-level plans.

The Importance of Balance

When writing a book such as this, it is very hard to avoid presenting the entire project as a simple, single pass through the cycle of "plan, execute, and evaluate" with all of the planning taking place before any execution. We were even worried about including this chapter on overall project planning because it can give the impression that the entire project is planned up front before any iterations take place.

The reality of the situation is that you must balance the high-level lifecycle planning of the project with the low-level execution of the iterations, the objective measurement of progress, and the aggressive reduction of project risk. In iterative projects you need to continually challenge your plans by asking whether they are good enough. The lifecycle plans must be good enough to reduce the risk that the project is economically unsound and to provide the framework for the individuals involved to make the correct decisions about the work they are asked to complete. As Voltaire suggests, "The perfect is the enemy of the good."

As the quote at the beginning of the chapter indicates, you are unlikely to get where you want to go if you don't know where you are going. This must be counterbalanced by the observation that if you obsess too much about where you are going to end up, you are unlikely to go anywhere.

To most of you, these principles of lifecycle planning will appear to be just common sense; certainly the first six show up in some form in all project planning methodologies we have seen, but the number of projects where common sense is the first casualty of the planning process is quite astounding. People under pressure to show results often try to ignore some of these principles—sometimes quite a few of them—in an attempt to accelerate their projects and to appear to be more successful than those around them.

Applying the Principles to Overall Project Planning

To complete the chapter, we would like to use the principles of lifecycle planning to illustrate how all the things we have examined so far can be pulled together to produce a credible, succinct overall project plan.

The example we present here is a new, improved Automated Teller Machine (ATM), the ACME Super ATM, which provides an extensible, flexible platform for the distribution of money and paper goods.

Some excerpts from the Vision for the ACME Super ATM are shown in Table 6-2 and Table 6-3.

Table 6-2   *The Problem Statement for the ACME Super ATM*

The problem of	Having convenient and secure access to banking balances to withdraw funds, manage accounts, or purchase automatically dispensed goods
Affects	Customers of financial organizations and vendors using transactional paper-based currency (tickets, paper-based goods, and so on) or electronic currency
The impact of which is	Low customer satisfaction and high transaction costs
A successful solution would	Provide customers with access to their assets and the ability to transform them into other forms of paper-based or electronic currency

Table 6-3   *The Product Position Statement for the ACME Super ATM*

For	Financial institutions and vendors of paper-based and other virtual goods
Who	Own or manage automated teller networks
The	ACME Super ATM is an automated teller machine
That	Provides lowered cost of ownership and flexible definition of new transaction types, virtual products, and dispensable paper goods
Unlike	Conventional ATM devices and ticket machines
Our product	Utilizes standard computing platforms and component technology to provide a flexible, generic, and extensible but low-cost platform for managing customer transactions and dispensing goods

Because this is a book on management rather than software development, we only provide a brief summary of the example as a whole. Sample lightweight plans for the ACME Super ATM project can be found in Appendix C, "Examples."

Principle 1: Understand the Desired Outcomes

What constitutes success can vary greatly from project to project, so it is essential to understand what the project needs to achieve to be successful. The project might have a hard deadline for the delivery of a new system or firm commitments made in an external contract. There might be a limited window of business opportunity beyond which the system will not be required. There might be a particular business problem that needs solving, or there might be a particular need to make savings or improve productivity. The project might even have a number of different, often contradictory success criteria required by the different stakeholders. Remember: like beauty, success is in the eye of the beholder.

Many techniques can be used to identify the desired outcomes for a project. These draw heavily on any work already undertaken on the project's vision, business case, or objectives. Regardless of the form that they take, it is always a good idea for the project manager to capture these desired outcomes, making them visible to the whole team and ensuring that they are not forgotten during the execution of the project and remain the focus of all the project's endeavors.

The Balanced Scorecard[13] approach provides a good way to summarize the desired outcomes for a project. It forces the project team members to consider a number of perspectives, some of which are often forgotten when planning IT projects. Its true power is that it enables you to explicitly *balance* any competing objectives facing the project.

---

[13]   Balanced Scorecard: A measurement-based strategic management system that provides a method of aligning business activities to the strategy and monitoring performance of strategic goals over time. See Robert S. Kaplan and David P Norton, *The Balanced Scorecard: Translating Strategy into Action* (Harvard Business School Press, 1996). See also www.balancedscorecard.org.

The Balanced Scorecard has four dimensions:

- **Financial perspective**—What is important to the sponsors and senior management? To succeed financially, how should the project appear to its stakeholders?

- **Customer perspective**—What is important to the users? To achieve the project vision, how should the solution appear to the customers?

- **Learning and growth**—Are both the project and organization innovative and ready for the future? To achieve the project vision, how will the project sustain its ability to change and improve?

- **Process**—Which processes can the project help to add value? To satisfy the stakeholders, what business processes must the products excel at and add value to?

We like the Balanced Scorecard as a framework for thinking about and expressing the desired outcomes for the project. The objectives for the Super ATM project are shown in Table 6-4. The objectives should then be complemented with measures and targets.

Table 6-4 *Balanced Scorecard for the ACME Super ATM*

Dimension	Objectives
Financial	Reduce total cost of supporting teller machines by 50%. Reduce cost of configuring devices to dispense different items. Penetrate new markets (ticket retailing and other paper-based goods).
Customer	To provide a modular, expandable, and customizable platform for ATMs and ultimately general-purpose "dispenser" kiosks configurable as bank teller (traditional ATM), ticket dispenser, postage dispenser, card charger, and so on.
Process	Replace existing systems. Increase availability to 99.9%. Introduce a shared architecture for teller machines.
Learning and Growth	Develop software iteratively. Pilot the Unified Process.

There are many other tools we can use to help to understand what the stakeholders need from the project; this is just one tool that can help us. The important thing is to choose a simple way to understand and capture the desired outcomes of the project and then communicate them to all project team members to help them understand why the project is being undertaken. Perhaps even more importantly, you should periodically come back to the desired outcomes as a way to assess the project's progress: is the project drawing closer to these outcomes, or is it moving farther away?

Principle 2: Identify and Assess Risks

Risks are external factors that threaten the project's ability to achieve the desired outcomes. To bring these risks under control, we must first identify and then assess their likelihood and impact. Initially this entails understanding the general risks and constraints on the project (time, resources, standards, process, and so on). As the project progresses, more detailed and specific project risks will be added to the risk list.

A good way to start any project is to hold risk-identification workshops where the stakeholders in the project brainstorm the risks that they feel are facing the project. The risk identification effort must be open and honest, involving all affected parties. A common mistake is for project managers to hide risks from other stakeholders in the project, as if acknowledging that the risks will make them look as though they are not in control of their projects or that they are not good project managers. This is one of the most prevalent, dangerous, and unprofessional practices in the software industry today. Stakeholders must learn not to react negatively to risks and should encourage the project manager share this information openly and honestly.

Table 6-5 and Table 6-6 present some of the business and technical risks facing the Super ATM project.

Table 6-5   *Some Business Risks for the ACME Super ATM*

ID	Risk	Overall Exposure
1	Market might be too crowded with competitors	Low-medium
2	Might not be able to price product aggressively enough to displace competitors: • Cost to develop might be too high • Profit margin might provide insufficient return on investment	High
3	Customers might not want a new or more flexible solution	High
4	No future market for paper-based goods (such as tickets)	Low-medium

Table 6-6   *Some Technical Risks for the ACME Super ATM*

ID	Risk	Overall Exposure
5	PC/Windows-based platform might not be reliable enough for remote/unattended use	High
6	System might not "fail gracefully" if power or network connection is lost in the middle of a transaction	High
7	System might not be able to be made "tamper-proof," especially the device "charging"	High
8	Might not be able to deliver a sufficiently flexible, component-based system at low cost	Medium
9	Underlying technology (J2EE) might not perform sufficiently well to meet needs	Low
10	Printing might not be flexible or reliable enough	Low

These are just some of the risks that would be captured in the risk list. Many approaches advocate capturing risks, but this is even more important for iterative projects because the risks are the dominant driver for iteration planning. We look at the particulars of risk management in more detail in Chapter 8, "Iteration Planning."

In addition to identifying risks, you should also identify the high-level project assumptions and constraints. This means identifying financial and time constraints as well as the technical constraints on the solution such as platform dependencies. The constraints will usually have a dramatic effect on the approach taken to delivering the solution. Table 6-7 presents some of the constraints facing the Super ATM project.

Table 6-7 *Some Constraints Applying to the ACME Super ATM Project*

Constraint	Source
A demonstrable prototype must be available for next year's International Rail Conference.	Marketing
Existing ATMs must be replaced by the end of next year as warranties on existing hardware cease.	Operations
The system must conform to the International Vending Platform Specification.	Marketing
The project must be developed using the Unified Process.	IT Director

Principle 3: Set the Management Strategy

The management strategy sets the standards for the management of the project including the approach to be taken toward the iterative development of the software.

For example, iterative projects can be operated with differing levels of formality, which affect the visibility of phases and related milestones in the project. *Formality* refers to the degree to which artifacts are used as an official vehicle for communication among project team members. This will vary depending on the project's risks, the organization's culture and degree of trust, and the size and distribution of the project team. It is common today to regard formality of artifacts as arising from bureaucratic inefficiency, but civilizations discovered long ago that the *grand oral tradition* of communication left much to be desired in terms of accuracy, bandwidth, and effectiveness. There is no substitute for close interpersonal communication, but there is great value in having written records of proposals and decisions to support the collaborations of even small teams. A conscious decision needs to be made about what evidence will be required at each milestone (sign-offs, contracts, approvals, and so on) and the level of involvement and availability required by the stakeholders.

The layering of the plans and management roles recommended for iterative and incremental projects enables the strategy to be set in a way that facilitates rather than hinders the project. Table 6-8 presents a summary of the management strategy defined for the Super ATM project; this reflects the presence of ACME corporate standards such as the QA and Risk Management processes.

Table 6-8   *Highlights of the ACME Super ATM Management Strategy*

Dimension	Decision
Style of Delivery	• Staged iterative and incremental delivery • Colocated teams
Level of detail and formality	• The project will be low ceremony with high levels of user and stakeholder involvement • Adopt standard QA process with central governance
Process selection	• Unified Process, small project tailoring • Risk management using Top 10 risks (see ACME corporate Requirements Management Plan and tooling)
Reporting and communications	• Primary reporting mechanism—iteration assessment • Management by exception
Product Acceptance	• Independent user acceptance and system test • Stakeholders involved in all iteration and phase reviews

The management strategy can be set once for the overall project. This removes some of the management overhead from the evolutions and enables their planning to focus on the efficient and effective development of the software.

As well as defining the exact management processes to be followed, the mechanisms for monitoring and control need to be established. In this case there will be a combination of iteration, phase, and status assessments with overall project direction provided by the steering committee, key members of which will attend the phase assessments as well as the evolution assessments.

Principle 4: Create an Achievement-Based Roadmap

An achievement-based roadmap is a simplified view of the overall project plan showing the fundamental things to be achieved. The roadmap should be kept focused on achievements and business events rather than the techniques or process to be followed. You don't want to see the roadmap presented as a picture of your selected process lifecycle because this would add little value.

The roadmap can be presented in many ways:

- As part of a Gantt chart

- As a milestone network

- As a list of events

Our preferred mechanism is to draw the roadmap as a milestone map using the Unified Modeling Language[14] state chart notation. Figure 6-7 shows the initial roadmap for the ACME Super ATM.

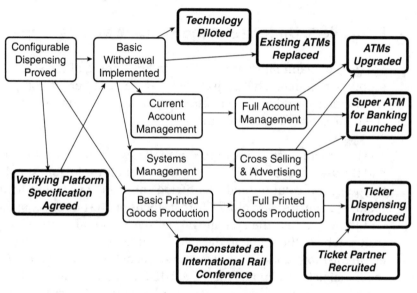

Figure 6-7   *Visualization of the roadmap for the ACME Super ATM*

The roadmap is quite simple. The items shown in italics inside the boxes with the bold borders represent external commitments and other external events that affect or impinge upon the project. They are a combination of

---

14   See www.uml.org for details and a free copy of the modeling specification.

the business results expected by the business (ATMs upgraded, ticket dispensing introduced) and the business constraints placed upon the project (demonstration at International Rail Conference). These are then complemented by the achievements to be made by the project itself, which are shown in a normal font within the boxes with a narrow border. Dependencies between the achievements and commitments are then examined, and these are added to the diagram as arrows from the earlier achievements to the later achievements that they enable.

The roadmap represents the commitments made by the project and the strategy it intends to adopt to meet these commitments in a simple, accessible way.

Principle 5: Understand the Solution and Its Scope

For project planning to proceed, an understanding of the solution and its scope is required. The project will have a number of complementary requirements products, elements of which all are required to really understand the scope of the solution.

The keys to understanding the scope of the system are the vision document and the use-case model. The Vision document is useful for establishing the theme of the solution and identifying the areas of achievement for the roadmap. The use-case model, with its focus on the boundary of the system and the value that the system will deliver to the business, is required to truly establish the scope of the solution and address the ambiguity inherent in the more sales-focused feature-level definitions. Figure 6-8 presents the initial use-case model for the ACME Super ATM. This level of use-case model, representing the primary use cases for the system, is typically included in the Vision document to complement the features and illustrate the key capabilities of the intended solution.

Supporting the use-case diagram is a more comprehensive model that will evolve to include detailed descriptions of the flow of events for each use case. The use-case model is complemented with a Supplementary Specification that captures the more global, and typically non-functional, requirements that do not readily fit into the use-case model. These artifacts will become more important as we plan the lower layers, especially the iterations that will actually elaborate and implement these requirements. For now we are looking for enough information to enable us to identify, scope, manage, and estimate an appropriate set of evolutions of the solution.

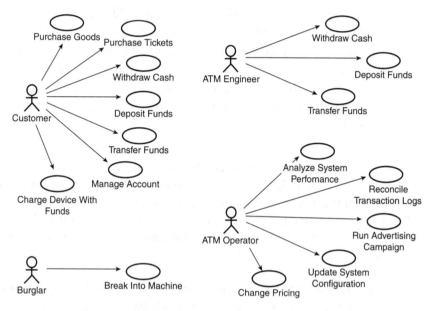

Figure 6-8 *Use-case diagram for the ACME Super ATM*

Principle 6: Assess and Estimate the Work to Be Done

To produce a credible overall project plan, you need to produce an estimate for the cost of the project as a whole.

At the overall project layer, estimates are primarily created using the folowing:

- **Analogy**—Compare the proposed project to previously completed similar projects in the same application domain. When using this technique, actual data from other completed projects is extrapolated to create a new estimate. This technique can be used at any level for any items where historical data exists. Be sure to record the assumptions used when producing the estimate.

- **Wideband Delphi**[15]— A technique relying on the judgment of experts who collectively create pessimistic, optimistic, and expected estimates. Estimates are created anonymously, and consensus is reached on the final estimates by a process of iteratively revising and adjusting the estimates. Wideband Delphi can be used to estimate anything and is particularly effective for generating the more abstract overall project and evolution estimates.

These techniques are used to create estimates for (1) the project as a whole and (2) each evolution identified, with a focus on the initial evolution. The techniques can also be combined: you can use analogy to extrapolate from a set of estimates generated using the Wideband Delphi technique. This can be very powerful when seeking an estimate for the later evolutions, given an estimate for the initial one.

For the ACME Super ATM, the following process was performed to create the initial estimate for the project as a whole:

1. Estimate size and complexity by analogy with previous projects. Create an overall estimate of effort and time required by extrapolating from previous projects' measurements of effort and schedule.

2. Perform Wideband Delphi with the architects and senior project managers to create an alternative estimate for the completion of the project as a whole.

3. Perform triage on the estimates to agree on an overall estimate and budget for the project as a whole.

---

[15]   For an accessible, succinct overview of the Wideband Delphi technique, see Karl E Weigers, "Stop Promising Miracles," *Software Development*, 8(2), February 2000, available from www.processimpact.com.

To verify initial estimates and the outline release plan, the following solution-based estimates were also created:

For each use case

- Prioritize from a customer perspective

- Assess the architectural significance

- Create an estimate of size and complexity

- For the high-priority or architecturally significant use cases, perform modified Wideband Delphi to create an estimate

- Estimate the other use cases by analogy to those estimated in detail

For each significant component[16]

- Assess size and complexity

- Perform Wideband Delphi to create an estimate

- Compare to earlier developments to create an alternative estimate

- Perform triage on the estimates to produce a consensus view of the overall cost and effort required to implement that component

These more detailed estimates will help in the creation of a credible plan for the evolution of the system.

---

[16] Here we are dealing with the very broad-brushstroke components identified by the candidate architecture. ACME has built ATMs before and therefore has a good understanding of what certain components, such as card handling and the banking interface, will cost.

Principle 7: Secure Agreement on the Project Plan(s)

To gain consensus on the project plan, you must work in both a top-down and bottom-up fashion. This means working simultaneously on the overall project plan, the development plan for the first evolution, and the iteration plan for the first iteration of the first evolution. The relationship between the plans is illustrated in Figure 6-9.

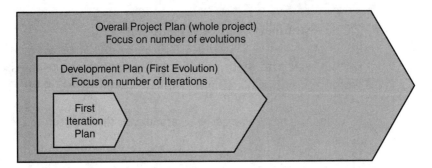

Figure 6-9   *The initial set of plans*

Working from the bottom up, you must start the first iteration of the first evolution to generate the information to enable the elaboration of the plans and estimates. Typically the project's first iteration creates the initial versions of the overall project plan and the evolution's development plan. We look at the process for bootstrapping an evolution in Chapter 7, "Evolution and Phase Planning."

Examine the business commitments and timescales for the project, and create an initial evolution-based release plan by laying out the work and assigning the milestones in the roadmap to one or more evolutions. This means selecting your evolution strategy and outlining the number of evolutions you will have. Typically there is a series of Unified Process evolutions, one for each major release of the software to be developed.[17] Figure 6-10 shows the initial evolution plan for the ACME Super ATM.

---

[17]   For larger projects, individual projects can be instantiated for each stream identified, especially where there are large amounts of non-software development work to be done. Here we are assuming that all the milestones can be achieved by a series of software development projects, which is the typical case where iterative software development processes are applied.

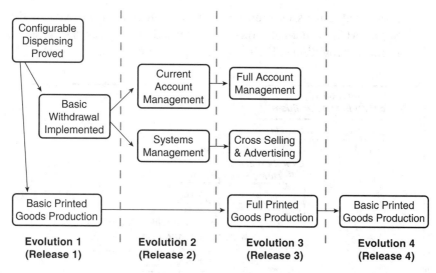

Figure 6-10 *Visualization of the ACME Super ATM evolution / release plan*

Based upon the commitments in the roadmap and the estimates for the development of the software, agree on some candidate release dates with the project's steering committee. In most projects, these dates are supplied as constraints against which the project scope and resources need to be negotiated. In this case the plan is for the major releases to be six months apart following the initial nine-month development of the first evolution. The first evolution is longer because of the architectural risks to be addressed.

Note:

The evolution release plan only focuses on the major releases of the project. It does not include the lifecycle and anchor point milestones discussed in Chapter 3, "Controlling Iterative Projects." These would be introduced during the planning of the evolutions themselves. Figure 6-11 illustrates the planned relationship between the overall project and the evolutions required.

At this stage, the focus of the planning is on the initial evolution and the planned alignment of subsequent evolutions; no other evolution planning is undertaken this early in the project. We do not consider planning anything other than our agreed commitments and the major business milestones at this point. By laying out and planning the evolutions, we indicate to the project's stakeholders the current planning horizon and the frequency of the management decision points. If a project is particularly risky, then more frequent assessments might be required. In the case of the ACME Super ATM, the evolutions are planned to deliver every six to seven months, providing sufficient overall project control.

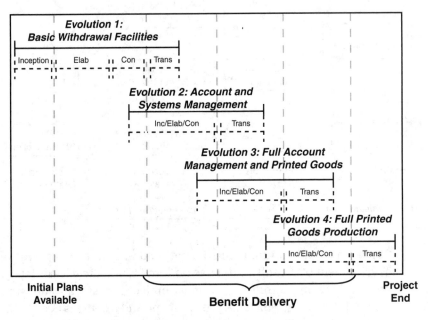

Figure 6-11   *Candidate lifecycle mapping for the ACME Super ATM*

In Figure 6-11, you should note that the first baseline of the overall project plan is not created until the end of the first evolution's Inception phase. By this point, the project has sufficient information to determine the overall contents of the phases and iterations in the first evolution, as well as a sketch of the contents of subsequent evolutions. This illustrates how the plans evolve, simultaneously influencing each other's contents and structure.

To enable the project to progress, the scope of the initial evolution must be elaborated to provide a more detailed and precise specification of the project's overall scope. This is where the use cases again have a significant role to play.

To define each evolution, you select an appropriate subset of the requirements; in practical terms this means selecting meaningful scenarios from your use cases as well as sets of related supplemental requirements. The selection of scenarios is illustrated by Figure 6-12, which shows the extent of the identified evolutions of the ACME Super ATM. It is this kind of dependency between the planning and work at each layer that requires the project to start iterating before the higher-level plans are complete. Without starting the first evolution to flesh out the requirements, it will be impossible to produce a credible release plan.

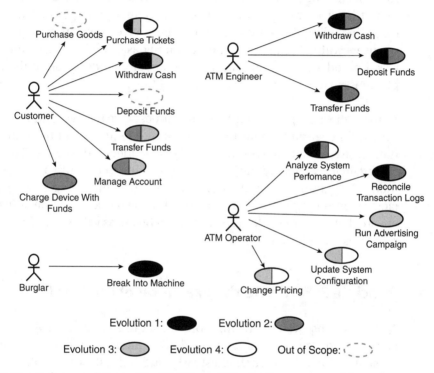

Figure 6-12 *Defining evolutions of the ACME Super ATM using its use-case model*

You should notice in Figure 6-12 that the evolutions share the same use-case model. Instead of a separate model for each evolution, one shared model is evolved through the series of evolutions alongside the product itself. The additive nature of the flows of events enables each subsequent evolution to be defined as a set of additions to the previously published models. This minimizes requirements rework and provides useful visibility of the future of the project, enabling requirements to be moved around the set of evolutions to tackle project risk. It also facilitates the estimation of the work required for each evolution because as flows of events are selected for inclusion into an evolution, their individual estimates can be used to challenge the overall estimate for the evolution.

You should also note from this example is that it is very rare for a release to be made up of a small number of *fully* implemented use cases. This would provide a very in-depth "bells and whistles" implementation of a very narrow selection of the system's services. To create a useful evolution of a system, it is far more typical to partially implement a larger number of use cases (including the basic and major alternative flows), thereby providing the users with a broader selection of more basic services. An emphasis on breadth and sampling important functionality is more useful than completeness in any one area.

As the project progresses and change requests are received, additional lessons will be learned about the nature of the required solution, and additional use cases and flows might need to be added to the model. This is OK, and again it is explicitly supported by the additive structure of the use-case model. By planning around a series of evolutions, the changes can easily be factored into the plans and the scope of the evolutions can be adjusted to ensure that the project delivers maximum business value with the time and resources it is allowed.

Principle 8: Facilitate the Execution of the Plan(s)

As we have observed many times previously, to enable the project to create anything, you must bootstrap your first iteration As soon as possible, you must start to address the highest risks and highest-priority objectives by producing a "release" of the software. To get anything done, a team must be put together and an iteration executed.

To get started, divide your first evolution into a series of time-boxed iterations. Use the project lifecycle to identify useful intermediate milestones for the project and to shape the iteration objectives. When planning iterations, we must be careful to observe the dependencies of our use cases and requirements. We must also consider the capacity of the iterations as well.

The planning of the phases and iterations is the subject of the next two chapters. This subsection is just intended to give a flavor of the kind of outcomes that can be expected when doing the initial planning of an iterative project.

Based on the framework provided by the initial risk list, roadmap, vision, and business case,

- Start to sketch out the overall project plan

- Start to sketch out the first evolution

- Start to sketch out the iterations

- Decide who will manage the evolution and the iterations

- Allocate and recruit resources

- Start iterating

Table 6-9 and Table 6-10 provide a brief overview of the contents and structure of the initial evolution's development plan. Table 6-9 shows how the risks are targeted onto the phases and mitigated by demonstrating end-to-end scenarios derived from the use-case model. Table 6-10 outlines the number and purpose of the proposed iterations and the increments that they produce.

Table 6-9 *Partial Project Plan for the ACME Super ATM*

Phase	Risks Mitigated	Scenarios Addressed
Inception	• Crowded market • Product pricing and profitability • Customer demand for configurable transactions	• Withdraw Cash • Configure Transaction
Elaboration	• Reliability of OS platform • Scalability of J2EE infrastructure • Fault tolerance • Tamper-proofing • Printing flexibility and reliability	• Break into Machine • Withdraw Cash + Bank System Stopping Responding • Withdraw Cash Basic Flow + Handle Transaction Log Failures • Withdraw Cash (scenarios in parallel) • Simple ticket printing
Construction	• Completing work on time, within budget	• All remaining scenarios

Table 6-10 *Summary of the ACME Super ATM's Release 1 Increments*

Phase	Iteration	Resulting Incremental Releases
Inception	I1	Proof of Concept: Basic cash dispensing
	I2	Proof of Concept: Configurable cash dispensing
Elaboration	E1	Prototype: Withdraw Cash Basic Flow
	E2	Prototype: Withdraw Cash with basic failure modes and protection + initial load testing
	E3	Prototype: Simple ticket printing + initial demo
		Prototype: Withdraw Cash with correction and reconciliation + load and performance testing
		Ticket printing flexibility and reliability testing
Construction	C1	Functional Release: Basic cash withdrawal Use Cases: Withdraw Cash, Refill and Service
	C2	Functional Release: Usable Cash Withdrawal Complete remaining use cases
Transition	T1	Patch Release: Bug fixes
	T2	Possible Patch Release: More bug fixes

The iterations are the wheels upon which the project rolls. If the project is not iterating, it is as though the project is up on blocks, and no matter how much work you do on the plans, it is not going anywhere.

The overall project plan would be left to focus on the evolutions and their milestones, as well as capturing the management strategy, organizational structure, and overall project estimates. Table 6-11 provides a brief overview of the overall project plan.

Table 6-11 *Highlights of the ACME Super ATM Overall Project Plan*

Evolution	Purpose	Milestone	Date
Evolution 1	Set up the project	Business case and plans agreed upon	Mar 31 05
	Demonstrate and pilot the new technology	Demonstration of printed good production	Jun 15 05
		Launch ticket facility at International Rail 05	July 12 05
		Evolution 1 Available	Aug 15 05
		Plans for Evolution 2 agreed upon	Sept 26 05

Evolution	Purpose	Milestone	Date
Evolution 2	Develop replacement ATM system	Technology pilot successful Operations and support trained in new system	Dec 30 05 Feb 27 06
		Replacement ATM accepted	Mar 27 06
		Plans for ATM replacement in place	Mar 27 06

Principle 9: Iteratively Evolve and Challenge the Plan(s)

The outline plans created by applying the earlier principles will need to be evolved as the project executes and as the project team learns more about what they are doing, how they are doing it, and how well they are performing. As the project progresses, the evolution plan will start to solidify as more clarity and precision are added to the phase objectives and release contents.

As the plans are adjusted according to project experience, two significant problems can occur. First, there is the overhead of continually updating the high-level plan to reflect the changes that are occurring in real time. Second, people at the appropriate levels of management need to be informed of the changes and need to know what the official plan of record is. Communicating this is important but easy to overlook because it can lead to a related problem: management in general will lose confidence if the plan changes too frequently or if they feel they have not had the appropriate sign-off and approval of the changes.

There is no magic answer to this problem. If the plans need to be adjusted, they need to be adjusted, but at the same time you cannot be re-planning on a daily basis. Re-planning at the ends of iterations and phases is essential, and if the changes in plans affect external project commitment, you will need to inform the affected parties of the changes. Producing only lightweight plans at each layer can significantly reduce the cost of physically changing the plans.

We return to the topics of assessment, measurement, and re-planning in Chapter 9, "Iteration, Phase, and Project Assessments," after you have learned more about the nature and consequences of evolution and iteration planning.

Summary

In this chapter we have presented an approach for delivering value through a series of major releases. Each release is managed by a smaller *development project* called an *evolution*. Various business risks can be managed by introducing evolutions. They are particularly effective in enabling important parts of a solution to be brought to market earlier and in enabling deployment and business change to be properly planned. They also help with the motivation of the team members by providing a sense of closure, showing business results, and providing a justified sense of accomplishment.

We have shown how a number of evolutions can be staged and coordinated to control the iterative cycle and enable the project to regularly deploy new versions of the system. From a senior management perspective, this is very powerful because it provides the control and visibility needed to integrate the project into the business, something that often gets lost when the project is seen as a continuous, undifferentiated series of iterations.

Finally, we introduced a set of principles for lifecycle planning and included an example that will help you to plan your projects. In the next chapter we expand upon these ideas by showing how to plan an evolution.

7

Evolution and Phase Planning

"If a man will begin with certainties, he shall end in doubts, but if he will be content to begin with doubts, he shall end in certainties."
—*Sir Francis Bacon*

At this point in the planning of the project, several decisions have been made:

- Whether to deliver the solution in one or more evolutions

- Whether to divide the work across one or more projects

Now that you have those decisions behind you, you need to make a number of decisions about how to structure the plan for the *initial* evolution:

- Which work should go in which phase?

- How will you know when the phase is done?

- How many iterations should you have in each phase?

- What does each iteration need to achieve for subsequent iterations to safely proceed?

- Which requirements and which risks does each iteration need to address?

- How can you organize the project to deliver the maximum amount of business value with the time and resources allocated to the evolution?

In the process of answering these questions, you will develop a plan for the evolution: an overview of all the iterations, their goals, major requirements, and risks, and a strategy for how and when you will make critical decisions.

In the last chapter, we showed how an evolution is composed of a complete software lifecycle, resulting in a "major release." Using the Unified Process lifecycle as our model, this means that an evolution is broken down into four phases (Inception, Elaboration, Construction, and Transition), each of which ends in a major milestone. Each phase is in turn broken into iterations, each of which ends with a minor milestone and delivers a "minor release." In this chapter we discuss the phases and how to plan and manage them.

What Happens Inside an Evolution?

The evolution plan is a project plan for the evolution, describing the phases and their end-of-phase milestones, including the number of iterations per phase and the iteration milestones. It is not necessary to plan the evolution in greater detail (that is done in the iteration plan). In the course of creating the evolution plan, estimates of time and resources needed across the evolution's lifecycle are developed.

Balancing Breadth and Depth Across the Phases

The key to successful iterative development is to achieve an appropriate balance between addressing the breadth and depth of the solution in the early phases of the project. Many unsuccessful projects exhibit either an overemphasis on research and development (all breadth and no depth) or an overemphasis on production without architecture (all depth and no breadth).

A balanced approach uses breadth to drive the major decisions and depth to actively attack specific risks. In the Unified Process lifecycle, the earlier phases focus somewhat more on breadth, while the later phases focus somewhat more on depth. This is illustrated by Figure 7-1, which shows how much the breadth (as represented by the horizontal dimension) and the depth (as represented by the vertical dimension) are typically addressed in each phase.

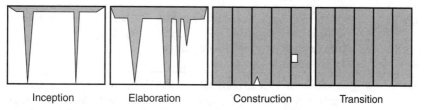

| Inception | Elaboration | Construction | Transition |

Figure 7-1   *Addressing breadth and depth across the phases*

In the Inception phase, the focus is mostly on breadth to understand the scope and extent of the proposed solution. A few specific issues are explored in depth to address risks that might threaten the very viability of the project. In the Elaboration phase, the breadth continues to be explored, completing the team's understanding of the problem and resolving the remaining issues that pose serious architectural threats. The additional spikes represent the depth added by the architectural prototypes created to prove the architecture.

During the Construction phase, subsets of the problem are selected, and their solutions are completed. In Figure 7-1, each Construction iteration is represented by a vertical column, reflecting that for much of the problem, a complete solution has been produced. The holes in the grid represent the missing pieces (typically bugs and defects) that remain in the solution at the end of the Construction phase. These are filled in during Transition to provide a complete solution to the entire problem.[1]

This variation across the phases is summarized in Table 7-1.

---

[1]   This illustration adopts a slightly simplistic view of the relationship between the problem and solution space, ignoring the fact that the boundaries might change as the project progresses, but it provides a nice representation of how the need to address both breadth and depth can be balanced across the phases.

Table 7-1 *Balancing Breadth and Depth Across the Phases*

Phase	Breadth	Depth
Inception	Wide and shallow to gain an understanding of the scope.	Narrow and deep if an architectural proof-of-concept is built.
Elaboration	Mostly wide and shallow to make sure the architecture covers the breadth of the requirements.	Selectively narrow and deep to attack risk areas with depth.
Construction	Occasionally wide to undertake impact analysis on changes. The main focus is on fully completing a verifiable increment for each iteration.	Narrow and deep to deliver functionality.
Transition	Occasionally wide to undertake impact analysis on changes.	Narrow and deep to correct problems based on feedback, defects, and change requests.

Achieving balance in the early phases enables the creation of a firm foundation for the rapid incremental development of the solution. A firm architectural foundation makes it possible to scale up the size of the development team, to geographically distribute development, and to quickly incorporate feedback.

The Type of Release Produced Varies by Phase

As you will remember, each iteration results in an "executable release." Just as the approach varies by phase, so does the type of release produced. The types of release produced in each phase are shown in Table 7-2.

Table 7-2 *Phases and Releases*

Phase	Type of Release	Effort Directly Contributing to Release[2]
Inception	Proof of Concept Prototypes	< 20%
Elaboration	Architectural Prototypes	> 50%
Construction	Deliverable System	> 80%
Transition	Usable System	Around 40%

---

[2] These figures are illustrative only; your experience might vary.

During the Inception and Elaboration phases, the releases produced are prototypes. These might be throwaway prototypes produced to illustrate some particular nuance of the architecture or evolutionary prototypes that will form the basis for the actual deliverable releases to be produced by later iterations. Being prototypes, they are not suitable for general release (either due to incompleteness or lack of quality).

After you leave the Elaboration phase, the releases produced by the iterations become deliverable releases. They have all the qualities required of a deliverable product: they have been tested, they have no missing pieces (nothing required is "stubbed-up"), they are documented, and they do something useful. If necessary, they could be deployed without change or amendment.[3]

The final column of Table 7-2 presents the percentage of the team's effort that directly contributes to the release produced by the iteration. The remaining effort is spent on various preparatory, management, support, and investigatory activities such as planning, estimating, project management, research, problem analysis, impact analysis, setting up environments, investigating new risks, performing impact analysis, user support, training, and familiarization.

These figures help to explain why the code growth curve, discussed in some depth in Chapter 2, "How Do Iterative Projects Function?" is S-shaped with its steep increase in productivity during the middle of the evolution when more of the teams' efforts are directly applied to the production of the release.

In the next chapter on iteration planning, it will become clear why it is so important to understand where the teams' efforts will be directed in any given iteration.

---

[3] In fact the only obstacles to their deployment are that 1) there is not yet enough functionality to enable the business to benefit from using the new system, 2) the users are not ready to receive the new system, or 3) the quality levels might not be sufficient for operational usage. These issues will, of course, all have been addressed by the last Construction iteration.

Effort and Schedule Across the Phases

Because each phase is focused on mitigating different risks, the effort required to achieve this will vary across the phases. For example,

- A project that is extending the capabilities of an existing solution will have significantly less business risk than one that is building a new product, and therefore the Inception phases of these two projects will differ greatly.

- A project that is addressing a new and unprecedented technology will have considerably more technical risk than one that is building on an existing architecture, and therefore the Elaboration phases of these two projects will differ greatly.

To determine the most likely spread of effort and schedule across the phases, you can use the standard figures published as part of COCOMO II,[4] MBASE,[5] and the Unified Process.[6] These are summarized in Table 7-3.

These figures are useful for validating the accuracy and completeness of your estimates.[7] They are easier to interpret when the project is shown graphically as a series of proportionally sized iterations as shown in Figure 7-2. This figure shows resource levels across the phases for a typical project. Each phase is shown as a number of iterations, each represented by a vertical bar on the graph. The number of iterations is illustrative only; it is the relative lengths and heights of the phases that are of interest. The height of an iteration bar represents the proportion of project resources expended during that iteration, whereas the length of an iteration bar represents the proportion of time spent in that particular iteration.

---

[4]   COCOMO II (the *Constructive Cost Model* II) is a model that enables one to estimate the cost, effort, and schedule when planning a new software development activity. See http://sunset.usc.edu/research/COCOMOII/.

[5]   The MBASE (Model-Based Architecting and Software Engineering) Method (Boehm-Port, 1998). See http://sunset.usc.edu/research/MBASE/.

[6]   The RUP figures are published in *The Rational Unified Process: An Introduction*, 3rd ed., Philippe Kruchten (Boston: Addison-Wesley, 2003) and *The Unified Software Development Process*, Ivar Jacobson et al (Reading, MA: Addison-Wesley, 1999).

Table 7-3 *Phase Effort and Schedule Distributions*

Phase	Unified Process		COCOMO II / MBASE		
	Effort	Schedule	Effort	Schedule	Explicitly Covered
Inception	5%	10%	6% (range 2%–15%)	12.5% (range 2%–30%)	No
Elaboration	20%	30%	24% (range 20%–28%)	37.5% (range 33%–42%)	Yes
Construction	65%	50%	76% (range 72%–80%)	62.5% (range 58%–67%)	Yes
Transition	10%	10%	12% (range 0%–20%)	12.5% (range 0%–20%)	No
Totals	100%	100%	118% (range 102%–135%)	125% (range 102%–150%)	

Source: *The Unified Software Development Process*, Ivar Jacobson et al. (Reading, MA: Addison-Wesley, 1999) and COCOMO II Frequently Asked Questions (http://sunset.usc.edu/research/COCOMOII/).

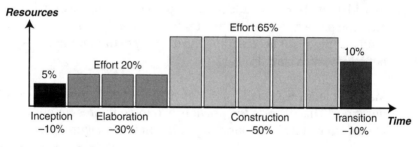

Figure 7-2 *A typical Unified Process project*

Adapted from *The Unified Software Development Process*, Ivar Jacobson et al. (Reading, MA: Addison-Wesley, 1999), page 335.

---

7   It is worth noting that the COCOMO/MBASE figures cover all projects, whereas the RUP figures are for a typical project of moderate size and effort, a single evolution, no existing architecture, and a moderate set of risks. The COCOMO/MBASE figures sum to more than 100%; the lowest number given for the total project effort and schedule is 102%. This is because the COCOMO II estimating model only estimates the size of the development work undertaken in the Elaboration and Construction phases. As a result, the effort in earlier phases must be added.

Figure 7-3 shows a project that has more challenging business issues (it requires an extra iteration to bring the business issues under control) and more challenging architectural issues (proportionally more time is spent in the Elaboration phase than the project shown in Figure 7-2). As a result, however, it spends proportionally less time in the Construction and Transition phases.

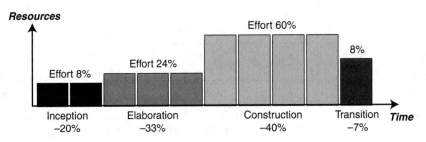

Figure 7-3   *A more difficult Unified Process project*

Adapted from *The Unified Software Development Process*, Ivar Jacobson et al. (Reading, MA: Addison-Wesley, 1999), page 336.

In both of these examples, the resource levels are adjusted across the phases, with more resources added to the project during the Construction phase after the project risks are firmly under control. This is not only a very powerful technique for accelerating the delivery of the solution; it is also a more effective way to staff projects.

Many projects, especially small ones, have fixed resource levels for their duration.[8] This distorts the previously quoted figures for effort and schedule, which results in the kind of profile shown in Figure 7-4.

---

[8]   Just because the approach is typical does not mean that it is the best approach. Projects with constant staffing often find themselves resource-constrained at the most critical times, usually resulting in inadequate testing and resolution of defects. Often the result is that quality suffers because of a largely arbitrary decision at the start of the project that workload can be leveled out across the project. As noted before, skills and staffing levels naturally vary, and maintaining constant staffing levels inevitably creates bottlenecks and reduces overall effectiveness of the project team.

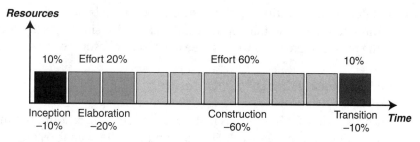

Figure 7-4 *Effort and schedule for a typical project with a fixed team size*

The effect of constant staffing levels is that either 1) the Inception and Elaboration phases are overstaffed, with a fair number of people sitting idle while the business problem, solution vision, and technical architecture are identified and evolved, or 2) the Construction phase is extended, delaying the delivery of the software.

Just as adding the right people at the right time can enhance a project's chances for success, adding too many people at the wrong time can "sink" a project by creating overhead and confusion before the project can usefully employ the people. It can add to project costs without corresponding improvements in results and can increase the probability that the project will fail. For example, having too many resources available during Inception and Elaboration creates a great deal of anxiety and pressure to *do something* with the idle resources, the result of which is usually that control over the project is lost as team members start to work on things without direction.

Iteration Duration and Frequency

As we saw in Part I, an iteration is like a mini-project: it produces some executable result, and it has a beginning, middle, and end. At the beginning of an iteration, the iteration plan is developed from the rough set of goals established for it in the development plan. In the middle, the actual work of refining and developing scenarios is accomplished, and at the end, the results are assessed. This basic beginning-middle-end pattern establishes some constraints on minimum iteration size and frequency.

Iterations also establish a *heartbeat* for the project—a rhythm of delivery that provides a mechanism to synchronize the efforts of teams working on different parts of the solution. For this reason, it is best to establish a common iteration schedule for the whole team. This simplifies the schedules of the project teams and makes it easier to share resources among them.

How Quickly Can a Project Iterate?

The length of an iteration is really a function of the amount of time needed to define, refine, agree on, develop, and test the scenarios and supporting artifacts identified to meet its objectives. To that basic measure, add a day or two for iteration startup (planning) and a day or two for closedown (post-mortem reviews of progress). In practical terms, we have found iteration durations of between two and six weeks to be optimal. Shorter than that, and the scenarios tend to be trivial; longer than that, and the work tends to lose focus.

Longer iterations are possible and are generally found where there is a very complex problem domain that requires a large project staff working as a single team or tightly coordinating across many teams. Before assuming that the team needs to be large or the iterations long, make sure that the solution architecture is well partitioned to enable teams to work in parallel on independent scenarios.

Other factors influencing iteration length include

- **Team size**—Larger teams introduce more overhead and therefore lead to longer iterations. It is generally recognized that the larger the team, the longer the iterations. In our experience, the following guidelines[9] provide a useful starting point:

    - 2 to 15 people: 2- to 4-week iterations

---

[9] Joe Marasco presents a thought-provoking discussion on typical iteration lengths and sizes in Chapter 10 of his book, *The Software Development Edge* (Boston: Addison-Wesley, 2005). Here he explains how he has found that the length of an iteration (in weeks) is related to the square root of the project's length (also in weeks). We have approached the problem somewhat differently but derive similar results: in our model, the length of an iteration is related to the number of people whose work you must coordinate. In the end, both methods are related to the overall scope of the work.

- 15 to 30 people: 4- to 6-week iterations

- 30 to 50 people: 6- to 8-week iterations

- **The iteration's objectives**—Some objectives require more time to complete than others.

- **Amount of overhead**—The more organizational reporting and other administrative overheads that are placed on the team by the owning organization, the longer the iterations must be.

- **Team distribution**—The more distributed the team, the harder communications become and the longer it takes to agree on decisions. This leads to longer iterations and increased levels of planning and documentation.

- **Resource availability**—The less dedicated time the project staff have to spend on the project, the more elapsed time the iterations require. Teams made up of people who are multi-tasking are less effective and harder to coordinate than teams that are dedicated to a task.

- **Project formality**—Some projects have more stringent requirements for formal reviews and project documentation, requiring that more time to be dedicated to these activities.

- **External dependencies**—The more dependencies the project has on external suppliers and resources, the harder the iterations are to plan and control. Often the lead times involved in accessing these external resources extend the length of the iterations. This includes regulatory interaction, coordination with partners, and so forth.

- **Project environment**—Agile and dynamic projects require an agile and responsive environment in which to work. This means that the facilities required to support the team need to be in place and available. This includes both the development facilities (build environment, test environment, configuration management, and so on) and the office environment (conference rooms, quiet areas, and so on). It is very hard to iterate on a four-week cycle if no meeting rooms or communal work areas are available to facilitate team interactions and communication.[10]

There is no universal iteration length. Some approaches[11] suggest that there is an ideal iteration length, but these usually assume a particular kind of project, with a particular size and structure. We feel that the iteration size should vary depending on the project risks, the work to be done, and the resources available.

If you are new to iterative development, we recommend starting with an iteration length of four to six weeks and then adjusting this based upon your experience as the project progresses. If four weeks is demonstrated to be too short, then consider using a longer iteration length. If six weeks appears to be too long, then reduce the length of the following iterations. In all cases, common sense should be applied and local circumstances taken into account.

Iterations need to be specified in terms of working days and therefore must take into account seasonal work patterns and holidays. Thus, a four-week iteration measured in working days might easily stretch to six or more calendar weeks when vacations and holidays are factored in.

---

[10] In fact, if you are working with a small team on short duration iterations, you should strongly consider moving the entire team into a single large room. You might also want to consider restricting access to e-mail and other distractions to specific times of the day to maximize collaboration time.

[11] For example, the iterative management method SCRUM makes the recommendation that all iterations, which it calls *sprints*, should be 30 calendar days in length. If you take into account the context within which the sprints are applied (small, dedicated development teams undertaking what we would call Construction iterations), then 30 calendar days is not a bad iteration length. For more information, see *Agile Project Management with Scrum* by Ken Schwaber (Redmond, WA: Microsoft Professional Press, 2004).

How Many Iterations in an Evolution?

Table 7-4 shows the typical numbers of iterations that we have observed.[12]

Table 7-4 *Typical Numbers of Iterations for Different Project Sizes*

Project Size	Inception	Elaboration	Construction	Transition	Total
Small	1		1	1	3
Typical	1	2	2	1	6
Large	2	2	4	2	10

Other authors report much larger ranges in the number of iterations a project can have. Craig Larman,[13] for instance, states that projects can have between 3 and 46 iterations and has personally been involved in a 2-year, 20-iteration project. In our approach, these much longer (in iteration number) projects would go through many Unified Process development cycles to provide for better control over risks and increased ability to deliver results.

There are a number of reasons why 10 iterations is generally considered to be quite large for a single evolution. One is related to the desire to deploy early and often. Having 10 iterations implies that either 1) there is a long time before the end of the Construction phase when the evolution is initially deployed or 2) there are a lot of iterations in the Transition phase, each deploying a minor upgrade to the system, and a long time to wait before

---

[12] These figures are consistent with those of other authors:

- Walker Royce in *Software Project Management* (Reading, MA: Addison-Wesley, 1998) observes 4 to 9 iterations overall with the following patterns:
  - Typical: 6 total arranged as 1, 2, 2, 1
  - Small: 4 arranged as 1 combined Inception/Elaboration iteration, 2, 1
  - Large: 9 arranged as 2, 2, 4, 1
- Philippe Kruchten in *The Rational Unified Process: An Introduction*, 3rd ed. (Boston: Addison-Wesley, 2004) observes 3 to 10 iterations, with the typical number being 6 to 8.

[13] See Craig Larman, *Agile and Iterative Development: A Manager's Guide* (Boston: Addison-Wesley, 2003).

any major changes can be made.[14] We prefer to constrain evolutions to no more than nine months to ensure that business value is delivered within a typical business budgeting cycle. This makes it difficult to organize the evolution into more than 10 iterations.

Forces That Add Iterations and Extend Phases

Phases do not have fixed durations, not even when stated as percentages of the total project duration; phases take as long as needed to mitigate the risks for which they are responsible. Some of the forces that extend phases are listed in Table 7-5.

Table 7-5   *Forces That Extend Phases*

Phase	Force
Inception	Highly volatile scope Poorly-defined business objectives Stakeholder disagreement
Elaboration	Unstable or unproven architecture Unstable requirements Unstable development environment Challenging non-functional requirements
Construction	No deployment window Large amounts of functionality to produce and test Poor architecture Inability to scale up the development team
Transition	Poor quality Hardware or system distribution and replacement Level and length of support required Number of deployment and installation sites Changeover strategy, such as incremental as opposed to "big bang" Large and complex databases to migrate Complex software requiring large amounts of user training

Because each iteration has a fixed length, there is a limit to the amount of risk each iteration can mitigate. Increasing risks usually means adding

---

[14] We examine a number of common iteration patterns for aligning iterations and phases in the next section.

iterations. This extends the length of the phases because phases cannot be exited until a set of risks is mitigated.

Staying on Schedule

Adding iterations or extending the length of phases to deal with risks creates a planning dilemma because most projects have a relatively fixed endpoint established by the time-to-market needs of the business or other regulatory or management directives. When the unknown occurs, the only way a project can be delivered on time is to reduce the scope or increase the resources. Even so, the latter rarely works, as Brooks notes in *The Mythical Man Month*[15]—adding people to a late project makes it later. In general, we have found that

(Fixed Scope) + (Fixed Duration) = Failure

In other words, the project team must be able to make trade-offs in capability delivered and risks addressed to complete the project in a fixed duration.

The good news is that not all requirements are equally important. It is usually possible to identify sets of requirements that can be either eliminated or postponed to future evolutions to meet the schedule, *provided that there is an atmosphere of cooperation and aligned goals between the business and the development team.* We have seen more than one project fail because the business took an *all or nothing* attitude regarding scope. As in any negotiation, insisting on everything often achieves nothing.

Faced with discovery of previously unknown risks, if you do not reduce scope or negotiate an extension to your schedule, you will fail. Some project managers fail to grasp this simple truth and, being afraid to confront the issues, keep going on the original plan without adapting to the new information. This not only postpones the inevitable—it tends to make it worse. Ignoring project risk is like ignoring a potentially terminal disease that can be treated if caught early but that becomes increasingly lethal the longer the symptoms are ignored.

---

[15] Frederick P. Brooks, *The Mythical Man-Month: Essays on Software Engineering*, 20th Anniversary Edition (Reading, MA: Addison-Wesley, 1995).

Planning an Evolution

Evolution planning is another form of lifecycle planning (as seen in the previous chapter) with a single evolution as the focus rather than the project as a whole. Planning an evolution is a process that involves the following:

- **Understanding the Desired Outcomes**—You need to understand what results the sponsoring organization needs to achieve and by what points in time they need to achieve these results. These staged outcomes inform the overall project milestones allocated to the evolution. This helps you to define the evolution's acceptance criteria.

- **Identifying and Assessing Overall Risk**—To effectively plan, you need to identify and prioritize the risks that affect the evolution.

- **Setting the Management Strategy**—Within the context of the strategy laid out by the overall project plan, you need to decide the strategy for the evolution and the iterations it contains. For example, how detailed will the iteration plans be? How much autonomy will the development team have? How are the iteration assessments to be conducted?

- **Creating an Achievement-Based Roadmap**—You need to sketch out the series of phases and iterations; each iteration should represent an achievement on the way to the creation of the major release to be delivered and deployed by the evolution. The evolution's development plan will partition the work across the phases, outlining the expected number of iterations in each phase and their dimensions.

- **Understanding the Solution and Its Scope**—You now need to look at the next level of detail for the use cases: use-case flows, scenarios, and supplementary requirements.

- **Assessing and Estimating the Work to Be Done**—You are now in the position to create a more precise estimate for the completion of the evolution. More detailed estimates are required for the work at hand, in particular this and the next iteration.

- **Securing Agreement on the Project Plan(s)**—As the evolution and iteration plans emerge, you will need to make sure that the stakeholders of the plans (the people affected by them) agree on them. In particular, the development team will need to agree with the evolution and iteration plans.

- **Facilitating the Execution of the Plan(s)**—The work will be done by the team undertaking the iteration, so the management team must do everything in its power to provide a suitable environment for the team to iterate effectively.

- **Iteratively Evolving and Challenging the Plan(s)**—The phase and iteration assessments will provide feedback on all elements of the project, particularly the evolution's development plan. The plans will be adapted to reflect the results of the iterations to date.

The evolution's development plan is actually created as a consequence of performing the evolution's initial iteration. Evolution planning is also undertaken in an iterative fashion. The principles of lifecycle planning make a nice checklist of the things to be done, but it is much better to approach the evolution planning from a more practical time-based perspective.

Bootstrapping the Evolution Plan

Each evolution starts with an initial Inception iteration that is used to establish the scope of the project, articulate potential solutions, understand potential risks to these solutions, and create an evolution plan. The initial plan demonstrates how the project intends to deliver the desired scope and deal with the risks in the time allotted to the evolution.

As we have noted before, most evolutions have a fixed delivery date that is established by external business objectives. If it has not been set by the business, then it will be established as part of the overall project's release plan. Given the target end date, you need to determine the number of iterations that will fill the time available to the project. To keep planning simple, assume that all iterations are of equal length; our preference is to assume an iteration length of four weeks until you find that a longer or shorter iteration is more effective.

If you do not have a fixed end date for the evolution, you need to estimate the completion date for the evolution based on your experience with similar projects or estimates of effort needed to deliver the desired outcomes. A precise estimate is not needed because after you start iterating, you will very shortly gather the information needed to make more precise estimates. Our experience is that evolution boundaries are usually established by external business factors, so it is unlikely that you will have the luxury of choosing the length of your evolution.

Next, you need to map the iterations to phases, at least temporarily, by assigning at least one iteration to each phase. If you have unassigned iterations, add iterations to the phases based on your relative assessment of risk: more business risk requires more iterations in the Inception phase, more technical risk requires more iterations in the Elaboration phase, and more deployment risk requires more iterations in the Transition phase. If you are not sure where to put the iterations, assume one iteration each in the Inception, Elaboration, and Transition phases, and put the remaining iterations in the Construction phase. You will have the chance to move iterations around as you gather more information during the initial iteration. In the next section, we look at some standard iteration patterns that help you to align your initial set of iterations with the Unified Process phases.

Estimate the resource profile for each iteration and use this to create an initial estimate of the capacity of each iteration. Use the phase-based resource profiles to determine whether to increase the size of the team as the project progresses. We look at the needed skills in more detail later in the chapter.

After you have this basic map of the iterations, look at the risks, commitments, desired outcomes, and constraints that apply to the evolution. These will have been passed down from the overall project plan, although they are typically fairly high-level and will need further refinement.

Flesh out the outline of the plan by assigning risks and desired outcomes to iterations, allocating higher-rank risks and desired outcomes to earlier iterations. Use the purpose of each phase to guide the mapping: business risks should be handled in the Inception phase, technical risks in the Elaboration phase, and deployment risks in the Transition phase. All remaining risks should be assigned to iterations in the Construction phase.

Give each iteration a name that reflects its *theme;*[16] this will help the team to keep in mind the purpose of each iteration. Also give the iteration a *number* within the phase. We like to number our iterations I1, I2, E1, E2, and so on because this gives each iteration a unique identifier within the evolution that doesn't change if we find that one of the phases requires the insertion of additional iterations.

Finally, you should create a more detailed estimate of the overall effort required to complete the evolution and compare this to the commitments and constraints imposed upon it. As part of this estimate, you need to estimate the effort required to resolve the risks or deliver the desired outcomes. You should use these rough estimates to validate the mapping of the risks and desired outcomes to the iterations. As you are doing this, you might see that there is too much work to do in a certain iteration. You might need to shift risks and desired outcomes between iterations and iterations between phases to balance the workload. You might find that there is too much work to accomplish in the evolution, which means that you might need to shift some desired outcomes to future evolutions. If you do this, make sure to update the overall project plan and confirm the decisions with the project stakeholders.

This process gives you an initial development plan, including the number of iterations and the length of each. This is more than enough to start the project iterating; in fact you need to perform the initial project iteration to be able to evolve a more detailed and credible plan. We expand on this pattern in subsequent sections. The patterns for planning the iterations themselves are covered in the next chapter.

---

[16] Example themes for iterations include Demonstrate Solution Feasibility (a good one for an iteration in the Inception phase), Prove Solution Scalability, (a good theme for an iteration in the Elaboration phase), and Deploy the Solution to Beta Test Users (a good theme for an iteration in the Transition phase). Construction iterations are usually themed around the subset of the functionality that they are intended to deliver.

Evolution Iteration Patterns

The divisions of iterations between phases can follow a number of patterns. Understanding these can help you to decide how to organize iterations into phases for your project. These patterns represent common responses to different sets of risks:

- **Inception Phase**—The number of iterations in the Inception phase depends on the number and complexity of the business issues and the problem domain. If the business domain is complex, highly regulated, or rapidly changing, the Inception phase will take longer. In addition, if the desired outcomes of the business are unknown or if the solution that will need to deliver these outcomes is hard to identify, the Inception phase will take longer.

- **Elaboration Phase**—The number of iterations in the Elaboration phase depends on the number and complexity of technical issues and the novelty of the technology to the development team. A solution that exercises technology in novel ways will be riskier than a proven solution.

- **Construction Phase**—The number of iterations in the Construction phase depends on the technical complexity of the architecture and the "mass" of functionality that needs to be developed. Estimation models such as COCOMO II are useful for estimating the amount of effort needed in the Construction phase.

- **Transition Phase**—The number of iterations in the Transition phase depends on the complexity of deploying the solution into a "production" environment.

Incremental Development

The incremental development pattern is illustrated in Figure 7-5.

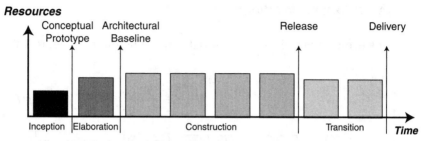

Figure 7-5 *The incremental development pattern*

Source: IBM Rational Unified Process

This pattern has the following characteristics:

- A short Inception iteration to establish scope and vision and to define the business case

- A single Elaboration iteration during which requirements are defined and the architecture verified

- Several Construction iterations during which the use cases are realized and the architecture fleshed out

- Several Transition iterations to migrate the product into the user community

This strategy is appropriate when

- The problem domain is familiar

- The architecture is already proven and familiar

- The team is experienced

- The risks are well understood and under control

This is the *ideal* iteration pattern. Applying the Unified Process lifecycle with very short Inception and Elaboration phases offers all the benefits of *rapid application development* while ensuring that the business and technical risks are kept under control.

Evolutionary Development

The evolutionary development pattern is illustrated in Figure 7-6.

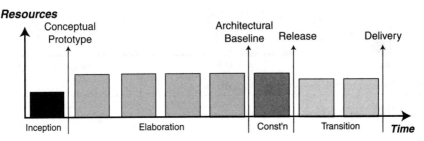

Figure 7-6   *The evolutionary development pattern*

Source: IBM Rational Unified Process

This pattern has the following characteristics:

- A short Inception iteration to establish scope and vision and to define the business case

- Several Elaboration iterations during which requirements are refined at each iteration and the architecture evolved until proven

- One or two Construction iterations during which the use cases are realized, the architecture is expanded, and the application is given a final polish

- Several Transition iterations to migrate the product into the user community

This strategy is appropriate when

- The problem domain is unfamiliar

- The architecture is unproven or unfamiliar

- The risks are not well understood

- The team is inexperienced

This is the pattern observed on most teams' first iterative project. It is also the most frequently adopted pattern when there is a strong need to establish an architecture for further evolutions of the product.

Incremental Delivery

The incremental delivery pattern is illustrated in Figure 7-7.

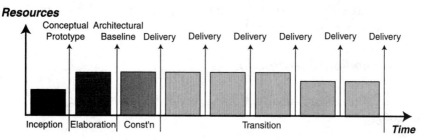

Figure 7-7   *The incremental delivery pattern*

Source: IBM Rational Unified Process

This pattern has the following characteristics:

- A short Inception iteration to establish scope and vision and to define the business case

- A single Elaboration iteration during which a stable architecture is baselined

- A single Construction iteration during which the use cases are realized and the architecture fleshed out

- Several Transition iterations, each of which delivers a new release of the product (with increased functionality) into the user community

This strategy is appropriate when

- Small increments have high value to the customer

- The architecture is already proven and familiar

- The requirements are stable and low risk

- The team is experienced in the architecture and the domain

This pattern is quite common for Internet site development where new content releases are expected every month and for incremental delivery of improvements to a system with a proven architecture. Tom Gilb advocates this style of delivery in his pioneering iterative and incremental development methodology EVO.[17]

Immediate Construction

The immediate construction pattern is illustrated in Figure 7-8.

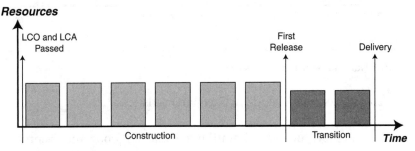

Figure 7-8   *The immediate construction pattern*

This pattern has the following characteristics:

- The completion of the Lifecycle Objectives (LCO) and Lifecycle Architecture (LCA) milestones before the evolution starts

- The immediate commencement of the Construction phase without the completion of any Inception or Elaboration iterations

- Several Construction iterations during which the use cases are realized and the architecture fleshed out

---

[17] Tom Gilb, *Principles of Software Engineering Management* (Reading, MA: Addison-Wesley, 1988).

- Several Transition iterations to migrate the product into the user community

This strategy is appropriate when

- The architecture is already proven and familiar

- The requirements are known and of low technical risk

- The team is experienced in the architecture and the domain

- The project is collaborative and informal

In some cases, anchor point milestones can be merged. As Barry Boehm[18] observes, a project deciding to use a mature and appropriately scalable fourth-generation language (4GL) or product line framework will have already determined its choice of lifecycle architecture by its LCO milestone, enabling the LCO and LCA milestones to be merged. This merging of the milestones is often enabled when another project (typically a feasibility project or the previous evolution) has already done the Inception and Elaboration work for you. In this case, the phases have been suppressed, but the milestones are still there, with reviews being undertaken before the set of construction iterations can commence.

No Elaboration

The "no Elaboration" pattern is illustrated in Figure 7-9.

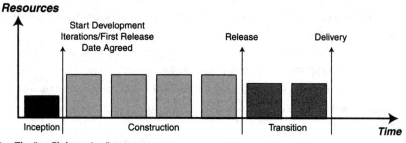

Figure 7-9 *The "no Elaboration" pattern*

18 Barry Boehm, "Spiral Development: Experience, Principles, and Refinements," Special Report, CMU/SEI-2000-SR-008, July 2000.

This pattern is our interpretation of the *Extreme Programming* lifecycle.[19] It has the following characteristics:

- A single Inception iteration to scope the project and agree on the release date

- The completion of the LCO and LCA milestones at the end of the initial iteration

- Several Construction iterations during which the use cases are realized and the architecture fleshed out

- Several Transition iterations to migrate the product into the user community

This strategy is appropriate when

- The architecture is already proven and familiar

- The requirements are known and of low technical risk

---

[19] In *Agile and Iterative Development: A Manager's Guide*, Craig Larman describes the XP Lifecycle phases, as defined by Kent Beck, as:

- **Exploration**—Purpose: Enough well-estimated story cards for first release, feasibility ensured. Activities: Prototyping, exploratory proof of technology programming, story card writing, and estimating.
- **Planning**—Purpose: Agree on date and stories for first release. Activities: Release Planning Game, story card writing, and estimating.
- **Iterations to First Release**—Purpose: Implement a tested system ready for release. Activities: Testing and programming, Iteration Planning Game, task writing, and estimating.
- **Productionizing**—Purpose: Operational deployment. Activities: Documentation, training, marketing …
- **Maintenance**—Purpose: Enhance, fix, build major releases. Activities: Might include these phases again for incremental releases.

For the purpose of this example, these have been mapped to the UP phases, with Exploration and Planning being interpreted as Inception, Iterations to First Release as Construction, and Productionizing as Transition. The Maintenance phase implies the possibility of further evolutions. Definitions taken from *Agile and Iterative Development: A Manager's Guide*, Craig Larman (Boston: Addison-Wesley, 2004).

- The team is experienced in the architecture and the domain

- The project team is small, and the project is collaborative and informal

This is another variant where the milestones have been merged, giving the impression that there is no Elaboration phase. This is the case for most Extreme Programming and SCRUM projects, where the architecture is already established before the start of the set of development iterations. This architecture is then adjusted by refactoring during the Construction iterations, as is typical of most iterative and incremental projects following the end of the Elaboration phase and the establishment of an architecture. Some Extreme Programming authors[20] allow technical concerns to affect the allocation of work to the initial development iterations, creating an informal Elaboration phase.

How to Use These Patterns

These evolution iteration patterns should be used when developing your initial plans for an evolution:

- Select the iteration pattern that most closely matches the characteristics of your current evolution. Consider your risks, think about your team's skills and experience, think about where your project is in the lifecycle, and select one of the patterns as a reference model.

- Adjust the model by adding or removing iterations to meet specific needs. It is quite possible that you might need to combine patterns to most closely match the characteristics of your project.

In practice, few projects strictly follow one evolution strategy. You often end up with a mix of patterns as the project progresses across a series of evolutions. An example is shown in Figure 7-10, where the project starts with the evolutionary pattern to enable the new architecture to be established.

---

[20] For example, Martin Fowler (for) and Kent Beck (against) agree to disagree about this in *Planning Extreme Programming,* (Boston: Addison-Wesley, 2000).

Subsequent evolutions follow other patterns to achieve specific objectives before adopting the incremental delivery pattern for maintenance and support.

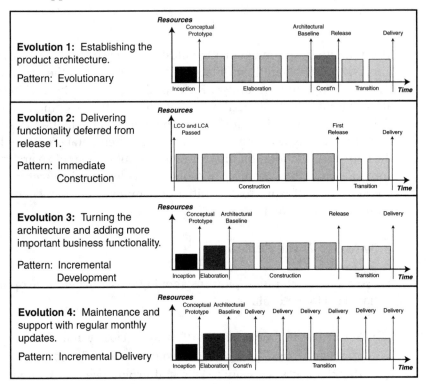

Evolution 1: Establishing the product architecture.

Pattern: Evolutionary

Evolution 2: Delivering functionality deferred from release 1.

Pattern: Immediate Construction

Evolution 3: Turning the architecture and adding more important business functionality.

Pattern: Incremental Development

Evolution 4: Maintenance and support with regular monthly updates.

Pattern: Incremental Delivery

Figure 7-10   *The evolution iteration patterns for a series of evolutions*

Among the advantages of the Unified Process's phased iterative model is that it accommodates a hybrid approach, simply by increasing the length and number of iterations in the particular phases where you face the most risk:

- For complex or unfamiliar problem domains, where a high degree of exploratory business work is required, increase the length of and the number of iterations in the Inception phase.

- For complex or unfamiliar technology problems, where a high degree of technological exploratory work is required, increase the length of and the number of iterations in the Elaboration phase.

- For more complex development technologies, where complexity is involved in translating the requirements and design into code, increase the length of and the number of iterations in the Construction phase.

- For situations where you need to deliver software in a series of frequent incremental releases, increase the length and number of iterations in the Transition phase.

Evolving the Evolution Plan

This planning process can be summarized in the following steps:

1. Set the iteration length. Start with a duration of four weeks and tune based on experience, team size, and risks.

2. Calculate the number of iterations to complete the project. To start, select an iteration pattern and an initial number of iterations based on the project's characteristics (size, complexity, risk, capability, and so on).

3. Estimate the capacity of each iteration in person-days. Don't forget to factor in organizational overheads, holiday periods, and any other factors that will reduce the number of working days available within the iteration time boxes.

4. Assess the risk and determine how to address it. Select the highest risks and then the scenarios, flows, and other artifacts that will force their confrontation and resolution.

5. Give each iteration a unique identifier and a name that reflects its theme.

6. Calculate how much effort the evolution will take to complete based on its current situation, its current rate of progress, and the experiences of the previous iterations. Either add iterations until there is enough capacity to complete the implementation of all the flows and scenarios or de-scope the set of flows until it fits the effort and schedule available.

7. Compare the plans and estimates to the reference models and adjust where applicable.

This process gives you an initial development plan, including the number of iterations and their lengths. Its iterative application also helps you to evolve your plans as the project progresses and more information becomes available.

Table 7-6 shows the initial development plan for the first evolution of the ACME Super ATM (last seen in the previous chapter). This includes a schedule and estimates for the effort available in each iteration (note that the figure in parentheses indicates the amount of effort that is expected to be dedicated to the implementation and testing of the new system). A complete development plan for this evolution is included in Appendix C, "Examples."

This initial plan is more than enough to start the evolution. The plan and the evolving requirements understanding, estimates, and capability measurements provide a firm basis for negotiation and scope management. As the project progresses, the plans and estimates will need to be evolved. The majority of the detail will be kept within individual iteration plans where the objectives will be clarified, evaluation criteria will be specified, and the detailed resource and activity planning will take place.

Table 7-6 *Initial Development Plan for Evolution 1: Basic Withdrawal Facilities of the ACME Super ATM*

	Iteration	Objectives / Risks	Schedule	Effort in Person-Days	Key Deliverables
Inception	I1: Scope Project	Establish the vision / 1, 4—Market perception	4 weeks Start: 31 Jan	80 (15)	Proof of Concept: Basic cash dispensing. Vision.
	I2: Agree on business case and evolution plan	Establish the business case / 2—Costs might be too high 3—Flexibility might not be desired	4 weeks Start: 28 Feb	75 (40)	Proof of Concept: Configurable cash dispensing. Agreed on business case. Development Plan.
Elaboration	E1: Demonstrate cash withdrawal	Establish the core architecture / 5—Platform suitability	4 weeks Start: 28 March	75 (40)	Prototype: Withdraw Cash Basic Flow. Fleshed out use cases and supplementary specs.
	E2: Prove basic ATM functionality	Prove suitability of architecture / 6—Failure modes 7—Tamper proofing	4 weeks Start: 25 April	75 (50)	Prototype: Withdraw Cash with basic failure modes and protection + initial load testing. Architecture Description.
	E3: Prove paper goods dispensing capability	Demonstrate reliability of architecture / 5—Platform reliability 10—Printing flexibility	4 weeks Start: 23 May	150 (100)	Prototype: Simple ticket printing + initial demo. Prototype: Withdraw Cash with correction and reconciliation + load and performance testing. Ticket printing flexibility and reliability test results.

Table 7-6 *Initial Development Plan for Evolution 1: Basic Withdrawal Facilities of the ACME Super ATM (continued)*

	Iteration	Objectives / Risks	Schedule	Effort in Person-Days	Key Deliverables
Construction	C1: Complete basic ATM functionality	Establish basic ATM functionality	4 weeks Start: 20 June	160 (130)	Functional Release: Basic cash withdrawal. Use Cases: Withdraw Cash, Refill and Service.
	C2: Deliver a supportable, robust ATM system	Establish a usable ATM and ticket dispenser	4 weeks Start: 18 July	160 (130)	Functional Release: Usable Cash Withdrawal. Complete remaining in-scope use cases. Dry run of rail conference demonstration. Pilot plans in place.
Transition	T1: Set up user acceptance testing	Support user acceptance testing	4 weeks Start: 15 August	75 (30)	Patch Release: Bug fixes. User acceptance testing.
	T2: Support user acceptance testing	Support user acceptance testing	4 weeks Start: 12 Sept	80 (30)	Possible Patch Release: More Bug fixes. User acceptance testing complete.
	T3: Support the technology pilot	Support the pilot	8 weeks Start: 10 Oct	64 (10)	Emergency fixes (if required). Successful pilot.

From a management perspective, you can expect to have a credible plan by the end of the Inception phase; put another way, you cannot successfully exit the Inception phase until you have a credible plan that demonstrates how you will mitigate the project risks. By the end of the Elaboration phase, you will have enough information for a more precise plan to be produced because the technical risks should be demonstrably under control by this time. To demonstrate his or her belief that the project has its risks under control, the project manager should be prepared to undertake the rest of the project for a fixed price. With the technical risks under control, the estimates should be within 25% of the actuals, enabling an accurate cost and schedule to be provided.

Typically, an evolution's development plan is issued at least twice: once toward the end of the Inception phase to support the Lifecycle Objectives milestone review at the Inception phase assessment, and once toward the end of the Elaboration phase to support the Lifecycle Architecture milestone review at the Elaboration phase assessment. It might also need minor rework to accommodate work shifting between iterations when exceptions occur or when sponsors or the steering committee members make major requests for change in scope.

Working with the Disciplines and Artifacts

At this point in the planning process, you might be feeling a little uncomfortable because you do not have detailed lists of project artifacts and deliverables yet, especially with regard to the various disciplines to be applied. As we have previously discussed, the core software development disciplines are applied continuously throughout the project. This is illustrated by Table 7-7, which is drawn from data provided by COCOMO II. These figures are useful for working out the skills and resources needed for each project phase and as an aid in assessing whether actual effort has occurred in the right places as part of your iteration and phase assessments. It is these figures that are used to create the estimates of the dedicated development effort and other project overheads in Table 7-2.

Table 7-7   *Percentage Effort by Discipline and Phase*

Discipline	Inception	Development		Transition
		Elaboration	**Construction**	
Management	14%	12%	10%	14%
Requirements	38%	18%	8%	4%
Analysis and Design	19%	36%	16%	4%
Implementation (Code and Unit Test)	8%	13%	34%	19%
Assessment [21]	8%	10%	24%	24%
Deployment	3%	3%	3%	30%
Environment / CM	10%	8%	5%	5%

Source: COCOMO II FAQ (http://sunset.usc.edu/research/COCOMOII/). The table is slightly modified from the figures defined by COCOMO II: We use Analysis and Design instead of Design; Analysis is not mentioned in the original breakdown.

Now although the disciplines are applied throughout the project, the loading is not evenly spread, even within the individual phases. This is illustrated by Figure 7-11, which shows how the effort applied to each discipline rises and falls across the lifecycle of a typical Unified Process project.

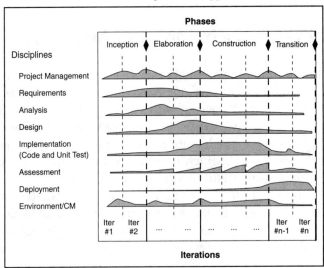

Figure 7-11   *The Unified Process effort profile*

Adapted from *The Unified Software Development Process*, Ivar Jacobson et al. (Reading, MA: Addison-Wesley, 1999).

---

[21] Note that "Assessment" includes all review activities, regardless of the type of review.

Of most interest is the distribution of the Project Management effort, which can be clearly seen to be at its most intense across the iteration and phase boundaries. This is because this is where the majority of planning, assessment, and management intervention takes place.

Within each phase, each discipline has a clearly defined purpose. Each milestone can be broken down to provide an objective for each discipline. If you understand these smaller objectives, it is much easier to work out the set of artifacts that you will require to pass the milestone review. In addition, the focus and purpose of the disciplines themselves change as the evolution progresses. As you proceed through the lifecycle, the depth and detail of the artifacts produced by each discipline will increase, as will their compatibility, cohesion, precision, and accuracy.

Table 7-8 presents an overview of the primary objective for each discipline in each phase. Some of these objectives are optional and are shown in italics. Some of the objectives might already have been achieved by early evolutions or the overall project, but these things are always worth checking before proceeding on the assumption that they are in place.

Figure 7-12 and Figure 7-13 complete the picture by identifying the artifacts that are typically required to demonstrate that the achievements have been made.

These figures are intended to a show a typical set of artifacts suitable for the execution of a controlled iterative and incremental software development project. Your projects might require additional or fewer artifacts to reduce their particular risks or to satisfy your favored development approach.

Table 7-8   *An Overview of the Phase Objectives by Discipline*

	Inception	**Elaboration**	**Construction**	**Transition**
Management	• Business Case Established • Management Strategy Defined	• Business Case Confirmed • Risks Under Control	• Project Under Control • Transition Plans Understood	• Project Completed • Stakeholders Satisfied
Requirements	• Vision Established • Scope Agreed On	• Vision Confirmed • Requirements Stable	• Requirements Correct	• Requirements Accepted
Analysis and Design	• Candidate Architecture Selected	• Architecture Communicated	• Design Recorded	• Design Tuned and Handed Over
Implementation (Code and Unit Test)	• *Executable Architectural Proof of Concepts Available*	• Executable Architecture Baselined	• Production Release Available	• Maintenance Responsibilities Handed Over • Major Problems Addressed
Assessment	• *Architectural Capabilities Assessed* • Test Mission Defined	• Architecture Verified • Test Strategy Established	• Release Verified • Deployment Strategy Verified	• Fixes and Changes Verified • Requirements Verified as Accepted
Deployment	• Deployment Scoped	• Deployment Risks Under Control	• Ready to Deploy	• Product Accepted
Environment	• *Process and Tools Selected*	• Environment Established	• Environment Tuned	• Project Archived

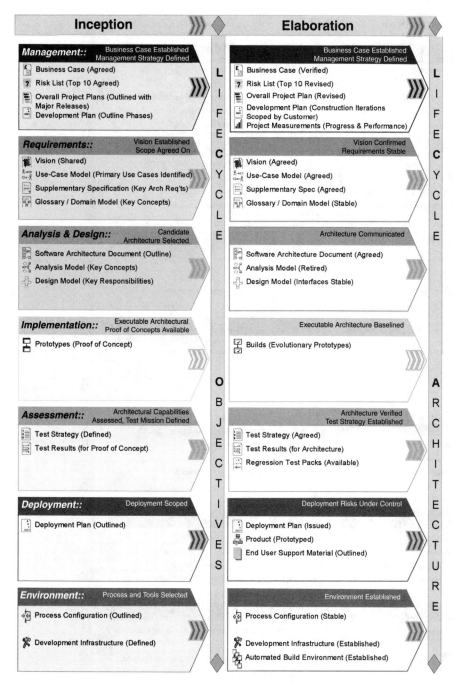

Inception

Management:: Business Case Established / Management Strategy Defined
- Business Case (Agreed)
- Risk List (Top 10 Agreed)
- Overall Project Plans (Outlined with Major Releases)
- Development Plan (Outline Phases)

Requirements:: Vision Established / Scope Agreed On
- Vision (Shared)
- Use-Case Model (Primary Use Cases Identified)
- Supplementary Specification (Key Arch Req'ts)
- Glossary / Domain Model (Key Concepts)

Analysis & Design:: Candidate Architecture Selected
- Software Architecture Document (Outline)
- Analysis Model (Key Concepts)
- Design Model (Key Responsibilities)

Implementation:: Executable Architectural Proof of Concepts Available
- Prototypes (Proof of Concept)

Assessment:: Architectural Capabilities Assessed, Test Mission Defined
- Test Strategy (Defined)
- Test Results (for Proof of Concept)

Deployment:: Deployment Scoped
- Deployment Plan (Outlined)

Environment:: Process and Tools Selected
- Process Configuration (Outlined)
- Development Infrastructure (Defined)

LIFECYCLE OBJECTIVES

Elaboration

Management:: Business Case Established / Management Strategy Defined
- Business Case (Verified)
- Risk List (Top 10 Revised)
- Overall Project Plan (Revised)
- Development Plan (Construction Iterations Scoped by Customer)
- Project Measurements (Progress & Performance)

Requirements:: Vision Confirmed / Requirements Stable
- Vision (Agreed)
- Use-Case Model (Agreed)
- Supplementary Spec (Agreed)
- Glossary / Domain Model (Stable)

Analysis & Design:: Architecture Communicated
- Software Architecture Document (Agreed)
- Analysis Model (Retired)
- Design Model (Interfaces Stable)

Implementation:: Executable Architecture Baselined
- Builds (Evolutionary Prototypes)

Assessment:: Architecture Verified / Test Strategy Established
- Test Strategy (Agreed)
- Test Results (for Architecture)
- Regression Test Packs (Available)

Deployment:: Deployment Risks Under Control
- Deployment Plan (Issued)
- Product (Prototyped)
- End User Support Material (Outlined)

Environment:: Environment Established
- Process Configuration (Stable)
- Development Infrastructure (Established)
- Automated Build Environment (Established)

LIFECYCLE ARCHITECTURE

Figure 7-12 *A phase milestone view of the Unified Process with key artifacts—Part 1*

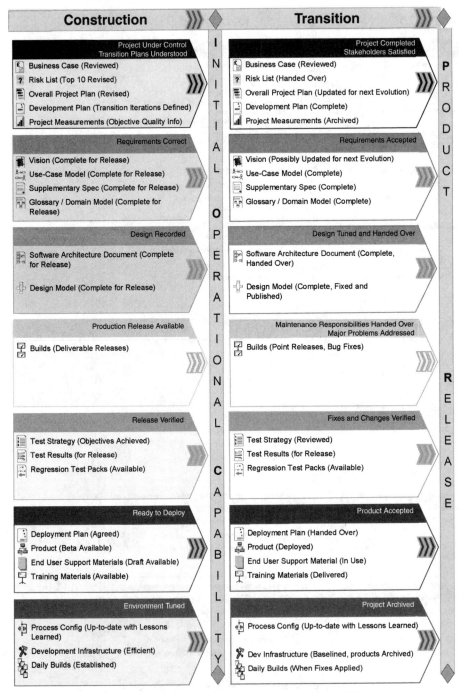

Figure 7-13 *A phase milestone view of the Unified Process with key artifacts—Part 2*

One point is worth stressing: the formality of representation used to capture these artifacts can vary widely, from whiteboard drawings to automated tooling. There are a variety of factors that drive these choices, but this is beyond the scope of our discussion. The important thing is that you decide which artifacts you need to drive out risk and that you decide the degree of precision at which you need to work.

Some people like to maintain a matrix of the artifacts to be produced and the phases and iterations of the project. A spreadsheet containing a list of the key artifacts and their state, progress, and estimate to complete is a very useful adjunct to the project plan. An extract of the deliverables table for the initial evolution of the ACME Super ATM showing the state and progress of the requirements products is shown in Table 7-9.

Table 7-9   *Artifact Planning for Evolution 1 of the ACME Super ATM*

Artifact	Inception		Elaboration		
	I1	**I2**	**E1**	**E2**	**E3**
Vision	Initial version	Agreed on			
Use-Case Model	Primary use cases and actors identified	Some architecturally and business-significant use cases detailed	Evolving to address project risks	All actors and use cases identified	Agreed on with all high-risk flows of events detailed[22]
Supplementary Specification	Initial version with key architectural requirements	Architectural requirements clarified	Evolving	Agreed on for evolution	
Requirements Management Plan	Agreed on				
Glossary / Domain Object Model	Initial version	Evolving	Evolving	Evolving	Agreed on

---

[22] The remaining low-risk flows of events will be detailed in the iterations that implement them.

Great care should be taken to focus on the key artifacts that will act as the permanent record for the project and not to get sucked into defining all the transient, work-in-progress artifacts that the team might use to facilitate their communication and teamwork.

Estimating and Work Breakdown Structures

Work breakdown structures tend to take on a different role in iterative projects from the one that they play in more traditional waterfall projects. For an iterative project, the work is broken down in two dimensions:

- **Time**—In this dimension, the work is broken down into iterations, which are then used to compose the phases. As we saw in the last section, these phases are estimated by length, effort, and development capacity. If a more detailed work breakdown structure is required in this dimension, then it is limited to the current iteration along with the detailed planning.

- **Artifacts**—In this dimension, the individual artifacts are identified and their development costs estimated and loosely partitioned across the iterations. This kind of "product breakdown structure" is limited to the artifacts that the project will deliver, ignoring any low-level, transient artifacts that the team might use to facilitate the execution of an iteration. Again if a more detailed product breakdown structure is required, then it is limited to the current iteration.

Within this structure, many estimating techniques can be used to create the estimates required to support the evolution planning. So far we have estimated the evolution as a whole and the team size and capacity of each iteration. More detailed estimates of the remainder of the evolution can be produced as the project progresses by estimating the effort required for the individual artifacts to be produced, the most significant of which is the software itself.

Estimating Effort

The evolving understanding of the requirements, the architecture, and the team's ability enables additional estimating models and methods to be applied. The collection of measurements from the iterations enables the estimating models to be calibrated and future trends to be predicted. Figure 7-14 illustrates the trends we expect to see for revised estimates produced as the evolution progresses through the iterations and phases.

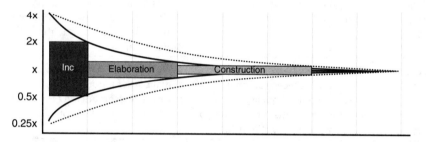

Figure 7-14 *Estimation across the phases*

As the evolution progresses, the techniques we can use and the accuracy of the estimates produced varies. Some of the more widely used techniques for each phase are summarized in Table 7-10.

Typically projects maintain estimates to complete for the various artifacts and for each requirement (use-case flow of events, supplementary specification) and change request. The significance of these more detailed estimates will become clearer in the next chapter when we look at iteration planning.

Table 7-10 *Estimating Techniques Across the Phases*

Phase	Applicable Techniques	Expected Results
Inception	• Analogy • Course-grained Wideband Delphi[23] • COCOMO II[24] Pre-Architecture Model • Use-case Points[25]	At the end of Inception, the estimates produced will typically have an error factor of 2 to 4.
Elaboration	• Fine-grained Wideband Delphi (on individual flows and supplementary specifications) • COCOMO II Post-Architecture Model • Use-case Points	At the end of Elaboration, the estimate will typically be within 25% of actuals.
Construction (to estimate completion)	• The same techniques are applied as during the Elaboration phase.	The estimation continues using the performance indicators and lessons learned from the last iteration and the overall project trends.
Construction (to estimate deployment and cost of ownership)	• The same techniques are applied as during the Inception phase. • Measurements of quality and maintenance costs can be used to tune the estimate for Transition.	At the end of Construction, we will know the actual cost of producing the system but will still have to estimate the cost of owning, maintaining, and deploying it.

The hardest phase to estimate is the Transition phase. This is because the models used for estimating the costs of software production (such as COCOMO II) only estimate these costs as a possible percentage of the development costs. Transition phase costs do not correlate well with development costs—the factors driving Transition phase estimates relate to the complexity of deploying the solution to the business, not the complexity of developing the solution.

---

[23] See the previous chapter for more information on analogy and Wideband Delphi estimating techniques.

[24] See http://sunset.usc.edu/research/COCOMOII/.

[25] A popular technique for estimating based upon use cases first published in "Metrics for Objectory" by Gustav Karner in 1993 (Diploma thesis, University of Linköping, Sweden, No. LiTH-IDA-Ex-9344:21) and popularized in many papers including "The Estimation of Effort Based on Use Cases" by John Smith (Cupertino, CA: Rational Software, 1999). Note: Other more traditional estimating techniques, such as Function Points, can also be used to estimate based upon the use cases and their flows. See for example "Mapping the OO-Jacobson Approach into Function Point Analysis" by Thomas Fetke, Alain Abran, and Tho-Hau Nguyen, published in the Proceedings of TOOLS-23'97 (Santa Barbara, CA: IEEE, 1998).

Effort in the Transition phase is a function of a number of factors, including

- The number of users and/or customers

- The number of deployment sites

- The complexity of data conversion/upgrade

- The business criticality of the operation supported by the system

- The complexity of supporting the product in a production environment

Transition phase costs are best estimated using the broader estimating techniques of analogy and Wideband Delphi. As the project progresses, these estimates can be tuned by including estimates of the cost of ownership made by extrapolating the project measurements collected during the iterations.[26] More detailed estimates can be derived in a bottom-up manner from a detailed deployment plan.

Staffing Levels and Skill Sets

You also need to estimate the skills and resources required. Because different types of work are performed in the different phases, the skills required of the project staff vary by phase as well. As a result, staff members tend to join and leave the project as their skills are needed. This is in contrast to the more conventional approach in which team members are assigned to the project for its duration, regardless of their skills and the needs of the project. The result is that excellent software developers are often asked to

---

[26] If the level of quality measured during the iterations is low, then the quality of the final product is likely to be low, increasing the costs of deploying the product. If the defects found during the early iterations are difficult and costly to fix, then those found during user acceptance testing or live operations are also likely to be costly to fix, again increasing the deployment costs.

become mediocre business analysts or deployment experts to the detriment of the project. Figure 7-15 illustrates how the relative size and importance of the teams change across the lifecycle.

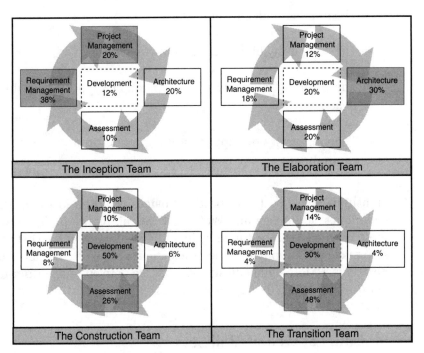

Figure 7-15   *Team emphasis across the phases*

To manage this virtual team of participants, you need a stable leadership team covering the four key areas of responsibility: Project Management, Architecture, Assessment, and Requirements Management, which were introduced in Chapter 4, "Are You Ready for Iterative Project Management?" This means instantiating a core leadership team consisting of at least a project manager—to lead the project and liaise with the customers—and a solution architect—to provide technical leadership. This leadership team needs to be supported by a "business representative" to provide an interface into the business and lead the vision for the project. For larger projects, all four leadership roles might have to be filled by different people.

With the leadership roles providing continuity, the project staffing can become more flexible and variable, enabling the right people to be added at the right time. Even if new people cannot be added to the team, the people already involved need to be prepared to move around and take on new responsibilities as the needs and dynamics of the project change.

Figure 7-15 illustrates how the relative size and importance of the teams change across the lifecycle:

- During the Inception phase, the project needs an organization focused on building the business case and assessing the viability of the project. This is reflected in the strong emphasis on the project management and requirement management teams.

- During the Elaboration phase, the project needs an organization focused on demonstrating an executable architecture and proving the selected approach. In this phase, the architecture team takes the lead and consumes the most resources.

- During the Construction phase, the emphasis changes to the production of completed, potentially deployable versions of the system. In this phase, the project needs an organization focused on building quality increments, with the vast majority of the resources concentrated on building and testing the iterations' releases.

- During the Transition phase, the project needs an organization focused on rolling out and supporting the early users of the system. In the model used in Figure 7-15, this leads to an emphasis on assessment to ensure that the solution is fit for purpose and for coordinating the transition to operations.

Because the figures used in this section are all percentages, they hold true regardless of whether the team can scale up and down in accordance with the risks it faces and the work it has to do.

Adapting and Revising the Estimates and the Plans

The key to effective evolution planning is evolving an appropriate level of detail to provide sufficient information to develop the individual iteration plans and place the results of the iterations into context. This enables the project to be effectively monitored and controlled. As the quote at the beginning of the chapter indicates, the project begins with doubts, not certainties. By accepting and acknowledging these doubts, the project can address them, building the confidence of the team in its ability to deliver.

This is true for the estimates as well as the plans. The estimates must be continually revisited and revised in light of the project performance and lessons learned. By layering the estimates along with the plans, the team can extrapolate from the results achieved against the lower-level iteration estimates to challenge and improve the higher-level estimates for the evolution and the project as a whole.

The plans themselves should be lightweight and should be evolved alongside the iterative development of the software. As the iterations and their assessments progress, the plans will need to be adjusted and revised to reflect the reality of the project. We return to this subject in more detail in Chapter 9, "Iteration, Phase, and Project Assessments," after we have looked at the planning and execution of the iterations themselves.

Summary

The purpose of evolution and phase planning is to create an overview of the evolution, including its iterations, phases, milestones, and objectives. The purpose is to create an outline, not a detailed plan of the project. The evolutions are planned using the lifecycle of the Unified Process and its predefined set of technical phases and milestones. These provide a roadmap for the development of the major release that is the primary goal of the evolution.

Each phase needs to be planned and managed a little differently: each requires a different mixture of skills and levels of resources, and each produces different kinds of results. As a result, it is not unreasonable to expect that different teams will staff each phase as long as there is a continuity of vision and expertise across phases.

In the next chapter, we continue exploring the management of iterative development by examining how to plan and manage iterations.

8

Iteration Planning

"He who desires but acts not, breeds pestilence."
—William Blake

Iteration planning is where the majority of the planning effort is expended. It is the most satisfying part of planning an iterative and incremental project because results are seen almost immediately. As the manager of an iterative project, you work with the iteration plans daily because they drive the actual work on the project. Iteration planning is a stripped-down, collaborative, focused form of lifecycle planning, tuned to exploit the short-term, time-boxed nature of the iterations.

As discussed in Chapter 1, "What Is Iterative Development?" and shown in Figure 8-1, each iteration goes through the management cycle of Agree, Execute, and Assess.

Figure 8-1 *The iterative management cycle*

Iterations are the epitome of the Shewart[1] cycle of Plan, Do, Check, and Act. This cycle is fairly common in most projects—iterative software development is distinguished by two things: the relatively short time period over which the cycle operates, and the degree to which the goals are driven by explicit risk reduction.

In this case, we have simplified the cycle for iterations to Agree, Execute, and Assess because

- There are several layers of planning and acting above the iterative cycle,

- The iteration objectives (goals and targets) must be agreed upon before the iteration is started, and

- We want to show that the detailed planning for an iteration can be done by the team members themselves after the objectives are agreed upon and understood.

In this chapter, we look at the first two elements of this cycle by walking you through the iteration planning process, examining some of the common iteration patterns for the various phases of the Unified Process, and discussing the role of the management team during the execution of an iteration.

Assessment is such an integral part of the iterative development process that we have given this subject its own chapter, Chapter 9, "Iteration, Phase, and Project Assessments," so we only cover the planning of assessments in this chapter.

Agreeing on the Iteration Plan

The development of an iteration plan involves six steps:

1. Assess the current state of project risks.

2. Agree on the scope (goals, time period) of the current iteration.

---

[1]   Quoted in W. Edwards Deming, *Out of the Crisis* (Massachusetts Institute of Technology, Center for Advanced Engineering Study, 1986), 88.

3. Agree on the iteration evaluation criteria.

4. Agree on the approach to be taken.

5. Agree on the work allocation.

6. Agree on when the assessment will take place.

This planning pattern repeats itself at the beginning of each iteration.

The first three steps involve the management team in setting the objectives for the iteration. This is the most important part of iteration planning because it enables the team members to agree on the purpose of the iteration and define a set of objectives that support the higher-level plans, ensuring that the iteration supports the goals of the evolution and the overall project, as well as the criteria that will be used to assess success. We look at these three steps in detail in the following subsections. The final three steps address the detailed planning of the iteration and are the subject of the later section entitled "Planning the Execution of the Iteration."

Assessing the Current State of Project Risks

The project's risks will vary over the course of the project: risks will be retired, and unanticipated risks will be exposed. Some risks that appear significant when first identified will be easier to deal with than expected, and some "easy to handle" risks will turn out to be more pernicious than was first thought.

Figure 8-2 illustrates the goal of risk management: to identify and address those risks to which the project has the highest exposure and for which it does not have a strategy in place to control. The tough part is that people are inherently poor judges of risk—we tend to underestimate their probabilities and impact and tend to be overconfident in our ability to resolve them. The countermeasure for these shortcomings is vigilance and requiring *proof* that risks have really been resolved. As the saying goes, "Hope is not a strategy."

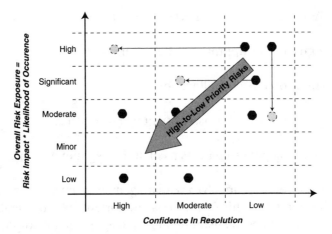

Figure 8-2   *Desired risk reduction over time*

There are many ways to manage project risks—too many to cover here.[2] The simplest way to effectively manage risk for an iterative project is to keep an active list of the top ten risks that can affect the project and that are within the project team's ability to control. If we always know what the top 10 project risks are, then we will always know which risks we need to attack in our next iteration. The short duration of the iterations means that 10 risks are usually more than enough for any iteration to deal with.

Table 8-1 shows an extract from a project's top 10 risk list. This simple tabular format can be used to track the state of the project's risks across iterations. The table shows the risk's current ranking, its ranking during the last iteration, and the number of iterations for which it has been in the top 10, as well as the risk exposure and mitigation plan.

---

[2]   If you are interested in learning more about risk management for software development projects, we recommend starting with *Software Risk Management: Principles and Practices* by Barry W. Boehm (IEEE Software, Jan. 1991), *Software Engineering Risk Analysis and Management* by Robert Charette (New York: McGraw-Hill, 1989), and *Assessment and Control of Software Risks* by Capers Jones (Upper Saddle River, NJ: Prentice Hall, 1994).

Table 8-1 *Excerpt from a Project's Risk List*

Rank This Iteration	Rank Last Iteration	Number of Iterations on the List	Description	Risk Exposure	Mitigation Plan
1	4	2	The team has never done iterative and incremental development before.	High	Appointed fantastic new manager.
2	7	4	External security threats and protection of data.	High	Next iteration, undertake "attack" testing.
3	New Entry	0	We've never written an online Bank System interface before.	Significant	Next iteration, prototype and demonstrate interfaces.
...	...	...	...	...	...
10	New Entry	0	Process experts do not have the experience advertised.	Moderate	Notice served. New suppliers being evaluated.

At the end of the iteration, the project's risks are reassessed and the top 10 adjusted to reflect the progress made during the iteration and to reflect any additional risks that have been detected. In each iteration, we would expect to see additional risks entering the top 10 to replace those that have been successfully addressed in the previous iteration. As shown in Appendix B, "Outlines, Templates, and Checklists," and Appendix C, "Examples," the top 10 risks can easily be captured as part of the iteration plan.

The easiest way to discover the top 10 risks is to ask everybody involved in the project what they think the biggest risks facing the project are, either by running a specific risk analysis workshop or as part of the ongoing iteration planning and assessment. Generally the risks that people are actively worrying about are those that most threaten the project.

After you have identified the biggest risks facing the project, you are ready to start planning what you will do about them in the next iteration.

Agreeing on the Scope of the Iteration

Three basic steps are involved in agreeing on the scope of an iteration:

1. **Refine the iteration's objectives**—Based upon the latest risk analysis of the project and the progress made so far, the initial set of objectives (as outlined in the development plan[3]) must be refined to provide a set of clear, measurable, achievable objectives for the iteration.

2. **Agree on the team's capacity**—Based upon the team's size, availability, and previous performance, its capacity for the next iteration must be determined and agreed upon. The best indicator of the team's capacity for an iteration is what it achieved in the previous iteration.

3. **Agree upon the iteration's deliverables**—Evidence is required to demonstrate that the team members have achieved their objectives. This evidence takes the form of one or more deliverables from the project. The deliverables' production cost must be estimated before their delivery is agreed upon to enable their cost to be compared to the team's predicted capacity.

Many people make the mistake of confusing the deliverables and other artifacts produced by the iteration with the iteration's objectives. It is important to separate the ends from the means. For example, it is common to see an iteration plan with objectives such as "Write the Vision," "Publish a Draft of the Software Architecture Document," or "Write the Development Plan." False objectives such as these obscure the real objectives of the iteration. The artifacts are just ways of recording and communicating the fact that work has been done and that decisions have been made. The objectives should communicate why the deliverables are required at this point in the project and the purpose that they serve.

For example, the reason the vision document is required is to establish a shared vision with the stakeholders and communicate to all the parties involved. We have seen a number of projects publish a vision document in their early iterations even though the project members knew that many of

---

[3]   As discussed in the previous chapter, the development plan contains an early mapping of risks to iterations. This mapping *should* be kept current, and the best way to do so is to revisit the mappings at the beginning of each iteration, adding new risks and retiring resolved risks.

the key stakeholders did not share the vision. It was as if they thought that publishing a vision would insulate them from disagreements. Artifacts are simply a means to an end; they have no value other than to document results. Focus on the results and let the artifacts follow.

Refining the Iteration's Objectives

The first step in agreeing upon the iteration's scope is to refine the iteration's objectives, outlined in the evolution's development plan, in light of the project's current highest-rated risks. Table 8-2 presents a selection of typical iteration objectives with some examples of the risks that they address.

Table 8-2   *A Selection of Iteration Objectives*

Objective	Description	Risks Addressed
Agree on the vision.	Establish a shared vision with all stakeholder representatives.	The business case cannot be agreed upon because there is disagreement about the scope of the system.
Provide basic cash withdrawal facilities.	Implement the next most important set of functionality.	The project doesn't implement the most important requirements.
Improve quality of unit tests.	Increase unit test coverage because it is currently insufficient.	System test is taking too long because the code is of insufficient quality to system test efficiently.
Prove the system's capability to keep data accurate and synchronized.	Ensure that data can be committed and rolled back against multiple data sources.	The existing legacy systems cannot be integrated into the new application.

You must ensure that the iteration objectives explicitly address the risks currently facing the project: the purpose of an iteration is to mitigate a particular set of risks. The objectives can be anything you want; they don't have to be derived from the selected development process or related to the expected set of artifacts. If the highest risk facing the project is quality, it is quite acceptable to establish as an objective the reduction of the number of open defects; if the highest risk facing the project is burnout due to overwork, it is quite acceptable to establish as an objective a reduction in the number of hours worked by the team during the iteration.

After you identify objectives, establish priorities to help the team understand where it should focus it efforts. Classifying the objectives as *essential*, *highly desirable*, or *desirable* is usually sufficient. We return to the subject of priorities when we look at setting the iteration's evaluation criteria.

Agreeing on the Team's Capacity

As we have discussed, an iteration is a time box in which work is performed. By definition, a finite amount of work can be done in a time box. Before too many objectives or too much work are assigned to an iteration, you must first understand the team's capacity.

The team's capacity for an iteration can be estimated by considering the following:

- **Availability**—The amount of time dedicated to the iteration. An estimate of this already exists within the evolution's development plan. This estimate should now be revisited in light of the current team size and circumstances.

- **Overhead**—The amount of the available time that will be consumed by other project activities instead of developing and testing the system. The project will incur necessary overheads for activities such as management, reporting, maintaining the development environment, and managing change.

- **Velocity**—The speed at which the team can implement and test requirements and change requests. The number of requirements the team can implement and test in a given time box is sometimes referred to as the *velocity* of the team.[4] As the project progresses, you will often find that scenarios and flows take less effort to implement and test, giving rise to an increase in velocity.

---

[4] This is the gradient of the team's emerging code-complete curve.

- **Contingency**—The amount of time to be set aside for unplanned work. In the early phases of the evolution, there might be a lot of unplanned work as new and unexpected risks arise and have to be handled. In the Construction phase, the amount of unplanned work should be minimized, reducing the need for contingency to be built into the iteration plans.

The best indication of a team's capacity is its members' performance during the previous iteration. Extreme Programming practitioners refer to this as *Yesterday's Weather*[5] based on the observation that the weather today is most likely to be the same as yesterday. The same holds for a team's performance—the performance for this iteration is most likely to be similar to that of the last iteration.

Another guide to the potential capacity of the team is the typical effort breakdown that has been observed for the different phases of the Unified Process, which we presented in Tables 7-3 and 7-7 in Chapter 7, "Evolution and Phase Planning." These figures can be useful in calculating the amount of overhead that can be expected in the iteration. In some cases, calculating the team's capacity is as simple as counting the number of days it has available to work on the project during the time box. Regardless of how it is done, the capacity of the time box must be accurately estimated before the plan can be agreed on.

Agreeing on the Iteration's Deliverables

The final part of agreeing on the iteration's scope is to identify the deliverables required to demonstrate that the objectives have been achieved. This is done by selecting the most appropriate scenarios, use case flows, and other artifacts to be developed by the team. Each will then need to be estimated so that the work intended can be balanced against the effort available.

---

[5] This concept is nicely explained and illustrated in *Planning Extreme Programming* by Kent Beck and Martin Fowler (Boston: Addison-Wesley, 2000).

Specifying the Release

The most important deliverable of any iteration is the release that will be developed. This is defined by the set of requirements that it implements.

Selecting the right set of scenarios to force the iteration's risks to be confronted and overcome is an art that improves with practice. In the early iterations, this requires collaboration among the team members to anticipate the scenarios (which have only just been identified but not fully described) that will cause the risks to be confronted. The right scenarios are those that enable the risks to be addressed with minimal implementation overlap, exploring as much new behavior as possible. In addition to these scenarios, supplementary requirements,[6] change requests, and defects are also selected that force the confrontation of the iteration's specific risks.

As the project progresses and risks are retired, the focus shifts to filling out the functionality of the solution (this can be thought of as addressing the risk that important capabilities might not be delivered) and addressing the change requests and defects raised against the earlier iterations (this can be thought of as addressing the risk that the quality of the product will fall below an acceptable level). As the project enters the Construction phase, specifying the elements to be implemented within the iteration becomes a simple task of selecting the most important items from the set of work remaining to be completed by the project.

To achieve this task, the various in-scope requirements, change requests, and defects must be prioritized and estimated. Table 8-3 and Table 8-4 illustrate the sort of information that is useful for the management team when iteration planning. The estimates are essential to comparing the amount of work to be done with the team's capacity. Summing the estimates for the elements remaining to implement and test also provides a useful estimate of the cost of completing the software development activities.

---

[6] Supplementary requirements are functional or non-functional requirements that are not described by scenarios.

Table 8-3 *Selecting Requirements to Deliver in the Iteration*

Scope	Unit	Business Priority	Technical Risk	Estimate (person-days)[7]
UC 1: Cash Withdrawal	Basic Flow	Must	Low	4 days
UC 1: Cash Withdrawal	Alt 2–6: Card Handling Errors	Should	Medium	7 days
Performance	SR1: Peak Loading	Must	High	10 days

Table 8-4 *Selecting Defects and Change Requests to Address in the Iteration*

Identifier	Description	Business Priority	Technical Risk	Estimate
CR 1075	Enable transaction to be canceled at any time prior to money being dispensed.	High	Low	2 days
Defect 7	Transaction logs are not recoverable when system power is lost in the middle of an update.	Must	High	9 days, plus hardware redesign to incorporate backup power

Change requests and defects should not be taken lightly: they can highlight deficiencies in the overall approach that, if ignored, might kill the solution. Balancing defect fixing against the need to implement new capabilities is also part of the art of iteration planning. Bear in mind that change requests and defects identified in earlier iterations are related to scenarios that, at the time, were considered the most important. If they are related to the correctness, performance, or usability of these scenarios, it may well be better for the project to address them immediately rather than continuing to add new functionality upon an already shaky foundation.

---

[7] In this and other examples, all estimates represent effort, not duration, and are for illustration only; your actual estimates and results may vary.

Specifying Other Deliverables

In addition to the software release, the iteration might need to produce other artifacts. Some of the risks facing the project might require mechanisms to address them other than the development of additional code. For example, the risks of not understanding the value of the solution might require the business case to be developed or updated, and the risk of not agreeing on the concepts underlying the design might require the creation of a software architecture description.

For each discipline, a number of context-setting communication and control artifacts might be required to address particular project risks or facilitate the achievement of particular objectives. Table 8-5 illustrates how additional artifacts can be factored into the iteration plan.

Table 8-5   *Selecting Artifacts to Deliver in an Early Iteration*

Discipline	Artifact	State	Estimate
Project Management	Measurement Plan	Complete definition of measurements to be used during Elaboration and Construction.	4 days
Requirements	Vision	Complete / agreed on by all stakeholder representatives.	7 days
Deployment	Deployment Plan	Outline significant events in and extent of the deployment of the proposed solution.	10 days

The majority of the required artifacts will have been identified in the evolution's development plan; the need for others might appear as the iterations progress and as the team learns more about what it needs to have in place to enable it to work efficiently and effectively. When identifying additional artifacts to be worked on during an iteration, it is essential to define the expected state at the end of the iteration. The intention is to produce artifacts that are fit for purpose and "good enough" to reduce the project risk. Many of the artifacts will evolve as the project progresses, being worked on and updated in many iterations, so the iteration plan should clearly identify what is required at this time.

To Artifact or Not to Artifact?

Artifacts are used to record the results of work efforts; they are important mechanisms for conveying information to other members of the project team by recording decisions and documenting shared understanding so that information is not stored only in people's heads. This pays off by forcing people to make explicit their understanding and assumptions and by reducing the amount of time needed to bring new team members onto the project. As a result, it should be possible for anyone on the project to explain what the artifact is for, how it is used, and what information it should contain.

At the same time, the surest sign of a project in trouble is producing lots of artifacts without understanding why. Too often, teams lose their way and simply go through the motions, producing artifacts that have no purpose or meaning and, as a result, no value. For every artifact, you need to make a conscious, collective decision about why the artifact is needed and what a team member can expect to get from the artifact. Don't fall into the trap of thinking, "Because our process defines this artifact, we must need it."

Be especially alert for artifacts that are being produced solely to satisfy management several layers removed. These are almost always spurious and not useful to managing the project and are probably not actively used by those far-removed managers. Instead, get them to focus on reviewing iteration results, risks, and issues, not on intermediate artifacts.

The Importance of Estimates and Priorities

When agreeing upon the scope of an iteration, keep these principles in mind:

- Do as much work as you can within the iteration time box, focusing on the highest-priority items first.

- It is better to complete one objective than to have started work on many objectives.

- If the iteration falls short of meeting all its objectives, those not completed will be moved to the next iteration.

- If the iteration exceeds its objectives, additional work will be brought forward from the next iteration.

To achieve the necessary planning flexibility, you must do three things:

- Ensure that all the activities and deliverables are clearly prioritized.

- Set a scale for success that enables the team to be successful even if the performance falls slightly behind the pace desired.

- Ensure that more work is lined up than can be done in the iteration in case performance outpaces expectations.

In addition, you should recognize that success is rarely binary: success spans a spectrum. Often teams will achieve most, but not all, of the objectives set forth in the iteration plan. The unexpected occurs, and reality rarely exactly matches plans. Is this the fault of the team or of the plan? In reality, it does not matter—what matters is to deliver a good enough solution in the time needed within the budget allotted. Everything else you do, including planning and measuring, should help you to achieve that goal. Assigning blame or determining accountability is irrelevant unless it helps you achieve a better end result. Instead, learn from mistakes and make sure to focus on root causes of problems, not symptoms.

Iteration objectives and evaluation criteria should be challenging but not impossible. Studies have shown that a goal which is slightly beyond one's grasp is more motivating than a goal that appears easy to achieve—most of us are motivated by the need to prove, and improve, ourselves. As a result, it should be possible to be successful without meeting all the objectives.

To set challenging objectives, you need to be able to view the objectives and work items from three perspectives:

- **Priority**—Which of the objectives are essential for the team to achieve, and which are only highly desirable or nice to have?

- **Effort**—How much and what type of effort is required to create the things needed to achieve the objectives?

- **Dependency**—Which objectives must be met before others can be addressed? Is there an explicit order in which the objectives must be addressed?

Prioritization

We recommend prioritizing the objectives using the categories shown in Table 8-6.

Table 8-6 *Prioritization of Iteration Objectives*

Priority	Description
Essential	The objective's achievement is essential for the iteration to be considered a success. If any of the Essential objectives are not achieved, then the iteration cannot be considered a success.
Highly Desirable	Objectives that the team would like to achieve in addition to the Essential ones. If the team manages to achieve all the Highly Desirable objectives, in addition to the Essential ones, then it is very successful.
Desirable	Additional nice-to-have objectives. These are included to provide visibility of things to come and to identify additional work to ensure that the team cannot run out of work before the end of the time box, even if it is extremely successful.

Prioritizing the objectives in this way ensures focus on the completion of the Essential objectives. Until you have completed all the essential objectives, you should not expend effort on the others. When using this prioritization scheme, you would expect any unsatisfied objectives defined for one iteration to be carried forward to the next, with the corresponding increase in their priorities. For example, what was considered Highly Desirable in the first iteration is likely to become Essential in the second.

Estimation

As we saw in Tables 8-3 to 8-5, detailed estimates are required for all the work elements selected for the iteration. These estimates of the effort to do the work and to document the results form the core of the iteration plan estimates.

Initially, the management team puts together the estimates using generic approaches such as Wideband Delphi and analogy or more parametric models such as use-case points.[8] These estimates support the initial iteration planning by enabling the management team to select an appropriate amount of work to include in the iteration when planning how to address the iteration's objectives.

These initial estimates can then be improved by considering which people will do the work and asking them to estimate how much of their effort will be required to do the work. This process enables the team to create a more precise and specific estimate to help with the detailed planning of the iteration.

Dependencies

The iterative approach minimizes the dependencies within the detailed plans by the very nature of the short duration of the iterations themselves. By judiciously selecting independent pieces of work that when integrated demonstrate the achievement of the iteration's objectives, the dependencies can be further reduced. Unfortunately, they cannot be eliminated entirely and must be addressed as part of the iteration planning.

Agreeing on the Iteration Evaluation Criteria

There is a saying that you can't control what you can't measure. The evaluation criteria measure how effectively the team has met the objectives for the iteration. Defining the evaluation criteria at the beginning of the iteration provides a clear focus for the team. This is the planning equivalent of the Extreme Programming practice "Write the tests first" or Steven Covey's "Begin with the end in mind."[9]

To this end, the objectives must be accompanied by evaluation criteria that define how their achievement will be measured and the levels of these measurements that will be considered a success. A good evaluation criterion is clear and fact-based: it does not require subjective interpretation.

---

[8]   These techniques were discussed in detail in Chapters 6 and 7 and can now be applied with more precision to the finer-grained deliverables identified for the iteration.

[9]   Stephen R. Covey, *The Seven Habits of Highly Successful People,* 15th Anniversary Edition (New York: Free Press, 2004).

Let's look at a couple of examples:

- **Good evaluation criteria**—Successful completion of all tests for the selected scenarios.

- **Poor evaluation criteria**—Sign-off from user that a scenario meets his or her needs.

The second example is probably a good idea, but it does not establish objective criteria for acceptance; it abdicates definition of success criteria to the user, and it does not give the team a target toward which to work.

Evaluation criteria must be objective and measurable; at the end of the iteration, the team should be able to clearly and objectively demonstrate its progress—there should be no room to debate whether the objectives have been met.

One of the most significant challenges for managers new to iterative development is the creation and definition of good evaluation criteria for the iterations. The thing to remember is that you can exploit the iterations to improve your own management capability as well as the team's development capability. If the evaluation criteria set for the initial iteration prove to be too subjective and open to interpretation, then this will become apparent at the iteration assessment, and you can learn lessons to help you define better evaluation criteria for the subsequent iterations. Table 8-7 provides a sample of example iteration evaluation criteria.

Table 8-7 *Qualifying the Objectives*

Objective	Evaluation Criteria	Evidence
Agree on the vision	All stakeholder representatives sign up to the vision.	Acceptance of the vision.
Provide basic cash withdrawal facilities	All of the iteration's Essential cash withdrawal flows are implemented.	Completed, successful execution of all related test cases.
Improve quality of unit tests	100% code coverage in unit tests.	Successful completion of static analysis.
Prove commit and rollback	Customer data successfully changed on all customer systems and then cancelled.	Completed, successful execution of all related test cases.

In Table 8-8, we have illustrated the evaluation criteria for different types of objectives; these are examples of the kind of evaluation criteria that might be appropriate for an iteration.

Table 8-8   *Defining Iteration Evaluation Criteria*

Type	Evaluation Criteria	Evidence
Scope	All Essential and 50% of the Highly Desirable requirements identified for the iteration.	Successfully passed system tests.
Quality	Zero priority-one defects; no more than three priority-two defects.	Number of new and open defects.
Stability	All regression tests are passed.	Distribution of new defects across flows, scenarios, and components.
Scalability	The system can handle 300 simultaneous users.	Test results from performance and load tests.

It is worth spending some time examining one or two of these in more detail, most particularly the areas of scope and quality.

Evaluation Criteria Relating to Scope

In most iterations, the most essential objective is to produce an incremental increase in the number of requirements that the solution fulfills and a decrease in the number of defects it possesses. Table 8-3 and Table 8-4 showed how each element will be estimated and prioritized separately, enabling the most important to be targeted on the iteration. Each element must be analyzed, designed, implemented, and successfully system tested to be considered complete. By defining the tests for each element, we give each its own evaluation criteria.

This can create a problem in the Construction phase when the team's velocity increases. As the number of individual elements targeted in an iteration increases, it becomes harder to succinctly define the success criteria for the iteration. To handle this issue, we recommend that you break the scope definition and evaluation criteria into two parts:

1. The list of requirements elements to be addressed, prioritized using the Essential, Highly Desirable, and Desirable schema suggested for the iteration's objectives. The evaluation criteria for each element are that it is integrated into the iteration's release and successfully passes all of its system tests.

2. An overall objective for the iteration identifying the percentage of these items that the team needs to complete to be considered successful. In Table 8-7, the overall evaluation criterion is that all the Essential requirements and 50% of the Highly Desirable requirements have been implemented. This provides flexible, challenging, but achievable objectives for the team.

This process gives two priorities to each requirement, one for its importance to the project as a whole (for which we recommend using the MoSCoW[10] prioritization scheme) and one for its priority within the iteration (using the iteration prioritization scheme outlined previously).

This layering of the objectives and their evaluation criteria enables the iteration plan to be very precise without becoming cluttered with endless lists of the scenarios, flows, and other items to be implemented. The information about the state of the requirements with regard to the iteration can be kept alongside the other requirements management information, providing additional context to the other ongoing requirement management activities.

---

[10] The MoSCoW rules are a method for prioritizing requirements used quite widely in the United Kingdom especially by followers of the Dynamic System Development Method (DSDM). In *DSDM: Dynamic System Development Method* (Reading, MA: Addison-Wesley, 1997) 28-29, Jennifer Stapleton introduces the MoSCoW rules as follows: "You will not find the MoSCoW rules in the DSDM Manual, but they have been adopted by many organizations using DSDM as an excellent way of managing the relative priorities of requirements in a RAD project. They are the brainchild of Dai Clegg of Oracle UK, who was one of the early participants in the DSDM Consortium."

When prioritizing requirements, the mnemonic has the following meaning: M = Must have, S = Should have, C = Could have, and W = Want to have but will not have this time around (although most practitioners actually take the W to stand for "Won't have").

Evaluation Criteria Relating to Quality

Evaluation criteria relating to the quality of the products produced by the iteration should be based on the level of quality appropriate for the phase of the project. When handling defects, it is better to set a threshold for the appropriate level of quality than to say which specific defects need to be addressed. If your goal is to improve the overall quality of the release being produced, it is better to have an objective with the evaluation criterion that the new release will have no unresolved priority-one defects than to have an objective to address the existing priority-one defects but to ignore any new ones that are created by the iteration.

The importance of the number of new and outstanding defects varies across the lifetime of a project. When addressing quality, you must remember that the releases produced during the Inception and Elaboration phases are prototypes specifically aimed at addressing and exposing project risks. Uncovering a priority-one defect, especially in any underlying reused or purchased components, early in the project is particularly beneficial and can help to reduce project risks. When the evolution enters the Construction phase, the releases should be of production quality, and the presence of large amounts of high-priority defects would be of particular concern.

Iteration Tolerances

By prioritizing and qualifying the objectives in these ways, we are implicitly defining a set of tolerances for the iteration. As time boxes, iterations have zero tolerance to schedule slippage; the iteration will always end when the plan says it should end. In these circumstances, it is essential that appropriate tolerances are set for scope and quality and that these tolerances allow the team some leeway during the assessment of the iteration.

Pulling It All Together into a Simple Plan

The first section of the iteration plan is the scope and objectives section where the materials considered in this section are captured and published. The most important part of this section of the plan is the objectives table where the objectives, priorities, and evaluation criteria are pulled together to provide a simple overview of the purpose and extent of the iteration. Table 8-9 presents a consolidated example based on the objective and evaluation criteria snippets we have been using throughout this chapter.

By presenting a consolidated view of the iteration's objectives and evaluation criteria, this table acts as a simple checklist that can be used to drive the iteration assessment, as we shall see in Chapter 9.

This scoping material is complemented by the second half of the iteration plan, which captures the detailed plan for the execution of the iteration. This is the subject of the next section.

Appendix B, "Outlines, Templates, and Checklists," provides a simple outline for an iteration plan. An example completed iteration plan can be found in Appendix C, "Examples."

Table 8-9 *Setting the Objectives for an Iteration*

Objective	Description	Risks Addressed	Evaluation Criteria	Evidence	Priority
Agree on the vision	Direction: Establish a shared vision with all stakeholder representatives.	The business case cannot be agreed on because there is disagreement about the extent of the system.	All stakeholder representatives agree to and support the vision.	Signed off vision document. Revised business case with estimates.	Essential
Provide basic cash withdrawal facilities	Scope: Implement the next most important set of functionality.	The project doesn't implement the most important requirements.	All Essential and 50% of the Highly Desirable requirements identified for the iteration.	Agreed on requirements statements and successfully passed system tests.	Essential
Improve quality of unit tests	Quality: Increase unit test coverage because it is currently insufficient.	System test is taking too long because the code is of insufficient quality to system test efficiently.	100% code coverage in unit tests.	Code coverage measured as 100% for all implemented or changed components.	Essential
Prove commit and rollback	Architecture: Ensure that data can be committed and rolled back against multiple data sources.	The existing legacy systems cannot be integrated into the new application.	Customer data changed on all customer systems and then cancelled.	Test results showing transaction consistency.	Essential
Prove scalability	Performance: Prove that the infrastructure will cope with the peak loads generated by the proposed network.	The architecture will not support the demands of the proposed ATM and vending machine network.	Greater than 1M transactions per second passing through an individual gateway.	Number of transactions per second.	Essential
Achieve production quality levels	Quality: No priority-one defects; no more than three priority-two defects.	Shipping a low-quality product.	Total numbers of open defects showing no priority-one defects and no more than three priority-two defects.	Number of open defects. Distribution of defects across scenarios and components.	Highly Desirable

The risks would typically be cross-referenced using their unique identifiers rather than listed here and in the risk list. The actual risk descriptions are included in this example to make the table readable without the inclusion of an additional table detailing the risks.

Planning the Execution of the Iteration

There are different styles and approaches to the detailed planning of an iteration, but regardless of the approach taken, it all boils down to agreeing upon the work allocation and ensuring that the assessment takes place.

Agreeing Upon the Approach to Be Taken

A discussion of the appropriate level of detail needed to plan an iteration generates a great deal of debate. There is no right or wrong answer; it is a function of project risk, personal preference, project size, project complexity, team capability, and team cohesiveness. Detailed planning cannot overcome other weaknesses, but other strengths can reduce the need for detailed plans. Overly detailed planning for a team in over its head can actually make things worse. Detail by itself does not make a plan good or bad; having the right activities in the right order is what makes a plan effective or ineffective.

We have seen iterations run very successfully off a simple task list with self-organizing teams selecting the appropriate tasks to do in an informal, *ad hoc* manner. We have also seen iterations run in a very formal fashion with Gantt charts, detailed formal work breakdown structures, and detailed activity networks that have been equally successful. In addition, we have seen both approaches applied inappropriately with equally poor results.

The style of planning and control adopted is a decision for the management team to make with the help of the development team and the organization's project governance authorities. This decision will be based on a number of factors:

- **Requirements for process auditability imposed by external governance bodies**—Certain industries or problem domains have greater demands for process auditability (being able to track what was done by whom and when). Typically these are domains in which safety-critical requirements dominate the solution, requiring greater formality in the way the project is managed.

- **Cohesiveness and proven capability of the team**—A team that has worked together before and has developed close working relationships is typically much more self-directing than a new team. A team that is made up of experienced individuals who have developed software in this way before will require less explicit guidance to ensure that it actually does the right things at the right time.

- **Organizational trust and accountability**—Trust is a funny thing—if you don't put trust in a team, the members will never develop the ability to make decisions for themselves, and ultimately they will probably fail. So many decisions must be made on a daily basis that everyone must be able to make countless small decisions on all matter of things. Along with the trust comes accountability—not for following the plan with great precision, but for delivering the desired results with the flexibility to adapt to change as necessary.

  No plan is so forward thinking that it can anticipate every possible outcome—in fact most plans do not identify more than one path to success. The only thing that can be said with certainty about projects is that they will never come out exactly as planned. As a result, trust and accountability are essential. If you can't trust team members and hold them accountable, you have either the wrong people or a dysfunctional organizational culture.

These factors will affect more than just the decision about the level and format to adopt for detailed iteration planning (be they task sheets or iteration Gantt charts). They will also influence other things such as the management style, the frequency and style of project reporting, and the technical approach. For example, will the management team adopt a hands-on or a hands-off approach? Will the team have informal stand-up meetings or produce regular documented reports? Will the developers adopt pair programming? Will there be collaborative team requirements and design workshops?

As part of agreeing upon the approach, any additional internal iteration milestones should be agreed upon. Typically, two types of intermediate milestones are introduced in the iteration plan:

- **Iteration milestones**—To define internal milestones and team events.

- **Build and integration points**—To indicate when the various strands of work will be integrated. In the Construction phase, daily builds of the software (at the minimum) are recommended.

Defining Iteration Milestones

The positioning, number, and style of these milestones vary according to the phase that the project is in. There is a basic pattern, which is shown in Figure 8-3.

| | Iteration
Readiness
Assessment | | Code
Freeze | Iteration
Assessment |

Figure 8-3 *The basic pattern for an iteration*

In this pattern, an iteration readiness assessment is undertaken with the team to confirm that all members agree with the objectives, evaluation criteria, plans, and estimates created for the iteration. This is carried out at the beginning of the iteration.

There typically needs to be a *code freeze* somewhere toward the end of the iteration to ensure that all the work undertaken during the iteration can be integrated to produce, test, and assess a consolidated release. This is the point where the development of new functionality for the iteration ceases and the testing of the release as a whole starts. This leads to the final iteration milestone, where the iteration's results are assessed by performing the iteration assessment.

There are a number of more detailed internal iteration patterns that can help when planning iterations. These patterns vary according to the phase of the project the iteration occurs in. We look at these in detail in the next section.

Working in Parallel Within Iterations

One classic mistake when planning iterations is to treat them as mini-waterfalls with highly serialized work from different disciplines. We recommend working in parallel to get the most benefit from the iterative approach.

The different emphasis between the two approaches is illustrated by Figure 8-4, in which the concurrent approach exhibits a very large degree of parallelism between disciplines, whereas the mini-waterfall approach exhibits serialization between disciplines.

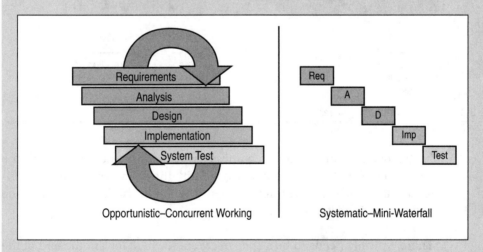

Figure 8-4 *Approaches to organizing work within the iteration*

The benefits of the concurrent approach include the following:

- More work occurs in parallel, so staff utilization is better.

- There is a feedback loop within the iteration, so errors in requirements and defects in code are found and fixed earlier.

- Parallel work requires more teamwork, which strengthens the team.

- The implementation, integration, and testing is continual and is not left until the end of the iteration where it would otherwise get squeezed-out.[11]

There are many problems inherent in adopting a waterfall approach to planning iterations, the most significant of which is the delaying of testing. If the iterations are treated as mini-waterfalls, the time box commonly ends without sufficient testing having taken place. The consequence of this is an ever-increasing test backlog and a false sense of progress: you may think that you've successfully implemented the requirements, but you won't know for sure until you test what you've built. The most common result of mini-waterfall thinking is the project having a series of iterations at the end dedicated purely to testing. The problem with this is that you may have gone off-course much earlier in the project and you won't know this until it's too late.

We feel that if you are not testing the results of an iteration within the iteration itself and considering these test results as part of the iteration assessment, then you are not really iterating.

Project managers new to iterative development have a tendency to over-plan the iterations. As with all the artifacts produced by an iterative project, the iteration plan only has to be good enough to record the decisions made, communicate the plans, and reduce the risk of the team members not doing the right things. A good indicator of the amount of planning required for an iteration is to consider the planning effort as a percentage of the total effort available for the iteration. If an iteration has 20 days of effort available, you should not be spending more than a day or two (5%–10%) planning and another day assessing. COCOMO II indicates that planning will

---

[11] Note that the time between the code freeze and the end of the iteration where the final release is tested as a whole should not be confused with the test period at the end of a mini-waterfall. Everything in the iteration release should have been tested by the time of the code freeze. The final short period of testing is just there to ensure that everything that has been done works together as a whole. We return to this subject when we look at the more detailed iteration planning patterns.

take around 14% of the project's entire effort; if you are spending more than this amount of time planning, you might be over-planning.

Agreeing Upon the Work Allocation

After the objectives, scope, and approach for the iteration have been agreed upon, the work needs to be assigned to the team members for completion. There are two basic approaches to achieving agreement upon work assignments within the team: assign work to the people or wait for people to volunteer. This has led to two dominant patterns for the planning and management of individual iterations, which we call "team-driven planning" and "top-down planning."

Team-Driven Planning

Team-driven planning is characterized by having the team members cooperate to develop the plan. It is characterized by the following behaviors:

- The team develops a prioritized list of tasks.

- Team members volunteer for tasks.

- Team members adjust estimates as they claim tasks.

- When team members complete a task, they take the next task off the task list and update actuals.

- The team leader keeps an eye on progress and productivity.

This approach is suitable for small, colocated teams, although it can be applied in distributed team settings when the team is experienced and a high degree of trust exists between team members. The approach is fairly disastrous when employed by inexperienced teams or teams that are unfamiliar with one another.

Top-Down Planning

The top-down planning approach is the more conventional approach in which a project manager assigns work to team members. It is characterized by the following behaviors:

- A project manager allocates tasks to team members.

- Estimation of task durations is provided by an expert rather than the person who will undertake the task.

- Iteration milestones and team events are used to synchronize and coordinate the work.

- Work breakdown structures are used to assign and track work.

- Formal work package definitions are used to allocate packages of tasks to particular resources.

This approach is more commonly employed on larger projects, where teams are more distributed or inexperienced. The top-down approach can be perceived to be "heavyweight," but if the team is inexperienced, then it is usually the only way that the project can move ahead.

Defining Units of Work

There are a number of different elements of the project that make good units for work allocation. When defining work units for the developers, there are two approaches that are particularly effective:

- **Grouping a set of related scenarios and supplementary requirements together into a unit of work**—This tends to be good for analysts because it provides a comprehensive view of part of the system. It is also quite useful for testers and assessment teams. It tends to work very well for developers working on small teams or teams working on systems to which a lot of new capabilities are being added.

- **Grouping requirements and changes assigned to specific packages and components together into a unit of work—** This tends to work well for systems whose architecture is mature and for those cases where the capabilities being added are easy to package along component or subsystem lines. This facilitates design, implementation, and unit testing and review at the subsystem or component level. It is also useful for addressing very specific defects that can be targeted to a specific subsystem or component. It is less useful in cases where the architecture is immature or where capabilities cross subsystems or components.

Packages and components are often "owned" by teams or individuals. Implementing a scenario or flow of events will often require the collaboration of many of the system's packages and components. Teamwork and shared ownership of the delivery of the requirements should be encouraged.

Agreeing Upon When Assessments Will Take Place

Iteration assessment is essential! It provides the feedback mechanism by which the team determines whether it is on track, and it enables the team to take any corrective action required to get back on track.

Iterative development is essentially a collaborative endeavor between the development team, the customers, and the project sponsors. To this end, the iteration assessment needs to involve representatives of all these stakeholder communities, including

- Stakeholders and users, who need to understand how the solution is progressing from a requirements and usability perspective

- Senior managers, who need to understand how the project is progressing with respect to overall budget and schedule

- All development team members, who need to understand the current state of the project and how the plans might need to be adjusted in subsequent iterations to deliver the right solution

Assessing an iteration includes the completion of several distinct activities:

- **Demonstrations of accomplishment**—Demonstrations of the results produced to ensure that the risks and objectives have been effectively addresses.

- **Retrospectives**—Open and honest discussions of what worked during the iteration and what needs improvement.

- **Acceptance reviews**—To determine whether the objectives and their evaluation criteria have been achieved and to assess the impact of the iteration's results on the higher-level evolution and overall project plans.

To involve all the appropriate stakeholders and cover all the assessment activities, a number of events might be required. For small teams with a small, integrated stakeholder community, a single event covering all aspects of the assessment might be appropriate. For larger teams or those with more complex stakeholder and team interactions, a number of separate events might be more applicable. Regardless of the approach adopted, the assessment events must be set up as part of the iteration planning at the beginning of the iteration to make sure that they happen and that the relevant people can attend.

We return to the subject of iteration assessment in more detail in Chapter 9.

Presenting the Detail as Part of the Iteration Plan

Highlights of the detailed plan will be presented as part of the iteration plan document. If the project is small, and a simple lightweight approach is adopted, then the entire detailed planning can be kept within the iteration plan in the form of a simple set of resource, task, and event tables. This is the format adopted by the outline iteration plan supplied in Appendix B, "Outlines, Templates, and Checklists."

If a more rigorous and detailed planning approach is required, then we recommend that you keep the detail in your preferred planning tool and just present a brief overview of the key dates, roles, responsibilities, events, and milestones in the iteration plan document itself.

Some people try to dispense with the iteration plan document and attempt to do all their planning within their chosen planning tool. In our experience, this is usually a mistake because the tools draw the plans away from time boxes and objectives toward the detailed planning of activities and dependencies. This is unfortunate because time boxing and objective setting are the indispensable planning activities for an iterative project.

Patterns for Iteration Planning

Because each phase addresses a different kind of risk, the iterations in each phase adopt differing approaches and styles.

Iterations in the Inception Phase

The work in the Inception phase can be thought of as proceeding along three parallel tracks: one dealing with the problem being solved, one dealing with solutions to the problem, and one dealing with managing the issues encountered on the project. Figure 8-5 shows how the Inception phase proceeds from an idea to a project strategy.

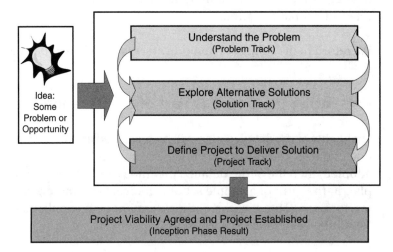

Figure 8-5   *Overview of Inception phase "tracks"*

The three tracks are aligned to the three distinct types of stakeholders affected by the project, last seen in Chapter 3, "Controlling Iterative Projects," when we considered the role of time boxes and the phases in controlling iterative projects:

- **Stakeholders of the problem**—People affected by the problem or who benefit from the solution.

- **Stakeholders of the solution**—People affected by the solution but who are not its principal beneficiaries (for example, those who have to support the solution).

- **Stakeholders of the project**—People engaged in project development who are not affected by either the solution or the problem but who are affected by how the solution is built.

Work in the Inception phase proceeds in parallel along the three tracks:

- The *problem* track, where the purpose is to **understand the problem**. This involves discovering the problem, understanding its symptoms and root causes, and describing the characteristics of a successful solution.

- The *solution* track, where the purpose is to **explore alternative solutions**. This runs parallel to the problem track to enable exploration of alternative potential solutions. As you identify and clarify possible solutions, you are often forced to ask more probing questions about the problem's root causes. These questions lead to a deeper understanding of the problem and point to new solutions.

- The *project* track, where the purpose is to **define the project to deliver the solution**. This involves evaluating the benefits and costs of potential solutions and determining what is required to deliver them. Eventually, a single solution is selected and the project is planned to deliver it.

As Figure 8-5 indicates, these tracks work mostly in parallel, occasionally interacting with each other. The problems to be solved affect the range of potential solutions, which in turn affect the way the project is organized to deliver the solution. Also, project organization and funding often constrain solution possibilities.

All Inception iterations will have objectives in each track, although the emphasis will vary dependent on the risks facing the project. The trick to planning Inception iterations is to derive iteration objectives that force the three tracks to converge and progress in synchronization with each other.

During the Inception phase, the project team is typically quite small, but the nature of the work required to address all three tracks typically leads to a much larger extended team being involved in the project. Identifying, coordinating, and managing the involvement of these external resources are some of the more significant challenges facing the management team when planning and executing the initial Inception iterations.

Iterations in the Elaboration Phase

The work in the Elaboration phase can be thought of as proceeding along the same three parallel tracks as the Inception phase. Figure 8-6 shows how the Elaboration phase proceeds from basic assumptions about the solution to a proven technical approach and a credible plan.

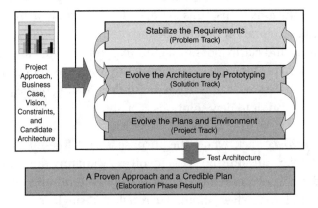

Figure 8-6 *Overview of Elaboration phase "tracks"*

Splitting the work into these three tracks helps to make the work performed in the phase more understandable. There is a tendency to equate the Elaboration phase with "Architecture," so considering the other tracks helps us to understand that a substantial amount of engagement with users and other stakeholders also needs to take place. In addition, conventional approaches tend to emphasize detailed planning early in the project, so emphasis on the "management" track helps to reinforce that the project plans still undergo considerable evolution in the Elaboration phase.

The overall result of the Elaboration phase is twofold. First, it defines the technical approach (the "architecture") to be used, and it proves that the architecture is appropriate. Second, based on this proven architecture, it produces a plan capable of delivering the solution. It might surprise some that a firm plan comes so late in the project (typically almost a third of way through the overall schedule). To this we pose a rhetorical question: if a plan is based on an unproven technical approach, is it credible?

Elaboration work proceeds in parallel along the three tracks:

- The ***problem*** track, where the purpose is to **stabilize the requirements**. This involves agreeing upon the extent of the requirements, settling "stylistic" issues—not detailed screen designs or UI specs, but issues relating to approach and consistency—and detailing those requirements that affect the choice of technical approaches. In the Inception phase, you will have drawn a sketch of the system capabilities, enough to understand the stakeholder needs and to confirm that the solution is worth building. This sketch is not enough to actually build the solution, however; more work is needed before you can determine the right technical approach. In the problem track, you focus on building an understanding of the full *range* of stakeholder needs.

- The ***solution*** track, where the purpose is to **evolve the architecture by prototyping**. This runs parallel to the problem track to define the architecture of the solution. The basic approach is to tackle the hard problems first, testing assertions about the candidate architecture and rejecting or modifying it as needed. There is a natural tendency to want to do easier things first, based on the assumption that in doing so you will gain experience and confidence. There are two problems with this approach: First, when you tackle the hard problems, you often find that the choices you have made already are wrong, invalidating much of the work already done. Second, it is easy to spend too long on the easy problems and run out of time to handle the hard problems. The reality is that in tackling the hard problems, the easy problems often look after themselves.

- The *project* track, where the purpose is to **evolve the plans and environment**. This focuses on elaborating the plans for the evolution and producing a reliable schedule. After the architecture is baselined, the rest of the project can be reliably planned and estimated. The reduction in technical risks enables estimates to be derived with greater accuracy so that now it is possible to produce a plan against which progress can be measured. Perhaps more importantly, it is now possible to scale up the project and work in parallel if necessary to meet the overall project delivery date.

As Figure 8-6 indicates, these tracks work mostly in parallel but frequently interact with each other. For example, the requirements to be stabilized first are those that will be prototyped to prove the architecture, and the first challenge in setting up the project environment is to provide the test environment to be able to prove the architecture.

All Elaboration iterations have objectives in each track, although the lead is typically taken by the solution track, where the architecture is assembled and proven. The trick to planning Elaboration iterations is to use the architectural prototyping to generate the information to reduce risk in the other tracks.

Many managers find the Elaboration phase the most difficult of the Unified Process phases to plan and execute because this is where the project addresses many of the most unpredictable and difficult risks. Because of this, the iterations need a few focused objectives, plenty of contingency, and a small, skillful technical team. This helps the team to execute the iterations successfully, and it builds team cohesion and morale. The focus must be kept clearly on aggressively tackling and reducing the risks by prototyping and experiment, not on slavishly completing long lists of artifacts.

Iterations in the Construction Phase

As you enter the Construction phase, the relevance of the three tracks diminishes as everybody lines up behind the development of production-quality releases of the software product. By this time, the problem is understood, the requirements are stable, and the architecture is proven and in place. There is still work to be done in all disciplines—requirements detail needs to be completed, architectural components need to be refactored, and plans need to be adjusted—but there is enough stability and robustness to the work completed that individual scenarios and components can be worked on individually, and the changes can be completed quickly enough that they can be integrated into regular (hopefully daily) builds that can be regression tested.

This leads to the overall iteration pattern shown in Figure 8-7, where the iteration is split up into four discrete chunks:

1. **Iteration Kick Off**—Where the risks are examined and the iteration plans agreed upon.

2. **Group Requirements and Analysis and Design**—Where the team gets together as a group to investigate and address any significant requirements or architectural issues and where the dependencies between the planned work items are examined.

3. **Frequent Regular Builds**—Where the individual requirements elements are taken, implemented, and integrated into builds and then independently tested. We revisit this section of the iteration when we examine the Construction cycle shown in Figure 8-8.

4. **Fix and Test**—Where, after the code freeze for the iteration has taken place, the final independent system testing of the complete release takes place. In response to this testing, any integration or high-priority defects are addressed before the iteration assessment takes place.

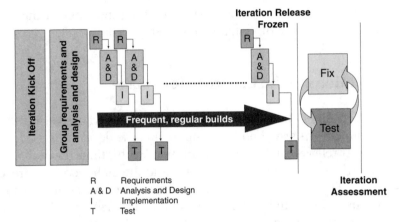

Figure 8-7   *A typical Construction iteration*

The majority of the iteration is spent in the productive middle section where the team is producing and testing the frequent, regular builds. Figure 8-8 drills down into this section in more detail to better illustrate the way that the disciplines interact with each other in a continuous cycle of construction and testing.

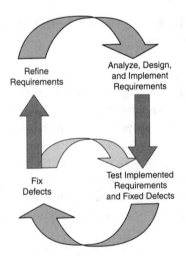

Figure 8-8   *The Construction cycle*

This cycle occurs daily, sometimes many times a day when fixing defects. Think of it as the "micro-cycle" of development. A set of requirements is selected, refined, and expanded. By the Construction phase, most of the requirements have been identified, but they usually lack some of the details that are needed to implement the solution. Use cases have been identified, including identification of all the alternative flows, but usually the flows lack full descriptions. That work needs to be completed now.

After the requirements are refined and detailed, they are analyzed, designed, and implemented. By the Construction phase, most parts of the system have been at least partially developed, so the work here is largely filling in the missing bits, extending existing code, adding new code to cover missing functionality, and refactoring the code to improve the architecture.

After being implemented, the requirements need to be tested. Developers will test their own work, and as the work of many developers is integrated, the results are typically tested by testing professionals. The result of the testing effort tends to be both verified requirements and identified defects. The defects are fed back into the code-fixing cycle.

As the developers finish one set of requirements, they select a new set of requirements for refinement and implementation.

This cycle continues until the code freeze for the iteration, where a final integrated build is produced and all the new requirements implemented in the iteration are given a final consolidated, integrated test to ensure that the release produced by the iteration is fit for purpose. The product of a Construction iteration should be a fully documented and fully tested production-quality release. To achieve this goal, some of the development work might need to be removed from the final build if it is incomplete or of insufficient quality.

If the team has been effectively system testing the code as it was initially integrated into the builds, then the final round of testing can be a simple case of assembling and running the new regression test suite, which is assembled by adding the new tests into the previous iteration's regression test suite.

If, as is sadly often the case, the Construction cycle has been applied in a more disconnected fashion, there might be a significant amount of independent system testing still to be done. It is essential that the test resources are factored into the plans and that the testing of the builds produced starts as early as possible. Regardless of the approach taken, there must be a code freeze to produce the iteration's formal release, and this release must be independently tested.

Iterations in the Transition Phase

Again, as we enter the Transition phase, we start to see the significance of the three tracks as they return to take a prominent role in the planning process. In this case, we have one track to deploy the product and gather feedback, one to maintain the quality of the solution, and one to hand over the project's responsibilities. Figure 8-9 shows how the Transition phase proceeds from the production of a deployable product to the completion of the project and the satisfaction of the project's stakeholders.

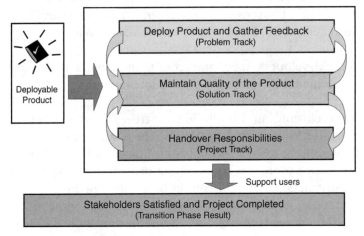

Figure 8-9   *Overview of Transition phase "tracks"*

Typically there are three tracks of work during the Transition phase:

- In the ***problem*** track, the team focuses on actively deploying the product, training users, supporting the deployment, and actively gathering feedback.

- In the ***solution*** track, the team focuses on responding to defect reports and change requests in an attempt to maintain the quality of the product.

- In the ***project*** track, the team leads focus on handing over the project's responsibilities, archiving the documentation, and shutting down the project.

All the tracks aim toward delivering stakeholder satisfaction and business benefit.

The end of the Construction phase marks the Initial Operational Capability (IOC) milestone. At this point, the solution becomes available for deployment. In the case of simple applications, this marks the beginning of a "beta test" period, which is followed by the publication of the General Availability version for download. For more complex and business-critical applications, there might be a lot more work to be done to successfully deploy the application, including training users and support staff in both system usage and new or changed business processes, data conversion, system migration, and the transition of the solution to a "production" environment, often at multiple sites.

The potential number and diversity of Transition activities is very high, which makes predicting the activities that will be required for your projects very hard. Some software development projects can deploy their software at the touch of a button through the Internet or their company intranet, whereas other projects might have to roll out new hardware or decommission existing systems. For example, Transition activities for the ACME Super ATM include

- Installation of ATMs in "parallel" environments to assess suitability to deploy

- Installation of ATMs at "live test locations" to assess suitability for wide-scale deployment

- Training of salespeople on new product capabilities

- Production of marketing materials (the preparation of these materials would have occurred earlier, in parallel with development activities in the Construction phase)

- Training of service and support staff in new ACME ATM capabilities

- Technician "boot camps" in which they experience real-world problems and gain certification

- Phased-in deployment of ATMs to "real world" locations, working closely with "early adopter" customers

- Monitoring of early deployments to enable fine-tuning of product roll-out

Now is not the time to let down your guard. If anything, precise attention to detail and the ability to successfully carry out a set of carefully planned Transition iterations is essential. All the effort put into the development of the software is wasted if it fails to be successfully deployed and used.

Using the Iteration Planning Patterns

As we have noted many times by now, the Construction phase is by far the most predictable phase of the development lifecycle. The patterns for this phase are much more mature and typically just involve selecting the correct requirement elements to be addressed, implemented, and tested. The priorities should be based upon the risks facing the project and the priority of requirements as determined by the customer and other users.

We have found that applying the three tracks (problem, solution, and project) in the other phases makes it much easier to come up with a balanced set of objectives to drive the iterations. Throughout the Inception, Elaboration, and Transition phases, we would expect all the iterations to have objectives in each track, and the relevant importance and weighting of each would be determined by analyzing the risks facing the project at the start of each iteration.

Executing the Iteration Plan

To conclude this chapter, we take a brief look at the role of the management team in the execution of the iteration plan. The management team and especially the iteration lead have a number of responsibilities during the execution of the iteration, including

- Planning the iteration

- Protecting the team from external influences and interference

- Leading the team and maintaining momentum

- Adjusting the plans to remove bottlenecks and other impediments to the team's success

- Monitoring and assessing the iteration and the performance of the team

As illustrated by Figure 8-10 and the various effort profiles shown throughout the book, the bulk of the management work is at the start and the end of the iteration, but there is plenty to do during the iteration itself.

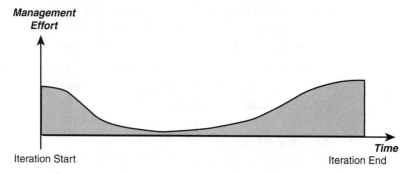

Figure 8-10   *The management effort profile for an iteration*

Planning the Iteration

The peak in effort at the beginning of the iteration represents the time the management team spends defining and agreeing upon the plans. This effort starts to tail off quickly after the iteration is underway.

Leading the Team

After the iteration objectives and their evaluation criteria have been agreed upon, the role of the management team is to lead the iteration. This involves doing whatever it takes to maximize the team's chances of success, including the following:

- **Helping the team to organize**—Many iterative development teams quickly become self-organizing, but often leadership is required to facilitate the effective organization of the team and to arbitrate when conflicts arise.

- **Removing obstacles**—The management team should do everything within its power to make sure there is nothing stopping the team from achieving the goals of the iteration.

- **Making decisions**—The success of the iteration often depends upon the team being able to build momentum and rapidly progress toward achieving the objectives. This requires decisions to be made efficiently and effectively. When teams are iterating quickly, the management must be able to make decisions quickly.

- **Balancing work**—The iteration lead needs to ensure that everyone in the team is playing his or her part and contributing effectively to the team's success. They must also make sure that individuals are not taking on too much and over-committing themselves and their teammates.

Protecting the Team

An important part of the manager's role during the execution of an iteration is to protect the development team from unnecessary interference and distractions. As Grady Booch observes,

> *Speaking of the individual developer, perhaps the most important thing that the management team can do is summarized in the following practice: Shield your developers from any and all distractions that keep them from their primary mission, namely, writing quality software.*[12]

Now of course the manager does other things that are important too, but this is an accurate reflection of the manager's role after the iteration is underway.

- Major changes of direction should be resisted during the iteration.

- The iteration handover point is the time to make major adjustments.

- Given the frequency of iterations, there is generally only two or three weeks to wait for items to be acted upon.

- The project manager and requirements manager are the external face of the team. The point where they interact with the team to steer the project should be the iteration boundary.

In other words, it is important for the team to finish the iteration and to leave the work in a stable state rather than risk constantly changing plans to try to adapt. The confusion and loss of confidence in the project direction and leadership can be considerable if the plan changes frequently during the iteration.

---

[12] Grady Booch, *Object Solutions* (Addison-Wesley, 1996).

Adjusting the Plans

As the iteration progresses, it is sometimes necessary to adjust the plans, if only slightly. Be prepared to fine-tune the scope of the iteration to keep the team focused:

- If the velocity is below that expected, make sure the lowest-priority tasks are deferred.

- If the velocity exceeds that expected, make sure the next highest-priority tasks are brought forward.

The iteration lead must be prepared to facilitate for the team: when bottlenecks appear, the leader must help the team to reorganize itself.

Typically the heartbeat of the project is such that most changes to plan can be left until the iteration assessment, but the management team must be prepared to make adjustments to help the project team to be successful. This can mean dynamically adjusting the iteration plans to react to unforeseen circumstances, such as the loss of a key project resource or the discovery of some unanticipated problem or risk.

Monitoring and Assessing the Iteration

If the iterations are longer than a week, some monitoring is required to ensure that tasks are being completed, to maintain estimates and actuals for the iteration, and to keep track of any unplanned work. On a daily basis, some focus is usually needed to keep the team on track and to adjust the daily work plan. These daily meetings tend to be short, ranging from a few minutes to a half hour, and they can be very useful for keeping a relatively small team on track for the daily work, especially when time is tight.

Because the daily work tends to vary in response to need, we strongly recommend that you not create detailed daily task plans. This is where trust and accountability come into play: *do* hold people accountable for results and hold them to milestones, but *do not* dictate the path they follow in achieving these results. Regular planning sessions can be used to dynamically adjust course as needed, but the results of these meetings are not changes to the plan of record (unless something really bad has occurred, but this should trigger a reassessment of the whole effort). If you find the plan of record changing on a daily basis, then it is likely that your plan is too fine-grained.

If the iterations are longer than the company's regular reporting schedule, then additional status assessments are required. If additional reports are required, try to produce them without interfering with the team's work on addressing the iteration's essential objectives.

The amount of management effort starts to rise as the iteration reaches its conclusion. This is due to the amount of work involved in assessing the current iteration and preparing the plans for the next iteration. Assessment is the subject of the next chapter, where we examine all aspects of iteration and phase assessments in more detail.

Summary

Iteration planning requires agreeing upon a target outcome for the iteration and then agreeing upon how the target will be achieved with the development team. The focus of an iteration should be small enough to achieve something measurable yet large enough to make progress toward overall goals.

Managing an iteration requires strong leadership to keep the team focused and remove any obstacles in their path. Perhaps more importantly, it requires patience and resolve to resist the temptation to re-plan every time something unexpected occurs. It also requires the management team to plan the iteration by specifying goals and then letting the team work out the right way to achieve these goals rather than by creating detailed task-level plans that become out of date almost as soon as they are created.

Iteration assessment is essential and must involve open and honest communication between all parties involved in the project. Along with this goes trust and accountability: trust the team to work out the best path but hold them accountable for results. By using this approach, teams are provided with the flexibility that they need to respond to change in a positive way.

Iteration, Phase, and Project Assessments

"Good judgment comes from experience, most of which comes from bad judgment."
—*Unknown*

By now you should understand that no plan is perfect, and every plan must be frequently adjusted to reflect new realities and risks. Assessment is the mechanism by which you take stock of where you are so that you can make course corrections to improve the chances that you will end up where you want to be. Assessments, at least in our context, are not undertaken to punish or blame but rather to learn and improve.

Assessment, of course, happens daily and informally on a moment-by-moment basis. Informal, personal assessment is important, but it is not enough when working with a team of people. People's perceptions differ. More importantly, because they differ, a problem that one person sees might not be seen by others, and this problem might have a large effect on the project's outcome. The inverse is also true; sometimes "problems" that people spend a lot of time worrying about turn out to be irrelevant. Part of the assessment process is the surfacing and dismissal of such non-issues.

Assessment is often seen as an "external" thing, coming from outside the project, often in the context of a compliance or capability assessment. It sometimes does, but the more valuable form of assessment is a team-driven self-assessment focused on improving capabilities. It is these kinds of assessments that are the focus of this chapter.

In this chapter we focus primarily on the more formal assessments performed at the boundaries and milestones of the project: the iteration and phase assessments. These provide natural points for reflection on performance to date, and they occur at points where the project is considering the planning of the next iteration, phase, or evolution.

We start with the iteration assessment because it is the most crucial assessment event for any iterative project. These are the inwardly focused assessment events that ensure that the team is iterating effectively and enable the results of the iteration to be put into the context of the overall project plans and action to be taken where necessary. Iteration assessment is so crucial to the well being of iterative projects that we do not consider a project to be iterating unless it is holding iteration assessments within the iteration time box for every iteration.[1] Iteration assessment enables the management team to "take the temperature" of the project and make small adjustments to its course to ensure smooth transition to the next iteration. The iteration assessments provide the oil that keeps the iterations rolling smoothly to the successful conclusion of the project.

The iterations take place within the phases of an evolution. If the iterations are successfully completed, the phase will be concluded with a more global, outward-looking phase assessment. This builds upon the results of the iteration assessments to make a go/no go decision about whether the project should proceed to the next phase. Phase assessments are more formal management events where project results are considered in the broader organizational context and validated against the project's business case and business drivers.

We conclude the chapter by looking at additional project assessments and why and when these might be needed.

---

[1]   We once came across an allegedly iterative project whose members were so pressed for time in their iterations that they kept postponing their iteration assessments in their enthusiasm to start the next iteration. Eventually they got around to running the iteration assessments for the first three iterations simultaneously in the middle of iteration four. Unsurprisingly, they found that they hadn't learned any of the lessons from the first iteration or taken any action to address the issues that they had encountered. In fact they found out that they hadn't really been iterating at all.

Assessing Iterations

The key to understanding the state of any iterative project is to assess the iterations themselves. The end of an iteration is the natural point to step back and see where you are and how things are going. This is essential to completing the plan for the next iteration, which is still just a set of tentative goals to accomplish. There is no way to develop the plan for the next iteration without assessing the current iteration.

The purpose of assessing the iteration is not purely to determine the success of the iteration itself; it also assesses the effectiveness of the process being followed, the dynamics of the team interactions, and the effectiveness of the overall project plan. Assessment is the key mechanism by which a team identifies problems soon enough to successfully correct its course. Without assessment, you are "flying blind" and cannot adapt to change.

The iteration assessment provides the opportunity for reflection on what is working as well as what is not working and needs improvement. This enables you to

- Re-plan the next iteration in light of what you have learned to date on the project

- Analyze project trends and their implications

- Reprioritize requirements and remaining work

- Reorganize the team

- Identify additional skills or experience that would help the team

- Identify rework required

- Adapt the process and working practices to solve specific problems

- Revise the estimates in light of what has happened

- Communicate openly and honestly about status and progress

- Reinforce and consolidate successful practices and ways of working

- Celebrate success

In short, the assessment gives you the data and forces the analysis needed to adapt your approach to the reality of where you are so that you can improve the probability that you will end up where you want to be. It also provides an opportunity to reward and celebrate the team's successes, building project momentum and team morale. Remember: *If you don't assess the current iteration, then you are not iterating.*

Assessing "In Flight"

Work and progress can start to be measured during the iteration itself. This continuous assessment gives you an idea how things are going and where corrective action is needed. There are a couple sources of data for this "daily health check"—data from the configuration management system, data from builds and unit testing, and subjective measures of attitude and morale. Useful things to look at include the following:

- **Progress on completing and testing scenarios**—Every iteration implements and tests a number of scenarios. It is unlikely that these will all be simultaneously completed at the end of the iteration. Although it might not make sense to impose strict intermediate milestones, you should still be able to get a sense for how each scenario is coming along. Talk to the development team every couple days and ask how things are going. As the work progresses, ask to see the prototypes. Don't turn these into formal reviews[2]—keep them informal and low-ceremony—but make sure to keep an eye on progress, or you might be surprised at the end of the iteration.

  A key issue to watch out for is whether the scenarios and prototypes being produced are actually testing the risk areas of the project called out in the iteration plan. If they are not, then you must find out why and redirect the team to focus on aggressive risk reduction and the iteration's essential objectives.

---

[2] Some managers like to have a more rigorous reporting mechanism with regular daily or weekly team meetings. The trick is to make sure that these additional meetings are kept lightweight and informal. One trick is to make these meetings "stand-up" meetings where no one is allowed to sit down and relax. This tends to keep the meeting focused and to the point. If the team is communicating effectively, then the need for endless formal team meetings should be reduced. Be warned: if you start with a lot of meetings, you will have a hard time getting rid of them.

- **General morale**—Assessing morale requires subtlety and indirect observation. Listen to the conversations for signs of enthusiasm or discouragement. Read body language and facial expressions. If you are close to the team, you probably have a sense for how people are feeling. If you are not close enough to the team member to read their attitudes, count that as a problem—you are disconnected from what is going on. If people don't feel that they can communicate openly with you, you have a problem to overcome and must use the iteration planning and assessment process to build trust and openness between the management and development teams.

  Also keep an eye on who is working overtime and understand why. If the team is running behind schedule, the overtime will start to creep up. You should make it a point to stay late sometimes just to see who is working late and why. We call this "assessing by walking around late"—it tells you a lot about what is really going on.

  If you have a good relationship with the team, you can have open, informal conversations with them about what is going on and what they think should be done about it. Most people are not shy about sharing their opinions, provided that an environment of trust exists.

- **Defect discovery and find/fix rates**—You should expect a lot of defects in the early phases of the evolution, but after the architecture is stabilized, you should see a pattern to defect discovery: new capabilities are introduced, causing defects to spike initially and then taper off as the functionality stabilizes and the defects are fixed. If defects start spiking and not leveling off, something might have happened to destabilize the architecture.

  The find/fix rate is also instructive: it shows the difference between the defect find rate and the defect fix rate. Early in the project, there will be a positive gap: defects are being found faster than they are being fixed. Later, the find/fix rate should be somewhat in equilibrium, and late in the project, the rate should be negative as fewer defects are found relative to the number fixed. A positive find/fix ratio is a bad thing late in the project because it means that you are not getting closer to delivering a successful solution.

A low defect discovery rate might not be a good thing, however; it might simply mean that you are not testing enough. Make sure that the capabilities being introduced are being tested and that you are not falling behind in your testing efforts.[3] When this becomes the case, you have no alternative but to either increase the testing rate or reduce the amount of functionality being developed. The most frequent way of doing this is to shift developers to testing until you catch up with the testing effort.

- **Relative rates of change of components**—Drawing on data from the configuration management system, you should examine the relative rates of component change. What you are looking for are any components that are changing a lot *when you would not expect them to be changing based on where you are in the project.* A key architectural quality is the localization of change. If you can't predict which components will be changed in response to a specific set of requirements or defects, then this is an indication that the architecture is not well understood and under control.

  In the Inception and Elaboration phases, components will change a lot, so this measure is of less value before the start of the Construction phase. In the last two phases of the evolution, you would not expect the core components and interfaces to change to any significant extent. In any phase, components that change several times more frequently than their peer components could signal instability in that part of the system. You should use this information to find out more about what is going on.

These measures help you to fine-tune the day-to-day execution of the project team and to reduce the number of surprises that are discovered at

---

[3] Also beware of its companion problem: testing that is "too friendly." Tests that are easily passed and that pad the statistics are rarely of much use.

the time the iteration is assessed.[4] You should resist the temptation to micro-manage the iteration and to continuously fiddle with the plans and the direction given to the team. The iteration boundary is the time to reflect on the results of the iteration and to undertake any major adjustments to the plans or to the team's working practices.

The Assessment Process

Iterations provide empirical evidence upon which the team can act. During the iteration, data and observations are recorded, so there are results from daily (or more frequent) builds, data that can be obtained from the change management system such as rates of change for components and numbers of defects and change requests, the results of the ongoing unit, integration, and system testing, and the experiences and observations of the development team. Risks and issues are documented as they arise. Automation can reduce the cost of collecting this data, but however it is captured, you should have some basic measures of project effort and results. This data serves as input to the assessment effort. Figure 9-1 shows the basic pattern for iteration assessment.

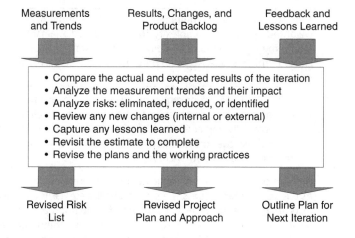

Figure 9-1 *The iteration assessment process*

---

[4] There are many other measures that you might find useful in managing your team (such as the ratio of planned to unplanned work, time spent on the project, cost, and so on), but you need to make sure that all measures collected are useful to the team and provide a level of benefit commensurate with the effort required to collect them.

Iteration assessments are based on a combination of subjective and objective measurements. Examples of these are summarized in Table 9-1 and Table 9-2.

Table 9-1 *Subjective Measurements*

Measure	Description
Lessons Learned	Lessons learned from the extended development team.
Customer Satisfaction	Feedback from stakeholders regarding their satisfaction with the project and progress to date.
Morale	Attitudes including morale, commitment, and confidence.
Risk Exposure	Risk exposure derived from the impact and probability of the identified risks. To be compared against acceptable levels of risk for the phase of the project.
Estimate to Complete	The estimate of the effort required to complete the delivery of the currently expected scope.

Table 9-2 *Objective Measurements*

Measure	Description
Absolute Progress	The actual number of requirements successfully implemented and tested—weighted by size and complexity. To be compared against the volume of requirements expected to be delivered at the start of the project and the current project scope. Absolute progress should increase over the duration of the iteration.
Relative Progress	The percentage of in-scope requirements that have been implemented and tested. To be compared (as a percentage) to the number of requirements expected to be successfully implemented (those currently in-scope). Relative progress should increase over the duration of the iteration. This should take the form of the classic code growth S-curve.
Breakage	Number of tests failed during the iteration's regression and system testing. As you can probably guess, more breakage is bad; less is good as long as the tests are representative. Be wary of tests that do not measure meaningful results because they could lead you to believe that things are better than they are. Toward the end of Elaboration and during Construction, the level of breakage for each iteration should be decreasing. If it isn't, then the project has some systemic quality problems.

Measure	Description
Scope Change	The mass of requirements currently in-scope. To be compared against the originally estimated volume of requirements and the total volume of identified requirements. Some scope change is expected, but large amounts of scope change indicate that something in the business environment might have changed, or it could be a sign that the original requirements were not the right ones. The trends for scope change are unpredictable, but the scope should be stable by the end of the Elaboration phase.
Effort Expended	Actual effort expended in each iteration. To be compared to the expected effort for the iteration. A useful indicator of planning accuracy, but don't fall into the trap of assuming that the plans were perfect so any deviation is due to poor execution. Estimates are usually somewhat wrong because people's ability to foresee the future is imperfect. If the amount of effort expended is continually falling short of that estimated for the iterations, then the project has little chance of completing on time.
Effort Profile	The proportion of the effort expended on each discipline in each iteration. To be compared against the standard Unified Process effort profile and the COCOMO effort distribution figures.
Overall Defect Trends	The overall number of open defects weighted by priority and the number of defects open, closed, and fixed in each iteration. To be compared with project quality tolerances. The number of defects tends to rise early in the project and should taper off toward its end. If defect levels do not taper off and defects are always carried forward from iteration to iteration, something is wrong: the architecture could be unstable, or the team might not really be working iteratively and might be more or less ignoring the test results. Some defect carryover from iteration to iteration is expected, but when it becomes the norm, it is a sign that the project is in trouble, and you need to stop all new work until you figure out what is wrong.
Find/Fix Rate	Defect find/fix rates—the ratio between the number of defects found and the number of defects fixed in each iteration. Used to track whether defects are being fixed as fast as they are found. A large difference between the find and fix rates also indicates that the architecture might be unstable or the project is in trouble (typically because it is implementing too much new functionality before the functionality already implemented is working).
Defect Density	The ratio of defects to the amount of code produced. Useful for tracking the overall quality level of the application.

Table 9-2 *Objective Measurements*   *(Continued)*

Measure	Description
Risk Discovery / Mitigation Rate	The ratio of new risks identified to risks retired during the iteration. This provides an indication of the validity of the published risk exposure. An increasing level of risk over the course of several iterations usually means that you did not understand risks very well to begin with. You need to look at this to decide whether you have a better understanding of risk now so that the discovery rate will come down in the future. You also need to make sure that the work you are doing in the iterations is directly addressing risk; if it is, you should be seeing *some* risks retired even though the overall number of risks might be increasing. Risk discovery is also phase-specific: you should expect a lot of new business risks in the Inception phase but not in later phases. Similarly, you should expect a lot of new architectural risks in the Elaboration phase but not in later phases.
Cost Profile	The costs incurred. The total cost of the iteration to date and the cost of each completed iteration. To be compared against the expected cost profile of the project.
Rework Trends	The amount of rework performed in each iteration as a percentage of the total effort. To be compared against the acceptable levels of rework for the phase of the project. You should see rework declining toward the end of the Elaboration phase as the work is stabilized. The rework in the Construction phase should be less than 25% of the total work. Excessive rework can often indicate an unstable architecture.
Estimate Accuracy	A comparison of actuals and estimates for each iteration calculated as the average margin of error for the iteration estimates. Useful for tracking the accuracy of the estimation and planning process. Estimation accuracy should increase as the project progresses.
Unplanned Work	The percentage of the effort in an iteration that was consumed undertaking unplanned work. To be compared against the contingency set aside for unplanned work in the iteration plan. Expect there to be more unplanned work in the early iterations of the project. The amount of unplanned work should be less than 10% after you enter the Construction phase.

For most of the project, it is more important to look at relative trends in each area than to focus on the absolute measures. As we discussed in Chapter 2, "How Do Iterative Projects Function?" and Chapter 3, "Controlling Iterative Projects," there are standard patterns for many of these measures across the phases of the process. By comparing project performance against these models, you can tell when the project is starting to run into problems, and you can extrapolate from the current position to predict where the project will end up if things continue as they are. By examining the trends, you can also spot "blips" in the project's performance, such as when the product quality suddenly decreases or the productivity of the team drops. By analyzing the other measures, you can often find the reason for the poor performance and decide whether any corrective action is required.

In the Transition phase, the focus on absolute measures becomes more dominant, so early in the evolution lifecycle, there is more of a focus on trends, and later in the evolution, there is a focus on absolutes.

To be effective and worthwhile, iteration assessments must be

- Objective and impersonal, backed up by facts and not *just* opinion (this is why measurement is so important to the management of iterative projects)

- Open, and conducted in a manner in which the sole goal is improvement

- Blame-free, with a singular focus on improvement rather than laying blame

- Honest, with a willingness to be self-critical

- Independent, so that at least some of the perspectives are provided by parties outside the project

- 360 degrees, that is to say performed from a number of different perspectives

These are difficult to achieve, and perhaps the hardest but most important thing to achieve is an open and blame-free environment with an honest focus on improvement rather than judging guilt. The social dynamics of a project in trouble often foster a culture of accusation and denial in which systemic problems are blamed on individual performance. It takes a great deal of skill to change this culture, but an insistence on ensuring that assessments focus on facts and not just opinions[5] is essential.

---

[5] We emphasize this because the emotional impact can never be ignored. Feelings are important, but ultimately you will need to support opinions with hard data so that you can improve.

The result of the iteration assessment is

- A statement of the level of success achieved by the iteration in meeting its objectives

- A revised risk list and estimate to complete

- Agreement on the objectives for and approach to be taken to the next iteration

And where necessary

- Reprioritization of the requirements and adjustments to the project scope

- The identification of areas of the solution to be refactored and reworked

- Actions to revise the project approach to address and reflect the lessons learned during the iteration

- Actions to revise the evolution development plan to reflect the actual performance of the project

This is all recorded in an iteration assessment document, an outline of which is provided in Appendix B, "Outlines, Templates, and Checklists."

Assessing from Different Perspectives

To achieve a rounded assessment of the iteration and its impact upon the project as a whole, an iteration assessment typically has three aspects:

- An internal assessment of the team's performance and working practices in the form of a retrospective

- External demonstrations of the products built and the capabilities implemented during the iteration

- An iteration acceptance review to formally "grade" and close out the iteration

You might find it odd that these three perspectives are only applied at the iteration level and are not repeated for the phase and project assessments. This is because the retrospectives and demonstrations carried out at the iteration level remove the need to repeat these kinds of events at the development project and overall project levels. The assessments at the higher levels are typically more formal management reviews and decision-making forums. This is not to say that these techniques are not useful at these levels, just that they are not mandatory. If you feel that a phase assessment would benefit from a demonstration to show those present the progress that has been made, then go for it, but generally it would be better to have invited these people to the iteration demonstration rather than extending the phase assessment.

Internal, Driven by Retrospective

At the end of the iteration, gather the team together to elicit their perspectives on what is working and what is not. This is usually best conducted as a facilitated session. Be careful to capture all perspectives and enable everyone to participate.

Creating an environment in which "facts are friendly" is important—don't let it degenerate into a finger-pointing exercise. Instead, focus on clarifying opinions with supporting data and identifying the root causes, rather than the symptoms, of the problems. Especially, don't let the discussions become personal; focus the discussions on identifying areas in which things are going well and those that need to be improved. Areas to probe include

- Architectural stability
- Quality
- Functionality
- Progress
- Process
- Working practices
- Environment

This feedback session should be short if you have kept up on the issues throughout the iteration; a couple hours is enough to identify the key issues. Briefly summarize the results and make sure that all participants are comfortable with the characterization of the issue; this is easier if you can stick to the facts. Consensus is important because a team split by major divisions will not be successful.

Retrospectives can be particularly powerful in spotting those areas of the project where teamwork and communications are not functioning as intended. For example, one project we reviewed was struggling to get to grips with use-case driven iterative development, especially the apparent lack of a functional specification for the developers to work from. The subject matter experts were writing the use cases, expecting them to be picked up and used to drive the development. Unfortunately, the developers were expecting to be supplied with formal interface specifications and were waiting for these to be produced from the use cases before starting any prototyping or development work. By bringing the whole team together to discuss what was and was not working in the project, this issue very quickly came to light, and a solution (which consisted of the subject matter experts and the developers working together to analyze the use cases) was volunteered by the team. Without the open and honest discussion fostered by the retrospective, they would have continued to blame each other for the lack of progress on the project, and the team would have become more and more divided and dysfunctional instead of the team members working together to address their shared problems.

External, Driven by Demonstration

Because each iteration will (or should) produce an executable release, you have the opportunity to engage users, obtaining feedback on how well the partially developed solution meets their needs. These reviews should involve direct users of the system as well as executive sponsors, all of whom will want to see how things are going. The external reviews should be structured around the scenarios for the iteration and should at least consist of a walkthrough of each scenario. If the solution is mature enough, you should actually let the users work on the system itself. Use as many sessions as needed to cover all the scenarios.

The nature of the demonstration should be driven by the objectives of the iteration and the nature of the risks being addressed. If there are concerns about the usability of the system, then inviting some users to come in and play with it in a controlled environment can provide very valuable feedback. If quality is becoming an issue later in the project lifecycle, then letting everybody loose on the system to undertake a "bug hunt" can illuminate lots of interesting and unusual quality issues.

Note:

In addition to these walkthroughs and usability exercises, formal testing of each scenario will be undertaken as a standard part of the iteration.

The demonstrations do more than just demonstrate the progress of the development to the stakeholders. They also

- Clarify the team's understanding of the requirements

- Generate discussions and surface misconceptions

- Check assumptions

- Build confidence in the team's ability to deliver

- Demonstrate that the risks are being addressed

- Demonstrate to everybody involved in the project that the solution is being developed iteratively

Demonstrations are particularly effective in bringing the entire development team together, convincing them of the benefits of iterative development, and building confidence in the team's ability to work together to deliver an effective solution. For example, one project that we were brought in to assess had been really struggling to build any momentum, continually writing and rewriting their use case and analysis models in an attempt to get grips with a complex problem domain. Analysis paralysis had started to set in, and the entire extended team (including all the developers and stakeholders) was becoming demoralized, disenchanted, and doubtful of the team's ability to deliver. For the next iteration, some of the primary scenarios were selected and a basic prototype produced that demonstrated some of the key characteristics of the proposed solution. The effects of the demonstrations were quite astounding; you could physically see the confidence growing within both the development team and the stakeholders. The emphasis of the conversations turned from being about why the project was difficult and couldn't be done to being about what could be done and by when. The discussions about requirements changed from being about whether they had captured all the requirements to being about whether the requirements were really needed and what they really meant to the business and the development of the solution.

There is an inclination in many iterative projects to not do sufficient prototyping in the early iterations, particularly in the Inception phase. This can lead teams to become demoralized and to suffer from "analysis paralysis" without ever getting to the heart of the problems facing the development team. Actually building something is a great antidote to this problem, which is why teams need to be writing code even in the earliest iterations of the project.

Acceptance, Driven by Iteration Objectives

Finally, you must make sure to review the iteration results with representatives of the various external stakeholders who have control over project funding or resources, such as a project review board, the program office, or the business sponsor. This is done to make sure that your funding and organizational support continues unencumbered. Nothing builds support like actual results.

These formal iteration acceptance reviews are the key to establishing management control of the iterations. They are the forum where the wider impacts of the iteration are put into perspective and decisions about what to do next are made. The iteration acceptance reviews are where the final status of the iteration and the evolution are agreed upon and recorded. They replace the need for the project to perform regular status assessments and produce the accompanying management reports. This means that the iteration assessment must be documented and the resulting documentation circulated to the stakeholders.

Without the more management-focused iteration acceptance reviews, the project can appear to be just rolling along with the occasional retrospective and demonstration. It is the iteration acceptance review that formally closes and documents the closure of the iteration. It is also the primary decision-making forum for any changes in the structure, direction, scope, or working practices for the project.

The iteration acceptance reviews are particularly effective in integrating the iterative project into the broader management structures of the overall project, program, and owning organization. They are the main event where the layers of our iterative management approach are brought together and given the opportunity to explicitly get involved in directing and assuring the project. In one organization we advised, there were a number of iterative projects that, to the senior managers, appeared to be directionless and running out of control. The projects were actually iterating quite successfully but were very private and inward-looking in their iteration assessments. They were not formally closing out their iterations, sharing the results of their measurements, or communicating effectively with any of the more senior managers in their particular program. This lack of visible monitoring and control mechanisms was threatening the future of the use of iterative techniques within the organization. By introducing the use of lightweight, focused, forward-looking development plans and formally documented iteration assessments, the disconnect between the iterative projects and the senior management was successfully addressed. In fact, the iterative projects started to be held up as exemplars of well controlled, responsive, collaborative, modern software development practices by the very people who had previously wanted to cancel them and revert back to waterfall development.

Planning the Iteration Assessment

In the last chapter we highlighted the importance of planning the iteration assessment as an integral part of the iteration plan. It is important that the correct people are involved in the assessment and that the assessment events are managed in a coordinated way. Although there are three important aspects to the assessment, the number and timing of the events can vary:

- For a small team, a single event covering all three aspects might be sufficient.

- For a larger team, separate events might be required.

In some cases, more than three events will be needed, especially if there is a large stakeholder community or many different aspects of the solution to demonstrate.

The most common pattern is to have a number of coordinated activities and events:

- One or more demonstrations to the various members of the stakeholder community

- An informal retrospective with the team

- A draft of an initial iteration assessment based on feedback and results

- A more formal iteration acceptance review with the key project stakeholders

- A revised iteration assessment to reflect the results of the iteration acceptance review

To help facilitate the planning of the iteration assessment, a project review table, as shown in Table 9-3 and included in the development plan template in Appendix B, can be useful.

Table 9-3   *Example Iteration Review Authorities*

	Overall Project Manager	Development Manager	Sponsor	Customer	User	Iteration Lead	Requirement Manager	Architect	QA Manager	Development Team	Anyone Else You Like
Iteration Acceptance Review (External)	Y	L	Y	Y	Opt	Y	Opt	Opt	Y	As required	Opt
Iteration Assessment— Demonstration (External)	Y	Y	Opt	Opt	Y	Y	L	Opt	Opt	As required	Opt
Iteration Assessment— Retrospective (Internal)	Y	Y	N	Opt	Opt	Y	Y	L	Y	Y	Opt

(L = Lead, Y = Yes, N = No, Opt = Optional)

This is a more detailed version of the summary chart we saw in Chapter 5, "A Layered Approach to Planning and Managing Iterative Projects."

Concluding an Iteration

The iteration is concluded by the iteration acceptance review, where the formal result of the iteration is agreed upon and recorded. This involves considering the results of the iteration and analyzing their impact on the project as a whole.

Measurement and Analysis

Measurements have a significant part to play in the overall assessment of the iteration and especially in assessing its impact on the project as whole. To help the assessors to understand how the project is progressing, the project measurements can be sampled on an iteration-by-iteration basis and then compared to the expected profiles. Figure 9-2 shows the expected trends (and some tolerance levels) for some of the key measures that we discussed in Chapter 2, "How Do Iterative Projects Function?" and presented in Table 9-1 and Table 9-2 earlier. Here we show the expected trends for a project with a fixed size team undertaking a nine-iteration project.

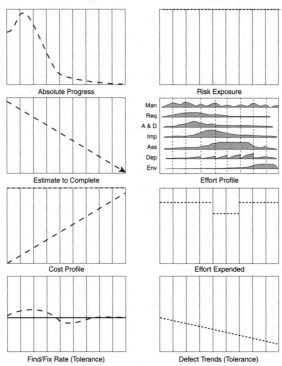

Figure 9-2 *Expected trends and tolerances for a selection of key metrics*

The trends shown include the following:

- **Absolute Progress**—As iterations are completed, progress is made. The absolute progress chart shows that the iterations produce measurable results, resulting in some set of scenarios being implemented and tested although significantly "stubbed out" in the early iterations. The dashed line at the top of the graph represents the mass requirements the project is expected to deliver.

- **Risk Exposure**—Risk exposure initially increases as more data becomes available, but within an iteration or two, it should decline as steps are taken to mitigate risk. Because many risks are driven by *unknowns*, the gathering of information in the course of the iteration reduces the risks related to the unknown, and the direct confrontation of risks in the course of the iteration further reduces the risks.

- **Estimate to Complete**—The inherent uncertainty of any initial estimate produced at the beginning of the project means that it potentially has a large error factor. This uncertainty should decline over the course of the project for a couple of reasons—first, there is less effort to estimate as the project progresses, and second, there is more information available on which to base the estimates. By tracking the current estimate to complete and comparing it with effort remaining available to the project, you can compare the expected completion date for the project with the dates to which you have committed. Because the team is of fixed size, the (possibly naive) expectation here is that the estimate to complete will be reduced by an equal amount during each iteration.

- **Effort Profile**—The composition of effort varies over time. Early on, it is more biased toward requirements, analysis, and architectural activities. Over time it shifts toward implementation and test activities. Keep in mind that there will still be some requirements work late in the evolution, and there will still be some testing early in the evolution.

- **Cost Profile**—Because the project has a fixed-size team, the project has (possibly naively) assumed a regular cost profile, with the costs increasing by the same amount each iteration. Because the only costs for this particular project are the wages of the staff, which need to be paid regardless of whether the staff is working or on holiday, this is probably a fair assumption. The dashed line at the top of the graph represents the project's spending cap and shows that the team members have some contingency available in case overtime is required.

- **Effort Expended**—The dashed lines show the expected level of effort predicted for each iteration. This doesn't really show a trend as such but does capture the initial project estimates for effort across the lifecycle. Iterations 5 and 6 show less effort available because in this example they cover the Christmas and New Year period.

- **Find/Fix Rate (Tolerance)**—There is no predictable trend for a project's find/fix ratio, but tolerances can be set. In this case, the dashed line shows the maximum acceptable find/fix ratio. This graph shows that it is acceptable to find more defects than are fixed in the early iterations but that after iteration number 4, the team must be fixing more defects than they find.

- **Defect Trends (Tolerance)**—Again, there is no predictable defect trend for a project. Ideally we would like there to be no defects at all. Tolerances can be set for the level of defects that are acceptable throughout the project, with the most important tolerance being the final acceptable level of defects when the product is released. In this case, a very low level of defects is acceptable at the end of the project.

As you can see from Tables 9-1 and 9-2, there are many other metrics that you might find useful in controlling your iterative projects. We present this set in more detail here because these are eight of the most common measurements used for understanding the relative progress being made by an iterative project and are typically those with which iterative projects start their measurement program.

Figure 9-3 shows some of the graphs at the end of the fourth iteration of an actual project. This was when the project hoped to conclude the Elaboration phase.

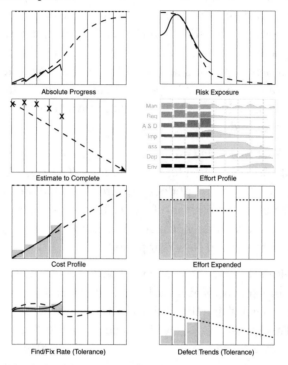

Figure 9-3   *Actual progress after four iterations*

The graphs show some significant deviations from the expected results and project tolerances. It is quite clear that if the project continues as it is currently progressing, there will be either a significant shortfall in the amount and quality of the functionality delivered or a significant overrun in the project's schedule and cost. To deliver on time, some corrective action is required. In this case, the project team decides to de-scope the requirements to be delivered, which in turn eliminates some of the outstanding risk facing the project. This also removes the need for one of the more problematic and low-quality components, thereby reducing the number of outstanding defects. After de-scoping, the project concludes with the profiles shown in Figure 9-4.

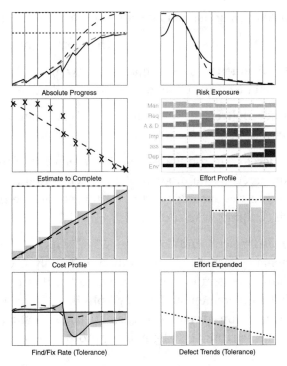

Figure 9-4   *Actual progress across a nine-iteration project*

In this case, the project concludes on time with a minor shortfall in the scope agreed upon at the end of the fourth iteration (the end of the project's Elaboration phase).

Conducting the Iteration Acceptance Review and Recording the Results of the Iteration

It is generally considered best practice to record the results of the iteration in a formal iteration assessment document. This is prepared before the formal iteration acceptance assessment meeting and is used to record the decisions made at the assessment.

The iteration acceptance review covers all the aspects of the iteration assessment:

- **Results**—Discuss how well the iteration did in meeting its objectives.

- **Risks**—A summary of how the iteration affected the risks.

- **Objectives**—A summary of which objectives have been met.

- **Requirements**—A summary of how many of the target requirements were implemented and passed testing.

- **Other Deliverables**—A summary of the state of the other deliverables.

- **Adherence to the Plan**—How the execution of the iteration compared to the original plan. Special attention should be paid to the accuracy of the estimates and the priorities in which things were addressed.

- **Measurement and Analysis**—Highlights of the measurements collected for the iteration and analysis of the trends across the iterations undertaken so far. It is recommended that measurement and trend graphs be collected for the eight key measures discussed earlier. The analysis should examine the measurements in light of any project tolerances that have been set.

- **Feedback from the Demonstration**—Capture the impressions gained from any demonstrations. Analyze any change requests that participants raised.

- **External Changes**—Describe any external changes that have happened during the iteration and that threaten to affect the project or its ability to deliver.

- **Lessons Learned**—Capture any lessons learned during the iteration and capture actions to address them.

- **Rework Required**—Based on the iteration's success, the measurement trends, the external changes, and the lessons learned, describe any rework that is required.

This format acts as an agenda for the iteration acceptance review and as the iteration assessment document used to capture the results of the assessment. An outline for an iteration assessment document is provided in Appendix B along with an iteration assessment checklist that can help you in preparing for and running an iteration assessment.

The structure of the iteration assessment document mirrors the structure of the iteration plan. The simplest way to populate the iteration assessment is to clone the key elements of the iteration plan and add information to summarize the actual results of the iteration.

The iteration assessment results in one of the following "grades":

- **Exceptional**—The iteration achieved results well beyond expectations, and the project is in exceptionally good shape to move forward.

- **Passed**—The iteration results were within acceptable ranges of expectations, and the project is on track.

- **Passed at risk**—The iteration did not quite meet expectations but is within acceptable reach of them; for example, all but one or two of the essential objectives were completed, and significant progress was made on the ones that were incomplete. Some adjustments need to be made in the next iteration to get the project back on track.

- **Unfinished**—The iteration fell short of meeting expectations (for example, many of the essential objectives were not completed), but the team has been doing the right things in the right way and would have been successful if they had had more time or more resources. The adjustments required to the development plans to get the project back on track are minor and within the project tolerances.

- **Failed**—The iteration failed to meet its objectives, and significant corrective action is required to get the project back on track. Major adjustments need to be made to the development plans and the project approach.

- **Abandoned**—The iteration failed to meet its objectives in very significant ways, significantly enough that the project or the approach has been determined to be infeasible. This is usually because the selected approach has been determined to be technically or economically infeasible.

If the iteration was *Unfinished, Failed,* or *Abandoned,* a recommendation about the continuation of the project must be made. For example, one of the following recommendations might be applicable:

- **Re-plan**—The project should be continued but requires major re-planning if it is to be successful.

- **De-scope**—The project should be continued, but significant numbers of requirements need to be de-scoped to enable the project to meet its other commitments.

- **Extend**—The project should be continued, but additional time and iterations are required to enable it to fulfill its commitments.

- **Try again**—The project should be continued, but the iteration should be attempted again with a different technology or approach.

- **Cancel**—The project should be cancelled.

It is impossible to provide a definitive list of all the possible actions that can result from the assessment of an unsuccessful iteration. A lot depends on the reasons for the failure and the relative importance of the project to the organization.

Common Iteration Problems

We have seen many problems that affect projects and teams new to iterating. To help you avoid them, it is worth looking at some of the most common:

- **Using iterative terms but "conventional" practices**—This usually manifests itself by having iteration goals such as producing a requirements specification or producing a design. Remember that we want to actually build and test something in each iteration. If the team fails to develop and test the scenarios selected for the iteration, you should make sure that they are not stuck in a "conventional" waterfall mindset. Evidence of this would include only applying one discipline per iteration or a belief that the system as a whole needs to be designed before implementation can begin. A potential solution to the second problem is to develop "stubs"[6] for parts of the system that are not immediately needed, enabling the other parts of the system to be executed and tested.

- **Gold plating**—Iterative development is about judgment; to enable the project to progress, the team has to be able to decide when artifacts are good enough to address the current risks and support the commencement of downstream activities. For example, a lot of project risk can be addressed by producing prototypes based on a simple outline of the requirements—in other words, the requirements do not have to be complete or perfect before they can be used to drive analysis, design, implementation, and test activities. The same holds true for the architecture and design. Many teams accustomed to working in a waterfall environment find this a very hard mindset to adopt; they have been conditioned to working in a way in which every aspect of one task is completed before the next task is started, and little judgment of the suitability of the artifacts produced is required as long as every last detail is completed. This problem typically manifests itself in an inability to make decisions and complete objectives without obsessively analyzing every possible aspect of the solution and documenting it to the minutest levels of detail.

- **Insufficient testing of those scenarios developed**—The most common problem that we see with project teams attempting to do iterative development is a reticence to give testing the visibility and emphasis that it deserves. It is very common to find a team reaching the end of an iteration having developed all the identified scenarios but failed to test any of them. Remember that the scenario does not count as complete until it has been tested. As the project manager, you should make sure that scenario testing is an integral part of the iteration's objectives and evaluation criteria, ensuring that the iteration

---

[6] Partial implementations of parts of the system that are not critical to addressing the risks targeted for the current iteration.

cannot be seen as a success unless appropriate levels of testing have been successfully completed. The only real solutions to this are 1) to enforce the code freeze before the end of the iteration and to focus the whole team on testing what has actually been completed, and 2) to start testing the scenarios individually as soon as they are completed.

- **Failing to treat the iteration as a time box**—If the iterations keep getting extended because the team can't finish them, they have failed to grasp the concept of a time box.[7] A time box ends at a specific date, no matter whether the work is completed or not. The iteration should not be extended to accommodate delivery. You might decide to re-plan the next iteration to continue the work, but this will likely have overall schedule impact because there is usually no way to make up for the lost time later. To address this problem, make sure that the objectives and scenarios are prioritized and addressed one by one, and make sure that the testing time does not get squeezed in an attempt to get more development time.

- **Uncertainty over iteration goals**—Iteration goals are simple: in the main, they consist of scenarios to be developed and tested, which in turn are driven by a set of risks to be mitigated. Even so, it is possible that the goals could have been poorly communicated or perhaps not even set. This manifests itself in the form of developers choosing the functionality that *they* want to develop based on personal preferences rather than risk or business value to be delivered. The iteration might produce *something*, but it is not what was expected, meaning that many test cases will fail.

- **Unclear evaluation criteria**—The evaluation criteria set for the iteration need to be unambiguous and objectively measurable. You can always tell that they are unclear when there is debate about whether they have been successfully achieved as part of the iteration assessment. Unfortunately, the setting

---

[7] Time boxing is discussed in more detail in Chapter 3, "Controlling Iterative Projects" and Chapter 8, "Iteration Planning."

of good objectives with suitable evaluation criteria is an art that can only be learned through practice. The feedback you receive about their appropriateness and effectiveness as part of the iteration assessment enables you to improve your skills as the project progresses. In particular, watch out for the use of completely subjective and practically meaningless evaluation criteria such as "draft" or "percentage complete." You want to complete things within the iterations if possible; if an artifact is to be partially developed within an iteration, you should clearly define which parts of it are to be completed or how its elements will be verified.

- **Too much or too little scope for the iteration**—The problem of too much scope will be fairly obvious—the team will not finish the work planned and will have a natural tendency to want to extend the iteration as discussed previously. You should look at why the scope was too large and adjust future iterations to the skills and work capacity of the team. The problem of too little scope is harder to discern because work tends to expand to fill the time allotted. Look for "extra bells and whistles" creeping in, especially in the user interface design, or other unplanned results. If the team members complete the work identified for an iteration, then they should pull forward things that need to be done in future iterations. If you find that they have invented new things to do that are outside the project scope, then they have missed the chance to get ahead on the project, and there will probably need to be a scope cut later when another iteration does not go as well as expected.

- **Too much or too little planning—overly detailed iteration plans**—Overly detailed iteration plans try to plan out every single task that the project team members will perform. Typically, detailed plans differ greatly from the actual tasks performed, resulting in their frequent revision. As we have discussed before, iteration plans should be simple and goal- oriented. There is no need to plan out exact tasks—you can leave it to the creativity and professionalism of the team members to figure out what they need to do. If the team members are not experienced enough to do this on their own, then you might need to do more detailed planning on their behalf.

- **Poor estimating and aggressive scheduling**—Successful iteration requires the team to be able to conduct reasonably accurate short-term estimating. To create a credible iteration plan, you need to be able to accurately judge the amount of effort available within the iteration and how long the objectives will take to complete. This can be an issue at the beginning of the project when the team is wrestling with many unknowns. Some project managers adopt a very aggressive approach to planning the iterations in which they continually overestimate the amount of work the team can do in the time box, continually setting the team up to fail before it has even started. Don't make every iteration objective essential. Use the Essential, Highly Desirable, Desirable prioritization scheme introduced in the last chapter to set achievable but challenging goals. Continually failing to achieve the iteration objectives quickly becomes very demoralizing for the team. At the start of the project, it is better to be modest in the team's objectives, thereby setting them up for success, rather than to be overly ambitious, thereby setting them up for failure.

- **Lack of focus**—Iterative development requires the team to continuously focus on the essential objectives, leaving the other less important objectives to be addressed after the essential objectives have been completed. It is not uncommon for teams to ignore the prioritization of the objectives and tackle the ones that suit their skills or meet their own interests or that they feel offer a quick win for the team. This leads to the achievement of desirable and highly desirable objectives, which sounds good at first, but it usually comes at the expense of really critical issues from getting resolved in the important early iterations. This leaves the project exposed to unnecessary levels of risk. There is a good chance that much of the apparent progress is an illusion that will be dispelled when the unresolved issues later cause much of the project's "progress" to be wiped out in a significant re-write of the solution.

There are other common problems that affect iterations in the specific phases of the process. We examine some of these in the following phase assessment sections.

Acting On the Iteration Assessment Results

Iteration assessments are pointless if the information gathered is not acted upon. The whole point of iterating is to enable results to be periodically assessed with the intent of redirecting the effort if it is headed in the wrong direction.

You must take into account the information from the iteration assessment as you adjust the plans for the next iteration. Even if the iteration and the project are to be abandoned, there will still be work required to conclude the project in a controlled fashion. In cases where significant corrections are required, you will probably need to make changes to the overall project plan as well.

As you move ahead, keep in mind the following:

- **Never confuse the map with the journey**—The project plan is only an outline (and a guess at that), so you should believe the team's results and not the plans. Remember, it is the achievement of the objectives that is important, not the production of artifacts or the completion of activities. Be careful not to confuse the ends (objectives) with the means (artifacts and activities).

- **Adopt the attitude that continuous planning is a good thing**—In every iteration, expect your plans to change (albeit in small ways if your planning is effective). Don't fall into the trap of thinking that the plan is infallible.

- **Mature your process alongside your team**—Tune the working practices alongside the plans; adapt your team's skills as necessary to improve over time.

- **Be prepared to cut your losses**—Canceling bad projects early is success because you save time, money, and resources that can be applied to better opportunities.

- **Be honest**—Without objectivity and honesty, the project team is set up for failure, even if developing iteratively.

As the iterations progress, you will pick up leading indicators for the success or failure of the project, which enable you to assess whether the project is and will remain within its tolerances. If the tolerances are exceeded, then the project must be put into exception, and the project review board must convene to decide whether the project should be abandoned.

Assessing Phases

The phases of the Unified Process provide a way of monitoring the state of the project. At the end of every phase is a formal phase assessment where a decision is made on whether to allow the project to proceed to the next phase.

The phase assessments differ from the iteration assessments in a number of ways:

- They judge the state of the project as a whole rather than of an individual iteration.

- They always decide whether to continue or cancel the project. Iteration assessments only consider canceling the project if the iteration has been a failure.

- They focus on the value promised by the delivery of the solution rather than the performance of the team developing the solution.

- They look outwards from the project, considering the broader business impacts of the project. Iteration assessments tend to be very inward looking, focusing on the issues facing the team rather than the broader issues facing the commissioning organization.

- They assess the project's success against the business case and the relevant lifecycle milestone rather than the iteration plan and its objectives.

It is important to realize that the phase assessment might decide to cancel the project even though the iterations have all been successful and the phase's objectives have all been achieved. Even if the project is successful, it might no longer make business sense.

As we have discussed before, iterations occur within phases. Each phase concludes with a major milestone that is achievement-based: risks assigned to the phase have to be mitigated before the phase can be concluded. A phase assessment (sometimes referred to as a Lifecycle Milestone Review[8]) is held at the conclusion of each phase to determine, following the completion of the final iteration of the phase, whether the milestone has been achieved and whether the project should be allowed to proceed to the next phase. The end of a phase represents a point of stability in the lifecycle of the project where the stakeholder viewpoints can be synchronized and where it is possible to consider redefining and even recontracting the project. By comparing the state of the project against the end-of-phase milestones, you achieve concurrence among all the stakeholders on the current state of the project.

Unlike iterations, which are time-boxed, phases are *achievement-boxed:* you cannot move on to the next phase without meeting the objectives for the current phase. Moving on to the next phase without concluding the current phase is one of the more common and serious problems that we see on projects. Moving on without mitigating risks is false progress, and it usually results in significant pain later because the uncontrolled risks will continue to cause problems until they are dealt with. Don't be pressured by the schedule into "declaring victory"—you will pay for it later![9]

---

[8] This is the name used within the IBM Rational Unified Process. We prefer to call it a phase assessment because it mirrors the activity undertaken to close out an iteration and reinforces the layered, recursive nature of the iterative project management process.

[9] As our colleague DJ de Villiers observes, "One common symptom is when the project 'officially' moves into Construction, but in hushed whispers the project team reassures each other that internally—unofficially—they are still completing Elaboration. Every single time I know of a team doing this, the tactic has failed and backfired on the development team by undermining the openness and honesty required for successful iterative development."

The management team needs to plan for the closure of the phase as part of the final iteration. The final iteration of a phase typically includes preparing for the phase assessment and ensuring that all the appropriate outstanding issues have been addressed and that no loose ends will be carried over into the next iteration, which will be in the next phase. In some circumstances, this might require the formal handover of various products and artifacts or the settling of the project financing, especially if the phase end is also the end of the current contract or outsourcing arrangement.

In addition to formally assessing the phase at its completion, the management team should be aware of any problems and issues that occur during a phase which indicate that the previous phase might have been exited prematurely. This is particularly important during the Construction and Transition phases because they are highly dependent on the successful conclusion of the Elaboration phase. We examine some of the common problems to watch out for during these phases when we discuss their specific phase assessments.

The Phase Assessment Process

As shown in Figure 9-5, the phase assessment process is very similar to the iteration assessment process. The emphasis is now on the evolution as a whole, and in particular its assessment against the phase's concluding life-cycle milestone, rather than on an individual iteration's objectives and evaluation criteria. Phase assessments tend to be more outward looking, focusing on how the project relates to and impacts upon the business and the commissioning organization, than the iteration assessments, which are more inward looking, focusing on the internal performance and issues facing the project.

The change in emphasis is reflected in the different output and the additional consideration of the business case and the project's overall success criteria. This is shown by the italicized elements in Figure 9-5.

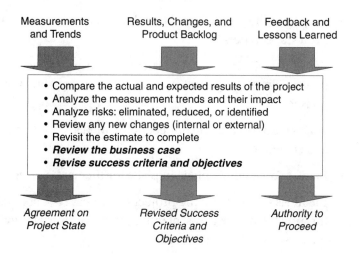

| Measurements and Trends | Results, Changes, and Product Backlog | Feedback and Lessons Learned |

- Compare the actual and expected results of the project
- Analyze the measurement trends and their impact
- Analyze risks: eliminated, reduced, or identified
- Review any new changes (internal or external)
- Revisit the estimate to complete
- *Review the business case*
- *Revise success criteria and objectives*

| Agreement on Project State | Revised Success Criteria and Objectives | Authority to Proceed |

Figure 9-5   *The phase assessment process*

It is the project manager's responsibility to bring the phase to closure by ensuring that

- The state of all artifacts is known

- Required artifacts have been distributed to the appropriate stakeholders

- The project's finances are settled if the current contract is ending (with the intent to recontract for the next phase)

- Stakeholder concurrence on the state of the project and the correct way forward is achieved and documented

The major issues to be considered during a phase assessment are related to the following:

- **Progress**—Has the project made adequate progress (in delivering capability, quality, and planned artifacts) across the phase?

- **Risk**—Is the project's risk profile acceptable to enter the next phase? Have the correct types of risk been addressed and mitigated?

- **Scope**—Is the project's scope well understood and acceptable to all stakeholders?

- **Baselines**—Have the right artifacts been produced, and are they in an appropriate state to allow entry into the next phase?

- **Performance**—Has the project performed acceptably on cost and schedule?

- **Plans**—Are credible plans in place for the next phase?

- **Business Case**—Does the project's business case still hold? If the project proceeds as planned, will appropriate levels of business benefit be achieved?

A more complete list of questions to be addressed in a phase assessment is provided in Appendix B.

It is essential that the business case is revisited to revalidate its assumptions and conclusions in light of any changes in the business or overall system's context for the project. Financial considerations are particularly important if the phase end also marks the end of a contract.

The key decision made by the phase assessment is whether the project should be allowed to proceed to the next phase.

Planning a Phase Assessment

A couple approaches can be taken for the phase assessment:

- **Formal Phase Assessment Meeting**—Schedule a separate assessment event.

- **Extension to an Iteration Assessment**—Add the phase assessment as an addendum to phase's final iteration acceptance review. If you do this, be sure that the iteration acceptance review is concluded before starting the phase assessment.

The phase assessment requires a joint decision to be made by all the stakeholders in the project. This usually entails having a meeting between the customer representative(s), the project's management team (the overall project manager, development lead, and iteration lead plus the team leads for the various functional areas of the project team), the user representatives, and the project sponsor. For small project teams, the second option is the most common because the entire project review board is typically involved in the iteration assessment as well. For larger projects or those with an extended project review board, a separate phase assessment is often required.

Whichever approach is adopted, make sure that the event is planned well in advance and that everybody is available. If the review is not undertaken with a suitable set of attendees, then it will be unable to make any concrete decisions about the continuation of the project, totally negating the purpose of holding the assessment in the first place.

To help facilitate the planning of the phase assessment, a project review table, as shown in Table 9-4 and included in the development plan (see Appendix B for further details), can be useful.

Table 9-4 *Example Attendees for a Phase Assessment*

	Overall Project Manager	Development Manager	Sponsor	Customer	User	Iteration Lead	Requirement Manager	Architect	QA Manager	Development Team	Anyone Else You Like
Iteration Acceptance Review (External)	Y	L	Y	Y	N	Y	Y	Y	Y	N	Opt

(L = Lead, Y = Yes, N = No, Opt = Optional)

This is a more detailed version of the summary chart we saw in Chapter 5.

Each phase has a different emphasis, which results in the phase assessments differing for each phase. In the next few sections, we look at performing the assessment for each of the four Unified Process phases.

The reviews are usually formal and conducted with some ceremony to demonstrate to all stakeholders that the objectives of the phase have been achieved.

Assessing the Inception Phase

In the Inception phase, you need to focus on "Business Risks." Table 9-5 illustrates the kind of questions that you should be asking. You must be able to answer these questions with reasonable certainty by the end of the Inception phase.

Table 9-5   *Questions to Ask at an Inception Assessment*

Risk	Questions to Ask
Value Proposition	Does the proposed solution solve a meaningful problem that people are willing to pay to solve?
Technical Feasibility of the Solution	Can the solution be built? Will new or unproven technologies be required?
Economic Feasibility of the Solution	Can we build the solution profitably? How much will it cost?
Time to Market	Can we deliver the solution within the window of market opportunity? How much time will it take?
Priorities	Given all the other things we need to do, should we fund this project?
Stakeholder Involvement	Are the right people involved in the project? Do they know what this project is about and do they care—are they involved and committed?

Appendix B contains an Inception Phase Assessment Checklist that includes a fuller list of questions to help you conduct your Inception phase assessments.

The ordering of the questions is significant—if there is no value proposition, for example, the rest of the questions are unimportant.

Too many projects don't spend enough time on these risks—they assume that others (usually the "business people") have already done all the work and that they would not ask to have the solution investigated if all these risks were not already resolved. This is rarely a good assumption, especially when you consider that the businesspeople cannot factor in any details of the team or its capabilities. More importantly, this underlines the need to build integrated cross-functional teams of technology and business people to solve a specific problem.[10]

At the assessment, the stakeholders need to explore all aspects of the viability of the proposed solution. Projects do not exist in isolation—a company must choose projects that will deliver the greatest value with the least risk. The project might be technically feasible and might solve a worthy customer problem but might still fail to be funded if better alternatives exist. For most projects, time to market is also very important. The value of a solution delivered later than expected is often diminished. There is usually a limited window of opportunity for most solutions—problems do not wait forever to be solved.

In assessing the Inception phase, you should focus on evaluating the following:

- **The scope of the solution**—This involves evaluating the primary use cases and key non-functional requirements.

- **The viability of the project**—This includes the alternatives that were evaluated to investigate the value of the solution, including reviewing the risks to the project.

- **The overall project and development plans**—This includes the releases, deadlines, estimates, constraints, and objectives. The first iteration in the Elaboration phase should be sketched out in some detail.

By the end of the Inception phase, there should be clear value in continuing the evolution. The main artifacts to review are the business case (which describes the value of a potential solution), the vision (which describes the solution), and the risk list (which describes the risks of building the solution).

---

[10] One technique for achieving stakeholder buy-in is for the project manager to try to convince the stakeholders why the project should *not* be done. The more arguments the stakeholders come up with for doing the project, the stronger their conviction and level of buy-in. This is not suitable in all circumstances, but in a closed environment where the project manager knows the stakeholders well, it can work very effectively.

Assessing the Elaboration Phase

In the Elaboration phase, you need to focus on "Technical Risks." Table 9-6 illustrates the kind of questions that you should be asking. In general, you want to verify that the team has proven that the selected approach is stable. The proof needs to be supplied by executed tests—design documents do not count because they do not prove anything.

Table 9-6   *Questions to Ask at an Elaboration Assessment*

Risk	Questions to Ask
Agreement on Capabilities	Do all parties share a common understanding of what will be built?
Selection of Components	Do we know what we are going to buy and reuse? Do we know what we have to build ourselves?
Technical Feasibility of Solution	Can the solution meet the requirements, including all functional and non-functional requirements?
Stability of the Architecture	Is the architecture stable enough to support the work that will be done in the Construction phase?
Stability of the Environment	Do we know what tools and processes to use and how?

Appendix B contains an Elaboration Phase Assessment Checklist that includes a fuller list of questions to help you conduct your Elaboration phase assessments.

By this time, the requirements should be stable: all use cases should have been identified and outlined, including alternative flows. Architecturally significant scenarios should have been detailed, analyzed, developed, and tested. This results in a partially completed design model, test cases, and tested and executed code. At the assessment, you must make sure that proposed development approach is suitable and that technical feasibility of the solution has been proven.

The technical aspects of the assessment are typically conducted as a number of walkthroughs and reviews of the prototypes, focusing particularly on the test results. "Paper reviews" of the architecture don't count—only through executed tests will you know that the architecture is stable. These technical assessments should be planned into the final iteration of the phase.

Areas warranting special focus include the following:

- Ensuring that all architectural scenarios have been covered.

- Ensuring that all non-functional requirements can be met. Special attention should be paid to matters involving scalability, security and authentication, fault tolerance, and responses to various failures. These are typically issues that need to be addressed in the architecture and cannot be easily addressed later without significant scrap and rework.

- Ensuring that the system produced will have an acceptable level of performance. At the end of Elaboration, we should have some confidence that the system produced will have the requisite performance under full load. Often this is glossed over, and when Construction is done, we have an ugly problem—a system that has all the functionality but is much too slow. This part of the architecture needs to be adequately vetted before closing out Elaboration.

At the successful conclusion of the Elaboration phase, the major technical risks have been mitigated, resulting in the establishment of a stable architecture. This stability enables credible plans to be put in place; at this point, it is possible to put together a firm commitment to delivery dates and scope to be delivered. It is also the point at which estimates become more reliable with the removal of major project risks.

Assessing the Construction Phase

After the Elaboration phase, the evolution takes on a "get it done" pattern, consisting of detailing requirements, analyzing and designing them, and implementing and testing them iteration by iteration. This pattern is enabled by the stability provided by the architecture: it actually enables the incremental work to produce accumulated results instead of creating rework.

During the Construction phase but before the end-of-phase review, you should keep an eye out for common problems, including the following:

- **Architectural instability**—If you're experiencing this problem, you probably never actually exited the Elaboration phase. Instability prevents effective parallel development and leads to "churn." The solution is to set the project "back" to the Elaboration phase. Often the project manager resists this solution because it appears to be setting the project back and might idle large parts of the team. The problem is that architectural control is difficult, if not impossible, to establish with lots of people working in parallel, so you have no choice but to halt the Construction phase work until stability is achieved.

- **Requirements instability**—If new requirements keep appearing, then you need to make a decision: if the new requirements do not affect the architecture, you might choose to continue the work, reprioritizing the requirements to shift some of the older requirements to later evolutions, or to add resources or iterations. If the new requirements cannot be satisfied within the current architecture and cannot be postponed to a later evolution, you have no choice but to go back to the Elaboration phase and establish a new architecture for this evolution of the solution.

- **Too much work, not enough time**—Sometimes the problem just ends up being bigger than you thought it was. The solution is to renegotiate the initial release scope or add resources (time and people). You should be mindful of *Brooks' Law*,[11] which observes that adding more people to a late project makes it later.

- **Not enough testing**—There is a tendency to equate the Construction phase with "Implementation" (writing code), postponing testing until the Transition phase—this usually results in serious problems cropping up in the Transition phase, in full view of users and executive sponsors. Other than the ill will that this situation creates, it also reduces the amount of time available to fix problems and usually results

---

[11]   Frederick P. Brooks, *The Mythical Man-Month: Essays on Software Engineering*, 20th Anniversary Edition (Reading, MA: Addison-Wesley, 1995).

in persistent poor quality. Sometimes this occurs because there are not enough testers on the project. A 2:1 ratio of developers to testers is a useful starting point in the Construction phase.

- **Too much rework**—Rework can occur in either implemented code or in test code. Some rework is expected early in the phase (up to 25%), but the percentage should decline over time as stub code is replaced with real code. Excessive rework in implemented code can be an indicator of individual quality problems, systemic quality problems, or architectural instability.

By the end of the Construction phase, the solution should be at a point where it is suitable for release (the minimum set of useful functionality)— all the capabilities should be implemented, and you should be ready to start the transition of the solution to its users. This means that you have a usable solution available—the solution is basically done, although you are probably still fixing defects. All the testing should have been completed, with the exception of the regression testing that you will do in the Transition phase as you fix defects.

Table 9-7 illustrates the kind of questions that you should be asking at a Construction phase assessment.

Table 9-7 *Questions to Ask at a Construction Assessment*

Risk	Questions to Ask
Solution Completeness	Have enough of the capabilities been implemented and tested?
Solution Quality	Is the solution of sufficient quality to begin the transition process?
Solution Stability	Is the solution stable enough to begin the transition process? Has the defect find/fix ratio begun to level out? Are defects being fixed faster than they are being found?
Transition Readiness	Are resources lined up for the transition phase? Has the user documentation been written? Are the users ready?

Appendix B contains a Construction Phase Assessment Checklist that includes a fuller list of questions to help you conduct your Construction phase assessments.

There is a strong tendency to push problems forward from the Construction phase to the Transition phase. We caution strongly against this: problems in the Transition phase are highly visible to all the stakeholders of the project; by moving into the Transition phase, you are basically telling people that the solution is ready to release. They will expect the solution to have some defects but to basically be usable. Excessive defects will undermine the solution and might even threaten it with cancellation. We have seen more than one project cancelled because of poor quality when the users finally got their hands on it. You should make sure that you are comfortable that the release is ready to be deployed before you release it, even in a preliminary form.

Assessing the Transition Phase

At the conclusion of the Transition phase, an evolution of the solution is complete, and a solution has been deployed to its users; the solution has been handed over to production support or the next project.

During the Transition phase but before the end-of-phase review, you should keep an eye out for common problems, including the following:

- **Installation and configuration of the solution**—These are "architecturally significant" issues that are often overlooked during the Inception and Elaboration phases. Upgrading a 24×7 system while it is running is a very architecturally significant issue. If these issues have not been considered, it might force the project *back* to the Construction phase or even the Elaboration phase.

- **Data conversion and production turnover**—In many systems, data conversion and production "cut-over" are complex problems that require significant attention. In shops supporting 24×7 customer access, how will users be transitioned to the new system? Often a parallel "conversion" environment will have to be established. When the application is ready to be made generally available, users are migrated to it. When significant amounts of data need to be converted, this turnover effort can be substantial. In complex cases, this turnover process can warrant a project of its own.

- **User and support staff training**—Few systems are so intuitively easy to use that their users do not require some training in their use. Systems accessed directly by customers must provide some way to lead customers through a tutorial the first time they access the new system. Operations areas will need training not only on the new system but also on any changes to the business process.

- **Ongoing system maintenance**—Like any other machinery, systems must be maintained. During the Transition phase, the project might need to integrate the rollout and patching of the new system with the ongoing maintenance of the old system.

- **Quick fixes**—Fixing defects often introduces more defects when people rush to fix them but do so carelessly. Be careful of quick fixes and patches to patches during Transition because this is a common cause of spiraling decreases in the quality of the system.

By the end of the Transition phase, these issues should be resolved. Table 9-8 illustrates the kind of questions that you should be asking at the phase assessment. The project cannot successfully exit the Transition phase until these questions have been resolved.

Table 9-8 *Questions to Ask at a Transition Assessment*

Risk	Questions to Ask
Delivery and Installation	Are the delivery mechanisms in place? Can the solution be installed easily? Can it be uninstalled easily?
Training and Mentoring	Have the users been trained? Are there procedures and supporting material to support the training of new users?
Operations and Support	Are procedures for system operation and maintenance in place? Have the staff members been trained? Are there procedures for system backup, recovery, and restoration?
Sponsor/ User Acceptance	Have the users and sponsors accepted delivery of the system?
Project Conclusion	Is the evolution over? Have all the project's responsibilities been handed over to someone else?

Appendix B contains a Transition Phase Assessment Checklist that includes a fuller list of questions to help you conduct your Transition phase assessments.

Upon the successful conclusion of the Transition phase, the solution has been transferred to an operations or production support process—it is "just another" application that the operations staff needs to support and maintain. The evolution is brought to a close, and the attention shifts to the next evolution or a new project.

You should encourage people to reflect on the processes followed, identifying what worked well and any things that need improvement:

- Focus on both good and bad.

- Be open and honest about what worked and what did not.

- Be non-judgmental; make sure that "what was done" is separated from "who did what."

You should make sure to learn from mistakes as well as successes. Don't sweep mistakes under the rug—be open and honest. Don't focus on assigning blame, but focus on what needs to be done to make the next evolution or project better. You should strive to create a learning culture in which experimentation for improvement is rewarded.

In preparation for the next evolution or project, develop recommendations about what should change next time; make decisions and put them into action. Learn from experience and communicate this knowledge to others so that other project teams can benefit from your experiences.

Concluding a Phase

The main purpose of the phase assessment is to decide whether to allow the project to proceed to the next phase. At the end of the assessment, the state of the project should be recorded, and the reviewers should decide whether to continue.

The result of the phase assessment can be one of the following:

- **Passed**—The customer representative agrees that the project has met expectations for the phase, and therefore the project can proceed to the next phase.

- **Passed at risk**—There is conditional acceptance of the completion of the milestone. The customer representative agrees that the project may proceed to the next phase, subject to the completion of specified corrective actions.

- **Failed**—The project has failed to achieve the expectations for the phase: either a further iteration is scheduled, or the various stakeholders have recourse to the contract to re-scope or terminate the project.

As well as establishing the state of the project (looking backward), the assessment must also establish the fate of the project. Regardless of the success or failure of the phase itself, the forward-looking status of the project must be determined. As a result of the assessment, the project itself should be classified as one of the following:

- **Approved**—Funding and commitment for the completion of the next phase.

- **Temporarily Approved**—Funding and commitment for the completion of the next iteration. This often occurs when there is a delay between the phase assessment and the formal allocation of the funds.

- **Extended**—Funding and commitment to address any outstanding issues and complete this phase.

- **Paused**—The project is not authorized to continue at this time but will be archived for resumption at some later date.

- **Postponed**—The project is to be archived for possible reactivation at some unspecified time in the future.

- **Cancelled**—The project is terminated.

Even if the phase's milestone is successfully achieved, and the phase is judged to have passed, the project itself might still be *cancelled, postponed,* or *paused,* such as if the funding is not immediately available or the project's resources are needed for a more important project.

If the phase is *passed at risk* and the project is *approved,* the management team might choose to initiate a new iteration to deal with the issues or simply might attempt to deal with them as part of the next iteration, the difference being in the amount of planning needed. Whichever approach is selected, the outstanding issues must be addressed and the milestone revisited at the next iteration assessment.

If the results of the phase are found to be unacceptable, but the project is not cancelled, the management team must initiate at least one additional iteration to attempt to conclude the phase. In this case, the project is classified as *extended,* and an additional phase review is also required to approve the project progressing to the next phase after the issues have been addressed.

In some cases, the resolution of the problems is taken out of the team's hands and is left to the customer and the project review board to resolve. This is particular common when the project has funding issues.

The results of the assessment should be recorded using the project/phase assessment document (see Appendix B for details).

Project Assessments

In the course of the project, additional project assessments might be required to complement the ongoing iteration and phase assessments. There are a number of reasons why these additional assessments might be needed:

- To handle *exceptions* raised by the iteration assessments

- Because the phase assessments are too far apart to provide sufficient management oversight for the commissioning organization or program

- To undertake *post-project reviews* of the evolution's effectiveness and delivered benefit

- To provide review points for the overall project, which might include more subprojects than just the software development

We look at each in turn after we have discussed the generic project assessment process.

The Project Assessment Process

The management team undertakes project assessments when additional project reviews are required to review the project in its entirety or handle exceptions. The main purpose of the project assessments is to ensure that the overall project risks are under control, that the evolutions of the project are in balance, and that the project is delivering measurable benefits back to the business.

The project assessment process is very similar to the phase assessment process, except that now the emphasis is on a particular set of issues rather than the conclusion of a particular phase.

The objectives of a project assessment are typically to

- Confirm that the need for the project has not changed

- Satisfy the stakeholders of the quality of the products delivered by the project

- Confirm that the business case is still viable

- Authorize the continuation or cancellation of the project

- Assess the benefits that the project has delivered

- Assess the overall effectiveness of the project

Project assessments are like generic phase assessments for the project as a whole, and they produce the same results as a phase assessment. Minutes of the state and fate of the project, including whether it is *approved* or *extended* or whether the project is to be *paused, postponed,* or *cancelled,* can be captured using the project/phase assessment document (see Appendix B for details).

When performing a project assessment, look collectively at the results of the evolution phases and iterations just completed: Are they all ready to proceed? Have they met their own success criteria?

Handling Exceptions

The most common cause of additional project assessments is handling exceptions raised by the iteration assessments. If an iteration assessment concludes that the project should be *extended, cancelled, postponed,* or *paused,* then it is probably wise to have this decision reviewed and ratified by a formal project assessment, including a broader selection of stakeholders than is typically included in the iteration assessment. Even if the iteration assessment includes all the relevant parties, more investigative work and reflection typically are required before the decision is made final.

Providing Additional Management Control Points

There is a subtle paradox inherent in the use of the Unified Process lifecycle: the more risk the project faces, the longer the phases will be, and the further apart the phase assessments will be. This is counter to most project management advice, which states that the riskier the project is, the more frequent the project assessments should be.

If a project has very high technical risk, it is not unusual for the Elaboration phase to last six months or more. This might be too long a period to go without convening the project review board for a formal project assessment. In this case, a mid-phase project assessment is probably a worthwhile addition to the plans. This would be conducted in exactly the same way as a phase assessment but without a predefined milestone to review progress.

Post-Project Reviews

The key to understanding the role of the post-project reviews is to understand the relationship between the development of an evolution of a software product and the actual realization of any business benefit to be derived from its deployment. The benefits of an evolution are not accrued until after the software product has been transitioned into the user community and typically not until well after the evolution itself has been finished. The relationship between the development and support costs and the generation of benefits is shown in Figure 9-6, where the costs incurred are shown as bars below the central line and the benefits accrued as bars above the line.

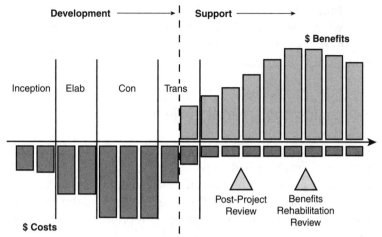

Figure 9-6 *Realizing the benefits from a software evolution*

It is the overall project's responsibility to carry out the post-project and benefit realization reviews for its evolutions and to ensure that the predicted benefits are actually realized. The results of these and the various sub-project phase and iterations assessments are among the primary inputs into the overall project assessment process.

To this end, shortly after the end of each evolution, you should conduct a post-project review to assess the benefits realized from the release, to learn how to improve project planning and execution in the future, and to enable reflection on the performance of the evolution as a whole.

As part of the measurement plan for the overall project, you should consider how you will measure the accumulating benefits that the project will deliver. This includes the planning and setup of the benefits realization reviews for the major releases to be delivered to the business. The types of benefits that can be derived from software products are so numerous that it is difficult for us to provide you with much more advice than to recommend that you consider how to measure the success of the project at the beginning of the project and set up appropriate mechanisms for measuring this success. Creating and monitoring measures identified as part of a project Balanced Scorecard acts as a great enabler for this task.

As part of the post-project review, you should also encourage people to again reflect on the processes followed, identifying what worked well and any things that need improvement. Now that the evolution has been over for a while, ask them whether they would approach the project in the same way next time. If they would adopt a different approach, ask them what things they would change.

Reviewing the Overall Project

Project assessments can also be used to review the state of the overall project as a whole. This is particularly important if the software development evolutions are only one part of a much larger endeavor. In this case you would also want to consider the other elements of the project. For example, are the non-software development subprojects on track? Are the inter-project dependencies under control?

The fact that the evolutions within the project have been subject to iteration and phase assessments means that little preparation is required to drive the overall project assessments, as long as the post project and benefits realization reviews have also been conducted. If these are not undertaken as part of the overall project, then additional work will be required to prepare the information needed to support the overall project assessment.

Summary

Assessment is a critical but sometimes neglected activity. Without assessment, you will miss the main benefits of iteration: the ability to learn from your mistakes and to take into account new information to improve subsequent iterations.

Informal assessment occurs day-to-day on the project, with a slightly different focus from phase to phase. Small corrections can be made without waiting until the end of the iteration, which will help you to anticipate problems. Major changes should be left until the iteration boundary.

Iteration assessments, conducted at the conclusion of the iteration, provide the ability to learn from experience. The iteration assessments help you to adapt the goals for subsequent iteration and develop effective iteration plans going forward. The iteration assessments are the major project monitoring and control mechanism and are essential to establishing any form of management control over iterative projects.

At the end of a phase, a more formal phase assessment is conducted, with the goal of deciding whether the team can proceed to the next phase. Phase boundaries are achievement-oriented, with certain results required before the evolution is allowed to progress to the next phase.

At the conclusion of the evolutions, business results are evaluated and compared to goals, which can in turn shape the plans of subsequent evolutions or phases and iterations within those evolutions.

Additional project assessments can be required to handle exceptions, to provide additional management control points for an evolution, to review the benefits achieved by the delivery of the software (post-project reviews), or to assess the status of the project as a whole (if it contains more than just software development). These are organized and handled in the same way as the phase assessments.

A Scalable Approach to Managing Iterative Projects

"Inside every large problem is a small problem struggling to get out."
—*Hoare's Law of Large Problems*

Projects come in all sizes. Large projects with more people, more products, and potentially more locations appear at first to be vastly different from smaller projects. But initial appearances can be misleading. Because communications between members of a large team must be very simple to be effective, the approach for managing a large project must actually be as simple as possible for the project to succeed. Scaling up the management approach to handle larger projects does not mean that you need a significantly more complex management approach. This chapter discusses how you can scale up the development effort without scaling up the complexity. A few simple techniques added to what we have presented so far enable very large projects to be handled without an equivalent increase in the complexity of the management approach.

By the same token, just because a project is "small" in size (scope, people, duration) does not mean that there is no need for management—small projects can face significant risks that require significant management attention. The main difference between very large and very small projects is that smaller projects tend to have fewer people, so the communications tend to be simpler, making a less formal approach possible. This is not an excuse to dispense with key management and architectural concepts, however, and small projects can require significant attention if the problem to be solved is poorly understood or changing rapidly, or if the architectural challenges are significant.

Managing Small Projects

The fewer people you need to coordinate, the fewer management problems you incur. Because the primary driver of headcount is work to be performed, you get the largest benefit out of reducing the scope of the project. You should first make sure that all the desired outcomes or needs are really essential and then figure out whether all the needs must be satisfied at the same time or whether a staged delivery is possible. Staging the delivery of benefits can enable you to staff the project with fewer people.

Your first strategy should be to manage the scope of the project, reducing the number of requirements that you need to implement. We find that many teams overlook this possibility, assuming that they need to deliver *all* the functionality the customer asks for. You need to question this assumption and find ways to challenge whether everything the customer asks for is really needed. Most systems are over-specified, and even on successful projects, up to 30% of the functionality delivered is never used.

The key to reducing scope is to focus on customer needs rather than the requirements they provide. For every requirement, you need to be able to identify the actual need—the outcome that the customer is trying to achieve. Many requirements, the proverbial "bells and whistles," are unrelated to a real customer need or a desired outcome. Any "requirement" that does not contribute to a material improvement in some task performed by a system user should be ruthlessly cut from the plan or at least deferred to a future evolution, freeing you from having to worry about it now (and giving you the option of cutting it later).

After you have confirmed the overall scope, take a look at the risks: if the business risks are few and manageable, you might be able to shorten the Inception phase. Smaller projects typically require less financial scrutiny and therefore have simpler funding models; this can greatly simplify the Inception phase. For most "maintenance" or "enhancement" projects where you are extending an existing solution, the Inception phase can be very short, perhaps as short as just a few days spent confirming that the enhancements requested actually have value.

Similarly, if you are enhancing an existing system with an existing architecture, the Elaboration phase might consist of ensuring that the changes will not break the architecture. But be extremely careful not to just skip over the Elaboration phase, no matter how small the project. At the very least, you need to validate that what is being modified or added is consistent with the underlying architecture and will not lead to instabilities.

After you have trimmed the scope, you can decide whether to deliver the functionality in one evolution or multiple evolutions executed in series. In Chapter 6, "Overall Project Planning," we discussed how to plan the delivery of business value in a series of evolutions. Delivering functionality in a series of evolutions can often provide results just as fast with less risk and with a smaller team than delivering the same capabilities in a single, large evolution with a much larger staff. Larger staff sizes introduce greater overhead, but sometimes this is the only way to get a large amount of work done in a short time period. If the achievement of the desired outcomes can be staged over a longer period of time, a smaller team can often get more done at a reduced cost by reducing overhead.

Figure 10-1 summarizes the multilevel planning approach introduced in Chapter 5, "A Layered Approach to Planning and Managing Iterative Projects." This layered approach enables the management and planning to scale up to cover multiple evolutions and longer time periods while keeping the planning and control simple and focused at each layer.

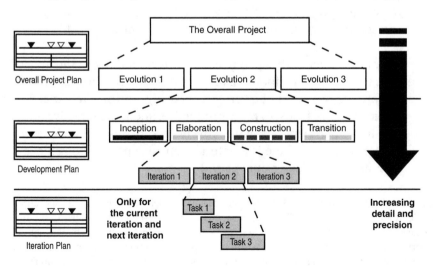

Figure 10-1   *A layered approach to planning*

The ability to serialize business value delivery through a series of evolutions is usually limited by the needs of the business. If there is a pressing need for a solution in a specific time period, perhaps due to regulatory or competitive pressures, then a larger project with more work being done in parallel might be the only solution.

How Small Is Small?

If you are producing a single software product and are working with a single team, then iterations can be relatively short, such as two to four weeks, and the overall project duration can be just a few months, especially if the Inception and Elaboration phase risks are already handled for you. The project team for this kind of project is probably just a few people, typically less than seven. If the team is colocated and has easy access to subject matter experts from the sponsoring organization, the formality of artifacts can be very low.

How small can a project become and still be a project? If it only takes a few days and only involves one person, it's probably just a task and doesn't require the application of the iterative software development lifecycle we have described. If the result can be delivered in a single iteration, as is the case with a fair amount of "maintenance" work, we also don't recommend creating a project with a lifecycle—a lot of good work can be done with a defect tracking system from which work can be assigned.[1]

Our experience is that you need to have something in the area of three to five people working for three or more iterations of three to four weeks each before the overhead of a "project" is really worthwhile. Smaller teams are typically more focused, more productive, and more effective, provided that the team members can achieve the necessary scope. Smaller teams require less process, but there is a natural team size needed to achieve particular results in a particular time period.

---

[1]   One way to handle maintenance backlogs is to create a project with a budget and a fixed number of iterations to explicitly address the backlog. This project can then have a brief Inception phase to set the budget and review the backlog, an Elaboration phase to address any architecturally significant changes selected from the backlog, a brief Construction phase to address the highest-priority items, and then an extended Transition phase to address the outstanding backlog. This would be one application of the Incremental Delivery pattern we looked at in Chapter 7.

Short iterations are very fragile: small perturbations can cause them to fail spectacularly. One-week iterations are possible but need to be very informal and very disciplined—and the combination of informal yet disciplined is hard to achieve—usually the people who can pull this off are very skilled and experienced people who have worked together very closely before. A two-week iteration is still very short and is probably on the outside edge of what is really practical.

To iterate quickly, project teams need to be able to make decisions and reach agreement quickly. Short iteration times, therefore, require dedicated resources (you can't share resources between projects and expect to get much done quickly). We have worked with some organizations in which team members are shared between multiple projects, so a person might be splitting his or her time between three or four projects. In some cases this makes sense; for example, it is common to share database administrators and operations support people between projects because no single project needs these resources full-time. For other project team members, splitting time between projects just makes everything take much longer. People need time to switch contexts, and each context switch makes the person less effective. Our recommendation is to devote each staff member to a single project to realize the business benefit sooner and make harder choices about deciding which projects not to do (or at least not to do now).

Finally, keep in mind that a small project still needs to consider all the same things as a large project, just on a smaller scale. Every project needs to consider business risks, requirements, architecture, development, testing, deployment, and so on. Every project must deal with risk. Just because the project is small does not mean that these things are unimportant; don't fool yourself by thinking that you can cut corners.

Scaling Up the Project

Sooner or later, you will find that to deliver the value needed by the business in the time frame needed by the business, you will need a lot of people working in parallel. Managing all these people is what makes a larger project complex, and the complexity doesn't grow linearly—it grows exponentially unless you can apply some organizing principles. There are many aspects to this complexity—more meetings and more artifacts to communicate among team members, more planning, more reviews, more work products, and so on.

There are a number of strategies for dealing with this additional complexity, which we describe in the following sections. We present the strategies in the order you should apply them. In other words, when faced with increasing amounts of work on the project, apply the first strategy, and then when you've exhausted the benefit of the first strategy, apply the second, and so on. In this way you will use the set of techniques that are appropriate to the task at hand and that are no more complex than necessary for your particular situation.

The "Core Architecture Team" Pattern

You will recall from earlier chapters that the primary result of the Elaboration phase is a stable architecture. A stable architecture enables you to add team members during the Construction phase, preventing changes made by one team member from undermining the efforts of other team members and causing rework. Failure to have a strong and persistent architecture will doom the entire effort. We cannot emphasize this enough because most of the scaling techniques that we discuss depend on having a strong, stable, and coherent architecture.

A stable architecture is the product of a small, highly focused, technically competent team; it is not the product of a committee effort.[2] The absolute size of this team will vary somewhat depending on the technical complexity of the problem space, but generally one cannot have dozens of people developing the architecture. A large architecture team simply cannot produce an architecture with the simplicity, consistency, and coherency needed to scale up the project team size.[3]

---

[2]   We have seen some organizations try and fail with this approach—starting with a number of originally separate projects and teams that must be brought together, each with its own "architect," they form an "architecture team" consisting of the set of project architects. Lacking a consistent vision and resources to actually create an executable architecture, they usually produce some nice documents or presentations but little in the way of a consistent code base suitable for scaling up a development effort.

[3]   Scaling up the team size is not the only reason for having an architecture; we focus on this aspect in this chapter to highlight its impact on scaling the project size.

As long as the project is small, the same team that develops the architecture simply continues the project work, developing the rest of the solution in the Construction phase based on the architecture established in earlier phases. As the scope of the solution to be delivered increases, though, there will be a point at which this *core architecture* team will not be able to do all the work on the project. Additional teams will need to be added, as shown in Figure 10-2.

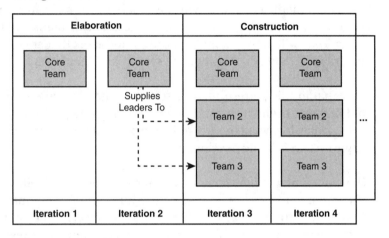

Figure 10-2   *Organization of a simple, multi-team development effort*

Adapted from: *Agile and Iterative Development: A Manager's Guide* by Craig Larman (Boston: Addison-Wesley, 2004).

Applying this pattern, you start with a small, colocated core team who will create the architecture for the solution, staffing the project during the Inception and Elaboration phases. To create and baseline the architecture, the core team must have the ability to implement and test as well as perform requirements, analysis, and design.

At the conclusion of the Elaboration phase, the architecture effort will have defined a number of major components that comprise the solution. The interfaces and key capabilities of these components will have been defined and partially developed as part of the architectural work, but there will still remain much work to do to fully complete the components. The architecture of the solution will have ensured the loose coupling of these components, enabling them to be developed independently and the project size to be increased with additional teams to undertake this work.

In the Construction phase, some members of the core team will move on to assume technical leadership roles for the component teams, while some members of the core team will remain to ensure that the architecture does not degrade as ongoing work is completed. In addition, members of the core team will ensure that the system is progressively implementing scenarios and that progress is being made toward solution delivery.

The component teams are typically made up of specialists whose skills align to the technologies or business areas encapsulated by the components. They will produce one or more components that are assembled and integrated into the final composite system and then tested.

Note that in this pattern there is still only one plan, one set of iterations, and one management team; there is still only one project. This pattern is most applicable when there is only one product being produced—that is, a single system is being developed.

There are limits to how large this pattern can be scaled. First, the number of component teams is limited by the number of components, which is limited by natural partitions within the solution space. Responsibility for a component cannot be subdivided between a number of teams, and you cannot draw arbitrary boundaries between components just to create more teams; if you try, you will simply increase the coupling between teams, effectively making several teams into one larger interdependent (but poorly organized) team. Note that every component must be owned by only one team, but each team can own a number of components. In assigning components to teams, you want to make sure that components owned by different teams are loosely coupled to minimize team coupling.

We find that in dealing with teams, there is a kind of *rule of seven* that provides a threshold at which things get a lot harder: any time you need to manage more than seven independent things, management gets a lot more difficult.[4] If you need to manage more than five to seven teams, you probably need the more explicit control structure provided by the "Core Project" pattern, which we discuss next.

---

[4] We arrived at this rule of thumb by observing teams and by an observation from the world of psychology: most people can remember seven plus or minus two things. This limit seems to be related to how our short-term memory works. We have noticed a similar effect in team size: a team with seven plus or minus two members seems to be fairly easy to manage, but when the team size grows to ten or more, it is usually time to think about splitting the team into two teams to reduce the communication overhead. To do this, however, the work needs to be divisible too.

The "Core Project" Pattern

As the project grows in size and needs to produce multiple products or larger-scale, independently packaged components, more management infrastructure is needed to coordinate the larger scope. In product development organizations, this can occur when developing a product line consisting of several products; in an IT organization, it can occur when a business process is supported by a number of systems. In either case, a number of products or systems, each potentially developed by a different team, are composed into some larger solution.

In this pattern, illustrated in Figure 10-3, a core project owns the overall solution and defines and develops a common architecture for the solution, much in the way that the core team owns the architecture of the simpler solution in the "Core Architecture Team" pattern. In fact, the project starts in much the same way—as a single project.

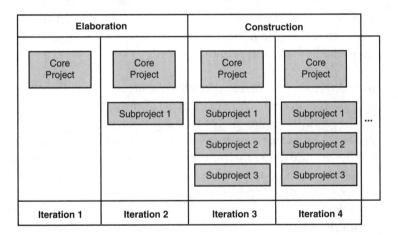

Figure 10-3 *A project with multiple subprojects*

As the architecture and the requirements start to stabilize, additional subprojects are spun off as required to independently develop the self-contained components identified by the core project. In this case the core project will do the integration and testing of the systems and components built by the subprojects.

The decision to use subprojects, as opposed to subteams, is really just a question of scale: if the solution is really large and requires the effort of more than 20 or 30 people[5] to develop, more effort will be required to coordinate the work, so it becomes worthwhile to consider a number of coordinated projects rather than trying to coordinate a number of teams.

Figure 10-3 shows the whole network of projects still sharing a common set of iteration boundaries, and the subprojects come together with the core project to integrate the entire system in every iteration. This might seem somewhat inflexible and of limited applicability; surely there must be some way to improve the efficiency of the overall project by staggering the iterations of the subprojects, possibly in line with layers of the architecture or the direction of the component dependencies?

Implicit in Figure 10-3 is the use of the iteration boundaries as synchronization points between projects. Within an iteration, subprojects are relatively independent. As they complete an iteration, their work products are integrated into the larger solution by the core project team. Note that in this figure, the core project and the subprojects still share the same iteration schedule and milestones.

In reality, the subproject schedules usually lead the core project's schedule to allow for successive integration of subproject components into the overall solution. In Figure 10-4, three subprojects are spun off from the core project to build three distinct sets of components; the dependency diagram on the left side of the figure shows the dependencies between components owned by the subprojects. Because Subproject 1 is dependent upon the components produced by Subprojects 2 and 3, those subprojects must complete their iterations slightly ahead of Subproject 1 to allow time for Subproject 1 to integrate their components. The core project must then integrate the results from Subproject 1 (as well as others not shown in the figure) to complete its iteration.

---

5 The *rule of seven* suggests that you could manage seven teams of seven, or 49 people, before needing to move to a project-subproject structure. Because teams are often smaller than seven members, we have found that somewhere between 20 and 30 people, you reach a practical limit on using subteams on a single project. The divisibility of the work often provides the deciding factor, as does the organization structure and financial governance model.

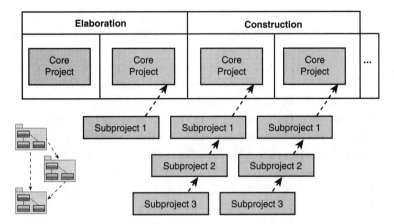

Figure 10-4 *Offsetting subproject iterations to reflect architectural layering*

It is worth noting here that there is an obvious cascade effect when an iteration on a subproject is late. If time boxing is not respected, the schedule slips progressively; if time boxing is respected, the danger is that the component might not be ready for delivery at the close of the iteration. In both cases, the dependent projects suffer.

We still have a one-to-one relationship between the core project iterations and the subproject iterations. The only real difference between Figure 10-3 and Figure 10-4 is the offsetting of the start and end dates for the subproject iterations.

The "Control Project" Pattern

As you continue to exploit the loose architectural coupling between the various components of the system being built and integrate components from more than one source, the core project becomes less and less the core of the entire development effort and more of a control mechanism to coordinate the assembly of a larger system from a number of other independently developed systems. In other words, as the number of subprojects grows, the core project develops less and less of the core functionality of the system and increasingly just plays a coordination role.

The "Core Project" pattern provides tight integration between the core project and the subprojects, with the number and size of the iterations of the subprojects being dictated by the core project. The key to making this work is defining a set of loosely coupled components that are then assembled into the overall solution. If the components are highly *independent*, the subprojects, including their phases and iterations, can also become more independent, with the core project playing less of a defining role and more of a pure coordination role, providing the management and architectural control needed to make sure that the components of the subprojects interact in a coordinated way. To achieve this, we introduce a "Control Project" to coordinate the work of multiple semi-independent subprojects. To facilitate the clear identification of those sets of components that can be delivered separately, we group sets of closely collaborating components into larger, courser-grained, independently deliverable groups of components that we call subsystems.[6] Figure 10-5 illustrates the relationship between the control project and the set of subprojects, where the subprojects are each responsible for a single subsystem and have their lifecycles bounded and controlled by the control project.

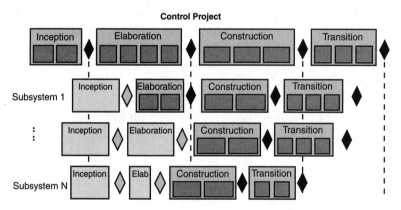

Figure 10-5   *The control project architects and integrates*

The project still starts with a single project (the control project) that captures the overall business needs for the project as a whole and creates the overall architecture including a partitioning of the solution into subsystems. As the subsystems boundaries become stable and their roles and responsibilities emerge, subprojects are created to develop them. This is

---

[6] In much UML and component-based development literature, the terms "component" and "subsystem" are used as synonyms. We reserve the use of the word "subsystem" to denote those sets of components that can be considered and delivered as a separate product. We hope this makes the text more accessible and not more confusing.

similar to the approach taken in the previous patterns with components; the difference here is that the subsystems are sufficiently complex to require a project of their own to manage their development. Each subsystem has an internal structure of components and potentially additional subsystems, which are in turn composed of components and possibly other subsystems, and so on.

The control project has two major roles to play in the creation of its sub-projects:

- Conceiving the subsystem projects within the confines of the overall architecture it creates

- Proving the overall architecture of the system as a whole

Because of the work done by the control project to define the architecture and the component subsystems, there is often very little work for the sub-projects to do to complete their Inception and Elaboration phases. In some cases the control project will perform these phases on behalf of the subprojects. This is a very common pattern, which is shown in Figure 10-5 by the presence of the grayed-out subproject phases. This leads to the appearance that the subprojects go straight into their Elaboration or Construction phase.

In fact, it is actually quite typical for the control project to perform the Inception phase and often the Elaboration phase for the entire project. Subsequent phases are then performed independently for each subsystem, with all the subprojects following the "Immediate Construction" evolution iteration pattern discussed in Chapter 7, "Evolution and Phase Planning."

Although the subsystem projects are relatively independent, their Elaboration phases (if they are undertaking these themselves) must be completed before the control project can complete its own Elaboration phase. It is very hard to prove the overall architecture of the system as a whole if the subsystem architectures are not in place. After the control project enters its Construction phase, it will assemble and test deployable releases of the overall system. Again this requires that the subsystems are deployable and therefore that they have exited the Elaboration phase. There are no such restrictions on the relationships between the Inception phases. The control project might choose to spawn an additional subproject at any time during its Inception or Elaboration phases.

In addition to establishing the overall architecture for the integrated solution, the control project provides the means for integrating the component subsystems into a complete solution. As the subprojects iterate and produce releases of their subsystems, these are delivered periodically (as frequently as possible, preferably continually) to the control project, which integrates them into a single system and then tests that system. The control project combines and integrates the subsystems from all the subprojects into a coherent deliverable. This leads to the subprojects transitioning their major releases to the control project, which has the responsibility for transitioning the solution as a whole to the user community. This is why all the subproject Construction and Transition phases end before the equivalent phases of the control project.

In this pattern, the project timelines are much less rigidly structured, with the subprojects adopting an iteration frequency and timeline that enables them to effectively address their risks while meeting their obligations to deliver to the control project. In many cases the subprojects can iterate at a higher frequency than the control project, which is often entirely dependent upon the results of the subproject iterations.

The control project also provides a project "heartbeat" (in the form of a common set of project phases and milestones), governing and coordinating the lifecycle for the project as a whole. This enables stakeholders to get involved in and review the state of the project as a whole rather than as a loose collection of collaborating projects.

The control project maintains overall responsibility for the architecture of the solution and continuously integrates the outputs of the subprojects by assembling, integrating, and testing them. These activities are continuous throughout the project, with each of the control project's phases playing a critical role in ensuring the delivery of an integrated solution, with its

- Inception phase-building the business case for the system as a whole and considering the various potential sources for the subsystems and components that could be used to facilitate its development

- Elaboration phase, focused on proving and baselining the architecture across the whole set of subsystems and subprojects

- Construction phase, focused on the continuous integration of the production-quality releases produced by the subprojects and the demonstration of the overall end-to-end threads of execution that their assembly supports

- Transition phase, focused on the delivery of the resulting composite system to its users

Many large projects fall into the trap of decoupling the architecture from the integration, testing, and deployment of the overall solution, thereby adopting the "anti-pattern" shown in Figure 10-6.

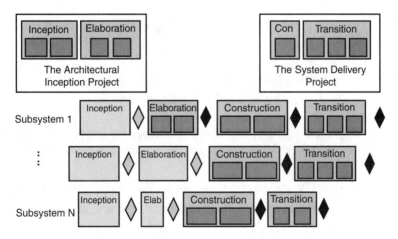

Figure 10-6   *An "uncontrolled" project anti-pattern*

In this anti-pattern, two discrete, disconnected (often by a considerable period of time), independent projects are created. First the project starts with an architectural inception project to define the architecture for the integrated solution. This project is limited to the very beginning of the project, identifying the boundaries and responsibilities of the subsystems to be built. The subsystem projects are then kicked off to independently develop the set of subsystems, and the architectural Inception project is concluded and shut down. Sometime later another project, the system delivery project, is started to integrate the various subsystems into a single composite system and then deploy it. This project is isolated to the very end of the project after the various subsystems have been independently constructed.

The problem here is the huge disconnect that occurs between these two separate projects. This causes many issues for the management team running the project, including the following:

- The lack of any ownership of the architecture. The architects are typically long gone before the ramifications of their decisions become apparent.

- The lack of any early integration of the products produced by the subprojects.

- The lack of continued ownership of the early decisions made by the architectural inception project.

- The lack of any ownership of the end-to-end threads to be implemented by the final composite system.

- The lack of any authority to resolve conflicts and disagreements between the various subprojects.

- The lack of visibility and commitment to overall project goals, and an everyone-for-themselves attitude among the subprojects.

By instantiating a control project to take the lead, these problems can be avoided, and even the largest projects can be run as a collaborating set of iterative and incremental development projects. The combination of both evolutions (enabling the project to scale in the time dimension) and subprojects (enabling the internal complexity to be managed) provides the flexibility required to enable the iterative and incremental approach to be applied to even the largest of endeavors.

This pattern is very flexible, allowing for both

- The development of highly coupled *systems-of-systems,* where only the overall system is released and deployed

- The development and integration of more loosely coupled application suites where, as well as being integrated by the control project, the individual subsystems are treated as products in their own right and transition to both the control project and their own user communities

The System-of-Systems Pattern

To enable the application of the Control Project pattern, the requirements and architectural approaches adopted must be layered and integrated in a similar way to the management approach. For the subsystems to be able to be independently developed in an iterative and incremental fashion, their corresponding subprojects must be able to identify end-to-end threads of execution for their subsystems and have a clear understanding of where their responsibilities begin and end.

Using the Unified Process and use cases, a recursive solution to systems development has evolved that supports this way of working. It is most commonly known as the system-of-systems pattern and is a form of systems engineering[7] using the Unified Modeling Language.[8] It builds upon the standard use-case driven development approach described in Appendix A, "A Brief Introduction to Use-Case Driven Development," to provide a recursive solution that promotes reuse and that scales to all forms of large-scale systems development.[9]

---

[7] See ISO/IEC 15288 Standard: Systems Engineering - Systems Life Cycle Processes—Standard BS ISO/IEC 15288:2002 British Standard / ISO/IEC 28-Nov-2002. ISBN: 0 580 40810 8

[8] www.uml.org

[9] The use-case approach to large-scale systems development is described in *Software Reuse: Architecture, Process and Organization for Business Success* by Ivar Jacobson, Martin Griss, and Patrik Jonsson (Reading, MA: Addison-Wesley, 1997).

Figure 10-7 illustrates how a system is completely composed of a number of collaborating but independent system elements, which we call components in our object-oriented, use-case driven approach.

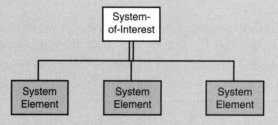

Figure 10-7   *Systems and system elements*

Source: ISO/IEC 15288 Standard: Systems Engineering - Systems Life Cycle Processes - Standard BS ISO/IEC 15288:2002 British Standard / ISO/IEC 28-Nov-2002 - ISBN: 0 580 40810 8

As a project starts to scale up and spawn subprojects to independently develop one or more of these system elements, we start to treat the system elements differently; in fact, we start to treat them as systems in their own right, which we call subsystems to differentiate them from the original system-of-interest. This promotion of system elements to formal subsystems is illustrated by Figure 10-8.

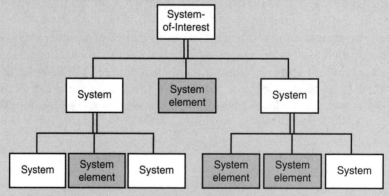

Figure 10-8   *Treating system elements as systems in their own right*

Source: ISO/IEC 15288 Standard: Systems Engineering - Systems Life Cycle Processes—Standard BS ISO/IEC 15288:2002 British Standard / ISO/IEC 28-Nov-2002 - ISBN: 0 580 40810 8

Note that not every system element is promoted to subsystem status, just those that are to be developed independently. Some system elements are always left to be developed as part of the original system-of-interest.

When applying use-case driven development techniques to this problem, the Unified Process can be applied to the system-of-interest and to those system elements selected for independent development. This is illustrated by Figure 10-9, where it can be seen that each of the selected subsystems has its own set of requirements, including its own use-case model, and that the subsystem interactions are coordinated by the use-case realizations created for the original system-of-interest.

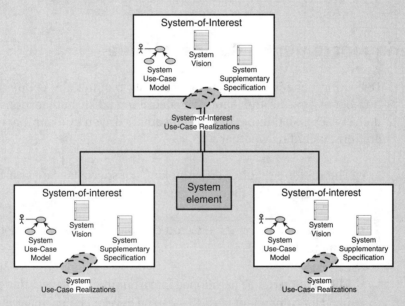

Figure 10-9   *The recursive application of use-case modeling techniques*

The detailed mechanics of system engineering and the techniques involved in its application are well beyond the scope of this book. We introduce these concepts here purely to illustrate that techniques are available to support the decomposition of large systems into networks of collaborating subsystems that can then be developed individually using iterative and incremental techniques.

The key to the effective use of these techniques is to use them in conjunction with the Control Project pattern to ensure that they are managed, governed, and controlled properly to the benefit of the overall project they are introduced to support. The injudicious application of these techniques can lead to additional complexity and exponential increases in the scale of the project. Again these techniques should only be used when really needed.

The positive thing about these techniques (and the reason that we mention them at all) is that just as with the management techniques discussed here, you always start with a small project to address the original system-of-interest. As the initial project evolves and the complexity of the problem and its solution becomes apparent, the development processes, the architecture, and the management structures can all scale up hand-in-hand with one another as needed to address the risks facing the project.

Delivering Incremental Business Value

Delivering benefit to the business usually requires the cooperation of a number of projects and teams. The decision to distribute responsibility for delivery across a number of project teams is driven by a number of considerations, including whether

- The solution requires different kinds of specialized expertise, often supplied by different teams or subcontractors

- The solution is too large or too complex for any one project team to deliver

- The solution can be partitioned into a number of relatively independent component parts that can be developed in parallel

Staged Delivery of Business Value

Although the subject of this book is software development, there will always be other non-software development activities that must be undertaken to make the project and the software a success. Often the software development must be integrated with non-software development activities, such as training, business change, marketing, hardware installation, operating system upgrades, and operational support. This is illustrated in Figure 10-10.

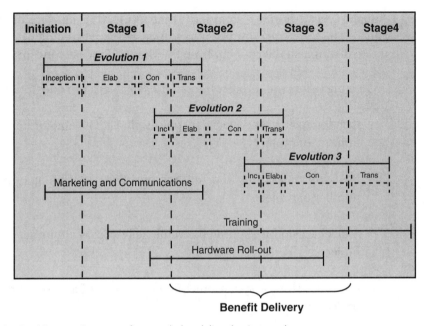

Figure 10-10 *Many projects are often needed to deliver business value.*

The separation of software development from the activities related to promoting business change often results in the situation where the deployment of the solution is turned over to another project team that is responsible for the rollout of the application.[10] The deployment team then has to undertake the business change and training required to enable the new product to deliver the expected business benefit. This usually results in a dedicated project to deploy the application and the related business changes.

Figure 10-10 structures the overall "business project" into a number of "stages," each of which delivers benefit to the business. This structuring of the overall project plan facilitates the integration of the non-software development project components into the plan.

We introduce the concept of the "stage" to coordinate the activities of a number of projects to deliver some specific business value. A stage can be

---

[10] In one project that we worked on, new buildings had to be built to hold the hardware to run the new software. As you can see, deployment can be a major undertaking that sometimes dwarfs the software development in terms of cost and complexity.

thought of as a *business* iteration[11] that results in a delivery of business value.[12] The term *stage* is chosen to emphasize the staged delivery of value and to distinguish the concept from the Unified Process concept of phases.

Organizing the overall project into a series of stages provides

- Regular review and decision points that span and unite a number of projects

- Planning milestones and funding horizons that can span a number of projects

- A mechanism for aligning the value delivered by a number of projects

- A mechanism for synchronizing the releases of a number of projects

The need to add stages is largely driven by the need to coordinate a number of otherwise disconnected projects that need to be synchronized and cooperate to deliver business value.

Stages are particularly useful in a number of circumstances:

- When there are discrete projects to be coordinated.

- When there is a sequence of evolutions that need to be overlapped.

- When the project is large and the Control Project pattern is not suitable to coordinate the diverse kinds of work needed to deliver business value. This is usually when there is a

---

[11] The concept of the stage is taken from the PRINCE2 project management methodology, which mandates their use to partition a project with a sequence of decision points. Unlike the Unified Process's fixed four phases (which also have sequential decision points), the number of stages is flexible and depends on the needs of the business.

[12] When we talk about products, we refer to things of value that the project delivers. Projects will also produce *artifacts,* but these are only intermediate results used to facilitate the project work.

multitude of software and other business projects that need to be coordinated.

- When the project is long-term and the overall project plan needs to be structured without using the more technical concepts of evolutions and phases, which are sometimes considered to be too technical for the project's business sponsors.

The example overall project plan for the ACME Super ATM project provided in Appendix C, "Examples," uses stages to structure the plan. This is because this project falls into the first two categories in the previous list.

Aligning Stages and Evolutions

The determination of a stage boundary is driven by two factors:

- When the value has to be delivered to the business. The end of a stage is partly determined by how soon the business needs the value to be delivered by the stage.

- When the software will be available for deployment. Typically the end of a stage has to align with the end of iterations in the Construction or Transition phase of the projects coordinated by the stage. If it doesn't, then there will be no release of the software to generate the business value.

For an iterative software development project, the most stable points in the project's lifecycle are the iteration and phase boundaries. These are the points when the project is "at rest"—the artifacts and releases produced are in a steady state, and objective measurements and results are available. When an evolution passes one of its lifecycle milestones, this ensures that a major set of risks and issues has been retired and that the results achieved are stable and verified.

When using stages to structure the overall project plan, the end of a stage needs to align with the end of at least one development iteration. It is most common to align the end of a stage with the end of an evolution's phase (or the iteration after the end of the phase to provide some contingency) because phase ends tend to deliver more stable and predictable results. These relationships are illustrated in Figure 10-11.

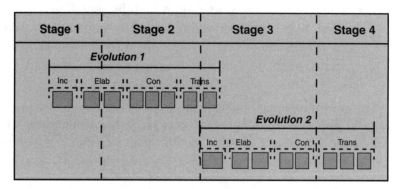

Figure 10-11   *Alignment of stage boundaries with iteration boundaries*

Typically an evolution does not produce results that are stable enough for delivery to the business until the Construction phase, and even then the solution is not complete enough to be fully deployed until the end of the phase. As a result, it is typical to align the end of a stage with the end of the Construction phase or one of the subsequent Transition iterations. Note the overlap between the last iteration in the Transition phase of Evolution 1 and the Inception phase of Evolution 2. This enables the second evolution to get started while the first evolution is wrapping up. Running these iterations in parallel provides continuity between the two evolutions.

Figure 10-11 is somewhat conservative—as we saw in Chapter 6, there can be more overlap between evolutions such as that shown in Figure 10-12. This illustrates the most typical pattern for the alignment of stages and evolutions, with the Inception phase of a subsequent evolution overlapping the Transition phase of the prior evolution, or even with the later iterations of the Construction phase of the prior evolution. This is acceptable because the Inception, Construction, and Transition phases do not affect the architecture of the overall solution, so dependencies are greatly reduced, enabling work to proceed in parallel.

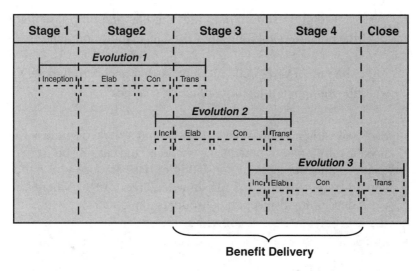

Figure 10-12 *Typical stage/phase alignment*

The inclusion of the next evolution's Inception phase in the previous stage enables the project to conclude its stage with all the information it needs to make the decision about whether to go ahead with the next stage. In addition to coordinating the set of projects to ensure regular benefit delivery to the business, the stages act as management review and control points for the project as a whole.

Handling Sequential and Parallel Evolutions

Aligning evolution cycles as described in the previous section is not really sufficient justification for adding the concept of a stage; evolution iteration alignment can be achieved without using stages. But as evolutions become increasingly independent and overlapped to optimize the project plans, enable the efficient use of resources, and reduce the total elapsed time for the project, the need for staging becomes more apparent.

As we saw in Chapter 6, there are rules that apply when overlapping evolutions:

- An evolution cannot complete a phase before the previous evolution has completed the same phase.

- An evolution should not enter the Elaboration phase before the previous evolution has exited its Elaboration phase.

- The more overlap, the more work that occurs in parallel and the more potential for conflicting changes.

As noted earlier, some projects require that several discrete software products be developed in parallel, as would be the case if you were developing a communication system consisting of base stations and handsets. Each could be evolved separately as shown in Figure 10-13, where a single project is developing two separate products in parallel.[13]

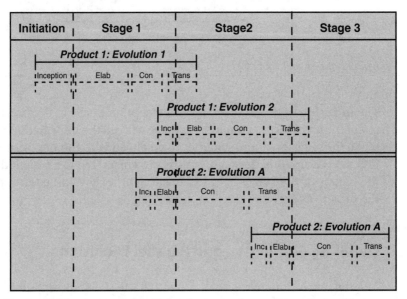

Figure 10-13 *Parallel development of multiple software products within a single project*

The overall project must manage any dependencies between the two streams of software development (as well as other training and marketing projects that are not shown). As new releases of the solution are delivered to the business, the benefit of using stages to align the development schedules of the two products (the handset and base station) becomes more readily apparent.

---

[13] If the two software products shared an architecture or could not be delivered without one another, then the Control Project pattern would be more appropriate.

This provides a simple mechanism for scaling up projects and for including additional self-contained streams of work under the control of one simple overall project plan. In this case, the two products are very loosely coupled and can be managed fairly independently. The "stage" concept adds a coordination point that enables relatively independent work efforts to synchronize with each other to deliver business value.

Managing Dependencies Between Iterative Projects

As a project manager, it can be useful to understand the mechanisms that iterative development practices supply to help us manage inter-project dependencies.

Figure 10-14 shows how iterations of one project can be set up to be dependent upon the results of another project's iterations and phases.

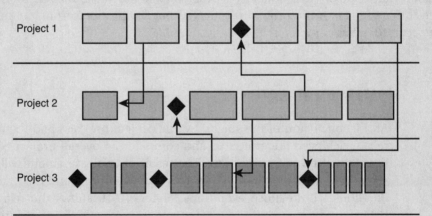

Figure 10-14 *Aligning dependencies with iteration and phase boundaries*

In this figure, the boxes represent the iterations of the projects, and the diamonds represent their lifecycle milestones, which are achieved when they exit the phases of the Unified Process. The arrows show how an iteration of one project is dependent on the conclusion of an iteration or the completion of a milestone in another project.

The iteration boundaries and lifecycle milestones of a project provide suitable points for defining inter-project dependencies because they are the most stable points in an iterative project's lifecycle, the points at which the project is in a steady state and its artifacts and releases are most likely to be in a fit state for reuse. If you have a dependency on another iterative project, then it is foolish to align yourself to anything other than an iteration end. This is because these are the only points of visibility into the other project plans and the only points where you can be confident that the other project will be at rest with a sensible baselined set of products and artifacts. The intermediate points in the iterations are too unstable to be useful when considering and addressing inter-project dependencies.

If a project manager knows that another project depends on the results of an iteration, he or she can make sure that the dependent elements are the highest priority for the team and do not get moved to a later iteration if things are not going so well.

From the perspective of one of the "consumer" projects, the fact that a project has passed one of the lifecycle milestones provides additional insight into the stability and state of the products it is producing. In fact it is quite rare for projects, other than an owning core project, to accept any products from another project until it has completed its Elaboration phase.

Assessing Stages

At the conclusion of the stages, overall project progress and the business results achieved are evaluated and compared to overall project goals and the state of the overall project. The result of this assessment will in turn shape the plans of subsequent stages and evolutions and the phases and iterations within those evolutions. Figure 10-10 shows the relationship between stages, evolutions, phases, and iterations of three evolutions of a software product and the non-software development subprojects that make up the overall project.

In this case, the stages are a management mechanism for planning, coordinating, and controlling the overall project as a whole. Stage assessments are undertaken at the stage boundaries to review the project in its entirety. The project assessment process described in Chapter 9, "Iteration, Phase, and Project Assessments," provides a perfectly good mechanism for performing the stage assessments.

The objectives of a stage assessment are to

- Confirm that the need for the project has not changed

- Satisfy the stakeholders of the quality of the products delivered by the subprojects

- Establish that the stage has been completed successfully

- Confirm the objectives and tolerances for the next stage

- Confirm that the business case is still viable

- Authorize the passage of the project into the next stage

When evaluating a stage, look collectively at the results of the evolution, phases, and iterations just completed: Are they all ready to proceed? Have they met their own success criteria? A stage cannot conclude successfully unless the phases and iterations of the project's evolutions successfully conclude. For the non-software development subprojects, are they on track?

As shown in Figure 10-10, the stage boundaries can cut across multiple evolutions of the software product and any non-software development subprojects commissioned by the overall project.

A stage assessment is concluded in the same way as any other project assessment, and it establishes and documents the state and fate of the project as a whole. This includes deciding whether the next stage is *approved* or this stage is *extended* or if the whole project is to be *paused*, *postponed*, or *cancelled*.

The fact that the evolutions within the project have been subject to iteration and phase assessments means that little preparation is required to drive the stage assessments as long as the post-project and benefits realization reviews have also been conducted. If these are not undertaken as part of the overall project, then additional work will be required to prepare the information needed to support the stage assessment.

Projects and Programs

A *project*[14] is not the sole management tool for organizing work: projects can be grouped together into *programs*. A program is a group of related projects managed in a coordinated way. Programs usually include an element of ongoing work.[15]

Examples of different kinds of programs include

- Strategic programs, in which projects share vision and objectives

- Business cycle programs, in which projects share budget or resources but might differ in their vision and objectives

- Infrastructure programs, in which projects define and deploy supporting technology used by many other projects, resulting in shared standards

- Research and development programs, in which projects share assessment criteria

- Partnership programs, in which projects span collaborating organizations

Of course this is just a sampling of the many different kinds of programs, and there are often variations that combine different aspects of them. The important thing to remember about a program is that it organizes projects to focus attention on the delivery of a specific set of strategic business results. True programs differ from large projects[16] in that they focus on the

---

[14]   A *project* is a temporary endeavor undertaken to create a unique product, service, or result (Source: Project Management Body of Knowledge (PMBOK); see www.pmi.org).

[15]   Project Management Body of Knowledge (PMBOK); see www.pmi.org.

[16]   There is often much debate about what differentiates a program from a large project, much of which is purely academic in nature. In reality, large projects can benefit from a lot of the best practices inherent in program management and vice versa. When programs are explicitly created by organizations, they are long-term, transformational endeavors aimed at producing a step change in some aspect of the organization's capability. When projects get very large, they might appear to transform into programs as program management techniques are applied to help manage their complexity, but in reality they are still large projects.

delivery of a step change in an organization's capability, which in turn can impact all aspects of the business including the business processes, financial structures, and information technology.

Another area that is often confused with and related to program management is *portfolio management*. This is typically a higher-level management oversight function that focuses primarily on allocating investments and reviewing results delivered to the business. It does not tend to get into project coordination activities but rather relies on the program and project management layers for this management. Iterative projects fit very easily into a portfolio management environment. The control and visibility provided by the layered management approach and the continual monitoring of project progress through the iteration and phase assessments enable the iterative project to be easily integrated into the portfolio.

The relationship between programs, projects, evolutions, and iterations was explored briefly in Chapter 5 and illustrated by Figure 5-1, repeated here as Figure 10-15.

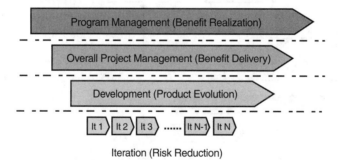

Figure 10-15 *A scalable process: planning at multiple levels*

Adapted from Laurence Archer, "Implementing Rational Unified Process Within a PRINCE2 Environment" (Oaks Management Services [previously Oak IT], 2001).

Organizing Programs Using Stages

Because we have already shown that projects can have subprojects, and stages can be used to align projects working in parallel to deliver some business benefit, why add the additional overhead of a program? The reason is that using subprojects and stages might not provide sufficient oversight for and coordination between the projects. Sometimes additional management is needed so that the benefits achieved by executing the projects in a coordinated way is greater than that which would accrue if the projects were all done individually. Within a program, projects often share objectives and have a common process. Because the projects in a program work together to produce a desired business result, they usually share a common vision and requirements, a common architecture and related components, and various assets and artifacts from the development process including common standards, style guides, and review criteria.

The concept of a stage aligns nicely with the notion of a program providing a long-lived management structure that coordinates business value delivery over time. In effect, a stage is to a program what an evolution is to a project. The relationship between program stages[17] and projects is shown in Figure 10-16.

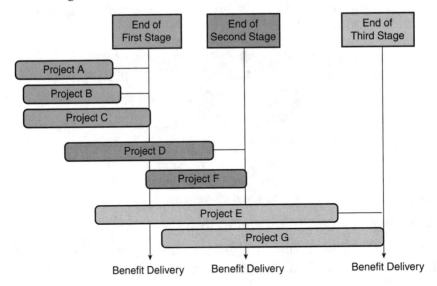

Figure 10-16   *The relationships between program stages and projects*

---

[17]   In the program management methodology described in *Managing Successful Programmes* by the UK Office of Government Commerce (The Stationery Office Books, 1999) and some other program management methods, the program stages are referred to as *tranches*. We decided it was easier to understand our approach if we didn't introduce another new term for a concept that already exists. If you are familiar with the concept of *tranches*, feel free to substitute this wherever you see the term "program stage."

Each stage delivers an incremental change in organizational capability. The end of a stage provides a major review point at which the program results can be evaluated and assessed against desired outcomes.

Stages can be used to group related projects together, as shown in Figure 10-17.

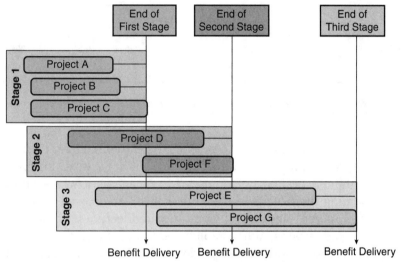

Figure 10-17   *Using program stages to group sets of projects with shared goals*

Just like the evolutions of a software development project, the stages can overlap, building upon one another and sharing objectives as they incrementally deliver products as part of a larger, coordinated program. The evolutionary nature of the stages and the inherent close coupling of the projects within them make them prime candidates for the application of the Control Project pattern and Unified Process iterative lifecycle.

Figure 10-18 shows how work can be organized within a stage, with the stage governed by a control project. Notice how the phases for the control project sometimes end a little later than the corresponding phases of the projects it manages. This enables the results from the managed projects to be *rolled up* to the control project.

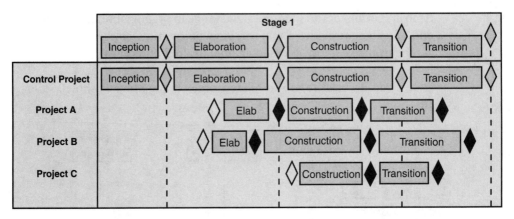

Figure 10-18   *Each program stage is governed by a control project.*

How is a stage managed in practice? As with our earlier discussion of control projects, the control project starts the stage by capturing the requirements and desired outcomes for the stage as a whole and creating or updating the overall architecture to be shared by all projects within the stage. As the subsystems within the architecture become clear and their roles and responsibilities stabilize, additional projects in the stage are initiated. As we saw when we introduced the Control Project pattern, it is typical for the Inception phase and sometimes the Elaboration phase of the subsystem projects to be performed by the control project. This leads to the subsystem projects having had some of their milestone achieved for them, which is shown in Figure 10-18 by the grayed-out diamond-shaped milestone symbols.

As the subprojects iterate and produce releases of their subsystems, these releases are delivered to the control project, which then integrates them into a single system and system tests it. The control project integrates the final results from the subsystem projects, delivering the result for the stage.

Just as the decision to split a single project into a number of evolutions at the project level was driven by the desire to deliver value earlier, the decision to organize the program work into a number of stages is driven by the desire to organize a number of projects to incrementally deliver value to the sponsoring organization. Stages also provide a way to manage projects working in parallel, providing a control and synchronization mechanism (through the control project) for related projects.

The Important Role of Architecture

As we have discussed at a number of points, a stable architecture is essential to support teams working in parallel. In these discussions we have shown the architecture of the overall solution being defined and developed by a core team, usually the control project team. Solution architecture by consensus or committee does not work—every attempt at working this way we have seen has resulted in failure. Because the architecture effectively defines the scope of the work that the subsystem and subproject teams perform, a single perspective that cuts across all teams working on the project is needed to make sure that the work will all fit together.

The cautionary tale here is that if the project structure and team responsibilities are determined before the architectural composition is worked out, conflicts are likely to arise. This is one of the reasons why it is difficult to combine a number of projects into a program after they are underway: each project team will already have a perspective on what they are doing, and they are unlikely to take direction from any other "peer" team. In cases such as this, a firm but fair dictatorial hand is needed from the control project. Failure to align the roles and responsibilities of the subsystem teams through an overall shared architecture will result in a system that cannot be integrated.

Summary

In prior chapters we have focused on managing the project itself. In this chapter we looked at how projects can be scaled up and even grouped together into programs using a small set of recursive, layered management techniques.

Project size has many dimensions, many of which are unknown at the start of the project. As a result, it is always best to start small and scale up as necessary. The techniques that we described show how the initial work can be conducted by a single project, which can evolve into a control project if it becomes apparent that more structure is needed. Because the mechanisms are the same regardless of the size of the endeavor being undertaken, starting small has no downside, and it gives you a better understanding of how big the problem really is without imposing too much overhead too early. If the project starts big, it will stay big.

The main lesson that we have learned over the years is that smaller projects are more successful, so the management team should do everything it can to try to ensure that their projects are no larger than they need to be. If we always start with the assumption that the project is reasonably small and manageable, then there is the possibility that it will stay that way.

Even when the project size expands, you can exploit the layering principles to keep things small at each layer. If the architecture is stable, each subproject can work relatively independently, coordinating with other subprojects at iteration boundaries and through the control project.

Finally, even for large projects, the plans must be small. A large project, properly layered, can still have a simple project plan. With the details pushed down to the subproject level, the overall project plan still consists mostly of goals, milestones, and dependencies organized at stage, project, phase, and iteration levels. Each plan need consume no more than a page or so, and at no time is there a need for a task-by-task, day-by-day schedule. No project manager can accurately plan at that level, and it is not necessary anyway. Detailed planning actually gets in the way of success rather than enabling it by obscuring the real issues with meaningless and usually out-of-date detail.

The good news is that regardless of the size of the project, everything starts the same; you always start with the same set of core products: risks, plans, business case, vision, use cases, architecture, and prototypes.

11

Getting Started with Iterative Project Management

"Desirable ends do not come of themselves. Men must conceive them, believe in them, further them, and execute them."
—Carl Van Doren

This book has presented an approach to improving business results through the systematic application of the principles of iterative development, but the principles do not apply themselves. In this final chapter we present practical advice on adopting these practices within your projects and your organization. We realize that you come to the subject of iterative project management with different goals and different constraints on how much change you can introduce. You might be someone who is

- Completely new to managing iterative development projects and about to start on your very first iterative project

- Already engaged in managing iterative projects and struggling to put the theory into practice

- Already managing iterative development projects and looking to improve and validate your approach

- Engaged in rolling out or supporting the rollout of iterative development techniques to your department or organization

To support all these views and more, this chapter looks at how to you can apply what you have learned to

- Implement your first project

- Build on your current success

- Help change your organization

We discuss how you can start to apply the techniques immediately to the projects that you manage and how you can build upon this success to progressively expand your use of iterative software development practices.

Embarking on Your First Iterative Project

Embarking on your first iterative project probably fills you with some uneasiness, and you might have some doubts about your project taking on what you might perceive to be additional risk. In this section we help you take that first step.

Why Iterate?

As we have noted a number of times in prior chapters, iterative development is undertaken to eliminate project risks early in the project, before they can have a chance to sink the project. By tackling risk explicitly, your project will be more likely to succeed. That alone should provide fairly powerful motivation. Other reasons for adopting an iterative approach include

- To achieve higher quality

- To achieve faster results

- To achieve results more reliably, or sometimes just to achieve results at all

- To reduce staff frustration and turnover

- To achieve greater flexibility and business agility

- To reduce costs

Understanding these and any other goals is important so that you can factor them into the actions that you and your team will take.

The impetus for change can come from any number of sources: from senior management wanting to achieve better business results, from senior technical leaders wanting to resolve recurrent project problems, or from project teams that want to improve themselves. Whatever the source, the stimulus for change tends to gestate until a sponsor picks it up.

There also needs to be a sense of urgency about the need to change; some crisis or significant opportunity is required to get the project team members to be interested in the extra work of learning how to do something new. Change is initiated for a variety of reasons. The reasons listed here are the major themes that lie behind most change initiatives. Often the reasons for the change are not well articulated or even well understood.

Unless there is a sense of urgency, the stimulus for change will never become great enough to overcome resistance. People become comfortable with the status quo, and it is difficult to get them to change unless they feel that they will personally benefit from the change. They need to believe that unless they change the way they work, bad things will happen, or in the case of opportunities, good things will fail to happen.

This is not to say that threatening or frightening people is an effective motivational technique (it is not). It merely observes that people need to feel that if they don't change, they will fail. In the early stages of a change, only a few people might feel this need to change. As long as the change is small enough that it only affects a small group, this is sufficient to move ahead.

Potential Barriers to the Adoption of Iterative Practices

Before you start, you need to understand the potential barriers to the change so that you can make the right choices of timing, project, and approach. Some of the more important questions to ask include in the following:

- **How supportive is senior management of the change?** The measurements and milestones they establish can easily derail an iterative approach, as is the case when they ask even seemingly innocent questions such as "When will the design be completed?" or "When will requirements be signed-off?"

- **What is the scope of your authority to make changes?** How much of the development lifecycle are you responsible for? For example, the requirements might have already been specified in a format and to a level of detail that would make it more difficult to adopt an iterative approach.

- **What are the team's feelings about the changes?** How enthusiastic is the team about iterating? To achieve the transition to iterative development, you will need the support of the team, especially the other members of the leadership team.

- **What else does the team have to do?** How many other projects and initiatives is the team involved in? If the team is not focused on and dedicated to the project, the transition to iterative practices will probably be slower and take more time and energy to complete.

- **What capability do you need to improve?** It is important to understand the capability of the team and how well the current capability supports the proposed iterative approach. For example, is there any testing capability in the team? Testing will be needed from the first iteration, which is often a problem in companies organized around the phases of a waterfall process where the expectation is that testers will only be needed late in the project lifecycle.

- **What work has already been done?** Few projects start from scratch. You need to know what products and artifacts have already been produced.

- **Where are you in the project lifecycle?** It is important to understand the state of the project. Changes are easier to make during an evolution's Inception and Elaboration phases than they are during its Construction and Transition phases.[1]

Selecting the right project and the right team members for the initial effort is important. Table 11-1 presents some of the key characteristics to look for in your first iterative project.

Table 11-1   *The Characteristics of a Good First Iterative Project*

Characteristic	Description	Reason
Attitude	Iterative development needs a team that wants to iterate (or at least to try new approaches).	"Unbelievers" will revert to their old ways of working, masking this by using "iterative" terms.
Project Size	The project needs to big enough to have at least four iterations but small enough that it will deliver results in four to six months. You want to choose projects that can demonstrate rapid success in dealing with real problems.	It will take a few iterations for the benefits to be accepted by the team. The team will need time to get used to the new ways of working.
Team Composition	Iterative development requires a full development team to be in place.	The team might be small but needs to cover all the software development disciplines all the time. Testers are needed early and throughout the project, not just at the end.

---

[1]   You can still evaluate a project using the Unified Process lifecycle even if the project is not being run using the Unified Process and even if it is not being run iteratively. The questions in the phase checklists can be applied to any project, and the answers will provide valuable insight into the project's state and outstanding risks.

Table 11-1   *The Characteristics of a Good First Iterative Project*   (continued)

Characteristic	Description	Reason
Technical Leadership	You need the support of people who can accurately gauge technical risk and help you to use this assessment to drive the definition and mitigation of technical risks.	The selection of appropriate risk reduction strategies requires a high level of technical knowledge about the proposed solution. The management team relies on the architecture team to successfully guide the project through the Elaboration phase.
Business Criticality	The project needs to be business-critical enough to get the attention and involvement of stakeholders throughout the project.	Stakeholder involvement is needed throughout the project if the full benefits of iterative development are to be achieved.

The lack of these characteristics does not, by itself, present an insurmountable problem, but it will slow the pace of the project, in particular extending the first two phases where the major business and technical risks are addressed.

When you start your first iterative project, factor the successful adoption of iterative techniques into the critical success factors for the project and the career development objectives for the team members. This is especially important if circumstances require an investment in training and mentoring the team to enable the transformation to take place.

Conventional wisdom suggests that you should choose low-impact, non-critical projects to be the focus of early change efforts to reduce the change effort's risk and the potential for failure. The problem with this is that although these projects are lower risk, their non-criticality usually means that they are starved for resources and not considered "mainstream" enough to ever be taken seriously as success stories. This dooms the overall change initiative. Low-priority projects are not visible enough to engender the support needed to drive the change forward.

Instead you should

- Look for a *small* number of must-do projects that have organizational focus and strong support

- Look for projects with a smaller set of stakeholders to keep communication simpler

- Look for projects with high internal visibility—ones that would make good success stories

- Choose projects that are short- to medium-term in length

- Staff the projects with the best people available (respected leaders)

- Organize projects to generate short-term wins—divide work into iterations

- Keep the project size small in the first few iterations and then scale up

- Focus on choosing the right projects and committing resources to them

Choosing critical projects sounds risky, but there is no sense in hiding from the fact that only critical projects will get the attention and resources necessary to succeed. The key is choosing projects critical enough to get resources but that can start small and then scale up in a controlled way, not becoming too large before the architecture and technical risks can be brought under control. Scaling up should be targeted for the Construction phase but not before.

Communicating the Goals of Change

To motivate the change in approach, you must be able to clearly and concisely communicate why a different approach is needed. If the business goal is to achieve better responsiveness to changing market needs, the goal for the iterative project effort might be something like *be able to go from idea to released product in nine months (or less!)*. The more precise and measurable the goals, the easier they are to achieve.

It's important for you to do a couple things when you are communicating the reasons for the change:

- **Be concise and articulate, and be able to explain it in a few minutes or less**—The vision needs to be precise and specific, without sounding like empty slogans exhorting people to "do better." It should set specific goals that can be translated into criteria by which people can make decisions.

- **Link problems to outcomes, such as "If we don't do X better, Y will happen"**—Linking problems to outcomes is essential to getting a sense of urgency to solving the problem. Being specific is also important. Generalization is easy but not very compelling. Ultimately you need to set specific goals. Being specific about the problem and its impact sends this message from the beginning. For example, "Our inability to deliver releases within X% of the projected date results in lost opportunities of Y million dollars per year" directly links the problem to its outcome.

You must communicate this vision at every possible opportunity, at every level of the organization. Everyone should understand what is being done and why. Learn to be able to concisely describe the vision in a few minutes and present it as an "elevator pitch"—think of a chance meeting in an elevator with a key decision maker. You have this person's undivided attention for, at most, a few minutes. The vision needs to be crisp, concise, and compelling enough to explain in just these few minutes. Everyone today is busy; they don't have time to carefully read pages and pages of reasoning and justification. Set it out for them, and your message will have a better chance of being internalized. The vision need not be very specific about how the change will be achieved, but it does need to be compelling.

John Kotter[2] observes that failure to communicate the vision is a key factor in failed change efforts. You will probably need to communicate the vision 10 to 100 times more often than you are planning to. People usually focus on the impact and cost of changing; everyone needs to understand the impact of not changing. Only when people feel that their outcomes will suffer if they don't change will the change really take root.

---

[2]   John P. Kotter, *Leading Change* (Harvard Business School Press, 1996).

Determining the Pace of Change

Every person and every project has a limited tolerance for change. People who have been successful with change initiatives in the past are more likely to embrace change, whereas people and projects that have a mixed or poor record of success with change will be more resistant to change. Trying to make too many changes too fast will be destabilizing and will make things worse, at least for a period of time. Most people have a threshold to the pace of change that they can sustain—try to push change faster, and the entire effort can stall and fall apart. The ability of the people to deal with change needs to be taken into account when planning change.

If the change is too large, people may lose hope that it will ever pay off and might abandon it. We have personally witnessed this many times, which is why we recommend an iterative approach to introducing change. This seems like simple common sense and no great innovation, but it remains a mystery to us why people so often try to push large changes in a single large initiative.

Expectations must be managed carefully. The tendency for teams to want to do everything immediately needs to be tempered; a sense of "proportion and pace" is crucial. The improvements must be driven fast enough to achieve the desired results as quickly as possible, but not so fast that the team gets confused or disheartened at the lack of progress caused by trying to do too much change at once.

Dealing with Skepticism

You will encounter skepticism and disbelief in the approach that you are proposing. You should be prepared to answer the skeptics because they are likely to become your biggest supporters if you can win them over. Everyone has seen grand new approaches that claim wonderful benefits but fail to produce results. The skeptics will ask, "What will be different this time?" The argument is based on the observation that every project manager starts every project with a new plan and the best of intentions, but the result is always the same: project slips, frustration, and failure. You must be able to answer the question, "Why should we believe you are doing something significant enough to affect the outcome?"

We have encountered this question often enough to have some thoughts on how to answer it. Appropriate responses include the following:

- "We recognize that change is inevitable, and we are taking an approach that recognizes that. We will set goals for our progress, we will measure ourselves against those goals, and we will adapt our approach in light of new information rather than assuming that we had all the answers at the start of the project, which you know is not true."

- "We will focus on the big risks early, while we can still do something about them, and we will take explicit action to reduce those risks. If our first attempts do not work, we will keep at them until we have dealt with the risks."

- "We will focus on delivering the most important things the business *really needs* in an agreed-upon time frame rather than delivering everything they want. This is an important change from how we have done things in the past."

In short, you need to say and show how the iterative approach is pragmatic and deals with the realities of the world. Although real convincing comes only with the proof provided by real progress, most skeptics find the honesty of statements like these to be refreshing, provided that they are backed up with action.

Starting with Just Iterative Development

As discussed in Chapter 1, "What Is Iterative Development?" iterative behavior can be thought of as starting from the activity of developers. For a project to be considered iterative, it is essential that the software be developed iteratively—that is, the core development disciplines of Analysis, Design, and Implementation (which includes developer-driven testing) are applied repeatedly to evolve the software. Fortunately, this is the most natural way for developers to work. As Figure 11-1 shows, when these disciplines are executed in an iterative fashion, additional disciplines can be added around the core development ones to get the whole team iterating in an effective and collaborative manner.

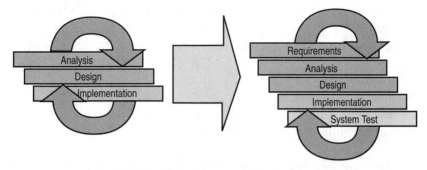

Figure 11-1   *Development (Analysis, Design, Implementation) lies at the core of the iterative approach.*

In some organizations, where waterfall development has become so entrenched that it has influenced the organizational structure and management responsibilities, you might find that

- The development work does not start until the requirements work is complete, and/or

- The other stakeholders and managers in the organization are very suspicious and don't believe that iterative development is suitable for them.

In this case you can still apply and benefit from iterative development and project management techniques by adopting the "requirements pipeline" pattern last seen in Chapter 1 and repeated in Figure 11-2.

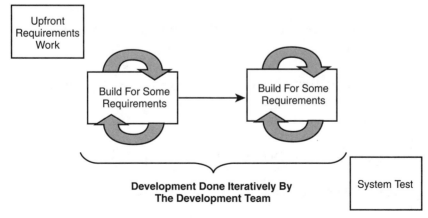

Figure 11-2   *Developing iteratively inside a waterfall requirements model*

This compromise is often adopted in organizations new to iterative development, and it reflects the fact that the desire to iterate commonly originates in the development teams. To prove their iterative development capability, they will start to develop the software iteratively while the requirements and overall system testing are done in the traditional manner. In this case, the job of the development team is made easier if the requirements are captured in a form that enables the identification of sensible chunks of work to be implemented in the iterations.

After the development team has demonstrated the capability to implement sets of requirements in an iterative fashion, you can then expand the scope of the iterations to include the requirements and assessment disciplines. The projects will not be truly iterative in the way we have described throughout the rest of the book until you change the way that the development team works with the business.

Bootstrapping an Iterative Project

Starting your first iterative project is really just like starting any other iterative project. You apply the "bootstrapping" process described in Chapter 7, "Evolution and Phase Planning":

- Start with a small team focused on the business and technical risks

- Challenge the team to start with a four-week iteration

- Adjust the iteration length in response to work and team culture

- Plan to deliver business benefit every three to six months

- Plan releases as well as iterations

- Start with a colocated team

- Address the architectural risks before scaling up

Regardless of how large the project might appear to be, remember the principles of scalable iterative project management presented in Chapter 5, "A Layered Approach to Planning and Managing Iterative Projects," Chapter 6, "Overall Project Planning," and Chapter 10, "A Scalable Approach to Managing Iterative Projects":

- **Start with the assumption that it is small**—If you start big, it will stay big, and generally the larger a project, the more likely it is to fail.

- **Do everything within your power to keep the project small**—If you don't fight to keep things small, they will naturally tend to get large.

- **Layer the plans and keep them succinct and focused**—To be comprehensible, plans must be small. Exploit the layering inherent in iterative projects to avoid unnecessary precision in planning the work.

The first iteration of your first iterative project will be the hardest to plan and manage; chances are you won't know exactly what to do and neither will your team, and this uncertainty is unsettling. It is also likely to be a new experience for the stakeholders as well as the project team, which will only compound the problems. To compensate for this, make sure that the iteration has modest objectives: whatever you do, don't set yourself and the team up to fail by setting ridiculously aggressive objectives.

If you are following the advice presented in this book, then the iteration should be of average length (we recommend four weeks but are prepared to accept four to six weeks as a starting point). It is common for initial iterations to run over their schedule. Allowing this to happen establishes a bad precedent. Keep an eye on progress during the iteration and be ready to scale back on ambitions even in the middle of the iteration to make sure that you will have time to assess results. This usually means moving some scope from the current iteration to the next in order to maintain the iteration time box. When you assess the iteration, you can decide whether to make future iterations longer.

Your first iteration will probably be over-planned. Don't worry; just keep learning and looking for ways to simplify the plans. The main trap to watch out for is overly aggressive planning, especially overestimating the productivity of a new team adopting new practices. If the team becomes demoralized, it will be impossible to get the project back on track, so set reasonable goals early and then ramp up expectations when the team is executing effectively.

Overly aggressive planning has other side effects on the expectations of external stakeholders. These stakeholders tend to focus almost exclusively on whether you did what you said you were going to do, and they will notice if you miss a milestone or if the project consistently fails to meet the commitments you have made to them and the other parts of the organization. The results of overly aggressive planning are illustrated by the following story.

> *We once met a project manager who, having failed to complete the Elaboration phase in the predicted number of iterations, needed to adjust his plans. The reason that the phase could not be completed successfully was that the architectural baseline could not be tested because no hardware was available to run the tests.*
>
> *On inquiring of the supplier when the hardware was likely to be available, the supplier responded that delivery would take at least six weeks, and that could only be achieved because they were such a valued customer and could be promoted to the top of the queue.*
>
> *Learning this did not stop the project manager from re-planning the phase by adding one four-week iteration to the plan. The hardware predictably failed to magically appear earlier than promised, and the project again failed to complete the testing. This repeated failure to achieve the milestone led to a complete loss of trust between the project manager and the steering committee, and caused the manager's removal from the project.*

It will take some time and effort to achieve the full benefits of an iterative approach. Your first evolution is unlikely to accomplish more than successfully producing the same amount of software in a non-iterative fashion, but there will be less rework, the project will be less risky, and the chances of delivering in the predicted timescales will be increased. As a result, it is important that you do not set unrealistic expectations for what can be achieved. Iterative development is not necessarily *faster* than traditional development, but you will be more certain of delivering the right result in an acceptable amount of time.

Maintaining Momentum

The more you iterate, the better you and your team will get at it. Each iteration results in management, planning, process adoption, and team interactions improving and iteration becoming easier. By struggling through the first few iterations, you and the team learn how to iterate and how to work together in an iterative fashion. Over time, the levels of planning, reporting, designing, and everything else will settle at a natural level suitable for the team and the project. You achieve this by reviewing results at the end of each iteration and adapting your tactics and plans, discarding or amending things that don't add value, and adding techniques as needed to resolve issues.

It will probably take you and your team a number of evolutions to become really proficient at iterating. The key is to keep going and use the evolutionary and iterative nature of the projects to evolve the team's capability alongside the solutions that they are developing. Achieving continuous improvement through iteration is the subject of the next section.

Adopting an Iterative Approach Iteratively

One of the most powerful things about iterative development is that it provides a platform for continuous process improvement. The adaptive nature of the management and development processes means that you can do more with your project's agility than just respond reactively to change—you can also respond proactively to the lessons learned and the trends exhibited by the project to continuously improve the project's working practices and performance.

Understanding Where to Start

Although we hope that by this point in the book you accept that iterative development and iterative project management are useful tools to deliver better results, we recognize that you cannot get there all at once. Your initial iterative projects are unlikely to exhibit all the desirable characteristics described in Chapter 2, "How Do Iterative Projects Function?"—let alone measure them. In our experience it takes the typical project team at least three evolutions to start to exhibit all the desired behavior and establish themselves as experts in iterative development. *Iterative development* covers a broad set of behaviors and cultural values that emerge over time when teams are focused on results. In choosing an approach to phase in improvements, we have found the model depicted in Figure 11-3 useful when thinking about what improvements must come first.

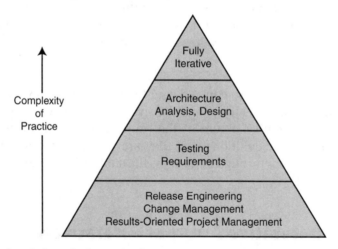

Figure 11-3 *The foundations of software development*

As shown in Figure 11-3, the foundation of iterative development is provided by a shift in project management focus away from creating detailed plans and measuring activities against these plans to results-oriented project management. As we have discussed in earlier chapters, software development is inherently creative and somewhat unpredictable. This means that the precisely appropriate approach is also not entirely predictable. Focusing attention on setting the right goals for each iteration and measuring achievements against those goals is the first and most important step in adopting iterative development.

Introducing effective practices in the areas of release engineering and change management (specifically basic versioning, baselining, and control over the things the project is producing) is essential to supporting this shift to becoming "results oriented." The ability to manage change across iterations (to determine which changes should be addressed in each iteration) and the ability to create executable releases (which requires a reliable build process) are essential to being able to make the shift to delivering objective results.

These basic skills can take you a long way, and in fact they provide most of what you need to perform maintenance and defect fixing across a series of iterations. This covers a great deal of software development activity, and most organizations would gain tremendous benefit if they only did these three things well.

If you are involved in new product development or are making larger and more significant evolutions to the software, you will need to add some additional skills, primarily the ability to understand needs and define requirements (referred to as "Requirements" in Figure 11-3) and requirements-driven testing. If you need to build a completely new solution, you will probably not have the luxury of building upon an existing architecture. You will need to have a more disciplined way of forming the architecture of the system and translating requirements into designs.

As the solutions become more complex, you will need to draw upon all these skills in a fully iterative approach that is able to dynamically respond to new risks and find creative solutions to new problems.

The main reasons for presenting this model are first, to illustrate that most projects can get a lot of value from a basic focus on the fundamentals of results-oriented project management, release engineering, and change management without formalizing the approaches used for requirements, testing, architecture, analysis, or design, and second, to demonstrate that improvements in requirements management, testing, analysis, or architecture must be built on a good foundation of the "lower-order" techniques.

Improving Practices Iteratively

When applying this model to make improvements in a gradual or "progressive" manner, you should not strive to first become "perfect" at the lower levels before moving up to the next level. Instead, we recommend the approach depicted in Figures 11-4 to 11-6.

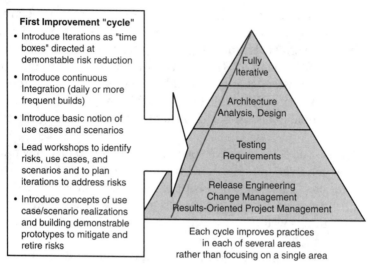

First Improvement "cycle"

- Introduce Iterations as "time boxes" directed at demonstable risk reduction
- Introduce continuous Integration (daily or more frequent builds)
- Introduce basic notion of use cases and scenarios
- Lead workshops to identify risks, use cases, and scenarios and to plan iterations to address risks
- Introduce concepts of use case/scenario realizations and building demonstrable prototypes to mitigate and retire risks

Fully Iterative

Architecture Analysis, Design

Testing Requirements

Release Engineering Change Management Results-Oriented Project Management

Each cycle improves practices in each of several areas rather than focusing on a single area

Figure 11-4   *Improvements in the first "cycle"*

We recommend introducing new practices iteratively, in a sense taking a "slice" of a set of the overall practices that are to be introduced and implementing them in a series of iterations. We refer to this "slice" as an "improvement cycle," which could be a single iteration or could be as long as an evolution depending on the scope of the improvements being made. An improvement cycle consists of one or more iterations over which you will introduce some changes and then measure the results. The concept of an "improvement cycle" aligned with a specific set of iterations enables change to be introduced gradually and in a controlled way so that you can make sure that a more basic set of improvements has been successful before you introduce additional change.

As noted in Figure 11-4, early improvement cycles introduce simple concepts such as the notion of an *iteration* as a time box in which specific results are achieved. The shift to a *results-oriented* perspective from an *activity-oriented* one is important, and it represents a big leap for many people, so you don't want to confuse people by introducing lots of other changes at the same time. We have found that the improvements listed in Figure 11-4 tend to be the most important changes to introduce first.

The early improvement cycles are specifically *not* focused on formality or matters of style because this tends to derail success and gets people focused on formality and not results. The key point is to introduce some improvements from each "level" in a lightweight way and only to the degree that the changes improve results so as not to introduce too much change at once. Figures 11-5 and 11-6 show that as the team becomes comfortable with basic skills, the scope of the improvement effort can expand. Improvement cycles continue as long as the team feels that the improvements are adding value and reducing risk.

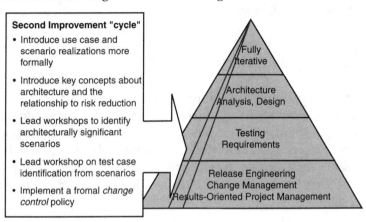

Figure 11-5 *Improvements in subsequent early "cycles"*

Specific improvements are driven by issues identified in iteration assessments to keep them focused on practical project needs. This approach enables the team to make progress and improve results while still getting useful work done. The boxes in the figures indicate the kinds of improvements that are *typical* in early and later improvement cycles.

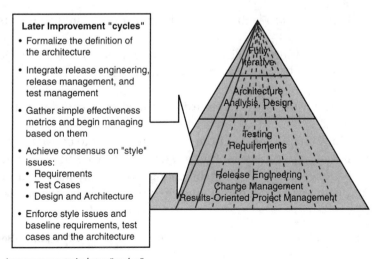

Figure 11-6 *Improvements in later "cycles"*

The essence of this approach is to introduce techniques in each improvement cycle to address the specific needs of the team rather than adopting a set of techniques wholesale. This enables the project team to show results *while* they are improving rather than letting the improvement effort stand in the way of producing results. This overcomes much of the traditional resistance to change.

Learning by Doing

The advantage of this approach is that people learn by doing, and they learn only what they immediately apply. The conventional wisdom (as practiced in much of the industry) is that change is introduced by defining the new processes, selecting supporting tools, and then training everyone on the new processes and tools. As it turns out, this approach actually increases the risk that the change will fail—the opposite of the intended result.

Training is necessary but on its own is not sufficient and is often over-emphasized at the expense of informal experiential learning. To understand why, let's consider five stages of learning:[3]

1. **Knowledge**—Basic knowledge of the concepts and the facts

2. **Comprehension**—Demonstrated understanding of concepts

3. **Application**—Ability to apply concepts in simple contexts

4. **Evaluation**—Ability to apply judgment on when and how to apply concepts to more complex contexts

5. **Innovation**—Ability to extend concepts to new contexts

All that can be expected from a training class is to convey basic knowledge and *maybe* to provide some practice in applying the concepts. Time and experience are needed for the change to actually take hold in the day-to-day activities of the team. Only when this occurs is the change successful.

---

[3] These are loosely adapted from Benjamin S. Bloom's *Taxonomy of Educational Objectives* (Boston: Allyn and Bacon, 1984).

To achieve sustainable results, change must be driven by doing real work. There are several reasons for this:

- People don't like to change, but they will change if they can see that change leads to positive outcomes. "Positive outcomes" means different things to different people. For management, it might mean more reliable schedules and improved delivery capability. For the people on the project, it might mean improved career development or improved quality of life. Successful change initiatives usually require the majority of stakeholders to achieve some positive result. The sooner positive results are shown, the sooner support for the change builds.

- Even positive changes are initially disruptive; few situations are so bad that change is not initially destabilizing. In addition, most changes take some time to produce results. While the changes are underway, a reserve of "good will" is gradually consumed until results become visible. The longer the change takes to show results, the more "good will" is consumed. While "good will" exists, the organization can afford to be patient, but after it is exhausted, impatience takes over and the change effort typically falls apart. The problem is that organizations that need to change the most typically have the lowest reserves of good will. As a result, it is essential that results be demonstrated throughout the change effort to maintain the momentum of change.

- Real change only occurs when people's daily habits change; habits change only with time and practice. As a result, change based on "telling and teaching" almost never succeeds. Real change requires "doing."

Achieving improved results is not inconsistent with introducing change. In fact, achieving improved results while doing real work is essential to achieving sustainable results and is at the heart of the iterative approach. At every iteration assessment, lessons will be learned and acted upon to improve the project's performance and results. By its very nature, iterative and incremental development encourages learning by doing for everybody involved in the project, which enables the approach to support its own adoption and improvement.

The Role of Coaching

When a new way of working is introduced, it is important to support the transfer of knowledge and application of new ideas. Workshops are an effective way to do this because they enable people to learn in the context of doing real work, and they accelerate the rate at which people can be productive using the new techniques.

To feel confident in the change, people need to be able to focus on "doing" and not be distracted by "figuring out what to do." Experienced practitioners who lead people through the new behaviors, getting them to apply the new process by doing, must provide guidance and coaching. Having experienced coaches available to the project team provides confidence in the outcome by providing experienced resources for the project team—people who have already been successful on other projects. A sense of confidence in the outcome is essential to building resilience within the team so that team members can recover from the inevitable setbacks that occur in any change effort.

To facilitate experiential learning, coaches enable the team to focus on "execution" instead of process definition. In addition, there are several other benefits of this approach:

- It builds support for the change by creating real success early.

- It lets team members focus on "learning by doing" rather than sending them to classes and hoping they can put the knowledge into action on their own.

- It builds expertise within the team so that over time the team can support the new way of working without external help.

- It reduces the risk of failures, delays, and quality problems resulting from the team's learning by doing.

- It accelerates the learning process by eliminating much of the uncertainty, discussion, and trial-and-error associated with learning by doing.

Some coaching is usually necessary to enable project team success. This will vary from team to team, but typically follow-on workshops are used to develop skills needed to execute the iteration plan. For example, in the Inception phase, project teams will need to understand how to understand the problem and create a vision for the solution; a workshop led by an experienced facilitator is often the most effective way to make progress toward this goal.

Sometimes the best coaches are on your own team in the form of the more experienced team members. Encouraging team members to work together to build team skills that improve team results also reinforces team cohesiveness. This does not happen accidentally, however; you will need to encourage it and plan for it.

Using the Iteration Plan to Provide a Roadmap for Change

The most effective method for introducing change is to tie the improvement effort directly to the work being performed. The most effective way to do this is to use the project and iteration planning effort (which must be done anyway) to drive the introduction of the new techniques just ahead of their need.

We have found that doing this through a series of focused workshops and subsequent hands-on mentoring jumpstarts results and facilitates skills transfer. For planning evolutions, an initial full-day workshop to bootstrap the development plan and the initial iteration followed by half-day workshops at the start of each iteration to review results from the previous iteration and plan activities in the upcoming iteration has proven to be most effective. The structure and contents of these workshops is as follows:

- Early in the evolution, a workshop is needed to create the development plan and the initial iteration plan and to outline the approaches to be adopted to requirements and change management (often in the form of requirements management and change management plans). Iteration plans are defined so that just enough process is introduced to meet the objectives of the iteration and support the goals of the current "improvement cycle." In this way, the project team learns the new ways of working by applying them.

- At the transition between iterations, a workshop is needed to review iteration results, plan the next iteration, and identify issues and action plans. This can include making mid-project adjustments to the process used by the project, adjusting approaches as well as the pace of change. Sometimes the change will be too slow and the pacing can be accelerated; other times the project team will feel that the change was too fast and the improvement plans for future iterations will need to be scaled back.

The key to making improvements is to use the iteration plan itself to map the change activities *as well as* regular project activities. Change activities need to be viewed as integral to the project—tasks that the project does to achieve better results, not something external that detracts from results. If we don't believe that improved results will be derived from a change, why would we want to pursue it?

The iteration plan can be a powerful reinforcement to the change—or the means by which the change is undone: if the plan supports the change, it will tend to succeed, but if it fails to reinforce the new desired behaviors, the change will not happen no matter how much support is otherwise given.

As we have discussed, the project is structured into a series of iterations that establish a kind of heartbeat for the project, enabling it to set intermediate milestones to check progress, to establish points at which non-essential requirements can be scoped out, and to enable mid-course corrections to the project plan. This also acts as the heartbeat for change, enabling 1) short-term improvement objectives to be set, implemented, and assessed, 2) the change to be tested, and 3) mid-course corrections to made to the improvement plans.

Finally, planning is nothing if the execution of the plan is poor. Some people act as if a good plan will implement itself. In reality, a mediocre plan with excellent execution is better than an excellent plan with mediocre execution every time.

Conclusion

Adopting an iterative and incremental development approach is a fundamental change in working practices for the management team and everyone else involved in the project. Successful iterative and incremental development requires a progressive and adaptive approach to be taken to the management of the project and requires the whole team to embrace change and the continual improvement that this change will hopefully produce.

In any change effort, it is essential to demonstrate the value of the change as soon as possible to overcome resistance and build support for the change. The only way that can be done is by achieving the desired technical and business results quickly and efficiently. The fastest way to reach these results is to introduce the change as part of getting real work done; if the change is considered separate from the "real work," it will never produce results. With the guidance and leadership of an effective coach, and with the support of management to measure and reward positive results and positive change, teams can improve their process while getting real work done. Process improvement and getting results should not be considered mutually exclusive.

To expand beyond individual projects, you will need enlightened but benevolent dictatorship coupled with the demonstration through real results to all involved that the future can be better. It also requires leadership, real leadership—not the phony slogans of motivational posters, but roll-up-your-sleeves, hands-on leadership from the front that shows that you have a stake in the outcome. No one is going to believe you if you sit on the sidelines cheering; you have to be in the game.

Iterative development is not hard, but changing the way that people work is. In this book we have provided you with the background information and the practical guidance necessary to deliver better results through your software development efforts. The next step is yours: you now get to put these concepts into action. We hope that the approaches and techniques we have presented in this book will help you and your organization to succeed and thrive by achieving the full promise of iterative development.

PART III

Appendices

A Brief Introduction to Use-Case Driven Development

The concept of use-case driven development was initially presented more than a decade ago by Ivar Jacobson at OOPSLA[1] in 1987 and then popularized in the classic *Object-Oriented Software Engineering.*[2] The concept of use cases has proven to be so popular that it has become the standard approach for modeling and capturing requirements for object-oriented development and a core part of the Unified Modeling Language (UML).[3] Use-case driven development itself forms the basis of many popular iterative and incremental development methods, starting with the Objectory Process and its descendents, the Unified Process and the IBM Rational Unified Process.

> **Note**
>
> The material in this appendix is adapted from our previous book *Use Case Modeling* (Boston: Addison-Wesley, 2002).

---

[1] Ivar Jacobson, "Object-Oriented Software Development in an Industrial Environment," OOPSLA, 1987.

[2] Ivar Jacobson, Magnus Christerson, Patrik Johnsson, and Gunnar Overgaard, *Object-Oriented Software Engineering: A Use Case Driven Approach* (New York: ACM Press, 1992).

[3] See www.uml.org for details.

Use cases are a practical technique for documenting requirements. They provide a way of discussing system users' goals and how the system works with users to achieve these goals. As a result, use cases are also helpful to people who ensure system usability, document the system's behavior, and design, develop, and test the system.

Use cases have an essential role to play in managing and controlling an iterative project by enabling the requirements to be gathered into meaningful subsets for delivery by an iteration. They also help to drive the project from within by unifying the project team and driving many of the development activities.

This appendix provides a brief introduction to the concepts of use cases and use-case driven development. It provides the awareness required to manage a project by applying the techniques and sufficient background to support the use of the concepts within the rest of this book.

Use Cases and the Requirements Discipline

The goals of the Requirements discipline are to

- Establish a shared vision

- Bridge the gap between the business and the supplier

- Communicate the intent of the system

- Define the capabilities required of the system

In essence, the goal of the Requirements discipline is to establish and maintain agreement with the customers and other stakeholders on what the system should do. This is typically done by creating and agreeing on a requirements specification.

To be able to successfully manage an iterative and incremental development project, the project manager needs to be aware of the requirements and how they are managed. Figure A-1 shows the key requirements artifacts used by the Unified Process, which we used as our reference model for this book.

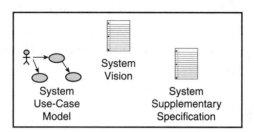

Figure A-1 *The key requirements artifacts of the Unified Process*

The most important of these is the use-case model because it defines the threads of behavior of the system, which are used to shape the iteration plans and to drive development activities within the iterations. The Vision complements the Use-Case Model by providing the "mission" statement and a roadmap for the product being produced. This helps us to understand the problems and opportunities that the proposed solution is to address, providing the context and justification for the solution defined by the Use-Case Model.

The Supplementary Specification complements the Use-Case Model by providing a home for any and all requirements that don't fit inside the Use-Case Model, either because they describe requirements that apply to all use cases (and so do not belong in any one use case) or because they describe requirements that are not easily expressed as threads of behavior or scenarios (such as performance, security, or other kinds of requirements that are generally expressed as declarative requirements). The role of the Supplementary Specification will become clearer as we look in more detail at the contents of the use cases and how they are structured.

The basic principles behind use cases are very simple: to get to the heart of what a system must do, you should

- Focus on who (or what) will use it or be used by it

- Look at what the system must do for those users to achieve something useful

To support these ideas, use-case modeling has two main concepts:

- Actors (things external to the system)

- Use Cases (what the system must do for the actors)

These are defined in more detail in Table A-1. The concepts and visual representations are defined by UML.[4]

Table A-1   *The Basic Building Blocks of a Use-Case Model*[5]

Icon	Definition
⚇ **An Actor**	An actor defines a role that a user can play when interacting with the system. A user can either be an individual or another system.
⬭ **A Use Case**	A use case describes how an actor uses a system to achieve a goal and what the system does for the actor to achieve that goal. It tells the story of how the system and its actors collaborate to deliver something of value for at least one of the actors.

Use cases are an incredibly powerful tool for requirements management. They provide a simple and intuitive way to achieve the following:

- **Establish the requirements of the system**—The use cases place the requirements into the context of the user's goals and the value to be delivered by the system.

- **Establish the system boundary**—The model identifies who or what interacts with the system and what the system should do.

---

[4]   See www.uml.org for details.

[5]   The UML 2 includes the slightly more arcane definitions:
- **Actor**—An actor specifies a role played by a user or any other system that interacts with the subject.
- **Use Case**—A use case is the specification of a set of actions performed by a system, which yields an observable result that is, typically, of value for one or more actors or other stakeholders of the system.

Taken from the UML 2.0 Superstructure Specification (The Object Management Group, October 2004).

- **Communicate the requirements to all stakeholders**—The use cases provide a common thread through all project activities, communicating with both the stakeholder community and the development community.

- **Visualize the value to be provided by a system**—The use cases themselves provide a visual index into the capabilities and value to be provided by the solution.

Figure A-2 shows a simple Use-Case Model representing the requirements for a simple telephone system. From this diagram alone you should be able to intuitively understand the value this system provides to its users and form your own opinion about the suitability of the proposed solution.

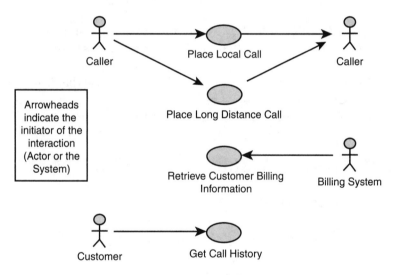

Figure A-2 *The use cases for a simple telephone system*

Figure A-3 shows an excerpt from the use-case model for a bank Automatic Teller Machine (ATM).

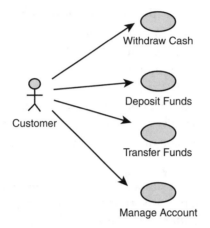

Figure A-3 *An excerpt from the use-case model of an ATM*[6]

Again you should find this quite intuitive, and you should be able to see immediately the value that the ATM system offers to the bank's customers.

There is much more to a use case than the ellipse that is used to represent it on diagrams such as Figure A-2 and Figure A-3. Each use case has its own specification (or use-case description) where the details of the requirements are captured.

A use-case description is composed of the following:[7]

- A basic flow of events

  - The normal way of attaining the value

---

[6] For a more complete model of the ATM, see our book *Use Case Modeling* (Boston: Addison-Wesley, 2002).

[7] There are other attributes that can be used to characterize and add more information to the use-case descriptions, but they are all optional and are beyond the scope of this brief introduction. The elements listed are the major components of a use case and the ones that the project manager should be aware of.

- The expected path through the use case

- The assumption behind the basic flow is that it will successfully enable the actor to achieve the goal and extract the value represented by the use case

- Alternative flows of events

  - Other ways of attaining the value

  - Exception and error conditions

- Scenarios that enumerate combinations of basic and alternative flows

  - A description of one particular path through the use case (the basic flow plus 0 or more alternative flows)

- Pre- and post-conditions

  - Statements describing the state of the system before and after the use case is performed

The structure of the flow of events is additive, with the alternative flows being defined in terms of their variance from the basic flow. Figure A-4 illustrates the typical structure of a flow of events. The straight arrow represents the basic flow of events, and the curves represent the alternative paths in relation to the basic flow. Some alternative paths return to the basic flow of events, whereas others end the use case.

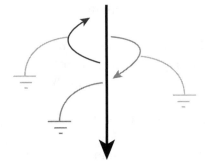

Figure A-4 *The typical structure of a flow of events*

Figure A-5 shows an outline of the Place Local Call use case and some of its alternative flows and scenarios. Note that the basic flow shown is just an outline, not the full use-case description.

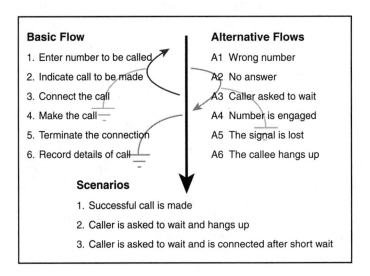

Basic Flow

1. Enter number to be called
2. Indicate call to be made
3. Connect the call
4. Make the call
5. Terminate the connection
6. Record details of call

Alternative Flows

A1 Wrong number
A2 No answer
A3 Caller asked to wait
A4 Number is engaged
A5 The signal is lost
A6 The callee hangs up

Scenarios

1. Successful call is made
2. Caller is asked to wait and hangs up
3. Caller is asked to wait and is connected after short wait

Figure A-5 *Inside the Place Local Call use case*

Each use case

- Describes how the actors and the system interact and the actions the system takes to deliver something of value to the actors

- Shows the system functionality an actor uses

- Models a dialog between the system and its actors

- Is a complete and meaningful flow of events

Use cases can be captured at an appropriate level of detail to reduce risk. Their narrative structure enables the detail of the requirements to be elaborated (within the structure defined by the structure of the flows of events) as the project progresses and needs the detail to address the project specific needs. Some projects can function with just an outline of the use cases flows, while others require much more detailed requirements specifications.[8] Regardless of the level of detail required by the project, the additive structure of the use cases enables a project to

- Iteratively evolve the requirements

- Manage scope using the definitions of the flows of events

- Plan the iterations by selecting specific use cases, flows of events, and scenarios that address the immediate project risks

Use Cases, Development, and Testing

As well as facilitating the elicitation, organization, and documentation of requirements, use cases can play a more central and significant role in the software development lifecycle. After you have identified, authored, and agreed upon a use case, scenario, or flow of events, it can be used to drive the other development activities. In these cases, the lifecycle of the use case continues beyond its authoring to cover activities such as analysis, design, implementation, and testing. This lifecycle is shown in simplified form in Figure A-6.

---

[8] Use-case descriptions evolve through a number of states, from brief description through outlines, essential outlines, and detailed descriptions until a fully described requirements specification is created. It is not always necessary to evolve the description all the way to fully described status, and in fact many projects find outlines or essential outlines to be sufficient. The project risks will enable the project team to select the appropriate state for its use cases. For a full discussion of appropriate levels of use-case description and when and where to use them, see *Use Case Modeling*, by Kurt Bittner and Ian Spence (Boston: Addison-Wesley, 2002).

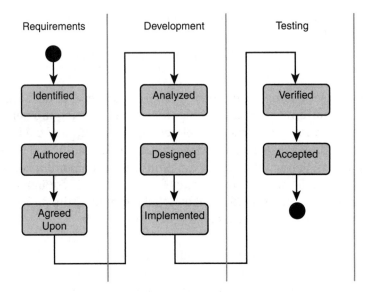

Figure A-6   *A use-case driven software development lifecycle*

This lifecycle is not intended to imply that analysis cannot be started until all the use cases have been agreed upon or even until any use cases have been agreed upon. It is just saying that you cannot consider the analysis of a use case to be complete before the use-case authoring has been completed and the use case itself agreed upon. Figure A-6 is arranged to emphasize the three main applications for the use cases:

- **Requirements**—The identification, authoring, and agreement of the use cases and their descriptions for use as a requirement specification.

- **Development**—The analysis, design, and implementation of a system based upon the use cases.[9]

- **Testing**—The use-case-based verification and acceptance of the system produced.

---

[9]   For more information on using use cases to drive the analysis and design of software systems, we recommend Doug Rosenberg and Kendall Scott's *Use Case Driven Object Modeling with UML: A Practical Approach* (Reading, MA: Addison-Wesley, 1999) and Craig Larman's *Applying UML and Patterns: An Introduction to Object-Oriented Analysis and Design and the Unified Process* (Upper Saddle River, NJ: Prentice Hall, 2001).

It is this ability for the use-cases to unify the development activities that makes them such a powerful tool for the planning and tracking of software development projects.

To fully understand the power of use cases, it is worth considering this life-cycle in a little more detail. Use cases can play a part in the majority of the disciplines directly associated with software development:

- **Requirements**—The use-case model is the result of the Requirements discipline. Requirements work matures the use cases through the first three states from Identified to Agreed Upon. It also evolves the glossary, or domain model, that defines the terminology used by the use cases and the supplementary specification that contains the system-wide requirements not captured by the use-case model.

- **Analysis and Design:** In analysis and design, use cases are realized in analysis and design models. Use-case realizations are created that describe how the use cases are performed in terms of interacting objects in the models. These models describe in terms of subsystems and objects the different parts of the implemented system and how the parts need to interact to perform the use cases. Analysis and design of the use cases matures them through the states of Analyzed and Designed. These states do not change the description of the use cases but indicate that the use cases have been realized in the analysis and design of the system.

- **Implementation (also known as Code and Unit Test or Code and Build)**—During implementation, the design model is the implementation specification. Because use cases are the basis for the design model, they are implemented in terms of design classes. After the code has been written to enable a use case to be executed, it can be considered to be in the Implemented state.

- **Test**—During test, the use cases constitute the basis for identifying test cases and test procedures; that is, the system is verified by performing each use case. When the tests related to a use case have been successfully passed by the system, the use case can be considered to be in the Verified state. The Accepted state is reached when a version of the system that implements the use case passes independent user acceptance testing. Note: if the system is being developed in an incremental fashion, the use cases need to be verified for each release that implements them.

These relationships are directly reflected in the lifecycle of the use case described earlier and are illustrated in Figure A-7.

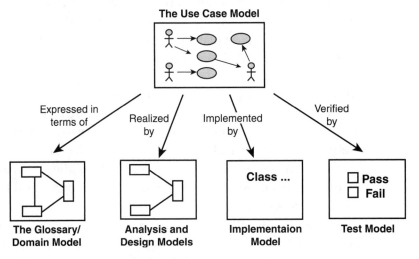

Figure A-7   *The use-case model and its relationship to the other software development models*

Adapted from *Object-Oriented Software Engineering: A Use Case Driven Approach*, Ivar Jacobson et al. (New York: ACM Press, 1992).

Use cases can also help with the supporting disciplines, although these disciplines do not impact the lifecycle of the use cases themselves:

- **Project Management**—In the Project Management discipline, use cases are used as a basis for planning and tracking the progress of the development project. This is particularly true for iterative development where use cases are often the primary planning mechanism.

- **Deployment**—In the Deployment discipline, use cases form a foundation for what is described in user manuals. Use cases can also be used to define ordering units of the product. For example, a customer could purchase a system configured with a particular mix of use cases.

Although primarily a requirement capture technique, use cases have a significant role to play in the ongoing planning, control, development, and testing of the system. It is this unification of the software development process that makes use cases such a powerful technique. To get the full benefit of using use cases, they should be placed at the heart of all the software development and project planning activities.[10]

One of the most powerful aspects of adopting a use-case driven approach is the way that the same use cases, flows, and scenarios are used to drive the analysis, design, implementation, and testing. As shown Figure A-8, the use cases close the loop on the development by driving the definition of the test cases that are used to verify the results of the development work.

---

[10] For more information on how use-cases can shape and drive the entire software development process, we recommend the following texts:

- Philippe Kruchten, *The Rational Unified Process: An Introduction,* 3rd ed. (Boston: Addison-Wesley, 2003).

- Ivar Jacobson, Grady Booch, and James Rumbaugh, *The Unified Software Development Process.* (Boston: Addison-Wesley, 1999).

- Ivar Jacobson, Magnus Christerson, Patrik Jonsson, and Gunnar Overgaard, *Object-Oriented Software Engineering: A Use Case Driven Approach* (New York: ACM Press, 1992). The first book to popularize use cases.

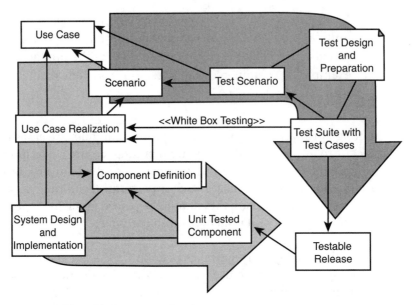

Figure A-8 *Use-case driven development and testing*

The large lower arrow illustrates how the use cases and scenarios are used to drive the development of a testable release that implements the functionality that they define:

- **Use-Case Realization and Component Definition**—Use cases are "realized" by collaborations of components that fulfill the use case. By stepping through the use case, you find the components that perform the use case, either reusing existing components with the right behavior or creating new components or new operations on existing components to achieve the desired result.

- **Unit Tested Components**—By using the use case-realizations to step through component interactions, you can know exactly how the component is used and therefore how to test it.

- **Testable Release**—By stepping through scenarios and use cases using the whole system, you have a means to evaluate whether the system does what it is supposed to do.

The use cases also provide a basis for identifying test cases and test procedures; that is, the system is verified by performing scenarios based on the use cases. Use cases provide us with a black box view of the system. The products of analysis and design provide a white box view of the system and relate the requirements to the individual pieces of the system.

The large upper arrow illustrates how the same use cases and scenarios are used to develop the tests that will verify the quality and suitability of the release produced by the developers:

- **Test Scenarios**—Black box system tests are derived from the use cases by identifying a set of test scenarios that will achieve the test objectives for functional and requirements coverage.

- **White Box Testing**—To create white box tests from the use cases, identify a set of design-level scenarios (from the collaborations documented in the use-case realizations) that will achieve the test objectives for design validation and component coverage. This relationship is shown with the dashed arrow in Figure A-8.

- **Test Suite with Test Cases**—The resulting tests are assembled into a test suite that can be used to verify the "testable release" produced by the development activities.

Based upon the use cases, the test design and preparation activities can proceed in parallel with the system design and preparation activities. This enables the test suite to be available when the testable release becomes available. Test cases derived from the use cases take advantage of the way that use cases gather together the requirements to ensure good functional test coverage of the system and to produce robust, repeatable test suites.

Within the framework provided by the use cases, a number of strategies are available for capturing the correct amount of detail to address the risks inherent in the project. For example, the following approaches are all compatible with the use-case driven approach:

- **Lightweight Requirements**—For many systems, outlines that clearly denote the responsibilities of the system and the actors (a form known as an Essential Outline or Essential Use Case[11]) is sufficient, with the detail of the specification being documented through prototyping and analysis modeling activities.

- **Formal Requirements**—The use-case specifications can be elaborated into a complete formal requirements specification that defines all the system's inputs, outputs, and responses. The use cases can then be used to act as a formal contract between the customers and the developers.

- **Test Driven**—Based upon use-case outlines, the requirements detail can be captured in test cases derived from the use cases' flows of events. The development team can then develop software to pass the set of test cases.

- **Creative Analysis and Design**—In some cases, it is impossible to define what the detailed requirements are without first developing the solution because no one has seen or experienced the kind of solution that needs to be developed. In these cases, capturing the goals of the stakeholders and the value to be realized by the system in the form of a set of outlined use cases provides a firm foundation for the creative design of the solution while also supporting its controlled iterative development.[12]

What is important in all cases is that the additive structure of the use cases and the flows of events enable the requirements, whatever their level of detail, to be considered in terms of the value that they deliver and to be

---

[11] Larry Constantine is most often associated with this formulation of use cases; see his article "The Case for Essential Use Cases," *Object Magazine*, May 1997 (New York: SIGS Publications).

[12] Note that capturing the goals in this way is also useful when using packaged solutions, where the detailed requirements of the customer are secondary to the current implementation of the package. The use case outlines enable the package to be verified against the user goals and the system's expected value without the overhead of creating irrelevant, detailed specifications.

approached as complete end-to-end stories that if implemented will enable that value to be realized.

This flexibility in the use of the early outline-level requirements statements empowers the team to approach the problem iteratively and to iteratively evolve the solution while continuing to iteratively evolve the requirements. Given even the briefest outlines of a set of use cases and their flows of events, it is possible to start to prototype candidate solutions and consider their impact on any existing components and solutions intended for use as part of the new system.

Use Cases and Unified Process Lifecycle

As well as unifying the various disciplines of the process, use cases have a key role to play in the lifecycle of the Unified Process. We saw this in the high-level overview of the Unified Process lifecycle presented Chapter 3, "Controlling Iterative Projects." We can now revisit these views of the lifecycle to illustrate the role that use cases play in facilitating the Unified Process lifecycle. Table A-2 builds on Table 3-2 to illustrate how the use cases are exploited to facilitate the phases of the process.

Table A-2 *Use Cases and Their Role in the Unified Process Lifecycle*

	Inception	Elaboration	Construction	Transition
Risk Focus	Business	Architectural	Logistical	Roll-Out
Requirements Focus	Scoping the project	Stabilizing the requirements	Achieving a correct statement of requirements	Completing the requirements
Key Requirements Artifacts (and their state)	Supplementary Spec (key architectural requirements) Use-Case Model (critical use cases identified) Vision (shared)	Supplementary Spec (agreed) Use-Case Model (agreed) Vision (agreed)	Supplementary Spec (agreed) Use-Case Model (agreed) Vision (agreed)	Supplementary Spec (complete) Use-Case Model (complete) Vision (complete)
Development Focus	Evaluating possible solutions	Establishing and proving the architecture	Incrementally completing the solution	Deploying and tuning the solution

Table A-2 *Use Cases and Their Role in the Unified Process Lifecycle* *(continued)*

	Inception	Elaboration	Construction	Transition
The role of use cases in the development activities	Use cases are used to scope the system, identify the architecturally significant threads, and provide a context for the production of any proof-of-concept proto-types used to de-risk the project.	Use cases are used to elaborate the requirements and provide the context within which the architecture is proved.	Use cases, flows, and scenarios are used to specify the contents of the releases produced by the iterations and to define the tests used to verify the quality and completeness of the releases.	Use cases form the basis for user guides and other instructions.
Outcome	Agreement to fund the project	A stable, proven, executable architecture	A useful, tested, deployable, and documented solution	The solution is in "actual use"

The three stakeholder perspectives—problem, solution, and project—are also useful for examining the role use cases can play in driving iterative software development. Table A-3 is an annotated version of Table 3-4, which provided an overview of the key *activities* to be undertaken for each area and each phase. Table A-3 *illustrates the impact that use cases can have on the planning and execution of a software development project* by calling out those activities that are directly driven by the use cases, those that directly benefit from the use of use cases, and those that are not significantly impacted by the project's use of use cases.

Out of the 61 key activities shown in the table,

- Eighteen are directly driven by the use cases. These are shown in bold.

- Twenty-six benefit from the use of use cases on the project. These are shown in italics.

- Seventeen are not significantly affected by the use of use cases. These are shown in a regular font.

Table A-3 *A High-Level, Activity-Based Overview of the Unified Process Project Lifecycle*

	Inception	LCO: Viability Establish	Elaboration	LCA: Selected Approach Proven	Construction	IOC: Usable Solution Available	Transition	PR: Project Completed
Problem	• **Identify the architecturally significant requirements** • *Understand the target environments* • *Define the problem* • **Determine the value of solving the problem**		• **Stabilize the requirements** • **Detail the critical requirements** • *Elaborate on the vision*		• **Complete the requirements** • **Author user documentation** • *Manage changing requirements* • *Assess user readiness* • *Request change requests*		• *Perform acceptance testing* • *Train users* • *Market the solution* • **Manage change in the user community** • **Suggest improvements** • *Report defects and deficiencies*	
Solution	• **Explore possible solutions** • **Evaluate alternative solutions** • **Synthesize the architecture**		• **Prove the architecture** • **Develop prototype(s)** • *Describe the architecture* • *Describe component interfaces* • *Select components*		• **Develop components** • **Test and assessment** • *Refine the architecture* • *Optimize component design*		• *Deploy to end users* • **Prepare for support and maintenance of the system after it is delivered** • *Correct defects* • *Tune the application* • *Parallel operation and application migration*	
Project	• **Establish the project's scope** • *Plan lifecycle* • *Establish project costs* • *Build the business case* • *Identify the critical risks*		• *Track progress* • *Improve estimates* • *Plan development* • *Control risks* • *Elaborate upon the process* • *Establish the project infrastructure* • *Establish metrics* • *Resource the project*		• **Impact analysis** • *Monitor and control development* • *Plan deployment* • *Optimize process* • *Monitor risks* • *Collect metrics* • *Optimize resource usage* • *Control costs*		• *Assess the impact of change* • *Schedule changes* • *Hand over to production support* • *Monitor and control deployment* • *Close down the project*	

By using use cases in conjunction with an iterative lifecycle approach to shape and influence the project plans, the project manager can ensure that development is driven by the requirements, the correct risks are being addressed, the project is converging on the correct solution, and the benefits promised by the iterative approach are realized.

Table A-4 shows the evolution of the use-case model itself and the state of the use-case driven development activities across the Unified Process lifecycle. These figures can be used to measure where a project is in the lifecycle and to balance the requirements and development activities to ensure that the project iterates effectively and does not revert to waterfall development practices.

Table A-4   *The Evolution of the Use-Case Model*

Use-Case State	Inception	Elaboration	Construction	Transition
Identified	60%	> 80%	100%	100%
Outlined	50%	20% – 80%	0%	0%
Authored	10%	40% – 80%	100%	100%
Analyzed	< 10%[13]	20% – 40%	100%	100%
Designed, Implemented, and Verified	< 5%[13]	< 10%	100%	100%

Source: Adapted from *The Unified Software Development Process*, Ivar Jacobson et al. (Reading, MA: Addison-Wesley, 1999), 358.

Use cases support the iterative development process in a number of other ways:

- Their additive, narrative structure supports the iterative evolution of requirements. The use cases start with an outline of their basic flow and the most important alternatives. This framework is then elaborated until a sufficient level of requirements detail has been captured to address the project risks. As can be seen in Table A-4, work on the use cases themselves is ongoing throughout the Inception, Elaboration, and

---

[13] A small percentage might be addressed for proof of concept purposes.

Construction phases, sometimes continuing into the Transition phase if there are late requirements changes.

- The use cases do not have to be fully described before they can be used to drive downstream development activities. Given even the briefest outlines of a set of use cases and their flows of events, it is possible to start to prototype candidate solutions and consider their impact on any existing components and solutions intended for use as part of the new system.

- The structure of the use-case model enables the team to drive down into detail where it will objectively reduce project risk. The 10% of the use-case model that is typically authored in the Inception phase is the most important 10% of the use cases as assessed by the customers and architects involved in the project.

This flexibility in the use of the early outline-level requirements statements empowers the team to approach the problem iteratively, evolving the solution while continuing to evolve the requirements.

Do You Have to Use Use Cases?

There are many different approaches to the iterative development of software, each with its own strengths and weaknesses and different situations where it is most applicable. Although the authors of these methods will tend to stress the drawbacks of other methods and the superiority of their own, it is actually far more useful to consider what they have in common. Table A-5 provides an overview of some of the most popular iterative and incremental software development methods.[14]

---

[14] We are only considering development methodologies here; these are methods that describe how to create software products based upon some representation of the required solution's requirements. The list, therefore, does not consider the various technique-neutral management frameworks such as Scrum (*Agile Software Development with Scrum* by Ken Schwaber and Mike Beedle, Upper Saddle River, NJ: Prentice Hall, 2001) and DSDM (www.dsdm.org).

Table A-5 *Popular Iterative Software Development Methods*

Software Develop-ment Method	Characteristics	Notes on Usage and Style
Essential Unified Process[15]	A stripped-down version of the Unified Process.	A lightweight, agile version of the Unified Process.
Extreme Programming[16]	A user story driven, test first, highly disciplined, lightweight iterative development process.	A developer-focused process popular with small development teams.
IBM Global Method[17]	A use-case driven, iterative and incremental, architecture-centric, component-based adaptable process.	IBM Global Method is IBM's proprietary internal method, which includes a use-case driven, object-oriented process for use on iterative projects.
IBM Rational Unified Process[18]	A commercially available, detailed version of the Unified Process.	Integrates the conceptual Unified Process with the IBM Rational Suite of software development tools.
Microsoft Solutions Framework for Agile Software Development[19]	A scenario-driven, context-based software development process.	Adaptive (agile) or refinement (formal) process variants are provided.
Unified Process[20]	A use-case driven, iterative and incremental, architecture-centric, component-based adaptable process.	Its component-based nature can be seen in its pervasive usage of the Unified Modeling Language[21] as its primary mechanism for specification and communication.

[15] See www.ivarjacobson.com.

[16] See www.extremeprogramming.org or www.xprogramming.com. For a good introduction to Extreme Programming, see *Extreme Programming Explained: Embrace Change,* 2nd ed., by Kent Beck and Cynthia Andres (Boston: Addison-Wesley, 2005).

[17] The iterative and incremental object-oriented elements were publicly published in *Developing Object-Oriented Software: An Experience-Based Approach* by IBM Object-Oriented Technology Center (Upper Saddle River, NJ: Prentice Hall, 1997).

[18] See www-306.ibm.com/software/rational/. For a good introduction and overview of the IBM Rational Unified Process, see *The Rational Unified Process: An Introduction,* 3rd ed., by Philippe Kruchten (Boston: Addison-Wesley, 2004).

[19] See www.microsoft.com.

[20] Widely used as a framework in many software development texts, the Unified Process is best described in *The Unified Software Development Process* by Ivar Jacobson, Grady Booch, and James Rumbaugh (Boston: Addison-Wesley, 1999).

[21] See www.uml.org.

All these methods can be called agile, and all consider their iterations to be driven by end-to-end threads of system execution (be they use cases, scenarios, tests, or user stories). Additionally, it is our assertion that all these methods can benefit from the application of the Unified Process lifecycle. In all these methods, it is the end-to-end threads of system execution that bind the disciplines together and ensure that the projects have a singular focus on delivering working software and value to the business.

All the methods listed here will work when applied by the right people to the right kind of problem. All the methods contain good practices that you could apply to your projects. All the methods are agile and adaptive in one way or another.

The iterative and incremental development process you select should be based on reducing project risk or, to put it another way, increasing the probability that you will succeed. Whatever your preferences on methodologies, we strongly recommend that your approach be scenario-driven. If it isn't, then the management of the project will be made an order of magnitude more difficult.

To support the controlled iterative development of the required solution, you must be able to choose a subset of the requirements to drive the development effort in each iteration. To ensure that releases provide value, you must implement end-to-end threads of execution through the system. Use cases, user stories, and scenarios will enable you to do this. Declarative statements of requirements typically will not.

Regardless of the software development approach you select, as long as you adopt some form of scenario-based approach, there is a wealth of practical guidance in Part II of this book to help you plan and control your iterative and incremental development projects. We use use cases in our discussions to provide concrete examples of the management process. From a project management perspective, you can gain the same benefits from scenarios or user stories.

Summary

This is enough to give you a foundation in Use-Case Modeling—what use cases are and how they are used to manage projects. In short, use cases are a way of describing the capabilities of a system and how users utilize those capabilities to get something done. Taken as a whole, use cases describe how the system is used (hence the term "use cases"). As such, they are essential tools to understanding what you need to deliver. In addition, the use cases can be used to drive development and test activities (and training and documentation, too), and they help to unify the project team around delivering something of business value.

More particularly, from a management perspective, they enable the following:

- **The definition of the scope of the system**—The Use-Case Model forms the basis of agreement and negotiation with the stakeholders defining both the internal and external releases.

- **The estimation and tracking of development effort**—The use cases provide a platform for producing detailed estimates and tracking the progress of the project.

- **The planning and management of iterations**—The use cases define the end-to-end threads of behavior that can be assigned to iterations for implementation.

If you would like to learn more about use cases and use-case driven development, then we refer you to our earlier work, *Use Case Modeling*, published by Addison-Wesley in 2002.

Outlines, Templates, and Checklists

This appendix provides a selection of reusable assets to aid in your adoption of iterative and incremental project management.

This appendix is split into three sections:

- **Template Role Definitions**—Extended role definitions to complement the roles introduced in Chapter 5.

- **Outline Plan and Assessment Documents**—Outlines for the various plan and assessment documents discussed in Chapters 6 to 10.

- **Checklists**—Some simple checklists to assist you in conducting the assessments described in Chapters 9 and 10.

The intention is not to provide definitive templates but to provide some useful assets to help you in the creation and population of your own templates and artifacts. Our intent in providing these resources is not to provide a "fill-in-the-blanks" process that substitutes for real understanding of the contents of the rest of the book but to make it easier to put what you have learned into practice. Some of the worst projects we have seen are those that have extensive templates but whose members simply blindly fill in the templates rather than thoughtfully considering how they will reduce risk and deliver value. On these projects, no one seems to know why they are filling in the templates, and the project makes little real progress even though it has extensive documentation.

Template Role Definitions

In Chapter 5, "A Layered Approach to Planning and Managing Iterative Projects," we briefly introduced the key management roles involved in an iterative and incremental software development project. These three roles are shown in Figure B-1 and are fully described in the subsections that follow.

Overall Project
Manager

Development
Lead

Iteration
Lead

Figure B-1   *Key management roles*

These role descriptions are presented in a simple format that is compatible with the IBM Rational Unified Process, which can be copied and adapted for use within your projects and organizations.

The role definitions are focused on the distribution of those management responsibilities that are most explicitly affected by the adoption of iterative and incremental development practices and are not intended to provide a definitive statement of a project manager's responsibilities. They should be used in conjunction with other sources to provide a full job specification for a project management post within an organization or project team.

Each role definition includes a list of the skills and experience typically required when fulfilling the role. These are not listed in order of importance. The relative importance of each quality will vary from organization to organization and project to project.

As seen in Chapter 5, these are abstract role definitions that can be assembled to create the appropriate management structure for your project. The separation of concerns created by having three distinct roles provides a scalable solution that supports all sizes of iterative software development project.

Overall Project Manager

This role covers the overall management of the project, including any elements of business change and benefits realization allocated to the project.

The overall project manager plans the project as a whole—structuring the project, identifying evolutions, allocating resources, shaping priorities, coordinating interactions with customers and users, and generally keeping the project team focused on achieving the project's desired outcomes. The overall project manager also establishes a set of practices that ensure the integrity of the products that the project produces.

The overall project manager has authority to run the project on a day-to-day basis within the constraints laid down by the owning program or commissioning organization. This role's prime responsibility is to ensure that the project produces the required products to the required level of quality and within the specified constraints of time and cost. The overall project manager is also responsible for ensuring that the project produces a result that is capable of achieving the benefits defined in the project's business case.

Staffing

The skills and experience needed to fulfill the role of overall project manager depend on the size and technical and management complexity of the project, but to play the role, to at least some degree you must

- Be experienced in the business domain and the culture of the commissioning organization

- Have risk analysis and decision-making skills with a history of making sound decisions quickly under stress

- Have management, estimation, planning, and scheduling skills

- Have presentation and communication skills

- Show leadership and team-building capabilities

- Have good interpersonal skills and show sound judgment in staff selection

- Have business and financial acumen, establishing a sound business case for the project

- Have good negotiation skills, liaising with the customers, senior management, the steering committee, and other projects to negotiate contracts and commitments

- Be objective in setting and assessing milestones, ensuring stakeholder and team buy-in

- Be prepared to take responsibility for overall progress and use of resources, initiating corrective action where necessary

- Be focused on the delivery of customer value in the form of usable products that provide real business benefit

- Have an awareness of modern software development practices

- Share the technical vision but be pragmatic in the scoping and implementation of plans and scrupulously honest in the assessment of outcomes

This is the purest of the three management roles and is often combined with that of the development lead when the management team is instantiated for small- and medium-sized projects.

Development Lead

This role covers the aspects of project management that focus on the management of the development of one or more evolutions of a software or software-intensive system.

The development lead ensures the production of the software and supporting artifacts defined by the overall project manager (as part of the overall project plan) to an appropriate level of quality in a time scale acceptable to the overall project manager and the project's steering committee. This involves directing, motivating, planning, and monitoring the development team's work on the creation of the software and supporting products.

Staffing

The skills and experience needed to fulfill the development lead role depend upon the size and technical and management complexity of the development, but to play the role, to at least some degree you must

- Be experienced in software development

- Be experienced in the domain of the application

- Be experienced in requirements management

- Understand the iterative software development lifecycle

- Have risk analysis, management, software estimation, and project planning skills

- Have good negotiation skills and be able to work with the stakeholders to establish project scope and commitments

- Have effective presentation and communication skills

- Show leadership and team-building capabilities

- Have good time management and triage skills and a history of making sound decisions quickly under stress

- Be adaptable to change, especially being able to adapt to new events and to recover from wrong decisions

- Be objective in setting and assessing work, ensuring team buy-in

- Be technical enough to understand the technical risks and architectural issues in order to understand which issues are most pressing and which can be relegated to later iterations

- Share the architectural vision but be pragmatic in the scoping and implementation of plans and scrupulously honest in the assessment of outcomes

- Be focused on the delivery of customer value in the form of executing software that meets (or exceeds) the customer's needs

More technical and specialized than the overall project manager role, the development lead role is focused on the delivery of working software and naturally requires a more hands-on, in-depth involvement in the creation of the software. This role is often combined with the iteration lead role when the management team is instantiated for small projects.

Iteration Lead

This role covers the aspects of project management focused on the management of one or more iterations.

The iteration lead is tasked with ensuring that an iteration delivers the expected results to the required level of quality. This covers

- Negotiating the objectives and evaluation criteria for the iteration

- Planning and allocating the individual activities and tasks required to execute the iteration

- Assessing the progress and effectiveness of the iteration

- Leading the development team from day to day during the iteration

Staffing

The skills and experience needed to fulfill the iteration lead role depend upon the size of the development team and technical complexity of the proposed solution, but to play the role, to at least some degree you must

- Be experienced in the intricacies of software development

- Be experienced in the domain of the application

- Be experienced in understanding and interpreting test results

- Have the ability to estimate the amount of time, resources, and effort needed to complete very technical development activities

- Have the respect of the developers and technical members of the team

- Be able to clearly scope and define evaluation criteria for individual objectives and activities

- Show leadership and team-building capabilities

- Be focused on establishing the minimal essential characteristics of the solution

- Be focused on the delivery of executable, tested software

The least managerial of the three management roles, the iteration lead is focused on leading the team to the successful completion of an iteration. In most cases, the iteration lead role is seen as more of a technical team leader role than a formal project management role. This is usually the first management role that senior developers assume because it acts as a good stepping stone when moving from a technical career to something more managerial.

This role is often combined with the development lead role when the management team is instantiated for small projects.

Outline Plan and Assessment Documents

Throughout the book, we have talked about the necessity to produce and work with lightweight plans at each level of project planning and to push as much of the detail down into the iteration plans as possible. In this section, we provide outlines for the key planning artifacts:

- Overall Project Plan

- Development Plan

- Iteration Plan

These are presented as outlines rather than templates because our intention is to highlight the most important elements of each plan with regard to planning an iterative and incremental project. This enables us to focus on the purpose of the plans rather than their format or detailed contents.

To complement the plan outlines, we also provide outlines for the matching assessment documents:

- Iteration Assessment

- Project / Phase Assessment (suitable for documenting Phase Assessments, Project Assessments, and Stage Assessments)

The purpose of these outlines is to highlight the most important topics to be covered in the assessments rather than to attempt to describe a definitive format for these events.

The important thing to remember when considering these outlines is that each project is different and presents unique management and planning problems. When preparing templates for use on your projects or in your organization, take what you need from these outlines and complement these ideas with your own experience and best practices from your organizational standards and management toolset.

These outlines should be read in conjunction with the examples in Appendix C because they put the outlines into practice, providing concrete examples of the contents of each section and illustrating the application of the ideas outlined here.

Overall Project Plan—Outline

The Overall Project Plan is a comprehensive, composite artifact that gathers together all the information required to manage a project. It encloses a number of other artifacts developed during the project's initiation and is maintained throughout the project.

This Overall Project Plan contains the following information:

- **Project Overview**—A brief description of the project and its key deliverables. This must include the following:

  - **Desired Outcomes**—A clear statement of the project's desired outcomes. As noted elsewhere, the more precise and measurable the outcomes, the better it will be for everyone.

  - **The Project Approach**—An outline of the management approach adopted for the management of the project as a whole.

- **Project Organization**—An overview of the organizational structure of the project team. This focuses on the managerial team and the team structures. A simple organization chart with notes on roles and responsibilities is sufficient.

- **Project Plan**—A definition of the stages and business-significant milestones for the project, explaining the estimated cost and schedule, including the following:

  - **A Roadmap**—A one-page (at most) pictorial representation of the goals the project will achieve and the order in which it will achieve them.

  - **A Release Plan**—Details of known releases, their purpose, and any agreed upon delivery dates.

- **A Stage Plan**—An outline of the stages, evolutions, business deliverables, and dependencies of the project. This includes estimates and details of the external releases and other business-significant milestones.

- **Estimates and Tolerances**—These indicate how much slippage is tolerable before a major re-plan is forced.

  This section should be kept brief and to the point. The detail will reside in the individual development and iteration plans.

- **Management Strategy**—A definition of how the project will be conducted, including the following:

  - **Project Monitoring and Control**—A description of the approach the project will adopt to monitor progress and control the project.

  - **Technical and Supporting Process Plans**—An overview of any particular processes to be followed by the project, including methods, tools, and techniques.

Most organizations follow their own project management standards for the production of the overall project plan; details of some lightweight representations of what is needed are included in the next few subsections. The overall project plan document itself should provide an accessible overview of the project as a whole; the majority of the supporting detailed information will be held elsewhere in the lower-level plans and other management artifacts and tools (such as spreadsheets and planning tools). A few pages, at most, should be sufficient for each section of the overall project plan.

Project Overview

The purpose of this section is to position and provide an introduction to the project. It usually starts with a précis of the project's vision and business case, and it needs to include the following sections.

Objectives and Desired Outcomes

Describe the purpose of the project, including its objectives and desired outcomes. We have found that preparing a Balanced Scorecard for the project enables this to be done in a succinct and accessible manner.

Project Approach

Describe the approach to be taken to the management of the project. This should position the software development work required against the other aspects of the project such as deployment, business change, and marketing.

If the project is to be staged, then a summary of the intended stages makes a suitable management summary of the plan and introduces the reader to the dynamics of the approach selected. A table such as Table B-1 is usually sufficient.

Table B-1   *Overview of the Planned Stages*

Stage	Purpose	Key Deliverables	End Date
The identifier for the stage.	A brief description of the purpose of the stage summarizing the milestones it will achieve.	A summary of the key products to be delivered by the project during the stage.	The date when the stage will end and any specific tolerances defined for the stage.

The purpose here is to provide a succinct overview of the plan that illustrates what the project is intended to deliver and when.

The Key Deliverables column of this table should include at least the major releases to be produced by the project and any other deliverables allocated to the project by the commissioning organization or program. In those cases where the delivery dates need to be more specific than the planned end of the stage, the additional dates can be included when defining the deliverables in the Key Deliverables column.

Assumptions and Constraints

Document any assumptions made about the project and any constraints applied to the project by the commissioning organization or program.

Evolution of the Plan

Detail the major milestones for the plan. Typically the plan is revised at the boundary of each stage.

Project Organization

The purpose of this section is to describe the overall organizational structure of the project and the teams that it contains.

Organizational Structure

Describe the management structure of the project team. Limit this to a high-level description of the key roles on the project and the expected extent of the teams because the structure might change stage-by-stage, evolution-by-evolution, and even iteration-by-iteration. Each evolution's or other team's details can be included in the appropriate development plan. Remember that the goal is to push the detail down into the lower-level plans.

Roles and Responsibilities

Clarify the organizational structure by including definitions of the roles used. A table such as Table B-2 is usually sufficient.

Table B-2   *Defining Roles and Responsibilities*

Job Title	Primary Responsibilities	Secondary Responsibilities	Comments
For each role identified, provide a job title	Describe the main responsibilities	And any secondary responsibilities	Adding descriptive comments where necessary

External Interfaces

The project will have many external interfaces. It is important that these are identified and the responsibilities of the people on the interfaces clearly defined.

Project Review Authorities

The project governance mechanisms must be clearly identified and resourced. At the very minimum, the project must appoint a project review board to conduct the milestone reviews and the project, phase, and iteration assessments. Summarize the key review points and reviewers here. Detailed procedures should be defined in the Management Strategy section or deferred to the lower-level plans.

Stakeholder Representatives

A similar process to the process for the project review authorities should be undertaken for the requirements elicitation and review process. This should be summarized here and detailed in the project's requirements management plan or delegated to one of the lower-level plans. The project's Vision document should contain an analysis of the stakeholder and user types.

Other Interfaces

Identify any other people who must be kept informed about project progress. This includes any executive oversight functions, finance functions, or other external teams that have a role in project chartering or governance.

Project Plan

The overall project plan needs to provide an overview of the plan to be adopted. We like to see a number of succinct representations of the project in the Overall Project Plan including the following.

Roadmap

A roadmap is a pictorial representation of the project as a whole—we tend to use a UML[1] state or activity chart for this purpose.[2] To explain the roadmap, a tabular format is used to complement the pictorial representation, describing the milestones and capturing the dates by which they need to be completed. A table such as Table B-3 is usually sufficient.

Table B-3   *Describing the Milestones in the Roadmap*

Milestone	Description	Acceptance Criteria	Assignment	Completion Date
For each milestone identified in the roadmap	Describe what it represents	How the completion of the milestone will be assessed	The stream, evolution, or subproject to which it has been assigned	And the date by which the milestone will be achieved

Stage Plan

If the project is to be staged, then the overall project plan must summarize the stages. A table such as Table B-4 is usually sufficient.

Table B-4   *Example of a Stage Plan Summary*

Stage	Purpose	Key Deliverables	Workstream	Milestone	Date (tolerance)	Comments
For each stage	Describe its purpose	Identify the significant products to be produced	And which work stream will produce them	For completeness align to the milestones from the roadmap	Define the delivery dates (and any related tolerances)	Add comments where required

---

[1]   For details of the Unified Modeling Language, see www.uml.org.

[2]   An example roadmap is shown in Appendix C.

Some methodologies, such as PRINCE2, recommend producing a detailed Stage Plan for each of the stages identified in the Overall Project Plan. We have found it better to decompose the project into work streams, each with its own series of development plans. These will often overlap the stage boundaries to enable the evolutions to be conceived before the stage starts and to fulfill their ongoing transition responsibilities, which often carry into the next stage.

Release Plan

If the project is purely a software development project, then a release plan is necessary to complement the overall project roadmap. As with the roadmap, we have found UML state or activity charts very useful for pictorially representing the release plan. If the project has other responsibilities, then the detailed release plan is usually delegated to the software development plans.

To further qualify the pictorial representation, details of the releases' purpose, contents, and delivery dates are necessary. A table such as Table B-5 is usually sufficient.

Table B-5   *Release Plan*

Release	Description	Delivery Date	Comments
Name and number each release	Describe its key characteristics	Define when it will be delivered	Add comments where required

Estimates and Tolerances

This section summarizes the overall estimates for the project. It is necessary to produce high-level estimates for the duration of the project, the resources needed (including staffing levels), and the overall cost and budget. As discussed throughout Part II, tolerances are important because actuals rarely exactly match estimates. You must decide how much variance is significant, or you will be constantly and pointlessly revising plans.

Dependencies

This section highlights any major dependencies inherent in the plan, such as dependencies on external resources or events that might add risk to the project. Highlighting dependencies calls out that they warrant special attention.

Management Strategy

You need to define the management strategy clearly and unambiguously to make the project easier to manage and to ensure an appropriate amount of stakeholder interaction. We have found the following elements of the management strategy to be particularly effective:

- Providing a summary of the overall management and technical approach adopted

- Clearly defining the project communication and assessment mechanisms

- Objectively analyzing and recording the need for additional management products and plans

Overview

In this section, you must summarize the overall strategy adopted, highlighting the key decisions made in each area of the management strategy: the style of delivery, the level of detail and formality, the processes selected, the reporting and communications strategy, and the approach to product acceptance.

Defining Communication and Assessment

It is generally worthwhile to describe the project review processes and the level of involvement required from the project members and stakeholders. At the very minimum, clearly identify the responsibilities and level of involvement of the management and other representatives appointed to the various project review authorities. A table such as Table B-6 is usually sufficient. This table includes an example row illustrating the types of people that you might want to involve in a phase assessment.

Table B-6 *Defining Regular Assessment and Reviews*

Assessment Event	Roles[3]									Timing
	Project Manager	Sponsor	Customer	User	Iteration Lead	Requirement Manager	Architect	Quality Assurance	Development Team	
Identify the assessment event (Stage Assessment, Phase Assessment, Iteration Acceptance Assessment, etc.)	Identify the various roles involved across the top of the table and then for each role define their attendance and role in the event. We typically use the following scheme: L = Lead (the chairperson and leader for the event) Y = Yes (a key participant in the event) Opt = Optional (they will be invited as required) N = Non-applicable (the event is not suitable for their involvement) See the example row below.									Clearly denote the frequency of the event.
Phase Assessment	L	Y	Y	N	N	Y	Y	Y	N	End of every phase.

[3] Examples of common project roles; your project might have greater or fewer roles.

A similar table can be used to show the management reports to be produced and their circulation.

Deciding What Other Management Products Are Required

Many other plans and processes might be required to enable a project to be successfully managed. Often these are established at a program or organizational level, at other times they need to be explicitly addressed for the project at hand, and at other times they are not needed at all. We have found it beneficial to create a checklist to record the decisions made in these areas and provide references to the organizational or local policies being followed. One or more tables such as Table B-7 are usually sufficient.

Table B-7   *Auditing the Use of Standard Control Artifacts*

Control Artifact	Usage	Justification / Reference
Identify the expected plan or control document.	Say how the artifact will be treated. We usually use the values: **Y** to indicate an artifact needed at the overall project level **N** to indicate an artifact not needed **Reuse** to indicate an artifact reused from another project or team **Delegated** to indicate an artifact to be produced by one of the subprojects	Justify the decision made and provide a reference to the relevant reused, delegated, or developed artifacts. Artifacts created at the overall project level can be created as an addendum to the overall project plan or as separate documents.

This section can become quite cumbersome, especially for high-ceremony organizations.

To illustrate the kinds of things that an owning organization might expect, we have provided the following lists (see Tables B-8 through B-10) of some of the more commonly requested control artifacts that are associated with some of the more popular software development and project management methodologies.

Table B-8 *Management Control Artifacts*

Control Artifact	Usage	Justification / Source
Risk Management Plan	As defined in Table B-7.	As defined in Table B-7.
Measurement Plan		
Documentation Plan		
Problem Resolution Plan		
Subcontractor Management Plan		
Process Improvement Plan		
Communications Plan		
Stakeholder Involvement Plan		
Resource Acquisition Plan		
Training Plan		
Schedule Control Plan		
Quality Control Plan		
Close-out Plan		

Table B-9 *Supporting Specialist Plans*

Supporting Plan	Usage	Justification / Source
Requirements Management Plan	As defined in Table B-7.	As defined in Table B-7.
Infrastructure Plan		
Configuration Management Plan		
Quality Assurance Plan		
Product Acceptance Plan		
Evaluation Plan		
Development Process Description / Development Case		

Table B-10 *Methods, Tools, and Techniques*

Standards and Guidelines	Usage	Justification / Reference
Business Modeling Guidelines	As defined in Table B-7.	As defined in Table B-7.
User Interface Guidelines		
Use-Case Modeling Guidelines		
Design Guidelines		
Programming Guidelines		
Test Guidelines		
Manual Style Guide		

Keeping Things as Lightweight as Possible

We know what you're probably thinking at this point—this is a lot of stuff. We agree that it looks like a lot of plans and guidelines, but it really is not as bad as it looks, and you might not need all of it. Here's how to keep the process manageable.

On smaller or less complex development efforts, most of the artifacts listed in Table B-8 can be collapsed into a single document, with each of the "plans" being described in a section within the document. Each section might be only a paragraph or two if you have a simple process.

Many of these plans can be reused across projects, especially if the organization has adopted a common approach across all its projects. This reduces the overall work the individual project teams need to do to get started. This is especially true for the plans in Table B-10. Always leverage whatever you can from a higher level within the organization.

In everything, do only what is absolutely necessary to reduce risk and produce better results. Don't define a complex process to handle every possible contingency. Instead, make sure that you can recognize when problems occur and then be flexible enough to react appropriately. No one can anticipate every contingency, and usually detailed plans prepared in anticipation of contingencies have to be adapted anyway.

If you're not actually going to measure whether people are following guidelines, don't bother to document them. People tend to do things that are reinforced by measurements, and presenting guidelines that no one really seems to care about (at least not enough to measure whether they are being followed) is confusing. Because you can really only measure a limited number of things, choosing the really important things reduces the amount of guidelines necessary.

Development Plan—Outline

The Development Plan is a comprehensive, composite artifact that gathers all the information required to manage the development of an evolution (major release) of a software product. It encloses a number of artifacts that are typically developed during the Inception phase, and it is maintained throughout the project. The Development Plan should be read in conjunction with the Overall Project Plan that defines the project as a whole and includes the release plan and the overall management strategy.

The Development Plan matches the Overall Project Plan in structure and contains the following information:

- **Project Overview**—Provides a brief description of the development project and its key deliverables. For a fuller description of the project's purpose, scope, and objectives, see the Overall Project Plan. This also includes details of any assumptions and constraints applicable to the plan.

  This section acts as the "Work Package" definition, or terms of reference for the evolution. It includes an overview of the approach to be taken and the project's development and delivery strategy.

- **Project Organization**—Describes the organizational structure of the development team.

  This section provides a more detailed view of the development team structure, complementing and refining the high-level organizational breakdown found in the Overall Project Plan.

- **Project Plan**—Defines the phases, milestones, and iterations for the project, explaining and clarifying the estimated cost and schedule. This includes the following:

  - **The Project Plan**—An outline of the phases, iterations, and deliverables of the evolution, including estimates and details of the internal releases and other internal milestones.

- **Estimates and Tolerances (for the development)**—This section provides more precise and detailed estimates to complement and challenge those found in the Overall Project Plan. Where necessary, it also refines the overall project tolerances and explains how they affect this particular development.

- **Management Strategy**—Defines how the project will be conducted.

- **Project Monitoring and Control**—Describes any exceptions or extensions to the Overall Project Plan's Management Strategy that are applicable to this evolution.

- **Technical and Supporting Process Plans**—Provides an overview of the software development process, including methods, tools, and techniques to be followed.

The Development Plan mirrors the structure of the Overall Project Plan qualifying and extending it where necessary and adding the detail of how the evolution will be developed. It is not necessary to repeat any of the information from the Overall Project Plan.

Project Overview

Objectives and Desired Outcomes

Describe the purpose of this particular development project, including the evolution's objectives and desired outcomes.

Project Approach / Development and Delivery Strategy

Describe the approach to be taken to the development of the software system. Include an outline of the iterative approach adopted for the development of this evolution. If you like what you've learned from this book, then you will probably select one of the iteration patterns described in Chapter 7, "Evolution and Phase Planning," and then tailor it to reflect the adjustments required to support your project.

Include a brief overview of the overall pattern of phases and iterations provides a succinct introduction to the plan to be detailed later in the development plan. The type of information contained in Table B-11 is usually sufficient.

Table B-11   *Summary of the Phases and Iterations*

Phase	Iteration	Resulting Releases	Risks Addressed
Name the phase.	Uniquely identify the iteration by numbering it within the phase (for example, I1 for the first Inception iteration) and then name it to summarize its intended purpose.	Categorize and briefly describe the resulting release.	Provide a brief summary of the type of risks addressed.

Add a row for each iteration, grouped by its intended phase. If you don't know what the plan is yet, then just summarize what you expect to happen without committing yourself too much. The purpose is to provide an overview of how the project will proceed (for review and discussion purposes) and not to define a prescriptive plan.

Key Deliverables

Summarize the key deliverables from the evolution. The type of information contained in Table B-12 is usually sufficient.

Table B-12 *Summary of the Key External Deliverables Required from the Development Project*

Deliverable	Milestone	Date and Tolerance	Comment
Name the deliverable.	Name the milestone (either internal or external) at which it is required.	Define the date by which delivery is required and any tolerances defined for the delivery.	Add any additional comments needed to make the plan understandable.

This table will include at least the major release to be produced by the evolution as well any other deliverables allocated to the evolution by the Overall Project Plan.

Assumptions and Constraints

Document any assumptions made about this evolution and any constraints applied to the project by the Overall Project Plan or other external forces.

Evolution of the Development Plan

Detail the major milestones for the plan. The type of information contained in Table B-13 is usually sufficient.

Table B-13 *Evolution of the Development Plan*

Version	Date	Milestone	Comment
1.0	End of Inception	Lifecycle Objectives	Initial plan for public circulation.
2.0	End of Elaboration	Lifecycle Architecture	Stable plan for the completion of the development.
3.0	End of Construction	Initial Operational Capability	Revised plan to cover transition and support.

Any minor revisions produced between these milestones will be point releases, which will be version numbered accordingly.

Project Organization

Team Structure

Describe the organizational structure of the development team. This structure can change phase-by-phase and iteration-by-iteration. Describing the key roles on the development team is usually sufficient. Each iteration's team details can be included in the iteration plan if required.

Roles and Responsibilities

Clarify the organizational structure by defining the roles and responsibilities of the people listed previously. The type of information contained in Table B-14 is usually sufficient.

Table B-14   *Development Team Roles and Responsibilities*

Job Title	Primary Responsibilities	Secondary Responsibilities	Comments
For each role identified	Describe the responsibilities	And any secondary responsibilities	Adding descriptive comments where necessary

External Interfaces

Clarify how the development project will assist the overall project in managing its external interfaces and add any detail required to clarify how the development project will interface with any other workstreams or subprojects within the overall project. The same format and structure as that applied in the overall project plan can be applied here.

Project Plan

The most important part of the development plan is the project plan. Fill in a table such as Table B-15 to outline the phases and iterations; add a row for each expected iteration. Be careful not to get too carried away with predictive planning; the purpose of this outline is to enable the negotiation of commitments and impact analysis of the results of the iterations. Remember that much of the detail will be added as the particular iterations draw near. This table is then complemented with release and deliverable plans to provide a complete picture and timeline.

Table B-15   *Phases and Iterations*

	Iteration	Objectives / Risks	Schedule	Effort	Key Deliverables	Plan Ref
Phase Name	I1: Name the iteration	Summarize the iteration's objectives and the risks it addresses as a bulleted list.	Define the duration of the iteration in weeks and its start date.	Estimate the effort available in the iteration in persondays.	Add a bulleted list of the iterations key external deliverables.	Provide a reference to the iteration plan.

Add a row for each iteration and group them by their intended phases. If you don't know what the plan is yet, then just summarize what you expect to happen without committing yourself too much. The purpose is to provide an overview of how the project will proceed (for review and discussion purposes) and not to define a prescriptive plan.

This table is typically defined using a landscape format to allow enough space in the columns to describe the objectives, risks, and deliverables.

Incremental / Iteration Release Plan

The most important deliverables are the releases, of which there will be one per iteration. Use Table B-16 to log the releases, their types, and their production dates.

Table B-16   *Iteration Release Plan*

Release	Production Iteration	Production Date	Type	Description
Name and number the release.	Detail the iteration that will produce the release.	Specify the date of its intended production.	Describe the type of release to be produced: proof of concept, prototype, internal release, or external release.	Add a brief description of the contents of the release.

Other Project Deliverables

It is often useful to provide a summary of the project's other key deliverables and their state by phase and iteration. An example for the Vision document is shown in Table B-17. If these deliverables are those mentioned in the project overview at the head of the document, then mark these in bold to indicate that they are external deliverables.

Table B-17   *Other Key Project Deliverables*

Artifact	Inception	Elaboration		Construction		Transition
	I1	E1	E2	C1	C2	T1
Name the artifact to be produced	Describe the expected state of the artifact at the end of each iteration. See the example given for the Vision document below. Add a row for each of the other important project deliverables.					
Vision	Initial version	Evolving	Agreed Upon and Signed Off			

Again be careful not to get too carried away with predictive planning; these are only outlines to allow the negotiation of commitments and the impact analysis of the results of the iterations. Many of these details can be added later as a record of how the project progressed.

The Iteration Release Plan and the Other Key Project Deliverables tables should each fit onto no more than two sides of standard letter-sized paper. If they don't, you are getting carried away and including stuff that really belongs in the iteration plan, or the project is way too big. If you really feel the need to have more detail, then we advise that you keep this in your project planning tool or some supporting spreadsheet.

Estimates and Tolerances

Include the course-grained estimates for the evolution as a whole. The finer-grained estimates will be associated with the requirement elements (use-case flows, scenarios, Supplementary Specifications, and so on). Typically the estimates are maintained in some kind of spreadsheet where the estimates for the individual artifacts, scenarios, use-case flows, and expected overheads can all be maintained and tracked. Based on these estimates, calculate the resource levels required throughout the project.

The estimates of the capacity (in person-days) of each iteration are included in Table B-15 in the earlier project plan section.

Management Strategy

The development will be managed in the context of the Overall Project and will only need to note any qualifications, exceptions, or extensions to the management strategy laid down in the Overall Project Plan. If the development project is being undertaken alone, without an overall project to provide context, you may want to duplicate the equivalent sections from the overall project plan, considering the need for explicit monitoring and control procedures and supporting plans as part of your development project.

Project Monitoring and Control

Describe any exceptions or extensions to the Overall Project Plan's Management Strategy that are applicable to this evolution. Any additional reporting needs above and beyond the Project Reviews and Assessments detailed in the previous "Project Organization" section should be defined. If required, the same tabular formats can be reused.

Technical and Supporting Process Plans

Provide an overview of the software development process, including methods, tools, and techniques to be followed. This section should complete the equivalent section in the overall project plan by providing more detail.

Iteration Plan—Outline

The Iteration Plan is the fine-grained, task-level plan for the iteration. The Iteration Plan contains the following information:

- **Scope and Objectives**—Defines the scope of the iteration in terms of what will be achieved, including the following:

  - **Risks**—A list of the risks specifically addressed by this iteration.

  - **Objectives**—A list of the iterations objectives, qualifying how the risks will be addressed.

  - **Requirements**—A list of the use-case flows, scenarios, and supplementary specifications to be implemented and tested in this iteration.

  - **Change Requests and Defects**—A list of the change requests and defects to be implemented and tested in this iteration.

  - **Other Deliverables**—A list of any other products that are to be produced in this iteration to complement the release developed and tested.

  For each of these, you should also describe the associated evaluation criteria that will be used to assess whether the iteration is a success. For example, certain requirements might be mandatory, and others might be "nice to have." You should be explicit about these distinctions.

- **Plan**—Describes the detailed plan for the iteration. Typically a high-level task list, team responsibilities, and schedule of group events are sufficient. Don't forget to include the assessment events in the plan.

Scope and Objectives

Start by introducing the iteration in an informal and accessible way. Explain where the team is in the project and outline the purpose of the iteration.

Risk Analysis

List the risks, 1-10, that you will be addressing. If you can tackle more than 10, then your iteration is probably too long. Typically this is a subset derived from the project risk list, usually referencing the overall project risk list rather than duplicating the details.

A template for a risk list that can be included in the iteration plan is shown in Table B-18.

Table B-18 *A Simple Iteration Plan Risk List Template*

Rank This Iteration	Rank Last Iteration	Number of Iterations on List	Risk	Exposure	Mitigation Plan
The current position in the risk list.	The position in the risk list at the start of the last iteration.	A representation of how long the risk has been one of the project's top 10 risks.	A description of the risk.	The project's exposure to the risk (typically Very High, High, Medium, Low, or Very Low).	A description or reference to any mitigation plan in place.

Iteration Objectives and Evaluation Criteria

Qualify what will be done about the risks by clearly defining the specific objectives for the iteration and their measurable evaluation criteria. A template for an objectives table that can be included in the iteration plan is shown in Table B-19.

Table B-19 *Defining the Iteration Objectives and Evaluation Criteria*

Objective	Description Addressed	Risks Criteria	Evaluation Evidence	Required	Priority
Name the objective.	Provide a brief description to illuminate the name.	List the risks that achieving the objective will mitigate (optional).	Describe the evaluation criteria that will be used to assess the achievement of the objective.	List the evidence that is required to support the evaluation criteria (optional).	Define the priority of the objective within the iteration (Essential, Highly Desirable, or Desirable)

Add a row for each objective defined for the iteration. An example taken from an iteration plan for an iteration in the Inception phase is shown below.

Agree on the vision.	Establish a shared vision with all stakeholder representatives.	The business case cannot be agreed on because there is disagreement about the extent of the system.	All stakeholder representatives agree to and support the vision.	Signed off Vision document. Revised Business Case with estimates.	Essential

To enable the objectives and priorities to be maintained across a number of iterations, we tend to keep a work-in-progress set of objectives in a spreadsheet, copying those agreed upon to the iteration plan when it is published at the start of the iteration.

Requirements, Defects, and Change Requests

Select the use-case flows, scenarios, supplementary specifications, defects, and change requests to be implemented and tested in this iteration to mitigate the selected risks. These should be individually estimated. This is often just a reference to a requirements management tool or spreadsheet where the requirements are prioritized and targeted onto specific iterations. Progress and quality can also be tracked there. The same holds true for defects and change requests.

If you don't have a set of such spreadsheets or more sophisticated tools, then we would highly recommend that you create some. Extracts from the tools can then be used to populate this section of the iteration plan. A table such as Table B-20 is usually sufficient.

Table B-20   *Allocating Requirements, Defects, and Change Requests to the Iteration*

Scope	Unit	State	Estimate	Iteration Priority
The owning artifact (for example, the use-case name).	The unique identifier and name of the item to be addressed (for example, Basic Flow or the name of an alternative flow or scenario).	The state the item should be in at the end of the iteration, typically implemented and tested.	An estimate of how long addressing the item will take.	The priority of the item within the iteration.

Other Deliverables

List any other artifacts (in addition to the software release) to be produced in this iteration. A table such as Table B-21 is usually sufficient.

Table B-21   *Allocating Other Deliverables to Be Produced by the Iteration*

Discipline	Artifact	State	Estimate	Iteration Priority
The discipline that owns the artifact.	The name of the artifact to be delivered.	The state the artifact should be in at the end of the iteration.	An estimate of how long producing the artifact will take.	The priority of the item within the iteration.

Implementing and testing a flow of events naturally includes updating the design, test specifications, and so on, so these don't need to be listed.

Plan

The scope and objectives need to be complemented with a plan describing how they will be achieved.

Capacity Estimate

You must provide an estimate of the combined effort available for planned tasks in the iteration. Create a table of the resources available for work during the iteration and their expected capacity. Don't forget to include overhead activities such as e-mails, time sheets, personal development, training, communications events, and support. There are also recurrent activities required to support the iterative way of working (such as iteration planning, iteration assessments, and regular team meetings) and software development (such as performing daily builds and checking the results of automated regression testing). Because these tend to be group or shared responsibilities, it is easier to treat these as an additional overhead rather than to include them in the capacity estimate.

A couple of simple tables, such as Table B-22 and Table B-23, are sufficient to capture the details needed and to enable an accurate estimate of the team's capacity to be created.

Table B-22   *Team Availability*

Name	Role	Availability			
		Week 1	Week 2	Week 3	Week 4
For each member of the team	Describe their role in the iteration	And then estimate how many days of each week of the iteration they will work on the project			

Table B-23   *Overheads and Contingency*

	Week 1	Week 2	Week 3	Week 4
For each type of overhead or group activity (such as those listed below)	Estimate the number of days that will be spent on it in each iteration			
Corporate Activities				
Generic Iteration Activities: Planning, Assessment, Communications, Builds, Admin, etc.				
Support				
Contingency				

Schedule

Create a schedule of any group events such as workshops, reviews, integration points, and system test dates, remembering to include the assessment events. Make sure you plan the assessment events as part of the initial iteration planning. You don't want the iteration to be delayed because people aren't available for assessments.

Again a tabular format, such as Table B-24 where a row is added for each significant event, could be used.

Table B-24 *A Simple Table of Events*

Week	Date / Time	Event	Description	Involves
Identify in which week of the iteration the event will occur.	Identify when the event will happen and its expected duration.	Name the event.	Describe the event.	List who should be involved.

Task List

A living tabular task list enables the state and allocation of tasks to be tracked throughout the iteration. One mechanism is to create a tabular task list in a format such as Table B-25 or a commercial task assignment tool. For the items (objectives, requirements, change requests, defects, and artifacts) listed previously, adding the owner and state of the work to the list might be sufficient.

Table B-25   *Simple Tabular Task List*

Task	Owner	Involves	Delivers	Estimate	State
Uniquely identify each task.	Assign it an owner (or leave it open for volunteers).	Describe anyone else who needs to be involved.	Describe the expected output of the task.	Estimate how long it will take to complete.	Record its current state (unassigned, assigned, in process, complete, etc.).

This kind of low-level task management is typically better performed in a project management tool or a spreadsheet. A reference to the task list or detailed plan is usually all that is included in the iteration plan document.

Many of you might feel that these tables are too lightweight, and others might feel that they are too detailed. The answer is that you can plan your iteration in whatever way works for you and your team. If you like using planning tools, then go ahead.[4] Just be sure that the amount of planning effort is proportional to the size of the iteration. If the iteration is two weeks long, then spending four days planning it is probably excessive. Always keep in mind that planning is just another tool to manage risk—when misapplied, it can add risk to the project just like anything else. More planning is not better than less planning, just as less is not better than more. Strive for *just enough* planning to make sure that there is a clear picture of what work needs to be done when and by whom. Remember that you only need to have identified the immediate tasks to be addressed and have their ownership distributed throughout the team to start the iteration. Additional material can be added to the plan as needed.

---

[4] But keep in mind that the section on Scope and Objectives is not optional and cannot be replaced by Gantt charts.

Iteration Assessment—Outline

The Iteration Assessment documents the results delivered by an iteration. It mirrors the iteration plan in that it reports on the objectives, deliverables, and plans defined by the iteration plan. Some people actually record the assessment as an addendum to the plan itself.

The Iteration Assessment contains the following information:

- **Iteration results**—Provide a summary of how the iteration performed and the "grade" given to the iteration; complement this with a detailed analysis of the results relative to the detailed objectives and evaluation criteria.

- **Findings**—Describe how the team performed during the iteration and anything that happened outside the project that is likely to affect the project or its ability to deliver. Make sure that you capture any lessons learned and note any rework required.

Iteration Results

Summarize how the team performed during the iteration, telling the story of what happened in the iteration, summarizing what risks were addressed, presenting the percentage of objectives achieved, and assigning a "grade" to the iteration. Some sections of the assessment duplicate the format of the iteration plan with the addition of extra columns; others are more independent. The important thing is that all the areas are considered and objectively assessed.

In Chapter 8, "Iteration Planning," we introduced the grading scheme presented in Table B-26.

Table B-26   *Iteration "Grades"*

Result	Description
Exceptional	The iteration exceeded expectations, completing all essential objectives and many others.
Passed	The iteration completed all the essential objectives.
Passed at risk	The iteration completed nearly all the essential objectives and can proceed to the next iteration without re-planning the project (such as adding or extending iterations).
Unfinished	The iteration fell short of completing the essential objectives but was doing the right things and would have succeeded with more time.
Failed	The iteration failed, and significant corrective action is required.
Abandoned	The iteration was abandoned.

If the iteration was *Unfinished, Failed,* or *Abandoned,* a recommendation about the continuation of the project must be made. For example, the project might have to be re-planned, de-scoped, extended, or cancelled. It is impossible to provide a definitive list of the possible actions that might result from the assessment of an unsuccessful iteration. A lot will depend on the reasons for failure and the relative importance of the project to the organization.

Results Relative to Evaluation Criteria

Be sure to analyze and describe how well the iteration did in meeting each of its objectives. The easiest approach is to copy the objectives from the iteration plan and add a column to capture the verdict of the assessment. Possible verdicts for an objective are shown in Table B-27.

Table B-27   *Results Relative to Evaluation Criteria*

Result	Description
Pass	The evaluation criteria were met, and it is agreed that the objective has been achieved.
Partial Pass	The majority of the evaluation criteria have been met, and enough of the objective has been achieved that the objective itself can be closed off and the remaining work subsumed into later objectives.

Result	Description
Fail	The evaluation criteria for an essential objective have not been met, and therefore the team has failed to achieve the objective. Note: this only applies to the essential objectives. If you fail to achieve a highly desirable or desirable objective, then this is *not* a failure.
Incomplete	Work has been started on the objective, but the objective has not been achieved. This is useful for acknowledging work that has been undertaken against non-essential objectives.
Not Started	The work necessary to achieve the objective has yet to be started. Typically this is the state of the majority of the highly desirable and desirable objectives at the end of the iteration because the team's efforts should be directed at achieving the essential objectives.

The evidence column can now be used to capture what actual evidence there is rather than presenting the evidence that was expected. This leads to the presentation of the results against the objectives and their evaluation criteria in a table such as Table B-28.

Table B-28   *Recording the Result of an Iteration Against the Objectives and Evaluation Criteria*

Objective	Description	Risks Addressed	Evaluation Criteria	Evidence Accumulated	Priority	Verdict
These columns are copied from the iteration plan.				List the evidence that has been produced to demonstrate that the objective has been met.	Copied from the iteration plan.	Record the project's success in achieving the objective: Pass, Partial Pass, Fail, Incomplete, or Not Started.

Remember that it is the assessment against the essential objectives that is most important. If all the essential objectives have been achieved, then the iteration is a success.

Results Relative to the Planned Deliverables

If the project is particularly large or important, it might also be worth summarizing how the project did with regard to the required deliverables:

- **Requirements**—A summary of how many of the target requirements were implemented and tested.

- **Other Deliverables**—A summary of the state of the other deliverables.

- **Test Results**—A summary of the results of the testing undertaken within the iteration.

A brief summary is sufficient because all the information will be available elsewhere within the project.

Findings

As well as documenting the result of the iteration, the iteration assessment should also present what has been observed and learned during the iteration. We find the following headings useful in structuring the assessment and focusing on what needs to be assessed:

- **Adherence to the Plan**—A summary of how well the iteration matched the original plan. Special attention should be paid to the accuracy of the estimates and the priorities in which things were addressed.

- **Measurement and Analysis**—A summary of the measurements collected for this iteration and analysis of the trends across the iterations undertaken so far. As discussed in Chapter 9, "Iteration, Phase, and Project Assessments," it is recommended that measurement and trend graphs be collected for progress, risk exposure, estimate to complete, effort profile, cost profile, effort expended, find/fix rate, and defect trends. The analysis should examine the measurements in light of any project tolerances that have been set.

- **Feedback from the Demonstration**—Capture the impressions gained from any demonstrations. Analyze any change requests they raised.

- **External Changes**—While the iteration is in progress, the world goes on around the project, and events that might affect the project happen. During the iteration, the team does everything possible to keep to the original iteration plan and to deliberately prevent external changes from affecting the project and distracting the team from meeting its objectives. The iteration assessment is the time to collect and reflect on any external changes that have occurred and how they affect the project. This can lead to new risks being added to the project's risk list.

- **Lessons Learned**—Capture any lessons learned during the iteration and capture actions to address them. This is possibly the most important part of the iteration assessment because it is what enables the team to improve.

- **Rework Required**—Based on the iteration's success, the measurement trends, the external changes, and the lessons learned, describe any rework that is required.

Project / Phase Assessment—Outline

The Project / Phase Assessment document provides a standard format for documenting the phase assessments, stage assessments, and any other project assessments that are required to handle exceptions or satisfy the project's stakeholders, owning program, or steering committee.

If the assessment is a phase assessment, then the assessment will include a formal lifecycle milestone review to assess the project against one of the lifecycle milestones (Lifecycle Objectives, Lifecycle Architecture, Initial Operational Capability, or Product Release). If the assessment is a stage assessment, then the project's state will be assessed against the end of stage milestone defined in the overall project plan.

The Project Assessment contains the following information:

- **Conclusions and Recommendations**—Provide a summary of how the project has progressed since the last management review. If the assessment is a phase or stage assessment, then give the phase or stage a "grade." Also document the assessment's recommendation of how the project should proceed.

- **Status / Milestone Review**—Review the project's state against the business case and the appropriate milestone. Also undertake a high-level review of the project's risk and issues and define any concrete actions the project needs to take.

- **Findings**—Describe how the extended project team performed during the time since the last assessment and anything that happened outside the project that is likely to affect the project or its ability to deliver. Make sure that you capture any lessons learned and note any rework required.

Conclusions and Recommendations

Provide a management summary of how the project has performed since the last assessment. Give the project a grade and clearly define the current state of the project. Document the assessment's recommendation for the continuation or cancellation of the project.

The conclusions and recommendations can be easily summarized in a simple table, such as that shown in Table B-29, which illustrates the successful conclusion of a phase.

Table B-29   *Summarizing the Assessment in a Simple Table*

Action	Result
Lifecycle Milestone Review	Passed
Recommendation	Approved
Corrective Action Required	None

In Chapter 8 we introduced the grading scheme shown in Table B-30, which can be used to indicate the result of a milestone review.

Table B-30   *Milestone "Grades"*

Result	Description
Passed	The project has passed the milestone review and is in a good shape to proceed to the next phase or stage.
Passed at risk	It is conditionally accepted that the milestone review has been passed, but additional corrective action is required.
Failed	The milestone review was failed, and the project will be either re-planned (with the phase or stage extended) or cancelled.

You must also clearly state the assessment's recommendation for the continuation of the project. As a result of the assessment, the project might be classified as *approved, temporarily approved, extended, paused, postponed,* or *cancelled.* Based on the project's success against the milestone and the assessment's decision on the future of the project, corrective action might be required. This can be as simple as adding an iteration or as complex as completely re-planning the project.

Status Review

The following reviews should take place as part of any project assessment:

- **Milestone Review**—Summarize how the project has performed against its milestones. If the assessment is a phase assessment, then review the performance of the project against the evaluation criteria for the appropriate lifecycle milestone. The phase assessment checklists later in this appendix can be used as a pro-forma for each of the Unified Process phases.

- **Business Case Review**—Review the project's progress and revised estimates against the business case to ensure that the project is still on course to deliver the expected business benefit.

- **Tolerances**—Review the state of the project against the defined tolerances, indicating how much of the tolerances have been consumed and what level of tolerance remains for the project going forward.

- **Risk Review**—Review the current state of the risks threatening the project.

- **Project Issues and Exceptions**—Review the current state of any issues and exceptions raised by the project.

- **Impact on the Plan / Corrective Actions**—Review the impact of the project's performance to date on the remaining plans and document any corrective actions required.

Findings

As well as documenting the current state of the project, the project assessment should also present what has been observed and learned during the time since the last assessments. This is particularly important when undertaking the regular phase or stage assessments.

We find the following headings useful in structuring the assessment and focusing on what needs to be assessed. These are very similar to those used as part of the iteration assessment. The project assessments shouldn't repeat the findings from the iteration assessments but should revisit the development project as a whole, summarizing what has been learned across all the iterations of the project.

- **Adherence to the Plan**—A summary of how well the project has matched the plan. Special attention should be paid to the number and length of the iterations used, the accuracy of the estimates, and the order in which things were addressed.

- **Measurement and Analysis**—A summary of the measurements collected for the project to date. Include some analysis of the trends across the iterations undertaken so far. The analysis should examine the measurements in light of any project tolerances that have been set.

- **Feedback from the Stakeholders**—Summarize the impressions gained from any demonstrations and other interactions with the stakeholders.

- **External Changes**—While the project is in progress, the world goes on around the project, and events that might affect the project happen. The project assessment is the time to collect and reflect on any major external changes that have occurred and how they affect the project.

- **Lessons Learned**—Capture any lessons to be learned that arise during the assessment process. These should complement the lessons learned during the regular iteration assessments and focus on broader issues affecting multiple iterations and the project as a whole.

Checklists

The following checklists provide simple questions you can use to review progress on a project. The checklists are not exhaustive or suitable for every kind of project but are presented here to give you an idea of the kinds of questions you should be asking.

Remember to factor local circumstances and policies into any checklists that you use in your organization. For example, if you are working in an organization committed to the use of CMMI, then you might want to include additional CMMI-related checks in the checklists.

The phase assessment checklists have been split into two sections:

- A generic checklist of items that apply regardless of the phase being assessed

- A series of phase-specific checklists—one for each Unified Process phase

To make the phase-specific checklists more usable, the questions have been grouped using the problem, solution, and project framework introduced in Chapter 3, "Controlling Iterative Projects":

- The problem questions are those that should be directed at the project's business representatives and other stakeholders.

- The solution questions are those that should be directed at the architect and the technical experts.

- The project questions are those that should be directed at the project sponsors and the management team.

Iteration Assessment

Assessing the results of the iteration:

- Has the iteration met its objectives (yes, mostly yes, mostly no, no) within the iteration time box?
- Have the risks identified to be mitigated during the iteration been mitigated or retired?
- Have you assessed whether the iteration has successfully mitigated the principal project risks?
- Was a demonstrable release produced?
- Were the test results satisfactory?
- Were the overall iteration goals met?

Assessing the effectiveness of the people, process, and plans:

- Were the evaluation criteria realistic, measurable, and achievable?
- Has the emphasis been on addressing all the essential objectives before any other work is started?
- Were the estimates of effort accurate?
- Have you compared actuals with estimates?
- Was the time box of an appropriate length?
- Did the iteration end on time?
- Were the right measurements collected?
- Were the right resources (both internal and external) available?
- Has the team been doing the right things?
- Is the team morale good?
- Have lessons to be learned been discussed and captured?
- Are the artifacts being produced useful and necessary?
- Are the processes being followed helping the project be successful?
- Are any impediments preventing the team from operating effectively?
- Are any additional skills needed by the team?
- Has the impact of any external changes been assessed?

Acting on the results of the iteration:

- Have all new risks been recorded?
- Have all new change requests and problem reports been assessed and prioritized?
- Has the need for any rework been factored into the plans?
- Have you carried forward all incomplete objectives to the next iteration?

- Have the measurement trends been analyzed?

- Is the remaining work achievable in the planned timescales?

- Does the amount of requirements completed and defects fixed exceed the number of new requirements or defects identified?

- Has the project risk exposure decreased?

- Are the project estimates and actuals converging?

- Are the measurements useful?

- Are the correct measurements being collected?

- Has a revised estimate been produced?

- Do the higher-level project plans need to be adjusted?

- Does the project scope need to be adjusted?

- Does the team need to be reorganized to become more effective?

- Does the project process need to be adjusted?

- Should the project be cancelled?

Generic Phase Checklist

Assessing the achievement of the milestone:

- Has the phase's related milestone been achieved?
- Is the business case still valid?
- Is the project scope still appropriate to fulfill the business case?
- Is the project's scope still acceptable to the stakeholders?
- Have all major issues for this phase been resolved?
- Is the project performance (in terms of cost/schedule/quality) satisfactory?
- Has the project risk exposure been significantly reduced?
- Is the project's risk profile acceptable for entry into the next phase?
- Have the right artifacts been produced, and are they in an appropriate state to allow entry into the next phase?
- Have the meeting participants agreed on the overall "grade" for the phase?
- Are plans in place for the next phase?

Assessing the effectiveness of the people, process, and plans:

- Was the milestone properly understood?
- Were the right resources (both internal and external) available?
- Has the team been doing the right things?
- Are the artifacts being produced useful and necessary?
- Did all the artifacts produced contribute to the successful conclusion of the phase?
- Are the processes being followed helping the project be successful?
- Are any impediments preventing the team from operating effectively?
- Has the impact of any external changes been assessed?
- Have lessons to be learned been discussed and captured?
- Were the right people involved in the assessment?
- Was sufficient time allowed for participants to prepare for the review?

Acting on the results of the assessment:

- If the phase was not accepted, has a follow-up review been scheduled?
- If the phase was accepted, is the funding in place for the project to continue?
- Have you logged all actions and issues arising from the review?
- Do the project plans need to be adjusted?

Inception Phase Checklist

Focus: Are the business risks under control?

Outcome: Agreement to fund the project

Milestone: Lifecycle Objectives—Project Viability Agreed

Problem

- Has the business case been established?
- Is there agreement on the business results to be achieved by the project?
- Does the proposed solution solve a meaningful problem?
- Is the project aligned with the business goals?
- Is the project financially viable? Can the solution be built profitably?
- Given all the other things we need to do, should we fund this project?
- Is there a credible value proposition?
- Is the solution feasible?
- How much is the solution worth?
- Can the solution be delivered within the perceived window of market opportunity? Will it be available in time?
- Is the scope of the solution understood?
- Is the problem understood?
- Do we agree on the scope of the solution?
- Have the critical requirements been identified?

Solution

- Is the project technically viable?
- Has the technical feasibility been assessed?
- Has a candidate architecture been selected?
- Has the development approach been agreed upon?
- Can we develop the proposed solution?
- Are the development and test environments in place for elaboration?

Project

- Is there a credible (low-fidelity) plan for delivering the solution within the time and financial constraints of the project?
- Have the assumptions behind this plan been tested?
- Is there an estimate of the cost and effort required to build the solution?
- Is the funding available?
- Are the desired outcomes for the project agreed upon and measurable?
- Are the objectives for the project agreed upon?
- Are the constraints placed on the project understood?
- Have the stakeholder and project responsibilities been agreed upon?
- Are the risks (business, technical, project, people, funding, etc.) understood?
- Have the critical risks been identified and assessed?
- Do we understand the scope and risks related to the deployment of the solution?

Key Artifacts

- Business Case (which describes the value of the solution)
- Vision (which establishes the scope of the solution)
- Risk List (which identifies the risks that threaten the success of the project)
- Project Plan (which outlines how the solution will be delivered)

Elaboration Phase Checklist

Focus: Are the technical risks under control?

Outcome: A stable, proven, executable architecture

Milestone: Lifecycle Architecture—Selected Approach Proven

Problem

- Do we know what we are building?
- Are the requirements stable?
- Do all the stakeholders agree on what it is?
- Has the business case been confirmed?
- Have the acceptance criteria been agreed upon?

Solution

- Do we know how we will build the solution?
- Has a sound architectural foundation been established and demonstrated?
- Has the technical architecture been proven through the development and evaluation of one or more architectural prototypes?
- Has it been proven that the solution architecture is sound?
- Has it been demonstrated that the solution can meet the requirements, including both the functional and non-functional aspects of the system?
- Have all architecturally significant scenarios been addressed (or de-scoped)?
- Has the architecture been tested and verified?
- Has the architecture been communicated to the team members?
- Have the deployment risks been addressed?
- Have the key architectural decisions been made?
- Do we know what we will buy and reuse?
- Do we know what we must build ourselves?
- Have the critical component interfaces been defined?
- Is the architecture stable?
- Has the architecture been baselined, such that any future changes to it will be under strict change control?
- Is a productive development environment in place?

Project

- Do all the parties share a common understanding of what will be built?
- Are the risks under control?
- Are there any risks or issues that prevent a production-quality release from being produced in the next iteration?
- Is there a credible development plan in place?
- Are there accurate estimates for the construction of the system? Do we know how much it will cost?
- Do we have enough time and resources to complete the project?
- Is the test strategy in place?
- Has the resource profile been agreed upon and sourced?
- Is the process being followed working?

Key Artifacts

- Risk List (which identifies the risks that threaten the success of the project)
- Project Plan (which clarifies how the solution will be produced)
- Use-Case Model (identifying all use cases and detailing those of architectural significance)
- Supplementary Specification (identifying the architecturally significant non-functional requirements)
- Architecture Description (capturing the key architectural decisions and explaining the architectural approach adopted)
- Architectural Prototypes (demonstrating the architecture)
- Test Results (verifying the architecture)

Construction Phase Checklist

Focus: Are the logistical risks under control?

Outcome: A useful, tested, deployable, and documented solution

Milestone: Initial Operational Capability—Usable Solution Available

---

Problem

- Are the initial users ready to receive the solution?
- Is the appropriate user documentation and training material in place?
- Are the acceptance plans agreed upon?
- Have the correct requirements been implemented?
- Is the solution complete enough to be useful?
- Is the solution robust enough to be usable?

Solution

- Is the solution functionally complete?
- Do any in-scope requirements remain unimplemented or untested?
- Do the stakeholders agree that the correct requirements have been implemented?
- Is a production release available?
- Is there any more work to be done?
- Is the solution ready to start the process of being transitioned to its intended users?
- Is the solution of sufficient quality to begin the transition process?
- Are defects being fixed faster than they are being found?
- Is the design recorded to a level that will enable the system to be supported and maintained?

Project

- Is the project under control?
- Are there quality problems?
- Are there performance or scalability problems?
- Has sufficient development been completed?
- Has sufficient testing been undertaken?
- Are production releases being produced every iteration?
- Is the impact of any outstanding work understood?
- Is the project ready to transition the solution?
- Are the resources and plans in place for the transition/deployment?
- Has the user documentation been written?
- Are the support resources in place?
- Is the transition environment ready to receive the solution?

Key Artifacts

- Risk List (which identifies the risks that threaten the success of the project)
- Project Plan (which clarifies how the solution will be delivered)
- Use-Case Model / Supplementary Specification (detailing all the requirements delivered)
- Designs (to support the evolution and maintenance of the solution)
- Code (to enable the solution to be altered and rebuilt)
- Tests (to enable the solution to be regression tested when changed)
- Test Results (verifying the quality and completeness of the solution)
- Training Materials / User Documentation (to educate users, potential users, and support staff)

Transition Phase Checklist

Focus: Are the rollout risks under control?

Outcome: The solution is in "actual use"

Milestone: Product Release—Project Completed

Problem

- Is the solution in use?
- Is there feedback from the users?
- Are the users happy with the solution?
- Are the users self-sufficient in their use of the system?
- Have the users and sponsors accepted delivery of the system?
- Have the requirements been accepted?
- Has the solution has been successfully transitioned to its users?
- Have the users been trained?
- Have the project's desired outcomes been achieved?
- Are the stakeholders satisfied with the results of the project?

Solution

- Has the development been completed?
- Are there any problems that need to be addressed?
- Have all fixes and changes made during transition been tested?
- Does the documentation (architecture description, design, etc.) reflect the delivered solution?
- Has the solution been successfully handed over to "production support"?
- Are the support mechanisms in place?
- Are procedures for system operation and maintenance in place?
- Are the support staff in place and trained?
- Are there procedures for system backup, recovery, and restoration?
- Are there procedures and supporting materials in place to support the training of new users?
- Have the architecture and design been handed over and communicated to the support and maintenance teams?
- Are the delivery mechanisms in place?
- Can the solution be easily installed?
- Can the solution be easily uninstalled?
- Can existing systems be easily upgraded and converted?

Project

- Has all project "handover" work been completed?
- Has the project been archived?
- Have all project responsibilities been handed over?
- Has all project accounting been completed?
- Is the project accepted as complete?

Key Artifacts

- Installers, including data converters (the product is complemented with easy-to-use installation and conversion mechanisms)
- Customer / User Surveys (to illustrate whether the users are happy with the solution)
- Defects and their resolution (to address problems that threaten the acceptance of the solution)
- Customer Acceptance (to document that the solution was accepted as complete)

Project and Stage Assessment

No specific checklist is supplied to support the more free-format project and stage assessments. The generic phase assessment checklist can also be used to support these events.

Summary

At this point, you might be feeling like there are a lot of things to do, document, and assess. We have tried to keep things as simple as possible, focusing on the minimally essential while supplying as much useful information as we can. At all times we have attempted to clearly indicate where information is optional. Multilayered planning as we have described removes the need to plan the entire project at once, so the work is spread more evenly across the whole project.

Most of the plans presented here are no more than a page or two long, especially if you use a project management tool and reference the details in the tools. Many project management tools do a good job of scheduling but a poor job of presenting the "big picture" in ways that are easy to grasp. We have tried to focus on simple presentation of information to close this gap.

Keep in mind that plans are like aircraft flight plans: they describe where you want to go and how you will get there so that you can evaluate whether you are on track at various points of the journey. Their main purpose is to help you get back on track if it turns out that the conditions are different from what you expected. They do not need to be a detailed listing of every turn and minor heading change that you plan to make. Think like a pilot: when you're flying a plane, you do not want to have to read through pages and pages of detail. The right information needs to be quickly accessible and comprehensible so that you can focus on the real task at hand: getting to where you want to go.

The checklists are supplied to help you with your iteration and phase assessments. Please don't mistake them as an alternative to thinking for yourself. Make sure each question is relevant before using it as part of your project assessments.

APPENDIX C

Examples

Throughout this book we have claimed that it is possible to produce lightweight plans that enable projects to be effectively managed without the need for excessive detail. In this appendix, we provide some examples to demonstrate how this can be done.

These examples are presented with some trepidation because they are not intended to be held up as examples of perfect project plans; there is no such thing as a perfect plan, and even if there were, it would be foolish to strive for it. You should instead aim for something that is practical and workable and that meets your needs. Our intention with these examples is to provide you with some ideas and experience of what lightweight iterative project plans look like.

The appendix contains

- An overall project plan

- A development plan for the first evolution of a software product

- An iteration plan and its matching iteration assessment

When you examine these plans and the accompanying assessment, you might experience one of a number of possible reactions, including

- Fantastic—This is just what I have been looking for!

- Oh dear, this is not enough detail to run a project as complex and large as mine.

- Where is the Gantt chart?[1] How can you possibly present a plan without a Gantt chart?

- Whoa, this is far too much for my small iterative project.

All these views are in some way correct. If you are working in a formal organization with a history of strong financial management and a rigid contractual framework, you might find the plans too informal and light-weight. You might be right, but please bear in mind that these examples are intended to be lightweight and have been created for educational purposes only.

If you are working in a informal organization with a small, well-organized team that has worked together for a while, and you are used to planning on a whiteboard, you might find the plans a little too formal. Remember these examples are attempting to cover all the aspects of project planning (including organizational structures, roles and responsibilities, and monitoring and control strategies) in a lightweight fashion and not just the identification of phases and iterations. There are a lot of things that you have probably been doing for so long that you've forgotten the importance of them. Go and work on a project with a completely new team, and you will probably rediscover the importance of some of the items that you think are "overhead."

The bottom line is that we would like you to take the good ideas and add them to your existing mechanisms and templates to enable your projects to adopt a more progressive approach to planning. If something is not needed for your team, or if you have a better way of doing it, feel free to ignore the

---

[1] Feel free to insert whatever your favorite planning aid is here.

inappropriate materials. It is our intention to give you a flavor of what a real set of plans might look like.

Before you start to look at the plans, here are a few things to bear in mind:

- Formal references and revision history have been left out to mimimize the size of the appendix.

- The emphasis throughout is on the software development aspects of the project because this is a book about planning and managing iterative software development.

- Each section of each plan is kept succinct and focused so that it would fit on one or two pages. This enables the relevant sections of the plan to be posted in the war room where necessary and prevents things from becoming overly detailed.

- You might benefit from looking at these examples in conjunction with the equivalent sections of Appendix B, "Outlines, Templates, and Checklists," because the two appendices support and help to explain each other.

- The overall project plan is the longest example document because it contains the most background and static information. The project plan section—outlining the roadmap, the stages, and the milestones—is only six pages long.

About This Example

We chose the automated teller machine (ATM) example for a couple of reasons: first, the problem domain, at least from a customer's viewpoint, is familiar enough that we would not have to spend a lot of time explaining it. Second, we used the ATM as an example in our earlier book, *Use Case Modeling,* and so by extending the example here, we could expand upon the earlier work and not have to contrive a completely new set of use cases. For the reader interested in more background on the use cases and requirements, we refer you to our earlier work.

To keep the example from getting bogged down in details that would obscure the overall message, we have omitted showing how plans evolve over time. This creates a real problem because it makes planning seem very static. In reality, none of the artifacts presented here would have started out in the form that you will see—all would have started as sketchy plans that were refined into their current form. For very informal projects, they would retain their "sketchiness," and for very large or complex projects, they would continue to evolve in detail beyond that presented here. Due to limitations of space, and to make the examples more understandable, we have reduced the range of appropriate detail into a single snapshot that is intended to show an "average." Just keep in mind that no project is ever really "average"—each has its unique challenges.

We are of the mind that some of the worst results on projects are produced by people who have picked up some template that they don't really understand and, thinking that the template will help guide them, have proceeded to simply fill out the template without thinking much about their goals. The result is usually utter nonsense: lots of documents with no real purpose.[2] What we want you to take away from these examples is an understanding of how the project can be moved along with relatively simple plans (you might debate the simplicity of these plans if you are accustomed to working very informally). We also want you to gain some insight into where the plans might need to be more formal or where they could be made less formal so as to improve the overall results.

We also believe it is very important to show you some realistic, true-to-life examples. The plans are by no means perfect, but they do reflect the realities of planning a realistically complex piece of software development as part of a larger technology transformation project.

---

[2] This behavior is sometimes reinforced by "process auditors" who view adhering to a process, whether it makes sense or not, as objective goodness. We feel that you need to understand what you must achieve and then adapt your process to help you to achieve those things. No process has a magic formula for success: the right skilled people doing the right things at the right time leads to success; the best a process can do is to help remind you of things that you might otherwise forget.

About the Sample Documents

This appendix contains four sample documents for the ACME Super ATM Product Development project:

- An Overall Project Plan

- The Development Plan for the first evolution

- An Iteration Plan for the first evolution's first Elaboration iteration

- An Iteration Assessment for the first evolution's first Elaboration iteration

These four documents are presented in a format as close to that of actual project documents as the design of this book would allow. A small amount of explanatory text has been added to make them easier to read in the context of the book. This includes the brief introductory paragraph on each document title page. Otherwise, they are published in as realistic format as possible, warts and all.

ACME Super ATM Product Development

Overall Project Plan Version 1.0

This example illustrates the overall project plan as it would likely exist near the end of the project's initiation (which coincides with the end of the initial evolution's Inception phase): the project is laid out and an overall roadmap and strategy have been established. Throughout the course of the project, slight adjustments will need to be made to accommodate changes in the surrounding business environment and our increasing understanding of the realities of the project.

Project Overview

The ACME Super ATM Product Development Project is set up to develop the next generation of generic ATMs suitable for vending a wide variety of financial products and other goods. The purpose and goals for the ACME Super ATM are described in the ACME Super ATM Vision and further illuminated in the evolving ACME Super ATM Business Case. The purpose of the ACME Super ATM is summarized in the product position statement shown in Table C-1, which is taken from the ACME Super ATM Vision document.

Table C-1   *The Product Position Statement for the ACME Super ATM*

For	Financial institutions and vendors of paper-based and other virtual goods
Who	Own or manage automated teller networks
The	ACME Super ATM is an automated teller machine
That	Provides lowered cost of ownership and flexible definition of new transaction types, virtual products, and dispensable paper goods
Unlike	Conventional ATM devices and ticket machines
Our product	Utilizes standard computing platforms and component technology to provide a flexible, generic, and extensible but low-cost platform for managing customer transactions and dispensing goods

This product is intended to address the problems analyzed in the ACME Super ATM Vision document and summarized in Table C-2.

Table C-2   *The Problem Statement for the ACME Super ATM*

The problem of	Having convenient and secure access to banking balances to withdraw funds, manage accounts, or purchase automatically dispensed goods
Affects	Customers of financial organizations and vendors using transactional paper-based currency (tickets, paper-based goods, and so on) or electronic currency
The impact of which is	Low customer satisfaction and high transaction costs
A successful solution would	Provide customers with access to their assets and the ability to transform them into other forms of paper- or electronic-based currency

The project includes the marketing and rollout of the new ATM platform including the replacement of all existing ACME ATM systems.

Objectives and Desired Outcomes

The objectives and desired outcomes for the ACME Super ATM Product Development Project are shown in Table C-3.

Table C-3   *Balanced Scorecard Summarizing the Objectives for the ACME Super ATM Project*

	Objectives	Measures	Targets	Priority
Financial	Reduce total cost of supporting teller machines by 50%.	Cost of support per "live" machine.	25% reduction in costs in year 2, 50% reduction in costs by end of year 4.	Essential
	Reduce cost of configuring devices to dispense different items.	Cost of setting up a new machine.	No more than installation + 10 minutes per product type.	Essential
		Cost of rolling out a new product.	Cost of enabling and testing a new product to be < $50,000.	
	Penetrate new markets (ticket retailing and other paper-based goods).	% transactions not related to dispensing cash.	25% non-banking by end of year 2, rising to 50% by end of year 4.	Highly Desirable
		Number of vendors supported.	Attract at least 3 new vendors each year after year 1.	
		Total number of transactions.	At least B and C by end of year 2, B and E by end of year 4.	
Customer	To provide a modular, expandable, and customizable platform for ATMs, and ultimately general-purpose "dispenser" kiosks configurable as bank teller (traditional ATM), ticket dispenser, postage dispenser, card charger, etc.	User acceptance.	0 priority-one defects or change requests outstanding on a release at end of UAT.	Essential
		Requirements coverage.	> 50% of each stakeholder's requirements included. All "Must Have" requirements satisfied in each release.	
		Number of transaction types supported.	All transaction types supported by Nov 06.	
		Number of types of goods supported.	> 3 out of 7 types of good by the end of year 2. All by end of year 4.	
		Diversity of location.	> 5 out of 10 key location types by the end of year 3.	
Process	Replace existing systems.	Number of original machines still live.	> 50% decommissioned by the end of year 2, all decommissioned by the end of year 3.	Essential
		Number of new machines deployed.	1,000 by the end of year 2, > 1,000 a year after that.	
	Increase availability to 99.9%.	Amount of downtime per machine.	< 7 hours per month down for live machines.	Highly desirable
		Number of defects.	< 30% of defects reported for equivalent previous generation release.	
	Introduce a shared architecture for teller machines.	Number of transaction types supported.	All transaction types supported by Nov. 06.	Essential
		Number of vendors supported.	< 3 vendor types by end of year 2, all by end of year 4.	

Table C-3 *Continued*

	Objectives	Measures	Targets	Priority
Learning Growth	Develop software iteratively.	Number of releases produced and tested.	Operational release at least every 9 months. After the initial release no more than 6 months between releases.	Highly Desirable
		Requirements progress. Regularity of iteration assessments.	At least 40% of the intended requirements implemented and tested by the middle of an evolution. Iteration assessment at least every 8 weeks.	
	Pilot the Unified Process.	Developer skills.	> 80% of development team with level 2 UP certification.	Desirable
		Style and content of the artifact set.	All artifacts conform to the ACME UP style guides.	

Project Approach

The overall project will be managed as a formal project using the ACME Integrated Project Management Process.

The project will be split into three streams:

- **Business Change (BC)**—Assisting in marketing, promotion, and product management of the next generation of ACME Super ATMs liaising with the ACME marketing department, the customers, and the development and deployment teams. The business change will be executed in accordance with the ACME Business Change and Marketing Process.

- **Software Development (SD)**—The development of the software to run the next generation of ACME Super ATMs and the integration of the software and the selected hardware platforms into a flexible, configurable, and maintainable system. The software and system's development will be approached iteratively and incrementally using the ACME Unified Process.

- **Deployment (Dep)**—The rollout of the new platform and the decommissioning of the existing ACME ATM machines. The intention is for this to be subcontracted because the installation and replacement of the physical machines is a very labor-intensive task. This stream will manage and assure the subcontractors using the ACME Supplier Agreement Management Process.

The project is expected to take four years to completely replace and revamp the ATM business and the existing ATM network. The project is to be staged, with each stage taking between four to eight months. Table C-4 provides a summary of the planned stages. Each work stream will be baselined and synchronized on the stage boundaries.

Table C-4 *Overview of the Planned Stages*

Stage	Purpose	Key Deliverables	End Date
	Start of project		Jan 3 05
Initiation	Set up the project.	• Business Case • Overall Project Plans	Mar 31 05
1—Demonstrate and pilot the new technology	Prove the overall project approach and then demonstrate and pilot the new platform including printed goods and basic withdrawal facilities.	• Demonstrable prototype with printed goods production • Printed Goods Marketing Plan • Super ATM Evolution 1: New Platform Pilot	Oct 10 05
2—Develop replacement ATM system	Develop replacement ATM system.	• Deployment Partner Agreement • Super ATM Evolution 2: Replacement ATM System • Marketing Materials for New ATM Platform • Deployment Plan	Mar 27 06
3—Develop and plan the roll-out of the Super ATM	Existing ATMs Replaced / Printed goods available / Super ATM Platform available and launched.	• Super ATM Marketing Plan • Super ATM Evolution 3: Super ATM Platform • Super ATM Deployment Plan	Expected Nov 06
4–7 (business as usual)	System enhanced, installed base increased, new vending products available, and problems addressed.	• Details to be added as earlier stages completed. • Each stage will produce a new evolution of the Super ATM.	Stages expected to be 6 months in length
Close down	Conclude project and hand over all responsibilities to operations.		Nov–Dec 08

Assumptions and Constraints

The following assumptions were made in the construction of this plan:

- Development times on the new delivery platforms are comparable to those experienced developing the last generation of ATMs.
- A low-ceremony iterative approach is appropriate for a project of this size.
- The market for printed and paper goods will be sustained for the next 10 years.
- A suitable partner can be found to decommission the existing systems and install the new systems.

The following significant constraints were placed upon the project:

- All existing ATMs must be replaced within four years.
- The deployment must be outsourced.

Evolution of the Plan

The overall project plan is designed to provide an overview of the project as a whole, providing a context for the individual work stream development plans. It will be revised at the end of each stage to 1) flesh out the plans for the next stage and the remainder of the project, and 2) capture the state of the project at the end of the stage. Table C-5 summarizes when it is expected that revisions of the plan will be available.

Table C-5   *Evolution of the Overall Project Plan*

Version	Milestone	Comment
1.0	End of Initiation	Initial plan to kickstart the project including plans for Stage 1.
2.0	End of Stage 1	Signed off plan for Stage 2.
3.0	End of Stage 2	Revised plan to cover Stage 3 and transition to business as usual.
4–8	End of previous stage	The plan will be continuously revised throughout the project.

Any minor revisions produced between these milestones will be point releases and will be version numbered accordingly.

Project Organization

The project structure is shown in Figure C-1. Roles are defined in Table C-6. Details of the Business Change and Deployment teams will be added in Stage 2.

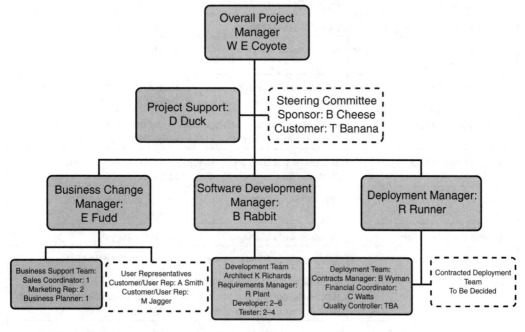

Figure C-1   *Organizational structure*

Table C-6 *Key Project Roles and Responsibilities[3]*

Role	Primary Responsibilities	Secondary Responsibilities
Overall Project Manager	Overall Project Manager	QA Manager
Project Support	Project Office	Administrator
Business Change Manager	Work Stream Manager	Marketing Manager
Software Development Manager Development Manager	Work Stream Manager	Iteration Lead
Deployment Manager	Work Stream Manager Supplier Agreement Manager	Deputy to the Overall Project Manager
Business Support Team	Implement business change / sales and marketing following the ACME Business Change and Marketing Process.	
User Representatives	Represent the business, providing subject matter expertise and direction on the overall project and the various work streams.	
Architect	Software Architect	Technical Advisor to the management team
Requirements Manager	Requirements Manager	Systems Analyst
Development Team	System and Software development following the ACME UP.	
Deployment Team	Monitor and control the deployment of the new systems and the supplier(s) contracted to undertake their physical deployment and the decommissioning of the existing systems.	
Contracted Deployment Team	Physically deploy the new systems and decommission the existing systems.	

---

[3] Detailed role definitions are available in the applicable process documentation.

External Interfaces

The project interfaces with a number of other projects, organizational units, and organizations. These interfaces are outlined here.

Project Review Authorities

The project is sponsored and directed by a specially formed ATM Steering Committee, as shown in Table C-7.

Table C-7   *Steering Committee Membership*

Reviewer	Responsibilities
Sponsor: B Cheese	Member of the project's steering committee, present at all stage assessments and reviews. Authorizes funding and has ultimate budgetary control.
Customer: T Banana	Member of the project's steering committee, present at all stage assessments and reviews. Approves the project and budgets on behalf of the business. Ultimate authority for requirements and business change decisions.
Technical Authority: A Brain	Overall technical authority for the project appointed by the ACME Technology Office. Ultimate authority for all technical decisions.
Corporate QA: B Picky	Undertakes mandatory quality and configuration audits as laid down by the corporate ACME governance standards.

The roles and responsibilities of the steering committee are further explained in the Project Monitoring and Control section later.

Stakeholder Representatives and Other Interfaces

The stakeholder representatives and their involvement in the project are defined in the project's Vision and Requirements Management Plan (delegated to the Software Development Work Stream with support from the Business Change Work Stream). The following external interfaces, shown in Table C-8, are also key to the success of the project.

Table C-8   *Other Interfaces*

External Body	Interface	Project Interface
International Vending Machine Standards Body	Attend standards body meeting as ACME representative; review and contribute to emerging standards.	Software Development Team
ACME Technology Office	Provide technical governance: invite to critical project reviews and support audits.	Software Development Team / Deployment Team
ACME Special Projects	Liase with the research and development team to ensure long life expectancy of products developed.	Business Change Team
ACME Security	Provide governance: invite to review products and support audits.	Overall Project Manager
ACME Quality Assurance Department	Provide project governance: invite to milestone reviews.	Overall Project Manager

Project Plan / Stage Plan

The project is expected to take four years to completely replace and revamp the ATM business and the existing ATM network. The project is to be staged, with each stage taking between four to eight months. An overall roadmap for the project is shown in Figure C-2 and qualified in Table C-9. Table C-10 describes the stage plan, including deliverables.

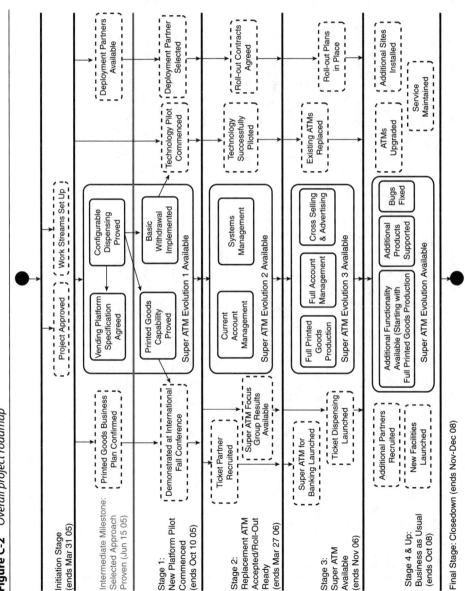

Figure C-2 *Overall project roadmap*

Table C-9 *Milestone Definitions*

Stage	Milestone	Assigned	Acceptance Criteria	Due Date
Initiation *Result: Project Underway* (ends Mar 31 05)	Project Approved	Pre-work stream.	Project approved by steering committee, funding in place.	31 Mar 05
	Work Streams Set Up	Pre-work stream.	Individual work streams set up, staffed and plans in place.	31 Mar 05
Stage 1—Demonstrate and pilot the new technology. *Result: Selected Approach Proven and New Platform Pilot Commenced* (ends Oct 10 05)	Printed Goods Business Plan Confirmed	Business Change	At least 2 partners signed up.	30 May 05
	Configurable Dispensing Proved	S/W Dev	Demonstration and testing of configuration utilities.	15 Jun 05
	Vending Platform Specification Agreed	S/W Dev	Specification signed off by the standards body and ACME.	15 Jun 05
	Deployment Partners Available	Deployment	At least 3 companies prepared to bid. Invitation To Tender Issued.	15 Jun 05
	Super ATM Evolution 1: Basic Withdrawal Implemented	S/W Dev	Demonstration and stress testing of cash withdrawal on the new platform.	10 Oct 05
	Super ATM Evolution 1: Printed Goods Capability Proved	S/W Dev	Demonstration and stress testing of cash withdrawal on the new platform.	10 Oct 05
	Demonstrated at International Rail Conference	Business Change	Demonstration of ticket printing at International Rail 05.	12 July 05
	Deployment Partner Selected	Deployment	Winner of deployment tender process decided and ready to start pilot rollout.	30 Aug 05
	Technology Pilot Commenced	Deployment	New Platform available in first 5 pilot sites.	10 Oct 05

Stage	Milestone	Assigned	Acceptance Criteria	Due Date
Stage 2—Develop Replacement ATM System *Result: Replacement ATM Accepted / Roll-Out Ready* (ends Mar 27 06)	Ticket Partner Recruited	Business Change	At least one ticket partner signed up.	30 Jan 06
	Super ATM Focus Group Results Available	Business Change	Results from at least 12 groups available.	27 Mar 06
	Super ATM Evolution 2: Current Acc't Management	S/W Dev	Accepted by user community.	27 Mar 06
	Super ATM Evolution 2: Systems Management	S/W Dev	Accepted by user community.	27 Mar 06
	Technology Successfully Piloted	Deployment	Technology successfully in use at 20 sites.	27 Mar 06
	Roll-out Contract Agreed	Deployment	Deployment partner contracts in place.	27 Mar 06
Stage 3—Develop and plan the roll-out of the Super ATM *Result: Super ATM Available* (ends Nov 06)	Milestones are likely to be as shown in Figure C-2. These will be detailed as the plan evolves. The purpose of this stage is to develop and launch the Super ATM with full banking and ticket dispensing facilities.			
Stages 4 +—Business as Usual (expected end Oct 08)	The sorts of milestones to be expected as the project enters business as usual are illustrated in Figure C-2. These will be detailed as the plan evolves. The purpose of each stage is to enhance, support, and maintain the Super ATM systems and their position in the marketplace.			

Table C-10   *The ACME Super ATM Stage Plan with Deliverables*

Stage	Purpose	Key Deliverables	Work Stream	Milestone	Date (tolerance)	Comments
Initial	Set up the project.	Business Case / Overall Project Plan	All	Project Approved	Mar 31 05 (none)	Project must be set up by March 31
		Work Stream Initial Plans	All	Work Streams Set Up		
1	Demonstrate and pilot the new technology.	Super ATM Prototype: Printed Goods Production	SD	Configurable Dispensing Proved	Jun 15 05 (2 weeks)	2-week schedule tolerance on demo
		Printed Goods Marketing Plan	BC	Printed Goods Business Plan Confirmed	Jun 15 05 (2 weeks)	Fate of printed goods decided
		Super ATM Evolution 1: New Platform Pilot	SD	Basic Withdrawal Implemented / Printed Goods Capability Proved	Aug 15 05 (1 month)	1 month tolerance on release availability
End of Stage		Stage and Work Stream Assessments / Plans for Next Stage	All	Stage Accepted as Complete / Plans for Stage 2 Agreed	Oct 10 05 (none)	
2	Develop replacement ATM system.	Pilot Results Analysis	Dep	Technology successfully piloted.	Dec 30 05	
		Deployment Partner Agreement	Dep	Roll-out contracts agreed	Jan 05 06 ($0.5M)	Costs must be within $0.5 M of business case estimate
		Super ATM Evolution 2: Replacement ATM System	SD	Super ATM Evolution 2 Available	Mar 27 06 (two weeks)	Replacement system must be available on time and rollout plans must be in place
		Operations and support trained in new system	SD	Super ATM Evolution 2 Available		
		ATM Replacement Deployment Plan	Dep	Roll-out Contracts Agreed		
End of Stage		Stage and Work Stream Assessments / Plans for Next Stage	All	Stage Accepted as Complete		Mar 27 06 (two weeks)

Stage	Purpose	Key Deliverables	Work Stream	Milestone	Date (tolerance)	Comments
3	Develop and plan the rollout of the Super ATM.	Super ATM Marketing Plan	BC	End of Stage 3: Super ATM Available	Nov 06 (1 month)	Launch date and end of stage will be firmed up as the project progresses
		Super ATM Evolution 3: Super ATM Platform	SD	End of Stage 3: Super ATM Available	Nov 06	
		Super ATM Deployment Plan	Dep	End of Stage 3: Super ATM Available		
	End of Stage					
4+		Deliverables will be agreed upon as the project progresses			Oct 08	
	Project End			Project Close-Down	Nov-Dec 08	

Allowable Tolerances

Tolerances are established to define rules for identifying and escalating exceptions. Within these tolerances, no action is required from the steering committee or sponsoring authority. If these tolerances are exceeded, oversight action will be taken.

Table C-11   *Overall Project Tolerances*

Type of Milestone	Tolerance/Permissible Variance	Comments
Overall Budget	10% overrun	The budget and spend profiles are detailed in the Business Case and the original project proposal.
End of Stage	10% schedule overrun	Schedule slippage might affect other stages.
End of Phase	10% schedule overrun; no skipped iterations	If phase overruns, assess cause for slippage and adjust plans for next phase accordingly.
End of Iteration	None	Iterations are strict "time boxes." If iteration objectives are not met, then adjust subsequent iteration plans.

Where applicable, more detailed tolerances are shown in Table C-10.

Dependencies

The project is highly dependent upon the following external decisions and activities:

- The international vending specification can be agreed upon in a timely fashion.

- Current customers are happy to have the ATMs replaced.

- Ticket and paper goods partners can be recruited.

- Additional ATM partners can be recruited.

Management Strategy

The project is to be conducted in line with the ACME Project Management processes and the ACME Unified Process. An overview of the management strategy is provided by Table C-12.

Table C-12 *Overview of the ACME Super ATME Management Strategy*

Dimension	Decision
Style of delivery	• Staged iterative and incremental delivery • Colocated teams • All streams will use the Unified Process lifecycle, although iteration is optional for the non-software development streams
Level of detail and formality	• The project will be low ceremony with high levels of user and stakeholder involvement • Adopt standard QA process with central governance
Process selection	• ACME Business Change and Marketing Process • Unified Process, small project tailoring • ACME Supplier Agreement Management Process (Progressive Incremental Model) • Risk management using top 10 risks (see ACME Corporate Requirements Management Plan and tooling)
Reporting and communications	• Primary reporting mechanism—stage and phase assessment supported by regular iterations or equivalent assessments • Management by exception
Product acceptance	• Independent user acceptance and system test • Stakeholders involved in all iteration and phase reviews • Marketing surveys, trials, and focus groups

Project Monitoring and Control

The key elements of the strategy for monitoring and controlling the project,

- Assessments and Reviews

- Regular Reporting

are defined in Table C-13.

This table defines the events and reports to be held by all the work streams in the project. Additional work stream-specific events are further defined in the work stream development plans.

Table C-13 *Regular Assessments and Reports*

	Overall Project Manager	Business Change Manager	Software Dev Manager	Deployment Manager	Sponsor	Customer	Requirement Manager	Architect	Technical	User Representatives	Team Members	Corp QA	Timing
Assessment Event													
Emergency Steering Committee Meeting	Y	Y	Y	Y	L	Y	Opt	Opt	Y	N	N	N	By exception as required
Stage Assessment	L	Y	Y	Y	Y	Y	Opt	Opt	Y	Y	N	Y	End of every project stage
Subproject Phase Assessment	Y	Y	Y	Y	Opt	Opt	Y	Y	Y	Opt	Opt	Opt	End of every work stream phase
Software Development: Iteration Assessments	Y	Y	L	Y	Opt	Opt	Opt	Y	Y	Y	Opt	Opt	At least every 2 months
Business Change: Regular Assessments	Y	L	Y	Y	Opt	Opt	Y	Y	Y	Opt	Opt	Opt	At least every 2 months
Deployment: Regular Assessments	Y	Y	Y	L	Opt	Opt	Opt	Y	Y	Y	Opt	Opt	At least every 2 months
Reports													
Highlight Report	Auth	Y	Y	Y	Y	Y	Y	Y	Y	Y	Y	Y	Fortnightly Report
Stage Assessment Report	Auth	Y	Y	Y	Y	Y	Y	Y	Y	Opt	Y	Y	End of every stage
Work Stream Highlight Report	Y	Auth	Auth	Auth	N	N	Y	Y	N	Opt	Opt	Opt	Weekly Report
Status / Phase Assessment Report	Y	L/Y	L/Y	L/Y	Y	N	Y	Y	Y	Y	N		At the end of every work stream phase
Iteration / Regular Assessment (Document)	Y	Y	Y	Y	Y	Y	Y	Y	Y	L	Y	N	At the end of every iteration or every month
Quality Audit	Y	Y	Y	Y	N	N	Opt	Opt	L	N	N	Auth	Once per stage (Carried out by the QA Team)
Configuration Audit	Y	Y	Y	Y	N	N	Opt	Opt	L	N	N	Auth	

(L = Lead, Y = Yes, Opt = Optional, Auth = Author, As Req'd = As required)

Monitoring and Control Processes and Supporting Plans

A number of additional plans are required to formally monitor and control the project. These are identified in Table C-14 along with those other artifacts defined by the ACME Project Management processes that the project does not require.

Table C-14 *Management Control Artifacts*

Control Artifact	Usage	Justification / Source
Risk Management Plan	Reuse	ACME Corporate Risk Management Plan.
Measurement Plan	Y	See Project Measurement Plan.
Problem Resolution Plan	Reuse	See ACME Problem Resolution Plan.
Subcontractor Management Plan	Delegated	See Deployment Work Stream development plan for details.
Process Improvement Plan	N	Built into project and work stream plans.
Communications Plan	Delegated	Project communications defined above. Stakeholder communications defined by the Business Change Development Plan.
Quality Control Plan	Delegated	See Project Quality Assurance Plan.
Stakeholder Involvement Plan	Delegated	See Business Change Development Plan.
Resource Acquisition Plan	Delegated	See work stream plans.
Training Plan	Delegated	See work stream plans.
Schedule Control Plan	N	Tolerances and procedures defined in project plans.
Close-out Plan	Y	See Project Close-Out Plan.

Technical and Supporting Process Plans

A number of additional technical and supporting plans are required for a project of this type. These are identified in Table C-15 and Table C-16 along with those other artifacts defined by the ACME Project Management and technical processes that the project does not require.

Table C-15   *Supporting Specialist Plans*

Supporting Plan	Usage	Justification / Source
Requirements Management Plan	Delegated	Software Development Project
Infrastructure Plan	Delegated	Software Development Project
Configuration Management Plan	Y	See Project Configuration Management Plan
Quality Assurance Plan	Y	See Project Quality Assurance Plan
Product Acceptance Plan	Y	See Project Product Acceptance Plan
Evaluation Plan	Delegated	See Project Quality Assurance Plan
Development Process Description / Development Case	Delegated	Defined for each work stream to support management strategy defined here

Table C-16   *Methods, Tools, and Techniques*

Standards and Guidelines	Usage	Justification / Reference
Business Modeling Guidelines	Reuse	The ACME Development Standards produced by the technology office are to be used in all circumstances.
User Interface Guidelines	Reuse	
Use-Case Modeling Guidelines	Reuse	
Analysis and Design Guidelines	Reuse	
Programming Guidelines	Reuse	
Test Guidelines	Reuse	

ACME Super ATM Product Development

ACME Super ATM Evolution 1: A Next-Generation Vending Platform

Development PlanVersion 1.0

This example illustrates the first evolution of the project. Breaking the project into a number of evolutions allows for the early introduction of the ATM system, with subsequent evolutions adding capabilities. Gradually introducing a new product, with basic capabilities provided initially, is a common strategy for getting a new product to market quickly.

This example illustrates the development plan as it would likely exist near the end of the evolution's Inception phase: the development project is laid out, and there is an initial mapping of work onto iterations. Over the course of the project, slight adjustments will need to be made to accommodate defect fixing and changes in requirements, so the development plan will need to be kept flexible.

Project Overview

ACME Super ATM Evolution 1: Next-Generation Vending Platform is the first evolution of ACME's next generation of universal automated teller machines, whose purpose is best summed up by the product position statement shown in Table C-17, which is taken from the ACME Super ATM Vision document.

Table C-17   *The Product Position Statement for the ACME Super ATM*

For	Financial institutions and vendors of paper-based and other virtual goods
Who	Own or manage automated teller networks
The	ACME Super ATM is an automated teller machine
That	Provides lowered cost of ownership and flexible definition of new transaction types, virtual products, and dispensable paper goods
Unlike	Conventional ATM devices and ticket machines
Our product	Utilizes standard computing platforms and component technology to provide a flexible, generic, and extensible but low-cost platform for managing customer transactions and dispensing goods

This evolution is to be developed as part of the software development stream of the Overall ACME Super ATM Development Project. The overall project plan (see the ACME Super ATM Product Development: Overall Project Plan) requires the system to be developed in a number of evolutions as shown in Figure C-3 and elaborated in Table C-18.

Table C-18   *Release Plan*

Release	Description	Delivery Date	Comments
Release 1	New Platform Pilot	15 Aug 05	1-month tolerance
Release 2	Replacement ATM System	27 Mar 06	2-week tolerance. Business-critical release
Release 3	Super ATM Platform	Nov 06	1-month tolerance
Release 4 & Up	To be defined	To be defined	6 monthly releases expected

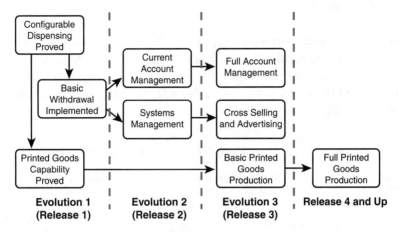

Figure C-3 *Release roadmap*

Project Approach

The system will be developed using the ACME Unified Process. Because this is the first evolution of the product and the development project faces significant business and technical risks, the Evolutionary Development pattern will be adopted. The number of planned iterations is shown in Table C-19. The project is expected to have a four-week heartbeat.

Table C-19   *Summary of the ACME Super ATM Release 1's Phases and Iterations*

	Iteration	Resulting Releases	Risks Addressed
Inception	I1: Scope Project	Proof of Concept: Basic cash dispensing	• Crowded market • Product pricing and profitability • Customer demand for configurable transactions
	I2: Agree upon business case and evolution plan	Proof of Concept: Configurable cash dispensing	
Elaboration	E1: Demonstrate cash withdrawal	Prototype: Withdraw Cash Basic Flow	• Reliability of OS platform • Scalability of J2EE infrastructure • Fault tolerance • Tamper-proofing • Printing flexibility and reliability
	E2: Prove basic ATM functionality	Prototype: Withdraw Cash with basic failure modes and protection + initial load testing	
	E3: Prove paper goods dispensing capability	Prototype: Simple ticket printing + initial demo Prototype: Withdraw Cash with correction and reconciliation	
Construction	C1: Complete basic ATM functionality	Functional Release: Basic cash withdrawal	• Completing work on time within budget
	C2: Deliver a supportable, robust ATM system	Functional Release: Usable cash withdrawal	
Transition	T1: Set up user acceptance testing	Possible Patch Release: Bug fixes	• Product quality • Acceptability of the pilot • Failure to function suitably in the live environment
	T2: Support user acceptance testing	Possible Patch Release: More bug fixes	
	T3: Support the technology pilot	Possible Patch Release: Emergency fixes	

Key Deliverables

The following deliverables, as shown in Table C-20, are expected from the evolution and identified in the overall project plan.

Table C-20   *Evolution 1: Key Deliverables*

Deliverable	Overall Project Milestone	Date and Tolerance	Iteration Alignment
Initial Development Plan	Work Streams Set Up	Mar 31 05 (none)	I2—End of Inception
Super ATM Prototype: Printed Goods Production	Configurable Dispensing Proved	Jun 15 05 (two weeks)	E3—End of Elaboration
Super ATM Release 1: New Platform Pilot	Basic Withdrawal Implemented / Printed Goods Capability Proved	Aug 15 05 (1 month)	C2—End of Construction
Next Evolution Development Plan	Stage Accepted as Complete	Oct 10 05 (none)	T2—Mid-Transition

Assumptions and Constraints

The following assumptions were made in the construction of this plan:

- The entire ACME ATM Development Team is available for use on the project.

- The team can scale up at the end of E2 for the final Elaboration iteration and the Construction phase.

The following constraints were placed upon the development project:

- The development project will follow a lightweight tailoring of the ACME Unified Process.

- All ACME Development Standards will be followed throughout the project.

Evolution of the Development Plan

The development plan is designed to provide an overview of the plans for a single evolution. It is an adaptive plan that will be revised at the end of each phase as needed to manage and control the project. Table C-21 summarizes when it is expected that revisions of the plan will be available:

Table C-21 *Evolution of the Development Plan*

Version	Date	Milestone	Comment
1.0	End of Inception / 26 March	Lifecycle Objectives	Initial plan to support the overall project initiation
2.0	End of Elaboration / 18 June	Lifecycle Architecture	Signed off plan for the development of Release 1
3.0	End of Construction / 13 August	Initial Operational Capability	Revised plan to cover transition and support

Any minor revisions produced between these milestones will be point releases and will be version numbered accordingly.

Project Organization

The development team structure is shown in Figure C-4. Roles are defined in Table C-22.

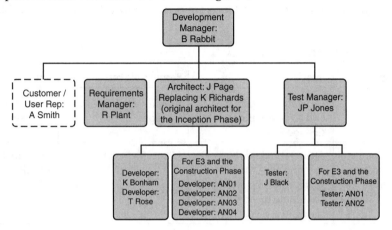

Figure C-4 *Evolution 1—Team Structure*

Table C-22 *Evolution 1—Team Roles and Responsibilities[4]*

Job Title	Primary Responsibilities	Secondary Responsibilities	Reviews
Development Manager	Development Manager	Iteration Lead	Requirements, Architecture, Tests
Customer / User Rep	User Coordinator	User Representative	Requirements, Tests
Requirements Manager	Systems Analyst Change Manager	Requirements Author Also overall project role	Requirements, Architecture, Tests
Architect	Architect	Release Manager Configuration Manager Also overall project role	Requirements, Design, Code, Tests
Test Manager Tester	Test Manager	Test Designer	Requirements, Architecture, Design
Developer	Designer Implementer	Requirements Author Integrator	Requirements, Design, Code, Tests
Tester	Test Designer Tester	Integrator	Requirements, Tests

4   Detailed definitions of the roles used in the Responsibility columns can be found in the ACME Unified Process Definition.

External Interfaces

The development team interfaces with a number of other organizations, projects, departments, and teams. These interfaces are outlined in Table C-23 and Table C-24.

Table C-23   *Evolution 1—Additional Interfaces*

External Body	Interface	Responsible Person	External Contact
Stakeholders and Users	Facilitate user groups and liase with Business Change Stream.	R Plant: Requirements Manager	A Smith: Customer / User Rep
International Vending Machine Standards Body (IVMSB)	Attend standards body meeting as ACME representative; review and contribute to emerging standards.	J Page: Architect	I Automate of the IVMSB
Overall Project	Attend project reviews and report on development progress / assist in overall project work.	B Rabbit: Dev Manager J Page: Architect R Plant: Requirements Manager	W Coyote: Overall Project Manager
Other Work Streams	Coordinate with other work streams. Attend their reviews and management	B Rabbit: Dev Manager J Page: Architect JP Jones: Test Manager	Other work stream managers

Table C-24   *Evolution 1—Project Review Authorities*

External Body	Responsibilities	Responsible Person
Overall Project	Attend project reviews and provide guidance and direction to the project.	W Coyote: Overall Project Manager
Customer / Users	Attend project reviews and provide guidance and direction to the project.	A Smith: Customer / User Rep
ACME Technology Office	Provide technical governance: invite to critical project reviews. Supports audits.	A Brain: Enterprise Architect

Project Plan

Table C-25 presents an overview of the plan for the evolution.

Table C-25   *Development Plan for Evolution 1: Next-Generation Vending Platform*

Phase	Iteration	Objectives / Risks	Schedule	Effort	Key Deliverables
Inception	I1: Scope Project	Establish the vision / 1, 4—Market perception	4 weeks Start: 31 Jan	80 (15)	Proof of Concept: Basic cash dispensing Vision
Inception	I2: Agree upon business case and evolution plan	Establish the business case / 2—Costs might be too high 3—Flexibility might not be desired	4 weeks Start: 28 Feb	75 (40)	Proof of Concept: Configurable cash dispensing Agreed business case Development Plan
Elaboration	E1: Demonstrate cash withdrawal	Establish the core architecture / 5—Platform suitability	4 weeks Start: 28 March	75 (40)	Prototype: Withdraw Cash Basic Flow Fleshed out use cases and supplementary specs
Elaboration	E2: Prove basic ATM functionality	Prove suitability of architecture / 6—Failure mode, 7—Tamper proofing	4 weeks Start: 25 April	75 (50)	Prototype: Withdraw Cash with basic failure modes and protection + initial load testing Architecture Description
Elaboration	E3: Prove paper goods dispensing capability	Demonstrate reliability of architecture / 5—Platform reliability 10—Printing flexibility	4 weeks Start: 23 May	150 (100)	Prototype: Simple ticket printing + initial demo Prototype: Withdraw Cash with correction and reconciliation + load and performance testing Ticket printing flexibility and reliability test results
Construction	C1: Complete basic Withdrawal ATM functionality	Establish basic ATM functionality	4 weeks Start: 20 June	160 (130)	Functional Release: Basic Cash Use Cases: Withdraw Cash, Refill, and Service
Construction	C2: Deliver a supportable, robust ATM system	Establish a useable ATM and ticket dispenser	4 weeks Start: 18 July	160 (130)	Functional Release: Usable Cash Withdrawal Complete remaining in-scope use cases Dry run of rail conference demonstration Pilot plans in place
Transition	T1: Set up user acceptance testing	Support user acceptance testing	4 weeks Start: 15 August	75 (30)	Patch Release: Bug fixes User acceptance testing
Transition	T2: Support user acceptance testing	Support user acceptance testing	4 weeks Start: 12 Sept	80 (30)	Possible Patch Release: More bug fixes User acceptance testing complete
Transition	T3: Support the technology pilot	Support the pilot	8 weeks Start: 10 Oct	64 (10)	Emergency fixes (if required) Successful pilot

Incremental / Iteration Release Plan

Table C-26 provides details of the releases to be produced by the iterations.

Table C-26   *Evolution 1—Significant Iteration Releases*

Release	Production Iteration	Description	Type	Production Date
0.0.1	I1: Scope Project	Demonstrate new system's ability to dispense cash and tickets	Proof of Concept	Available week 4 starting 21 Feb 05
0.0.2	I2: Agree upon business case and evolution plan	Demonstrate the new system's flexibility and configurability	Proof of Concept	Available week 8 starting 21 March 05
1.0.1	E1: Demonstrate cash withdrawal	Basic online cash withdrawal	Prototype	22 April 05
1.0.2	E2: Prove basic ATM functionality	Robust online cash withdrawal	Prototype	20 May 05
1.0.2	E3: Prove paper goods dispensing capability	Flexible ticket printing suitable for demonstration to potential customers	Prototype	17 June 05
1.1.0	C1: Complete basic ATM functionality	Production quality release with complete, basic ATM functionality	Internal Release	15 July 05
1.2.0	C2: Deliver a supportable, robust ATM system	Production Release for user acceptance	External Release	13 August 05
1.2.1+	T1: Set up user acceptance testing	Placeholder for bug fix and emergency releases that might be required during transition	Bug Fix / Emergency Release	TBD

Other Project Deliverables

Table C-27 shows the expected evolution of the other key deliverables across the planned set of iterations.

Table C-27   *Evolution 1—Significant Iteration Deliverables*[5]

	I1	I2	E1	E2	E3	C1	C2	T1 / T2 / T3
Development Plan	Draft	Initial Plan	Evolving	Evolving	Development planned	Possibly Revised	Revised to cover support	–
Vision	Initial version	Complete for Evolution	–	–	–	–	–	–
System Requirements	Evolving	Evolving	Scope Agreed	Complete for Evolution	–	–	–	–
Architectural Description	Outline	Evolving	Evolving	Established	Published / Proven	–	–	–
Design Model	Evolving	Evolving	Evolving	Evolving	Evolving	Evolving	Complete	–
Super ATM Software	–	–	Evolving Arch Prototype	Evolving Arch Prototype	Final Arch Prototype	Production Quality Release	Production Quality Release	Bug Fixing
Test Strategy	Evolving	Evolving	Established	–	–	–	–	–
Test Environment	–	Investigated	Established	Proved	–	–	–	–

5 Every iteration will produce an iteration plan, iteration assessment, test results, measurements, demonstrable software, builds, and release notes.

Estimates and Tolerances

The software development was estimated in a number of ways using the ACME Estimating Process and tools including COCOMO II and Wideband Delphi. Full estimates can be found in the estimating spreadsheet, and the results are summarized in Table C-28.

Table C-28   *Summary of Initial Estimates*

Phase	Person-Days	Comments
Inception	155	For a project such as this, which is risky from both a technical and business perspective, 25% of the estimated development costs are typically required for Inception.
Elaboration	620 (+ or – 20%)	Development cost based on a combination of COCOMO and Wideband Delphi from the initial use-case model and supp spec.
Construction		
Transition	155	Based on the needs for extensive user acceptance testing and our experience piloting new technology of this sort.
	930	

Allowing for a regular four-week heartbeat and an increase in team size in the middle of the project generated the estimates presented in Table C-29 for iteration lengths and team sizes. Note that the final iteration was added to enable the project to support the extended pilot required by the business and is in addition to the estimates.

Table C-29   *Adjusted and Unadjusted Estimates*

	Iteration	Unadjusted	Seasonally Adjusted	Dedicated Team Size	Team Size with 20% Contingency / Absence
1	I1	80	80	5	6
2	I2	80	75	5	6
3	E1	80	75	5	6
4	E2	80	75	5	6
5	E3	160	150	10	12
6	C1	160	160	10	12
7	C2	160	160	10	12
8	T1	80	75	5	6
9	T2	80	80	5	6

To enable the project to meet its commitment to support the pilot through to the end of November, an additional eight-week iteration with a team of two people was added to the development plan.

Additional Capital Costs

The project will also incur some additional capital costs for hardware to support the development and testing of the software:

- **Capital Costs**—Additional Hardware and Test Environments: $79,856.

All other costs (such as office space) are covered as part of operating the IT department and do not need to be covered here.

Management Strategy

The project will be managed using the ACME Unified Process in accordance with the management strategy laid down in the ACME Super ATM Overall Project Plan.

Project Monitoring and Control

The key elements of the strategy for monitoring and controlling the project,

- Assessments and Reviews

- Regular Reporting

are defined in Table C-30.

Monitoring and Control Processes and Supporting Plans

The following additional management artifacts and supporting plans are required for the evolution.

Resource Acquisition Plan

The team will be seeded with the current five-person ATM development and support team. Additional resources will be obtained from the central ACME development team to scale up the team at the end of iteration E2 (by 21 May 05).

The existing ATM development environment is suitable for the new development environment with the installation of the new tools and libraries. Development licenses have already been centrally purchased by the ACME Technology Office.

Additional test environments are required and will be defined as part of the project's Test Strategy. These will be ordered at the beginning of the evolution and installed and tested during iteration E1 (starting 28 March 05).

Training Plan

See project Training Plan. The initial team members will need training in the new development process and the new development languages and tools. The training of the additional team members joining for iterations E3–T1 will be planned as they are assigned to the team and their experience levels become known.

Requirements Management Plan (RM Plan)

The RM Plan will be established alongside the vision by the Requirements Manager and the Customer / User Rep. This will be based on the standard ACME Small Project RM Plan.

Infrastructure Plan

The project will reuse the existing ATM Development Infrastructure and will reuse (amending where necessary) the existing ATM Development Infrastructure Plan.

Development Case/Process Configuration

The project is following the standard ACME small project development case. This will be tuned during the initial Inception and Elaboration iterations as the development plan evolves.

Table C-30   *Evolution 1—Regular Assessments, Reviews, and Reports*

(L = Lead, Y = Yes, Opt = Optional, Auth = Author, As Req'd = As Required)

		Overall Project Manager	Development Project Manager	Other Work Stream Managers	Sponsor	Customer / User Rep	Other Users	Tech Office	Required Manager	Architect	Test Manager	Development Team	Others	Timing
Assessment Events	Phase Assessment	Y	L	Y	Y	Y	N	Y	Y	Y	Y	N		End of every phase
	Iteration Acceptance Review (External)	Y	L	N	Y	Y	Opt	Y	Opt	Opt	Y	As Req'd		End of every iteration
	Iteration Assessment—Demonstration (External)	Y	Y	Opt	Opt	Opt	Y	Opt	L	Opt	Opt	As Req'd		End of every iteration
	Iteration Assessment—Retrospective (Internal)	Opt	L	N	N	Opt	Opt	Opt	Y	Y	Y	Y		End of every iteration
Reports	Highlight Report	Y	Auth	Y	N	Y	N	N	Y	Y	Y	Y		Weekly Report
	Phase Assessment (Document)	Y	Auth	Y	Y	Y	N	Y	N	N	N	N		End of every phase
	Iteration Assessment (Document)	Y	Auth	Y	Y	Y	N	Y	Y	Y	Y	Y		End of every iteration
	Quality Audit	Y	Y	Y	N	N	N	Y	Opt	Opt	Opt	N	Customer	As required by the ACME QA Team
	Configuration Audit	Y	Y	Y	N	N	N	Y	Opt	Opt	Opt	N		

ACME Super ATM Product Development

ACME Super ATM Evolution 1 Iteration E1—Demonstrate Cash Withdrawal

Iteration Plan Version 1.0

This example presents an iteration plan as it would appear during the first week of the iteration after the team planning activities are completed.

We have selected the initial Elaboration iteration because it is from the period of the project where the planning consists of more than just selecting requirements, change requests, and defects from the project backlog.

Scope and Objectives

This iteration is Iteration E1—Demonstrate Cash Withdrawal, the third iteration of the first Evolution of the ACME Super ATM Development Project. It is intended to reduce the technical risk facing the project by

- Establishing the core architecture of the product

- Demonstrating the ability to provide basic cash withdrawal facilities using the new system components

- Fleshing out the use cases and supplementary specifications of Evolution 1 to help to define what is needed to enable the new system to complete a successful pilot in a live environment

The iteration is to last four weeks, from March 28 to April 23.

Risk Analysis

The top 10 risks currently facing the project are shown in Table C-31.

Table C-31 *Iteration Risk List (Top 10)*

Rank This	Rank Last[6]	Risk	Exposure	Mitigation Plan
1	–	Supporting previous ATM versions	Very High	Ring fence resources
2	–	Keith leaving	Very High	Hand over to Jimmy
3	5 (2)	Test Strategy, resources, and environments	Very High	Do initial testing and draft Test Strategy
4	6 (2)	It might be harder than we think (estimates)	Very High	Build Withdraw Cash
5	8 (1)	Reliability of the O/S platform	Very High	Build Withdraw Cash
6	9 (1)	Scalability of J2EE Infrastructure	Very High	Build Withdraw Cash
7	10 (1)	What are the requirements?	High	Complete primary use cases
8	–	Fault tolerance	High	Address next iteration[7]
9	–	Tamper proofing	High	Address next iteration[7]
10	–	Printing flexibility and reliability	High	Address next iteration[7]

[6] The number in parentheses is the number of iterations for which the risk has been in the top 10.

[7] Or possibly this iteration if the more essential objectives are completed early.

Iteration Objectives and Evaluation Criteria

The iteration objectives and evaluation criteria are presented in Table C-32.

Table C-32 *Iteration Objectives with Evaluation Criteria*

	Objective	Description	Risks	Est	Evaluation Criteria	Required Evidence	Priority
1	Demonstrate basic cash withdrawal facilities.	De-risk the technical platform by implementing and demonstrating basic cash withdrawal facilities.	4, 5, and 6	32	Successful Cash Withdrawal regression test suite created and tests passed.	Test Results / Build / Regression Test Suite	Ess
2	Establish the Test Strategy.	Demonstrate that the facilities are available to test the new system by conducting initial system, load, stress, and performance tests.	3 and 6	10	Environments Available / Initial load test results available.	Load and Performance Test Environment / Initial Load Test Results	Ess
				5	Test Strategy in place.	Test Strategy	HD
3	Understand the requirements.	Flesh out the important (Must Have and Should Have) requirements for the evolution.	7	10	Architect agrees with all architecturally significant use cases and supp specs documented / Users happy with prioritization.	Use-Case Model / Supplementary Specification / Requirements Tracking Spreadsheet	Ess
4	Hand over technical leadership from Keith to Jimmy.	Ensure that Keith's knowledge and authority is handed over to Jimmy.	2	6	Jimmy able to present architectural overview as part of iteration assessment.	Architecture Presentation	Ess
5	Get control of support commitments.	Get the team support commitments under control by ring fencing the amount of effort available to support the existing system.	1	16	Support costs are no more than 4 days a week and declining over the course of the iteration.	Time spent on support activities	Ess
6	Ensure software minimizes the chance of external tampering with the machine during cash withdrawal.	Implement the basic functionality to prevent people tampering with the machine.	8	4	Successful system test of all flows plus passing of attack and device insertion tests.	Test Results / Build / Regression Test Suite	HD

	Objective	Description	Risks	Est	Evaluation Criteria	Required Evidence	Priority
7	Add card failures to basic withdrawal handling.	Add card handling alternative flows to ensure exercise of mechanical card devices.	8	6	Successful system test of all card handling alternative flows.	Test Results / Build / Regression Test Suite	HD
8	Ensure that loss of connectivity or critical resources does not allow phantom withdrawals.	Add essential error handling to withdraw cash.	9	10	Successful system test of all Must Have cash withdrawal error handling flows.	Test Results / Build / Regression Test Suite	HD

Ess = Essential

HD = Highly Desirable

Requirements, Defects, and Change Requests

Table C-33 shows the requirements, defects, and change requests to be addressed in the iteration.

Table C-33 *Report of Requirements, Defects, and Change Requests*

Scope	Unit	State	Priority	Est	Obj
Use Case	Authenticate Customer: Basic Flow	Fully Tested	Ess	2	1
Use Case	Authenticate Customer: Alt Flow 2.1 No Connection to the Bank	Fully Tested	Ess	2	1
Use Case	Authenticate Customer: Alt Flow 2.3 —Inactive Card or Account	Fully Tested	Ess	2	1
Use Case	Withdraw Cash: Basic Flow	Fully Tested	Ess	20	1
Use Case	Withdraw Cash: Alt Flow 4.1—Handle Authentication Failures	Fully Tested	Ess	1	1
Use Case	Withdraw Cash: Alt Flow 4.2—Handle the Bank Not Approving Withdrawal	Fully Tested	Ess	5	1
Supp Spec	Performance 1.1: Peak Loading	Demo	Ess	See notes	2
Supp Spec	Performance 1.2: Transaction Service Levels	Demo	Ess	See notes	2
Use Case	Withdraw Cash: Error Handling Alt Flow 4.7—Handle Security Breaches	Fully Tested	HD	4	6
Use Case	Authenticate Customer: Alt Flow 2.5— Invalid Card Information	Fully Tested	HD	2	7
Use Case	Withdraw Cash: Card Handling Alt FLow 2.1—Handle Card Jam	Fully Tested	HD	2	7
Use Case	Withdraw Cash: Card Handling Alt Flow 2.2—Handle Unreadable Bank Card	Fully Tested	HD	1	7
Use Case	Withdraw Cash: Card Handling Alt Flow 2.3—Handle Invalid Card	Fully Tested	HD	1	7
Use Case	Authenticate Customer: Alt Flow 2.2— No Comm's with Customer's Bank	Fully Tested	HD	2	8

Table C-33 *Continued*

Scope	Unit	State	Priority	Est	Obj
Use Case	Withdraw Cash: Error Handling Alt Flow 4.5—Handle Running Our of Critical Resources	Fully Tested	HD	4	8
Use Case	Withdraw Cash: Error Handling Alt Flow 4.11—Handle Transaction Log Failure	Fully Tested	HD	2	8
Use Case	Withdraw Cash: Loss of Connectivity Alt Flow 5.1—Handle Bank System Stops Responding	Fully Tested	HD	2	8

Ess = Essential

HD = Highly Desirable

Notes on Supp Spec Estimates: Estimates for addressing the design and implementation of the supp specs are included in those for the Cash Withdrawal use case, and those for the specific performance and load testing are included in the estimate for the initial load and performance test results.

Other Deliverables

Table C-34 lists the other deliverables to be produced.

Table C-34 *Other Deliverables*

Discipline	Artifact	State	Priority	Est	Obj
Assessment	Load and Performance Test Environment	Available	Ess	5	2
Assessment	Initial Load and Performance Test Results	Delivered	Ess	5	2
Assessment	Test Strategy	Signed Off	HD	5	2
Req'ts	Use-Case Model	Agreed	Ess	5	3
Req'ts	Supplementary Specification	Agreed	Ess	5	3
Analysis and Design	Architectural Presentation	Delivered	HD	6	4

Ess = Essential

HD = Highly Desirable

Plan

This section describes how the objectives will be achieved.

Capacity Estimate

The team has 73 days available to work on the iteration (see Table C-35) after the project and team overheads are taken into account (see Table C-36).

The estimate to complete the essential objectives and prepare the essential deliverables is 58 days, which leaves 15 days of contingency to address the highly desirable objectives. The estimate to complete all the highly desirable objectives and deliverables is 25 days, providing plenty of work for the team to do if things go better than planned.

Table C-35   *Team Availability*

Name	Role 1 Apr[9]	Availability[8]			
		28 Mar – 8 Apr	4 Apr – 15 Apr	11 Apr – 23 Apr	18 Apr –
Brian Rabbit	Dev Mgr / Iteration Lead	3	2	2	3
Jimmy Page	Architect	3	4	4	4
Robert Plant	Requirements Manager	3	4	4	4
John Paul Jones	Team Leader / Test Manager	3	0	4	4
John Bonham	Developer	3	4	3	4
Tim Rose	Developer	3	4	4	4
Jeff Beck	Tester	3	2	4	4
Keith Richards (former architect)	Architect	3	3	0	0
Total Available		24	23	25	27
Team Total (overheads deducted)		18	17	19	19

[8]   ACME, Inc. only allows work to be planned for four out of every five days. The fifth day is assigned for corporate and personal development activities.

[9]   This week is only a four-day week because March 28 is a company holiday.

Table C-36   *Overheads and Contingency*

	Week 1	Week 2	Week 3	Week 4
Generic Iteration Activities: Planning, Assessment, Communications, Builds, Admin, etc.	2	2	2	4
Supporting Previous Versions	4	4	4	4
Contingency	0	0	0	0

Schedule—Key Events

The schedule of the iteration's key events is presented in Table C-37.

Table C-37   *The Schedule of Key Events*

Week	Event	Description	Involves	Date
1	*Iteration Start*			*18 March 05*
1	Iteration Planning Workshop	Workshop to set iteration objectives, analyze risks, and identify immediate tasks.	All plus Wiley[10] and Arthur[11]	18 March 05
1	Analysis and Design Workshop	Analyze the impact of selected requirements and make significant design decisions.	Jimmy, Keith, Robert, John, Tim, and John-Paul	20 March 05
2	Planning Review	Review iteration plan and development plan.	Brian, Jimmy, Robert, Wiley, John-Paul, and Arthur	25 March 05
2	Use-Case Workshop	Evolve the architecturally significant requirements.	Robert, Arthur, Keith, and Jimmy plus user reps	25 March 05
4	Code Freeze	Stop development and produce initial release for system testing.	All	8 April 05
4	Requirements Review	Review and prioritize the requirements with the stakeholders.	Brian, Robert, Arthur, Keith, and Jimmy	8 April 05
4	Demo to stakeholders	Demonstrate iteration release.	Robert, Jimmy, and Arthur plus user reps	10 April 05
4	Iteration Assessment / Plan next iteration	Workshop to assess the iteration (acceptance and retrospective) and outline plan for next iteration.	All plus Wiley and Arthur	12 April 05
4	Architectural Presentation	Presentation of architecture to team.	Jimmy to deliver as part of iteration assessment	12 April 05
4	**Iteration End**			**12 April 05**

---

[10]   Overall Project Manager

[11]   Customer / User Representative

Task List (Info Only)

The team undertakes their task planning, estimating, and allocation using a simple spreadsheet-based task management tool (the task tracker) that enables tasks to be identified, estimated, assigned, and tracked. This includes the collection of actual effort expended and the regular update of the estimate to complete.

Table C-38 shows the state of the task tracker at the completion of the iteration kickoff/planning meeting, which was used to populate the bulk of this plan. At the planning meeting, the risks, objectives, deliverables, resource availability, and schedule were all discussed and the relevant tables populated. Initial tasks were identified and then volunteered for or assigned. Table C-38 shows that work has been identified for all team members for the first week of the iteration. Several other more obvious tasks have been identified but not assigned yet.

Table C-38   *Extract from Task Tracker Showing Initial Task Identification and Allocation*

Task	Owner	Estimates / Actuals			State
		Orig	**TC**	**Effort**	
Planning workshop / iteration kickoff	Brian with whole team	4	0	4	Complete
Plan Iteration	Brian	2	0	0	Underway
Analysis and Design Workshop	Keith + 5	3	0	0	Underway
Hand over architect role	Keith / Jimmy	6	6	0	Underway
Flesh out requirements	Robert	7	7	0	Underway
Create Test Strategy	John-Paul	5	5	0	Underway
Set up Test Environment	Jeff	5	5	0	Underway
Develop Cash Withdrawal	John with Keith / Jimmy	10	4	0	Underway
Create Cash Withdrawal Test Suite	Jeff	5	5	0	Not Started
Support Previous Versions	Tim	< 2 a week	–	0	Underway
Develop Authenticate Customer	Tim	6	6	0	Underway
Prepare for planning review	Brian	1/2	0	0	Not Started

Table C-38   *Extract from Task Tracker Showing Initial Task Identification and Allocation (continued)*

Task	Owner	Estimates / Actuals			State
		Orig	TC	Effort	
Develop Error Handling					Identified
Develop Card Handling					Identified
Prepare Release					Identified
System Test					Identified

As the iteration progresses, the task tracker is updated by all team members on a daily basis, and new tasks are identified and added as required. This enables the team to dynamically manage the work undertaken within the iteration to maximize the team's chances of successfully completing their essential objectives and hopefully many of their highly desirable ones.

ACME Super ATM Product Development

ACME Super ATM Evolution 1 Iteration E1—Demonstrate Cash Withdrawal

Iteration Assessment Version 1.0

This example shows a hypothetical assessment of the iteration defined by the preceding plan. It is shown here to illustrate the kind of information that would appear in an iteration assessment.

Iteration Results

The iteration is adjudged to have passed at risk with the successful completion of all but one of the essential objectives. There is still the need to get the support overheads under control; otherwise additional team members will need to be added to the team.

The project risk has been significantly reduced, but the cost of supporting previous versions of the ATM system is still compromising the team's ability to focus and concentrate on developing the replacement system.

Risk Analysis

Table C-39 shows the effectiveness of the iteration in addressing the target risks.

Table C-39   *Iteration Risk Status*

Rank at Start	Risk	Mitigation Results
1	Supporting previous ATM versions	Some progress made, but need to make better progress; keep top position on list
2	Keith leaving	Responsibilities successfully transferred; remove
3	Test Strategy, resources and environments	Risk acceptably mitigated; remove
4	It might be harder than we think (estimates)	Risk seems to be under control; keep on list but lower rank
5	Reliability of the O/S platform	Some progress made, but need to make better progress; raise rank in next iteration
6	Scalability of J2EE Infrastructure	
7	What are the requirements?	Risk acceptably mitigated; remove
8	Fault tolerance	Some progress made; keep on list but lower rank
9	Tamper proofing	Risk acceptably mitigated; remove
10	Printing flexibility and reliability	No progress

Results Relative to Evaluation Criteria

Table C-40 presents the results of the iteration relative to the objectives and their evaluation criteria.

Table C-40 *Iteration Objectives, Evaluation Criteria, and Results*

	Objective	Est	Actual	Evaluation Criteria	Evidence Accumulated	Priority	Verdict
1	Demonstrate basic cash withdrawal facilities.	32	35	Successful Cash Withdrawal regression test suite created and tests passed.	Tests passed and regression test suite available.	Ess	Pass
2	Establish the Test Strategy.	10	8	Environments Available / Initial load test results available.	Environments set up and load test results available (system exceeded predicted performance when under load)	Ess	Pass
		5	3	Test Strategy in place.	Test Strategy developed, to be implemented next iteration.	HD	Partial Pass
3	Understand the requirements.	10	13	Architect agrees with all architecturally significant use cases and supp specs documented / Users happy with prioritization.	Use-Case Model / Supplementary Specification created and reviewed with users. Requirements Tracking Spreadsheet in use. Some issues needing resolution identified.	Ess	Pass
4	Hand over technical leadership from Keith to Jimmy.	6	4	Jimmy able to present architectural overview as part of iteration assessment.	Architecture Presentation completed; some issues uncovered that need to be resolved.	Ess	Pass
5	Get control of support commitments.	16	18	Support costs are no more than 4 days a week and declining over the course of the iteration.	Support needs still not fully defined. Support load increasing, not decreasing. Additional work needed in this area.	Ess	Fail
6	Ensure software minimizes the chance of external tampering with the machine during cash withdrawal.	4	3	Successful system test of all flows plus passing of attack and device insertion tests.	Test Results / Build / Regression Test Suite gathered. Goal was determined to be too vague:"minimize" is not measurable. Risk of tampering was determined to be acceptable.	HD	Incomplete
7	Add card failures to basic withdrawal handling.	6	3	Successful system test of all card handling alternative flows.	Coding of flows started	HD	Incomplete
8	Ensure loss of connectivity or critical resources does not allow phantom withdrawals.	10	4	Successful system test of all Must Have cash withdrawal error handling flows.	Initial work started	HD	Incomplete
	Plan/actual To complete essential objectives	89 74	91 78	Variance on overall effort within 5% Variance on individual estimates within 10%	Variance was 2.25% Variance was 5.4%.		
	To complete all objectives	99					

Ess = Essential

HD = Highly Desirable

Results Relative to the Planned Deliverables

All the essential requirements were successfully completed and tested. Initial load and performance testing went very well. All essential and highly desirable artifacts were delivered. Quality levels were very good, with only two priority-two and three priority-three defects outstanding at the end of the iteration.

Findings

The following findings were made during the iteration.

Adherence to Plan

Overall, the project is on track and within acceptable tolerances. Some attention needs to be paid to subsequent iteration plans: although progress is being made on reducing risks, the top risk was not addressed at all in this iteration.

The estimates are within the expected tolerance, and the team worked well together to ensure that the essential objectives were addressed before work started on the highly desirable ones.

Measurements and Analysis

Some estimates appear to have been too optimistic, specifically in the area of understanding requirements and support commitments. These are fairly typical areas that can take much more time than expected. Adjust future estimates accordingly.

The initial progress trends indicate that the project has a good chance of completing the essential requirements within the planned timescales.

If the support overheads are ignored, the effort profile is consistent with that expected for a Unified Process project in the Elaboration phase. If the support overheads continue to grow, as they have for the last few iterations, then the project's ability to accelerate after the technical risks are under control will be severely compromised.

Feedback from the Demonstration

User and technical reviewer feedback was very positive. Some minor issues, to be expected at this point on the project, were identified. These will be addressed in subsequent iterations.

External Changes

Keith has now left the project, and the handover to Jimmy has been completed.

Andrew Smith has been promoted and will no longer be the user rep for the project. His replacement Arthur Tolhurst attended the iteration assessment and will be picking up Andrew's responsibilities over the next few weeks.

Three partners have already signed up for the printed goods pilot, making it even more important that work is started on the printed goods demonstrator next iteration.

An initial draft of the Deployment / ATM Replacement ITT has been issued.

Lessons Learned

The new approach to team-based iteration planning was judged to have been an overwhelming success and should be repeated every iteration.

Objectives and their evaluation criteria must be clearly defined.

Developers adopting a "test first" approach can clearly improve the quality of the code entering system test.

Automated regression tests should be run every night to spot potential build problems.

Rework Required

A revised architecture description is required to address the issues uncovered during the handover.

Index

BOOKS ONLINE

ENABLED

THIS BOOK IS SAFARI ENABLED

INCLUDES FREE 45-DAY ACCESS TO THE ONLINE EDITION

The Safari® Enabled icon on the cover of your favorite technology book means the book is available through Safari Bookshelf. When you buy this book, you get free access to the online edition for 45 days.

Safari Bookshelf is an electronic reference library that lets you easily search thousands of technical books, find code samples, download chapters, and access technical information whenever and wherever you need it.

TO GAIN 45-DAY SAFARI ENABLED ACCESS TO THIS BOOK:

- Go to **http://www.awprofessional.com/safarienabled**

- Complete the brief registration form

- Enter the coupon code found in the front of this book on the "Copyright" page

Addison
Wesley

If you have difficulty registering on Safari Bookshelf or accessing the online edition, please e-mail customer-service@safaribooksonline.com.

Register
Your Book

at www.awprofessional.com/register

You may be eligible to receive:

- Advance notice of forthcoming editions of the book
- Related book recommendations
- Chapter excerpts and supplements of forthcoming titles
- Information about special contests and promotions throughout the year
- Notices and reminders about author appearances, tradeshows, and online chats with special guests

Contact us

If you are interested in writing a book or reviewing manuscripts prior to publication, please write to us at:

Editorial Department
Addison-Wesley Professional
75 Arlington Street, Suite 300
Boston, MA 02116 USA
Email: AWPro@aw.com

Visit us on the Web: http://www.awprofessional.com

Rational Minds and Addison-Wesley
What a Combination!

0-321-32127-8

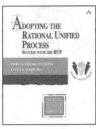

0-321-20294-5

0-321-26888-1

0-321-32130-8

0-805-35340-2

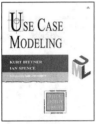

0-201-70913-9

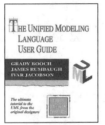

0-201-57168-4

0-201-73038-3

0-201-79166-8

0-201-42289-1

0-201-54435-0

0-201-92476-5

0-201-57169-2

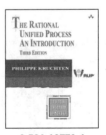

0-321-19770-4

0-321-12247-X

0-201-72163-5

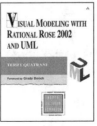

0-201-72932-6

0-201-30958-0

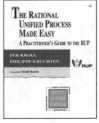

0-321-16609-4

0-321-24562-8

inform IT

YOUR GUIDE TO IT REFERENCE

Articles

Keep your edge with thousands of free articles, in-depth features, interviews, and IT reference recommendations – all written by experts you know and trust.

Online Books

Answers in an instant from **InformIT Online Book's** 600+ fully searchable on line books. For a limited time, you can get your first 14 days **free**.

Catalog

Review online sample chapters, author biographies and customer rankings and choose exactly the right book from a selection of over 5,000 titles.